A

HISTORY OF PHILOSOPHY.

ANCIENT AND MODERN.

BY

JOSEPH HAVEN, D.D., LL.D.,

LATE PROFESSOR OF SYSTEMATIC THEOLOGY IN THE THEOLOGICAL SEMINARY, CHICAGO, ILL., AND LATE PROFESSOR OF INTELLECTUAL AND MORAL PHILOSOPHY IN AMHERST COLLEGE, AND IN THE UNIVERSITY OF CHICAGO—AND AUTHOR OF "MENTAL PHILOSOPHY," "MORAL PHILOSOPHY," AND "STUDIES IN PHILOSOPHY AND THEOLOGY."

NEW YORK:

SHELDON & COMPANY.

NO. 8 MURRAY STREET.

1876.

Newburgh Stereotype Company,

INTRODUCTORY NOTE.

THE preparation of the following work ran parallel with the studies which filled the life of the author, and its completion and revision for publication was his last work. It is now put forth as a fitting complement to the "Studies in Philosophy and Theology," and to the treatises on "Mental Philosophy" and on "Moral Philosophy" which have been so favorably received by the public. It will, as we think, be welcomed not only by those who have been the pupils of its author, either through his lecture-room or through its works, but by that large and increasing class of thoughtful minds who will be interested in the history of what the human mind has done in "the noblest study of mankind."

The labor and enthusiasm of Dr. Haven's life was largely given to the presentation of that history, as viewed from his own characteristic stand-point of full loyalty at once to the word of God and to the convictions of the human mind, first to his classes in collegiate and professional study, and afterward to those intelligent thinkers, who are still pursuing "liberal education" in the midst of the activities of adult life. It is hoped that this book may not only be found valuable for study and reference in educational institutions, but that it may continue and extend that usefulness in the general community upon which its author seemed to be entering when he was called away.

J. EMERSON.

BELOIT COLLEGE, WIS., February, 1876.

AUTHORITIES.

In the preparation of the following pages, the works of the authors themselves, so far as extant and accessible, have been the chief source of authority as to their respective systems. In addition to these, the historical statements of Aristotle, Diogenes Laertius, Plutarch, and Cicero among ancient writers—the historical works of Ritter, Tennemann, Fries, Krug, Schwegler, and Ueberweg among the Germans—of Cousin, Tissot, Renouvier among the French—of Archer Butler, and Lewes, in England, have been carefully studied in the preparation of the chapters on ancient philosophy; of whom Ritter (History of Ancient Philosophy, 4 vols.), Tennemann (Manual of the History of Philosophy), Schwegler (Geschichte der Philosophie), and Ueberweg (History of Philosophy, Vol. i.) have been the chief guides; while in modern philosophy, Schwegler (as above), Cousin (Histoire de la Philosophie, 2 vols.), Lewes (Biographical History of Philosophy), and Morell (History of Modern Philosophy) have been the principal aids. Damiron (Histoire de la Philosophie en France au XIX. Siecle), Renouvier (Manuel de la Philosophie Moderne), and Hegel (Geschichte der Philosophie, 3 vols.), have also been consulted.

INTRODUCTORY NOTE.

THE preparation of the following work ran parallel with the studies which filled the life of the author, and its completion and revision for publication was his last work. It is now put forth as a fitting complement to the "Studies in Philosophy and Theology," and to the treatises on "Mental Philosophy" and on "Moral Philosophy" which have been so favorably received by the public. It will, as we think, be welcomed not only by those who have been the pupils of its author, either through his lecture-room or through its works, but by that large and increasing class of thoughtful minds who will be interested in the history of what the human mind has done in "the noblest study of mankind."

The labor and enthusiasm of Dr. Haven's life was largely given to the presentation of that history, as viewed from his own characteristic stand-point of full loyalty at once to the word of God and to the convictions of the human mind, first to his classes in collegiate and professional study, and afterward to those intelligent thinkers, who are still pursuing "liberal education" in the midst of the activities of adult life. It is hoped that this book may not only be found valuable for study and reference in educational institutions, but that it may continue and extend that usefulness in the general community upon which its author seemed to be entering when he was called away.

J. EMERSON.

BELOIT COLLEGE, WIS., February, 1876.

AUTHORITIES.

In the preparation of the following pages, the works of the authors themselves, so far as extant and accessible, have been the chief source of authority as to their respective systems. In addition to these, the historical statements of Aristotle, Diogenes Laertius, Plutarch, and Cicero among ancient writers—the historical works of Ritter, Tennemann, Fries, Krug, Schwegler, and Ueberweg among the Germans—of Cousin, Tissot, Renouvier among the French—of Archer Butler, and Lewes, in England, have been carefully studied in the preparation of the chapters on ancient philosophy; of whom Ritter (History of Ancient Philosophy, 4 vols.), Tennemann (Manual of the History of Philosophy), Schwegler (Geschichte der Philosophie), and Ueberweg (History of Philosophy, Vol. i.) have been the chief guides; while in modern philosophy, Schwegler (as above), Cousin (Histoire de la Philosophie, 2 vols.), Lewes (Biographical History of Philosophy), and Morell (History of Modern Philosophy) have been the principal aids. Damiron (Histoire de la Philosophie en France au XIX. Siecle), Renouvier (Manuel de la Philosophie Moderne), and Hegel (Geschichte der Philosophie, 3 vols.), have also been consulted.

CONTENTS.

PART FIRST.—ANCIENT PHILOSOPHY.

PERIOD I.—PRE-SOCRATIC PHILOSOPHY.

PERIOD II.—THE SOCRATIC PHILOSOPHY.

CHAPTER II.

CHAPTER III.

CHAPTER IV.

PERIOD III.—POST-SOCRATIC PHILOSOPHY.

CHAPTER I.

CHAPTER II.

CHAPTER III.

CHAPTER IV.

CHAPTER V.

CHAPTER VI.

PART SECOND.—MODERN PHILOSOPHY.

CHAPTER I.

CHAPTER II.

CHAPTER III.

CHAPTER IV.

CHAPTER V.

CHAPTER VI.

CHAPTER VII.

CHAPTER VIII.

CHAPTER IX.

INTRODUCTION.

GENERAL OUTLINE AND DIVISIONS OF THE COURSE.

THE most general and obvious division of the history of philosophy is into *ancient* and *modern*; the former extending from the earliest times of which we have historic record to the Christian era; the latter embracing the course of philosophic thought within that era.

For us, with the records and resources at our present command, the history of Ancient Philosophy must be chiefly that of Grecian philosophy. It was there that, so far as known to us, speculative inquiry into the origin and causes of things first assumed a scientific form. That it first commenced there, is not at all probable. No nation, it is reasonable to suppose, has ever existed, possessing any considerable degree of civilization and culture, which has not also exercised itself upon those great problems of human thought which in all ages present themselves to the reflecting mind. Egypt undoubtedly had her philosophy before the days of Abraham and the Pyramids; India had hers. But neither in Egypt, nor in India, did philosophic speculation assume, so far as yet appears, a strictly scientific form; nor do we know what was, in the earliest times, the philosophy of either.

The same may be said of China. A philosophy of some sort undoubtedly existed in all these countries long prior to the Grecian; but it would seem to have been rather of a theological or mythological, than of a scientific and rational character.

Of the Indian philosophy, if such it may be called, sufficient is known to satisfy us that, whatever its treasures, it casts little light on the progress of the human mind, in its search for truth, and has little to do with the subsequent course of philosophic investigation. The attempt to trace back to a Hindoo origin the subsequent Grecian speculations is neither necessary nor reasonable. Ritter, while he admits that the derivation is very doubtful, attaches too much importance to the Indian cosmogonies as the possible source of subsequent theories. Much more probable is it that the Grecian philosophy had its roots in the valley of the Nile, where, as we know, some of its chief thinkers wandered, and for a time dwelt and studied.

Nor can we with better reason trace the ancient philosophy to Hebrew sources. The Hebrew and Patriarchal families had what was better than a philosophy, a revelation. For them, if not for us, the first verse of the first chapter of Genesis settles the whole question, so long in discussion in the schools of philosophy, as to the origin and first cause of things. A philosophy in the scientific sense the Hebrews certainly had not; nor was the Hebrew mind of a speculative or philosophic character.

For reasons now stated, we begin, then, the history of ancient philosophy with that of Greece. It is the first pure philosophy known to us, the first earnest attempt to reach by speculative inquiry the sources of knowledge and the causes of things, of which we have any full and satisfactory account. It is the earliest definitely known philosophy which exerts a positive influence on the subsequent efforts of the human mind in its search for truth. The reasons for such a course are well stated by Schwegler (Geschichte der Philosophie im Umriss, § 2).

Of the Grecian philosophy, the most natural and obvious

division is that into the three periods most distinctly marked in the progress of the Grecian mind, each having characteristics of its own by which it stands apart and forms an epoch by itself. These are, the period prior to Socrates; the period of Socrates and his immediate disciples and successors; the period subsequent, which also closes the history of Greek philosophy. Taking Socrates as the central standpoint, and reckoning each way from him, we have the *Pre-Socratic*, the *Socratic*, and the *Post-Socratic* periods or epochs.

These again are divided into several schools, and each school numbers its several philosophers, differing somewhat in their views, yet so far agreeing as to admit of being classed together. Under the first, or Pre-Socratic period, there are four of these schools: the *Ionian*, the *Italian*, the *Eleatic*, the *Sophistic*. As designated according to their general character, rather than their geographical origin, these might be named the materialistic, the mystic, the rationalistic, and the sceptic schools; for such were their prevailing tendencies. Under the Socratic period, there were, besides that of Socrates himself, the *Cyrenaic*, the *Cynic*, and the *Megaric* schools, the school of Plato, called also the *Academy*, and that of Aristotle, or the *Peripatetic* school. Under the Post-Socratic period, there were the *Sceptic*, the *Epicurean*, the *Stoic*, the *New Academy*, as also, later, the Jewish-Alexandrian, schools.

These schools follow each other in the logical development of thought, and in the main also chronologically, though not always strictly so—one school sometimes overlapping or partly contemporaneous with another—the principle of arrangement being that of the doctrines taught, rather than a strictly chronological succession. Indeed it is impossible to adopt any classification except the most general one; nor is it necessary. In fact, scarcely two historians agree in their classification of the different schools, and the different philosophers under each.

PERIOD FIRST.

THE PRE-SOCRATIC PHILOSOPHY.

If we compare the schools of the first period with each other, we find it characteristic of them all to search for the first principle or ground of things. The Ionian sought it in some form of matter; the Italian in number; the Eleatic, in pure being; the Sophists in the subjective thought—(*Ich-Reit,* as Schwegler expresses it). The *Ionian* school was materialistic, and empiric; speculated on the outer world, its origin, nature, cause, and essence—the first principle which lies beneath all its changing phenomena;—made this external world the chief object of inquiry, but not without reference to the general law of our own being. The chief names included under this school, if we take this as the general characteristic, are Thales, Anaximander, Anaximenes, Heraclitus, Diogenes of Apollonia, and Anaxagoras.

The *Italian* school was mathematical and ideal in character, mystic withal; speculated on nature, but in another direction and method; found in number the essence of all things; applied its theories to practical matters, to society and the state. Pythagoras is the chief name, disciples are numerous, but no writings remain.

The *Eleatic* school was in general tendency rationalistic. It carried out yet further the trains of inquiry started by the preceding schools, and was itself in some measure the natural result of these schools. It brought out distinctly the difference, already indicated by the Italian school, between reason and the senses, and gave the preference to the former, allowing little faith in the latter. Its chief teachers are Xenophanes, Parmenides, Zeno, and Empedocles.

The *Sophistic* school,—named from the Sophists who composed it,—was sceptical in character, carried yet further the doctrine of the preceding schools, and denied the credibility not only of sense, but of reason; denied the reality of truth and the possibility of human knowledge. Protagoras and Gorgias are the chief philosophers of this school.

With this general comparison of the several schools we proceed to the more careful study of each in its order as already named.

CHAPTER I.

THE IONIAN SCHOOL.

Epoch of this school.—Its place in history occupies about two centuries; from about 600 to 400 B. C.

In the first of these centuries Cyrus and Darius were in power, and Daniel, Jeremiah, and Ezekiel were prophets. Afterward came Artaxerxes and his successors in power, and the later Jewish prophets appeared.

It was also the era of Confucius and Zoroaster.

The Ionian colonies at that time were independent, flourishing, commercial; the birth-place of Grecian philosophy and science.

The point of view of this sect of philosophers, as already stated, is experimental or physical. It was the philosophy of nature. It was reasonable and natural—nay, almost a matter of necessity—that the first inquiries should take this course. Yet not solely, or indeed chiefly *naturalists* were these men. They were naturalists with a *higher aim* and end than merely to understand physics. They made this the starting point and stepping stone to much higher results. "To find the law of his own being by meditating on the external world," says Maurice, "was what each proposed to himself." What did they attain? Much, I answer. They began with nothing, that is, they they had no past speculations and philosophies to fall back upon. They took the first steps in a new field and a new direction. Of course their first attempts were imperfect and crude; must so appear to us with our philosophy of the nineteenth century. Strange if in twenty-five centuries the human mind had made no progress in speculative research, yet with these rude beginnings, this school, at the very outset of the course of human philosophy, did reach certain very important results. They made the discovery of an ordaining, directing intelligence, *mind* in distinction from *matter*, the origin and first cause of mundane existence,—intelligence *immaterial*, eternal, supreme, one. Is not this a grand discovery for those early speculators to make? They discovered also the *immateriality* of the soul. In conducting their physical researches they likewise arrived at some conclusions which you will readily recognize as anticipations of modern science, as that the earth has passed through a series of tranformations in reaching its present state; that man is the last result, the successor of races less perfect,—of which he is perhaps the crowning result and transformation.

These Ionians may be again divided into two classes, as they pursued two different lines of thought and inquiry: the dynamists and the mechanists—a distinction much insisted upon by the former historians. The former find the vital principle of the world, the essence and origin of things, in some one simple principle, as air, fire, etc.—a principle susceptible of modification and transformation, out of which result the present various systems of things. The latter, mechanists, instead of deriving all things from some one single principle, admit many such, more or less, and these immutable (See Mallet, Hist. Ion., pp. 17, 18).

§ 1.—Thales.

Epoch or time when he flourished. According to Apollodorus, he was born 35 Olymp., and died at 70, that is, born about 639 B.C. But this, according to Ritter, is doubtful.

Was born at *Miletus*, at that time a flourishing commercial city of considerable importance in Asia Minor, not yet under foreign domination.

Thales was one of the seven wise men of Greece. This shows his general reputation and influence among his countrymen. He was a man of note and mark in his native city; possessed no little political power and influence, and saved the city from a compact with Crœsus against Cyrus. He was noted as a geometer and astronomer, and, according to Laertius, was the first to determine the length of the solar year, and to note with precision the equinoxes and solstices (Diog. i. 24. 27). Herodotus makes him predict a great eclipse of the sun. Tradition makes him owe his mathematical science to Egypt. This is very probable, as the Greeks derived both their mythology and science chiefly from Egypt. He was the first *Baconian* philosopher in physics, *i. e.*, he took OBSERVATION, as the *point of his departure* and the *method* of his inquiry. The very *first* of the philosophers adopted this principle, and it was that of the entire school, in fact. Thales left no *written* works, but taught orally. Writing, especially prose writing, was not then common in Greece.

His *general theory* as a philosopher.

Thales and all the early philosophers sought for the first or elementary principle of things, to reduce to *unity* the manifold plurality and variety of natural phenomena. There must be some ground principle at the basis of all these phenomena of nature ; some root, some fountain, some hidden source whence they all proceed. This, whatever it be, from which all things proceed and to which all things tend, the one substance that under all modifications remains unchanged—this, if you can but find it, is the first principle of all. And what can this be, what more likely to be it, than *water*, by which all things are begotten and nourished.*

The view of Thales is thus stated by Aristotle. The sustenance of all things is moisture, from moisture warmth proceeds, from warmth everything living draws its life; also all seeds are moist; but the source of moisture is water (Metaph. i. 3). It is thus stated by Fries (vol. i. 103), "Simple analogy seems to have guided Thales. The ground under our feet is mostly formed of water. Water gives and holds all lives. From heaven it comes. To heaven it mounts; and back again to the earth it must descend, ever changing. From the water, the clouds; from these the lightnings; to the lightnings perhaps that heavenly fire of the stars is itself allied." Very simple idea, you will say, but what more natural?

The Ionian philosophy, remarks the same writer, seems from the first to have fixed upon the unity of the law of natural phenomena through evaporation, which, indeed, in *sacrifice* gave the idea of the *communication of man with the gods.*

The idea of Thales, according to *Ritter*, is that the world is produced from water, as anything is produced from its seed ; water being the seed of the earth, which is but a growth, a development of a preëxisting form of life. The entire world, according to this, is a living thing, a being gradually forming from an imperfect seed-state, and possessing a sort of vitality and soul.

How nearly, in this view of the gradual formation of

* Sextus Empiricus, Adv. Math. vii. 5; Diog. Laertius, i. 27; Cic. Acad. ii. 37; Aristotle, de Cœlo, 11, 13; Cic. de Nat. Deorum, lib. i.

the earth from a previous imperfect and, as it were, seed-state, and of the important agency of water as the prime element of this transformation,—how nearly in this does the old Greek philosophy come to certain modern geological theories respecting the aqueous origin and formation of the earth. "Could anything," says an eloquent writer, "be more naturally present to an Ionian mind than the universality of water? Had he not from boyhood upward been familiar with the sea?"

> "There about the beach he wandered, nourishing a youth sublime,
> With the fairy tales of science, and the long result of time."

"When gazing abroad upon the blue expanse, hearing the mighty waters rolling evermore, and seeing the red sun, having spent its fiery energy, sink into the cool bosom of the wave, to rest there in peace, how often must he have been led to contemplate the all-embracing, all-engulfing sea, upon whose throbbing breast the very earth itself reposed. This earth how finite, and that welling sea how infinite!

"Once impressed with this idea, he examined the constitution of the earth. There also he found moisture everywhere. All things he found nourished by moisture; warmth itself he declared to proceed from moisture; the seeds of all things are moist. Water when condensed becomes earth. Thus convinced of the universal presence of water, he declared it to be the beginning of things."

It is possible to refer this theory of water as the ἀρχή, or first principle, to the ancient tradition that the sun and stars are born of the sea, out of which they seem to rise.

The essential points in this theory are not peculiar to Thales, indeed, but common to the Ionian philosophers, viz.: 1, That the world is a living thing; 2, That it proceeds from some simple primary substance, the seed of things not yet developed. The peculiarity of his theory, in distinction from others, is that he discovered or supposed water to be this first principle. In common with the ancients, he conceived of matter, not as we do, extended, impenetrable, moist, but only as a form of life. He had no idea of *inert* matter. Nor was water with him what the chemist means by it, a fluid having such and such properties, but rather the parent and seed of all life. The soul with Thales is the *principle of motion.* Whatever *moves,* then, and of course whatever *lives,* has a soul. The universe has; this great, broad, beautiful earth—what is it but a moving, a living thing, with a soul animating its giant frame. Simple idea this, but not without its beauty and sublimity.

Plutarch (de Plac. Phil. i. 8), makes Thales the first to distinguish between θεος, δαίμων, and ἥρως; the soul of the world, a spiritual being, and a human soul separate from the body. Yet this distinction is probably of earlier origin, as in Hesiod. Nothing hindered Thales from teaching the immortality of the soul, since death is only a change of existence, a transformation of the soul. Diogenes, accordingly, ascribes this doctrine to him, and Plutarch intimates or implies it in the above. Schwegler considers the ideas of a world-soul, of a personal God, and the immortality of the soul, to be of *later* origin; so also Fries. Aristotle ascribes the idea of a creative intelligence to a later origin; yet he admits Thales to hold the idea of God—as world-soul or *nous;* and all things to be *full of divinity* (de Anim. i. 5, 15; so Diog. L. i. 27, and Stobæus, Ecl. Phys. i. 2, νοῦν τοῦ κόσμου).

Was Thales a theist or an atheist? Lewes says not the latter; Ritter and Cousin deny that he was the former, and with reason; so Mallet; for his gods are not intelligent, self-existent, independent of the world; nor are they creators. The cosmogony of Thales corresponds to that of the poets and the priests of the age—they made Ocean and Tethys the parents of the gods; so Homer. Diogenes Laertius contradicts himself in ascribing to Thales the apothegms: that God is unbegotten, and that the world is the work of God; for he elsewhere says that *Anaxagoras* was the first to recognize an intelligence above matter. Cicero contradicts himself in the same way,—probably having in view the maxims now cited,—yet ascribing the same discovery to Anaxagoras. Aristotle explicitly says (Met. i. 3) that Anaxagoras was the first who held this: "When a man comes to announce that there is in nature, as among animals, an intelligence which is the cause of the order and arrangement in the universe, this man seems alone to have preserved his reason amidst the follies of his predecessors. Now we know *with certitude*, that Anaxagoras was the first to enter upon this point of view." Was Thales then an atheist? Rather, we should say, a pantheist; his view is not that of a creator, but of a spirit, or soul, pervading all, and filling all, and this is his deity (See especially Mallet, Histoire de la Philosophie Ionienne, article Thales).

The gods of Thales, like man, proceed from the elementary moisture; hence not self-existent, but subject to destiny—the blind moving force of the universe.

The following apothegms are ascribed to Thales, but perhaps with insufficient, at least doubtful, authority (Diog. L. i. 35, 36, 37; Plutarch. Conviv. c. 9). They are beyond doubt very ancient proverbs.

The *oldest* of beings is *God*, the *unbegotten*,
The *fairest*, the *world*, the work of God.
The *greatest*, *space*, the all-embracing;
The *swiftest*, *spirit*, the all-penetrating;
The *mightiest*, *necessity*, the all-controlling;
The *wisest*, *time*, the all-discovering.
No thought of man is concealed from God.
What thou condemnest in another, that do *thou* not.
What is the hardest? To understand thyself.
What is the easiest? To advise another.
Death distinguishes not itself from life.

§ 2.—ANAXIMANDER.

In placing Anaximander next to Thales, I do but follow the voice and verdict of antiquity, which have assigned him that place. It is very doubtful, however, whether he does properly rank next in point of time; still more doubtful whether he is to be regarded as the disciple of that master. The doctrines of the two, however, are nearly enough allied to admit of his being classed with the former philosopher as of the same school. Apollodorus makes him the contemporary and friend of Thales; so all antiquity. He was born at Miletus, about 611 B. C.; died 547. His general line of thought places him with the *mechanists*, rather than the *dynamists*, the first of that school. He did not, like Thales, inquire for some one simple element, as air, water, etc., from which all things proceed by a *living force*, a development theory, but explains the formation of things by the changes and transformations which occur in the diverse parts of a whole, composed, not of some few simple principles, as air, water, etc., but of an indefinite number of elements. (So Ritter.) His elementary principle is an abstract one. The *Infinite* or unlimited; τὸ ἄπειρον (and this is *one*), (Aristotle, Phys. i. 4, 5; Sext. Emp. Hyp. Pyrr. iii. 30; Adv. Math. vii. 5, ix. 360; Cic. Acad. ii. 37).

Diogenes Laertius, Plutarch, Eusebius, all state the same. The latter says (Præp. Evang. i. 8), "Anaximander, friend of Thales, says the Infinite contains likewise the first cause of all things as to generation and destruction." It is the all-embracing, the God-like in nature (Arist. Phys. iii. 4), (without form or qualities, so Arist. Phy. iii. 4) (Cic. de Nat. Deor. i. 10). How does he derive the universe from this ἄπειρον, the Infinite? Not by development of one substance or element into all other things, as Thales, by a power inherent in itself, but his *apeiron* is a sort of primitive chaos, according to Aristotle (Met. xii. 2), a melange of elementary substances.

According to him, says Simplicius, "the formation takes place, not by transformation of the first principle, but by the separation of contraries, by the law of eternal movement." He supposes, evidently, a necessary movement going on incessantly and eternally in the bosom of the infinite, which has the effect to disengage from each other, elements of a diverse nature and to bring together those that are like, and in this way comes to pass the organization and arrangement of material nature. To this effect Theophrastus is cited (Simplicius, Phys. 6, 6), "Anaximander teaches that by the separation of the infinite, particles of the same nature are borne to each other, and so what in the all, *ἐν τῷ παντὶ*, was gold becomes gold, what was earth becomes earth, and all things in like manner, not as things produced but formerly existing," *i. e.*, in their elements. Eusebius thus states the doctrine of Anaximander: "The stars, heavens, earth, all the worlds which fill immensity, disengage themselves from the bosom of the infinite. The generation and destruction are attributed by him to a movement circular and inherent in the infinity of things." This movement is circular. The earth is cylindrical in form. The *efficient causes* of this disengagement of matters are the eternal principles of heat and cold. The idea is evidently that of a *chemical* transformation or process of change, by which certain particles having like nature, or, as we should say, having affinity for each other, are first by the law of movement set loose or separated from the infinite, from the chaotic whole, and then in consequence of that affinity are brought together, this separation or movement being itself occasioned by the laws of heat and cold eternally operating.

The formation of the heavenly bodies is on this wise.

A sort of igneous sphere expands itself above the air that surrounds the earth, like the outer rind of a tree, which, being broken in many places and into circular fragments, there result the sun, moon, and stars (Eusebius, Præp. Evang, i. 8).

A crude theory this, you will say, of the first formation of things, yet, viewed as a whole, this chemical theory of the world's formation, is it altogether an absurd view for one to form who had no revelation, no first chapter of Genesis to guide him; who had no facts, or experimental philosophy to assist him, or, if any, but the most limited; who could at best form only a mere conjecture, could only imagine how by this possibility or that the great universe was formed? Nay more, this theory of separation and aggregation going on by the eternal laws of nature and the eternal movement of the infinite, is it altogether unlike some modern theories, which bear the proud name of science? Does it not remind one at once of the nebulous theory of Laplace and of the author of Vestiges of Creation.

Still nearer the modern scientific theories does our old Greek approach, when he comes to speak of the origin and formation of man. Man proceeds originally, he thinks, from *some other form* of animal life—some other species or race,—since he is not able at first, like other animals, to provide himself with sustenance. So Plutarch (de Placit. v. 19): "The first animals, according to Anaximander. had birth in the watery element, were covered with a sort of thorny rind, but after a time they elevated themselves to a drier region and their covering burst." Origen, lib. i., says that, "he taught that men existed first under the form of fishes, and that they inhabited the earth, not until they had become able to provide for themselves."

Ritter, however, maintains that Anaximander did not mean that men were born of fishes, but like them had at first a scaly or thorny hide, and like them proceeded from the mud.

The doctrine of Anaximander seems to connect itself here with that of Thales, viz., that humidity, or that the watery element, is the source of the first life. A direct consequence of this doctrine is that man, in his present form at least, was not at first in existence but is an ulterior form of life; that, in a word, there are successive phases in the organization of nature, and that man is the last result. In this broad and general principle does he not again anticipate the conclusions of modern science! Whatever may be said of the fishy theory of man's origin, which, by the way, is essentially reproduced in the Vestiges of Creation, is not the grand principle of successive formation one that all science goes more and more to confirm?

Anaximander was the first, it would seem, to use the term ἀρχή for the principle of things. His primary being or existence is a *unity*, the τὸ πᾶν, whence everything proceeds, and to which everything tends to revert. The contraries, as heat and cold, counteract each other. The sun dries the earth, etc. And so all contraries neutralize each other and all resolves again, at least such is the tendency, back to unity or chaos. The infinite is always in a state of incipiency, moreover, tending to a new phase of things, a new modification. His system approaches that of Thales, then, in these two essential points: 1, It assumes the unity of the primitive principle; 2, It admits humidity to be the source not indeed of all existence, but at least of all animal life. The difference, in the main, is that Thales takes the concrete, Anaximander, the abstract, view of things.

Anaximander seems to have been a fatalist. This eternal movement of the infinite is governed by a sort of fatalism. There is no trace in all this theory, of the intelligent *nous*—the conscious mover and orderer of things, the self-existent one of the later philosophers, nor even of the all-diffused mind or soul of the world of Thales. In this respect Anaximander is far behind Thales, He is neither a theist nor a pantheist, but an atheist. So Eusebius affirms, borrowing the language of Plutarch. "Anaximander," say they, "suppresses all efficient cause. In fact, the infinite is, after all, only matter. Now matter produces nothing, unless we admit at the same a being who is the producing cause" (Euseb. Præp. Evang. xiv. 14). Aristotle also takes the same view, viz., that Anaximander admits no divinity except the infinite, which is divine because immortal and incorruptible.

Renouvier, however, thinks that he may have admitted the existence of the popular gods, but made them subject to his law of necessity; and also that he and Thales are alike in this, both making their one principle to be the single cause and element of all that is.

Anaximander was great also as an astronomer.

Eusebius (Præp. Evang. x. 14) attributes to him the construction of gnomons, by which to mark the course of the sun and the seasons, and to indicate solstices and equinoxes. Diogenes Laertius (ii. 1) makes him the first to determine the perimeter of the earth and the sea, and to construct a sphere, also maps of the earth, and globes. In his system, the earth, as in most ancient systems, is placed in the centre of the universe and stands fast, because in the centre, other globes moving around it (Aristotle, de Cœlo, ii. 13), and is spherical, or, as Eusebius says (Præp. Evang. i. 8), cylindrical, having its diameter one-third its height. According to Plutarch (de Plac. Phil. ii. 21, 25), the sun is twenty-eight and the moon nineteen times greater than the earth. In all this you perceive the leading tendency of the whole school of Ionian philosophers, *i. e.*, to physical inquiry. The problem with them was to account for the universe.

§ 3.—Anaximenes.

The friend and pupil of Anaximander, according to some authorities; according to others, not born till after the death of the latter, and so of course not his pupil. Ritter dates his birth in the 63d Olympiad, about 527 B. C. Fries dates it about twenty years earlier, in the first year of the 58th Olympiad. In his general system, he seems more nearly allied to Thales than to Anaximander. Hence Ritter and others place him next in succession to the former. So also does Aristotle. *Chronologically*, at least, he does not belong there, however.

His problem and grand endeavor are the same with those of the whole Ionian school—to account for the various phenomena of nature as to their cause and origin; to hit upon the one prime element of all, whence all proceeds. In common with Thales and Anaximander, he assumes the *unity* of that first principle; in common with Thales, he assumes the concrete, abandoning the abstract principle of Anaximander. It is no longer *the infinite* that is the source of all, but some specific and individual element, viz., the *atmosphere* or air, the surrounding and all-embracing ether (Arist. Met. i. 3; Sext. Emp. Hyp. Pyrr. iii. 30; Adv. Math. vii. 5; Diog. L. ii. 2; Cic. Acad. Quest. ii. 37). By the condensation and rarefaction of this element may all the phenomena of the external world be explained. So thought Anaximenes, and he was, so far as we know, the first to take that direction. This air, or ether, whatever it be that surrounds us and all things, as a robe, in its invisible folds, is the beginning, whence all things proceed, to which all things tend, in which all things are again lost. Through condensation the cold particles precipitate themselves in the form of wind, cloud, water, earth. Through the opposite process—rarefaction—the atmosphere becomes fire and tends upward. The earth thus once formed, a vapor exhales; this expands, begets fire; the fire, meteorizing itself, becomes stars. On the contrary, the air, compressing, forms clouds; if the process goes on, rain is expressed in the same way; earth and even rocks result from the same process carried to its last degree. Thus incessantly *transformed*, the air dwells in an eternal movement which produces life—all beings—the souls of men—the gods themselves. All its physical qualities, as heat, cold, etc., are only diverse modes of its being. In fine, it is the one existence, the being unique and primary, of which the natural qualities are only so many inherent and ever-varying modes.

Plutarch (de Plac. Phil. i. 3) makes him say, Our soul is air, as such it governs us. The whole world is encompassed and governed by air, so that even, says Plutarch, he names the air God (so also Cic. de Nat. Deor. i. 10), and makes the gods proceed from it. Here seems to be a comparison of nature with self; the soul governing us, as the air does the universe. Maurice regards this as a new and important step in philosophy.

As to the general plan of the universe, he held, according to some, that the orbits of the stars were above, the air in the middle, water and earth below. Aristotle (de Cœlo, ii. 13), however, makes him teach, that the earth reposes in the midst, lying upon the lower air and upborne by it on account of its breadth (like a board on the water). He also represents him as giving to the earth a perpendicular, rather than a circular motion. According to most, he gives the earth a flat figure. The sun, moon, and stars proceed from the earth, inasmuch as composed of earth and fire. The sun keeps its heat by means of the swiftness of its motion. He seems to have discovered the borrowed light of the moon, and to have explained its eclipses by the intervention of the earth. According to Ritter he also discovered the obliquity of the ecliptic.

On the whole we agree with Ritter that the system of this philosopher seems to be an advance on that of Thales in two points: 1, It does not regard the world after the analogy of a seed-state, but of the human soul; 2, Does not, with Thales and one may add, Anaximander, derive all things from a state of unevolved life, but regards the principle of production as being from all time fully evolved and developed.

Plutarch is authority for the fact, that Anaximenes

recognizes the air as the elementary or first principle—the infinite. So Cicero de Nat. Deor. i. 10. So Diog. Laertius. Sext. Emp. classes him with those who held to a single principle, and adds that his principle is air. (See passage Adv. Math. ix. quoted in Mallet, 101.)

§ 4.—Heraclitus.

Epoch not precisely ascertained. According to Diogenes Laertius (ix. 1) he flourished in the 69th Olympiad, or about 500 years B. C. We may suppose him to have been born some thirty or thirty-five years before; or about the time that Babylon was taken by Cyrus, and the Persian empire founded. This makes him subsequent to Thales, Anaximander, Anaximenes, and Pythagoras, and contemporary with Parmenides. Belonged to the first family in Ephesus. Averse to social intercourse, with little sympathy for the race to which he belonged (Diog. L. ix. 2), of melancholy temperament, and possessing a taste for philosophical reflection, he had no ambition for political honors and power, and therefore, at his father's death, declined the magistracy of the city. Subsequently the city besought him to draw up a code of laws, but he declined; giving as a reason the not very flattering opinion that the corruption of the Ephesians was so inveterate as to be beyond remedy.

Now Ephesus was, beyond question, not a pattern of morals and virtue, but for that reason all the more in need of good law; and we cannot help suspecting that the fault was partly in the man and not wholly in the city, corrupt as it was. (He was one of nature's reformers, cut out for that; a regular Garrisonian by birth, a sort of Wendell Phillips or Carlyle.) Still it is not impossible that the prevailing corruption of the cities of Greece was *one cause* of his profound melancholy. On the banishment of his friend Hermodorus he broke off all intercourse with the citizens, and passed his time playing with the children before the temple of Diana. Finally quitted Ephesus and retired to the mountains, living on roots and herbs. This sort of life induced dropsy. He returns to Ephesus, but his complaint is incurable, and he dies at the age of sixty. With all his cynical propensities and acerbity of temperament, he still loved his country and his native city, and would not consent, bad as Ephesus was, to go to Athens, where he was in high repute; nor to the court of Darius, then in the height of his power as conqueror of India. The letter of the king inviting him, and his reply, are given by Diog. Laert. and may be regarded as probably authentic. "The king Darius, son of Hystaspes, to Heraclitus of Ephesus, a man renowned for his science: Salutation. Thou hast written a book on 'Nature,' difficult to comprehend and explain. In certain passages, interpreted literally, this book seems to furnish a remarkable explanation of this universe and of the beings that it contains, and of the laws divine which preside over the movements which are going on in it. But many other passages are obscure, so much so that men, even the most versed in science, *know not how to find there thy thought.* Wherefore, I, Darius, son of Hystaspes, wish to become thy disciple in the science of the Greeks. Come, then, at once to my presence in my royal abode. The Greeks, for the most of the time, have little esteem for sages, and look with disdain on their admirable instructions. With me, on the contrary, every distinction awaits thee. Thou shalt find here every day new honors, and a life accommodated to all thy tastes."

If Darius really wrote this letter, he deserves to be had in everlasting remembrance of all philosophers and poverty-stricken men of letters—deserved, at any rate, a more civil reply than he got, according to the following. "Heraclitus of Ephesus to King Darius, son of Hystaspes: Salutation. All men forsake truth and justice, to abandon themselves—fools that they are—to avarice and vanity. As for me, stranger to every thought of this kind, and desirous of shunning the disgust and envy which always accompany high distinctions, *I shall not come* to the court of Persia, content as I am with the little that I possess, and which is amply sufficient for my desires." (The fellow should have been sent to the Ephesian State Lunatic Asylum, says the indignant nineteenth century, which he was not, for two reasons, as it seems to me; first, the said asylum was nowhere to be found; and secondly, he was not such a fool after all, for preferring a life of independent poverty to one of dependent ease and affluence.)

After perusing the above response of Heraclitus, we perceive the force and latent shrewdness of a remark of Aristotle, which, if that grim logician ever indulged in wit, we should certainly pronounce a capital piece of satire. As it is, we think the old Greek must have drawn down one eye-lid a little at the corner when he wrote it: that Heraclitus was one of those men with whom *their own opinions are as valid as science itself*. Darius and his wise men were not alone in finding it difficult to understand Heraclitus' book. It was universally acknowledged to be one of the obscurest books, as it was one of the first, ever written. The fragments that remain of it are sufficient to justify that opinion. Euripides sent a copy of it to Socrates, who with his accustomed keenness said of it, "What I understand of it is very good, and I am willing to believe the same is true of what I do not comprehend." This obscurity may have been owing, as Ritter supposes, partly to the early infancy of prose philosophical writing, partly to the lofty range of speculation in which he indulged; hence his thoughts were unable to express themselves adequately. His style is concise and broken, abrupt, of course obscure. Not unaware of this, he compares himself to the Sibyl, who "speaking with an inspired mouth, without a smile, inornate and unperfumed, doth pierce through centuries by the power of the God." Others, as Mallet in his very able work on the history of the Ionian philosophy, ascribe this obscurity to an intention of the author not to make his work the common property of vulgar and the reflecting, but to confine it to the capacity of those only who could appreciate it. So Descartes subsequently. He deposited his book in the temple of Artemis. (On the obscurity of Heraclitus, see Aristotle, Rhet. iii. 5; Cic. de Fin. ii. 5.)

There is much dispute as to the title of his work and its chief contents. By some it is regarded as a treatise on morals (Diog. L. ix. 12; Sext. Emp. adv. Math. viii. 7); by others, on physics; by others, as highly metaphysical in character. The probability is, it was neither exclusively, and all at once—a heterogeneous and confused collection of the opinions of the author on all subjects connected with philosophy. So Ritter i. 234. Diog. Laert. says the work was in three parts: physics, politics, and theology. On the whole, we may, with Mallet (Hist. Ion. Phil. 131), regard Heraclitus as the first Grecian philosopher who gave philosophy a wider range than it had previously traversed, and included in its sphere, not physics merely, but morals also.

The point of connection between his philosophy and that of the school to which he belongs is not difficult to discover. Like all the Ionian philosophers, he seeks a physical ground of all phenomena, a principle pervading and inherent in all natural phenomena. As with them all, this principle is with him a unity. Moreover, as with the dynamists all, and in distinction from the mechanists, it is a living principle or unity, a principle of life, growth, development that he seeks to discover. Not satisfied with tracing all things back to one first principle, as the others had done, he seeks for the *law of development*—how all things come from this first principle. This principle is FIRE, which seemed to him the most powerful, subtle, and pervading of all elements. So Aristotle affirms (Met. i. 3, de Mundo, c. 5), as also Plutarch (de Plac. Phil. i. 3), Diog. Laert. (ix. 7–9), and Cicero (Acad. ii. 37). Clement of Alexandria (Strom. v. 599), cites him as saying: "The world is not the work of gods or men. It always has been and always will be. It is an eternal fire, shining and going out by regular laws." (So also Plato, Symposium, p. 187; Diog. Laertius ix. 7–9.) From this element of fire, by transformation, proceed water, earth, and air. Both Clement and Plato notice the resemblance of this to Orpheus. Plato, in the Cratylus (p. 402), represents him as holding that all things proceed, by development and transformation, from this one principle, and are again resolved into it, by virtue of a perpetual flux. Nature entire resembles a river, which flows incessantly. From this perpetual flux of things result life and death; or rather there is neither life nor death—they are in fact one and the same thing; just as waking and sleeping, youth and age, they follow each other. So Plutarch cites him (Consol. ad Apoll. 10). And in yet another passage, cited by Plutarch (de Is. et Os. 45), he makes the movement of things in the world analogous to the vibrations of the chord of a bow, or of the lyre—all things in the world returning in like manner to the same point, only to go forth again, and so in an indefinite series of harmonious movements, ruled by necessity or destiny (see also Arist. Met. iv., 5; de Cœlo, iii. i; Plutarch, de Plac. Phil. i. 27, 28; Cicero de Fato. c. 17).

According to this philosophy, then, fire is the generating principle, which by rarefaction and condensation produces all things. Condensed, it becomes vapor. Assuming greater consistence, it becomes water. Still more condensed, this water becomes earth. This he calls the *movement from high to low*. Inversely, earth, rarefied, becomes water, and so on to the rest by evaporation from the sea. This is the movement *from low to high*. Fire is also the destroyer, as well as producer of the world; and this at certain alternate periods, in the eternity of time, fixed by the laws of destiny.

It seems to have been his idea that by opposition of parts results harmony of the whole; as in music, the combination of opposites, the sharp and the grave tones, produce harmony (Thus explained by Plato in the Symposium, and by Aristotle, de Mundo, c. 5. Compare Nic. Ethics, viii. 8). So in life, there are the opposite natures of male and female; and so throughout. These opposites or contraries in nature pass over to each other; life becomes death, death becomes in its turn life. Sleep passes into waking, and waking into sleep; and so on. Thus universally it is by the action of two opposite principles that all movement is produced. That principle, of these two opposites, which produces generation, he calls *war* or *strife;* that which produces death, *peace* or *concord.* Thus fire, in producing all things, passes through a series of transformations, by a law of repulsion or alteration: this is strife. So also by the law of affinity or assimilation all things resolve again into unity, cease to exist individually, die out; and this law of assimilation or death, is peace.

True, true, we exclaim. It is even thus. Life is war and a struggle—is tumult and confusion; the very principle of activity is strife. Death, on the contrary—is it not the principle of peace? the strife and tumult end—all is at rest. "For now should I have lain still and been quiet. With kings and counsellors of the earth. There the prisoners rest together; there the wicked cease from troubling and the weary be at rest."

Fire is a *restless* thing, incapable of permanence, longs to pass into other forms, struggles, strives; and the strife goes on, the restless activity, till again by the opposite law of affinity, like resolves itself again into like, and peace comes, and unity, and death. Ritter supposes that by fire he means, not flame but a sort of dry vapor. If so, his doctrine nearly resembles that of Anaximenes. He supposes also that Heraclitus uses the word in a symbolic sense, to denote the principle of universal vitality—something more than the mere ἀρχή of the previous philosopher, not a mere beginning, but a *life* pervading all.

As to the nature and arrangement of the various parts of the universe according to Heraclitus,—what we may call his natural philosophy. He supposes the heavens to be basins or bowls, the concave part toward the earth, so as to catch the evaporations from it, which form flames or stars. The sun is the purest of these flames. The stars, being farther off, fare not so well, get only poorer and impurer evaporations, and of course give light *accordingly.* The sun is just so large as it appears to be, and no larger, 12 inches in size, (Diog. L. ix. 7); it is kindled every morning and goes out every night (Arist. Met. 11. 2; Plat. de Rep. vi. 498). Eclipses of the sun and moon are caused by the basins turning round the other side toward us, while the monthly changes of the moon are produced by the revolution of its basin or reflector round itself (very much as a revolving light in a modern lighthouse). Day and night, seasons, winds, etc., are all produced by difference of evaporation. The evaporation of the sea, being impure and humid, extinguishes the lights, while that of the land, being pure, rekindles them. So crude and imperfect were the notions of that age respecting the structure of the universe. As crude and imperfect would ours have been, had not observation taken the place of theory, and science of conjecture. Viewed as mere conjecture, the bright thought of a mind speculating *a priori* on this subject, I know not why the hypothesis of the old Greek is not as reasonable and as probable, in itself considered, as any other. The trouble is, that it did not happen to be the correct one, and so seems to us a childish affair, because we happen to *know* another explanation to be the true one.

On the question of the legitimacy of our natural faculties, Heraclitus reasons thus. We are endowed with two means of attaining truth—sense and reason. The latter is the sole criterion of truth. The testimony of sense is not worthy of credence. "The eyes and ears of those having uninformed or imperfect souls are evil witnesses to men"

(Sext. Emp. adv. Math. vii. 126), which may mean simply that a man must know something in order to be a good observer and hearer, or it may mean to disparage the senses generally as not reliable, inasmuch as men generally have barbarous souls.

Reason, then, is the criterion of truth. What reason? not that of the individual, but the universal and divine reason, *i. e.*, the air or medium that surrounds us, which, drawn into us by inspiration, we become intelligent. This takes place at least during our waking hours. But in sleep we lose what we have acquired; the soul separates itself from that community of being which it has with the surrounding element, and we become irrational, because the senses are obstructed and the commerce is broken off between our souls and the universal soul. When we wake, the senses, the windows of the soul, open, and permit the soul to commune with the universal soul. Then we become rational again; just as coals kindle or go out at the approach or removal of fire. That which is the criterion of truth, then, is the universal reason,* or that which seems true to the judgment of all, but the conceptions of the *individual* reason are not to be relied on. The *universality* of a belief is the criterion of truth, a doctrine revived two thousand years afterward in opposition to the Cartesian doctrine in France. This idea of the senses as not reliable, is one which we shall afterward find carried out further in the Eleatic school, and made a very prominent doctrine, in fact, in subsequent Grecian philosophy. Heraclitus seems not to have conceived of Deity as an intelligent being distinct from nature. He was a pantheist. Hegel says there is not a position assumed by Heraclitus which he (Hegel) has not laid down in his logic. The following maxims are ascribed to him. It is necessary to be more on our guard against pride, than against a conflagration (Diog. L. ix. 2). To be wise is a great virtue,

* As authority for this whole statement, see Sext. Emp. adv. Math, vii. 129, 130, 133. Also Mallet, Man. Phil. p. 150.

and wisdom consists in conforming our words and actions to truth. The best thing for men is not to realize all their wishes. There await us at death such things as we neither hope nor expect. A people ought to battle for their laws as for their walls (Diog. L. ix. 2). His ideas of moist and dry seem to have been rather peculiar. A dry climate and soil he thinks most favorable for wisdom, *for there the soul* is *driest* and *best.* The soul, with him, is only a modification of air or fire, and so, of course, the drier is the purer and brighter. He accounts for the incapacity of the drunkard by his having a *moist soul!* (Stob. Serm. v. 120.) (See some fine observations on H. in Maurice, Encycl. Metrop. vol. ii. pp. 571–572).

§ 5.—Diogenes of Apollonia.

Born at Apollonia in Crete; time uncertain. According to Diog. Laertius, he was contemporary with Anaxagoras, and disciple of Anaximenes. Ritter regards him as successor of the latter. Renouvier and Mallet make him the successor of Heraclitus, which seems on the whole most probable. Tennemann fixes his date at the 77th Olympiad, about 472 B. C., which is probably not far from the truth.

He wrote several works, some on natural science, which continued till 600 of the Christian era. He came to Athens, which then began to be the metropolis of Greece in letters and science, as in power. Here, however, he was subject to envy and persecution, and his life even in danger.

Diogenes, the last of Ionian dynamists or naturalists; of those who saw in nature a being unique, material, living. Like the other Ionians, he takes a simple element as the principle of all things. The reason he assigns for so doing is the necessity of recognizing among things a series of mutual and reciprocal actions and reactions, which could not be, unless all proceeded from one common principle. So cited by Simplicius and Aristotle.

What, then, is his first principle? Like Anaximenes,

he takes *air*, meaning by it, not the simple atmosphere, but something intermediate between air and fire, something more refined than the grosser physical element, more ethereal and subtle, like the fire of Heraclitus, using the term symbolically, perhaps, rather than literally. Herein, as Ritter thinks, is seen the progress of philosophy from Thales onward, in that the whole school, while seeking the first principle in some one element, make that element less and less literal.

How was he led to take air as the first principle? By analogy. Soul is air or breath; so both Anaximenes and Diogenes. Life consists in the soul; hence they conclude that air is the universal life. Diogenes makes it the soul of the world, which, like the human soul, has consciousness and thought. So Simplicius (Phys. i. 33) and Cicero (de Nat. Deorum i. 12) represent him. No animal can live without air, hence he supposes air to be the soul. Even the blood, the source of vitality, contains air. Simplicius (Phys. i. 32) thus cites: "Man and the other animals who breathe, live on air, and the air constitutes their *soul and their thought*, and if respiration ceases life and thought cease at the same time." Aristotle (de Hist. Anim.) thus: "Diogenes established that thought is produced by the circulation of air, with the blood, through the body along the veins." Plutarch also the same (de Plac. 4, 5). This theory is remarkable. It accounts for the formation of thought in a singular way, and also presupposes the circulation of the blood, a discovery of two thousand years later date. According to Plutarch and Aristotle, he makes the heart, by virtue of circulation of air, the seat and centre at once of life and thought. But Ritter disputes it.

Simplicus (Phys. i. 33) makes him confer on the air the attributes of divinity, greatness, power, knowledge, eternity, etc. By virtue of intelligence, *this supreme principle is regarded by him as author of the order and har mony in the universe.* "Without intelligence," says he, "it is impossible all things should be distributed as they are, each having its bound and law, as summer, winter, night, day, rain, wind, etc." (Phys. i. 32). Hence he infers the origin of things from an intelligent being, νόησιν ἔχον, a *soul which vivifies all and knows all.* "And to me it seems that the intelligent principle is that which men call *air;* it is *it* that *regulates* and *governs* all, pervades and penetrates all, and *there is nothing which partakes not of its essence*" (Phys. i. 33). In this last we have the element of pantheism. Taking the whole together, however, we have in it a grand advance, in philosophy, upon anything that we have yet found. From the doctrine of the previous philosophers, as Anaximenes and others, that the first principle was a mere force—vitality, physical development—to this doctrine of intelligence as the chief characteristic of that principle, the advance is striking. From mere action of blind fatality and eternal necessary movement, giving rise to the production of the universe; from that, to this idea of wisdom and intelligence ordering all these movements and appointing the seasons and their bounds, the difference, the progress is great.

Yet even here we have not as yet the idea of a *distinct spiritual existence,* such as we designate by the title of Deity, but rather, only a material being endowed with intelligence—a corporeal principle uniting with itself an intelligent element. So also thinks Mallet, see 175. The distinction between the mind and body, as separate essences, does not occur to him. His deity, or first cause, is merely corporeal or physical *nature,* endowed with the higher properties of intelligence, etc. He originates the idea, hitherto unknown to philosophy, of an efficient cause, but gets *not so far* as to perceive that it must be itself *immaterial.* This was the next and the next higher step in progress of the human mind, unaided by revelation, seeking after God. To make this final discovery was reserved for another studious and thoughtful man. But it is interesting to pause even here, and see how, by careful steps and slow, little by little, the mind by light of nature has wrought out its painful way thus far *toward* the knowledge of the true God.

Combining the two elements of spirituality and materiality in his first principle, Diogenes makes it, as *material*, originate the worlds in much the same way as Anaximenes had done; excepting always, that the various transformations take place, not by fixed and fated laws of movement as with him, but by intelligent and powerful will, assuming the double function of cause material and cause efficient.

Condensation of air produces *water;* further condensation, *earth;* rarefaction of air gives fire, etc. This process goes on continually, all things returning again to air whence they proceeded; nothing remaining *in statu quo;* but the primordial whole itself infinite and unchanged, notwithstanding the finite nature of the modifications.

The place of the different elements is determined by their relative density, water and earth taking the lower, air and fire the higher spheres. From these lighter and upper elements result the sun and stars.

From the different qualities of the air, which is not always and in all forms the same, but diverse, result the differences of species and individuals. The degree of warmth and dryness and rarity varies in the souls of different animals and in those of men, and hence a difference among them in activity, habits, intelligence, and bodily form, (Simplicius, Phys. lib. i. fol. 33).

The earth was formed by condensation from the warm surrounding sphere. This condensation produced motion, and so earth, as heaviest, was fixed in the centre. The sun, acting on the primitive moisture, formed the sea. This is gradually drying up and will finally disappear. Living creatures were formed out of the earth, before its oblique declination.

§ 6.—Anaxagoras.

Birth-place, Ionia, as with so many other ancient philosophers; town or city, Clazomenæ; time, Olymp. 70, or 500 B. C. So Apollodorus and Diogenes Laertius, followed by Brucker, Ritter, and Tennemann. Death, 428 B. C., at 72. The most notable in many respects of the Ionian school; the most perfect development of it. A life, a system, every way worthy of study, and perhaps you will say, with me, of admiration.

Of illustrious family, like Heraclitus, and like him he renounced riches and greatness for philosophy. Affairs public and private, says Mallet, rank, fortune, family, he abandoned all for science, and some one asking him one day if there was no longer for him any such thing as country, he replied, pointing at the same time to heaven, "My country is, on the contrary, the object of all my thoughts."

His youth was spent at Clazomenæ, and the other Ionian cities. Uncertain now who were his teachers, and what his travels, which were extensive. Diogenes Laertius makes him the pupil of Anaximenes, yet by oversight fixes the death of the latter at 538, or thirty-eight years before the *birth* of the former. Brucker not much better, for according to his dates Anaximenes must have been over eighty when Anaxagoras became his pupil. Yet, if not the pupil, he doubtless received the current philosophy of Anaximenes, Anaximander, Thales, etc. He finally emigrated to Athens, at about forty or forty-five. Athens was about to become the literary metropolis of Greece. Here he had, as tradition relates, pupils of distinction, as Pericles, with whom he was intimate, Euripides, Archelaus, Democritus, and even Socrates. Such is the testimony of Diogenes Laertius and of Suidas, as to Euripides and Socrates. Cicero bears the same testimony as to Euripides, and both Diogenes and Cicero affirm the same of Pericles.

Anaxagoras is the first Athenian philosopher of note,

although of Ionian origin, as were in fact the founders of all the great schools of the first age of Greek philosophy. From Miletus alone went forth Thales, Anaximander, Anaximenes, and Archelaus; from Ephesus, Heraclitus; from Clazomenæ, Anaxagoras. Ionia gave birth also to Xenophanes, founder of the Eleatic school, and Pythagoras of the Italian. Thus does this little province of Asia Minor give Italy her first two philosophers, Xenophanes and Pythagoras, and also Athens her first.

Anaxagoras passes his old age in poverty and want, and at the decline of the fortunes of Pericles, his friend and patron, suffers persecution. Accused of impiety toward the gods for saying that the sun is a burning stone, or mass of incandescent matter, according to one account he was con-condemned to death. Sufficiently cool his reply on receiving that sentence: that "nature had long ago pronounced against him the same sentence." According to the more probable statement, Pericles appears in his behalf, defends him boldly before the judges, and procures his liberation; but Anaxagoras goes into exile immediately, some say voluntarily, out of chagrin. Exile he was, however, at Lampsacus in Asia Minor, where he ended his days; Suidas says he put an end to his own life. Some one regretting that he should die afar from his native land, he replied, "the way to Hades is much the same from every place." Citizens of Lampsacus gave him funeral honors, and inscribed on his tomb, "Here lies Anaxagoras, who of all men penetrated farthest into the celestial world."

Was Anaxagoras, then, chiefly an astronomer? His epitaph might seem to convey that idea, but it was not so. It is related also by Diogenes Laertius and Aristotle, that when one asked him to what end he was born, he replied, "to this end, to contemplate the heaven, the sun, and the moon." This certainly indicates a leading propensity of his mind. Yet astronomy was but the preface and prelude to the grand oratorio. He studied nature in her external arrangements, only as the handmaid to a loftier and grander philosophy. The first philosophers, as we have seen, were all naturalists, and generally astronomers; but it was cosmogony rather than astronomy, the science of the *grand whole*—the ground and origin and genesis of the great universe ; whence it proceeded ; how it came to be ; that they had chiefly in view in all these inquiries.

Anaxagoras belongs to the class of philosophers whom we denote mechanists, regarding the universe not as the development of a unique element, but the result of the combination of many elements.

The primitive state of the universe was chaos, according to Anaxagoras; within the bosom of which chaos are contained an infinite number of material elements, of extreme tenuity, infinitely small and so imperceptible to sense. (In this last he holds a doctrine kindred to that of the *atomists,* Epicurus and Democritus, who give the name of atoms to these elements which he calls *τὸ σμικρὸν ἄπειρον* (the small infinite). These little fellows are all in a heap and confusion. Air and ether, however—by which last he means probably, as Aristotle and Plutarch suppose, what Heraclitus calls fire—envelope the whole, and are distinguished from the confused mass as elements special and determined. (Here his theory unites with that of Heraclitus and Anaximenes.)

In this jumble or chaos, everything is in all, *i. e.*, every part is like the whole, and contains a portion of the whole, and so to these infinite littles he gives the singular name homœomeriæ, *αἱ ὁμοιομερίαι* denoting that of which *the part is like the whole* (Plato. Phædo.c. 17 ; Arist. Phys. i. 4 ; Arist. Met. i, 3, 7, iv. 4 ; de Gen. An. i. 18 ; Sext. Emp. Hyp. Pyrr. iii. 32 ; Adv. Math. ix. 368 ; Diog. Laert. ii. 8 ; Cic. Acad. ii, 37). These are the elementary seeds of things. The whole mass of them a unity, yet each by itself a reproduction of the whole on a small scale. This is the point of departure. How comes the *world* out of this ? By movement, and this movement is the work of *mind.* Repose is

2*

the primitive state; repose in confusion, in chaos; by movement, things thus jumbled together in confusion separate themselves and become order; and this movement is not any principle inherent in matter itself, but the work of an *immaterial* existence—of mind (Plato, Phædo, 46, 47; Arist. Phys. i. 4. viii. 1; Met. i. 3, 4; Sext. Emp. adv. Math. ix. 6, 7; Diog. L. Proœm. 4, ii. 6; Cic. de. Nat. Deor. i. 1). *Duality* is thus established. *Matter* and *mind: a great point gained in philosophy.*

This movement is circular. By means of it the particles that are homogeneous, the cold, the wet, the dark, unite and form the earth, stones, etc.; while the light, warm, dry, uniting, ascend to the upper regions. Cold converts the clouds to water, water to earth, earth to stones, etc. Dissolution succeeds to aggregation in the same way—one follows the other continually. Nothing is born, nothing perishes; it is aggregation or dissolution; the reunion and separation of parts—nothing else. The things themselves are eternal.

The reciprocal action of fire, water, and earth, produces animals, which afterward propagate themselves. The fire, or ether, is highest, then water and air, then, lowest of all, the earth. Water being thus intermediary between earth and air and fire, is in constant state of motion. The sea, *e. g.*, continually changing its locality, retreating from some places and encroaching on others—sea and land changing places—(just as geology teaches at the present day). The sea would one day, if the world stood long enough, cover the mountains of Lampsacus.

In meteorology also we find Anaxagoras anticipating the results of modern science; that winds are produced by the sun's rays acting on the air, that thunder is caused by the shock of the clouds, etc. He predicted the fall of a certain meteoric stone. Regarded the sun itself and the stars as incandescent stones; and the moon, habitable, as the earth, with hills and valleys. Even conceived the existence of intelligent beings on other planets. "There are in other worlds than ours, men who have, as we, their cities, their habitations, their labors; for them as for us, there is a sun, a moon, stars; for them likewise the ground produces fruits of all kinds, which they gather and use as they need." Shooting stars he thinks are scintillations flying through the air; the milky way, the reflection of the sun's rays from stars not themselves luminous.

As to the great problem of the veracity of our faculties, he is more Eleatic than Ionian; decides that the testimony of sense cannot in any way conduct to certitude, and fixes on reason as the criterion of truth (Arist. Met. iv. 5, 7; Sext. Emp. Hyp. Pyrr. i. 33; Adv. Math. vii. 90, 91; Cic. Acad. i. 12; Tusc. Quest. iv. 23, 31). We see in this a tendency to the idealism of Zeno, and of Berkeley, Hume, and others among the moderns. That such was his view, is sustained by passages cited by Aristotle, Simplicius, Cicero, and others, about the snow appearing white, while in reality it is composed of water which is black. Lewes, however, thinks that he did not mean to deny that the senses are *subjectively* true—that they give correct reports of their impressions, that is, of phenomena—but only that they are not objectively to be relied upon. They perceive *phenomena*, but not *noumena*. If so, however, he is still not far from modern idealism; for this which is just now stated was really the position of Hume and Berkeley, and must be that of every consistent idealist. No one can deny the *subjective* truth of the senses; that were to deny consciousness.

What, finally, was his idea of God? The earlier philosophers had admitted only material causes. Anaxagoras, as Diogenes had also done, added to this an efficient cause. So say Aristotle, Simplicius, Diogenes Laertius, Proclus, and Cicero. He makes mind, in distinction from matter, an object of thought—immense, omnipresent mind. In this respect—and it is a grand step forward—his theory is wholly and totally distinct from, and in advance of the *pantheism* of many of the earlier philosophers and the atheism of others. Yet even with him the world and God are so related to each other, that while there would be no world without God, so also no God without the world. His idea of mind,—so Ritter—was not that of an entity existing apart from and *independent* of matter, pure spirit, but that of mind as exhibited in finite phenomena of animate material objects. This world-soul lives in every living thing. Individual souls differ in degree, not in nature, from this (So Arist. de Anima. i. 2. iii. 5). It is dependent on the bodily organization, and is set in motion by external impressions. It accompanies all bodily organization. Plants have mind, have pain, desire, pleasure, etc., even knowledge also. Ritter, accordingly, makes his discovery of mind to be much less of an advance on the previous systems, that of Heraclitus, *e. g.*, than I have represented it, and than it is generally regarded. Aristotle unjustly charges him with introducing *other* causes beside mind to account for things. But mind *originates* the *first* motion, and all other effects are results of that motion, mind is the first and efficient cause, not of matter, for matter and the *nous* or mind are coëternal, but of order and arrangement. The essence of mind is simple, pure, without mixture, containing in itself the knowledge and principle of the movement of all things, still not strictly creator, but only *ordainer* or *builder*, arranger of the world. It is not the *moral* providence of Plato, but only the metaphysical one, the *nous* pure, that puts things in motion and makes the laws of nature ; hence Plato dissatisfied with him. Yet in him is the germ of what Plato fully developed, for Aristotle makes him say that the *nous is the source of* the *beautiful* and the *good.* Here at least is the presentiment of the grand discovery of Plato (See Mallet, Hist. Ion. Phil. p. 244; also 237, 8).

CHAPTER II.

THE ITALIAN SCHOOL.

PYTHAGORAS.

THIS school, whose general characteristics have been already given (see introductory outline), was contemporary in part with the former. The later Ionian philosophers were subsequent to Pythagoras. To have introduced this school, however, at an earlier moment, and precisely in its chronological place, would have violated that unity which we wished to give to the Ionian philosophy, as a distinct system. Nor can the precise chronology of this school be determined. On no point are authorities more divided. The period variously assigned for the birth and epoch of Pythagoras ranges between the limits of the 43d and 64th Olympiads, a range of eighty-four years—somewhere within which period he was born. With Ritter and Tissot, I am inclined to place it in the 49th, or about 584 B. C. So Ueberweg 582. (But Schwegler and Butler prefer 548.) It is sufficient to say that while the Ionian school was flourishing and in its full vigor and prime in the Grecian colonies of Asia Minor, there arose in one of those islands of the Ægean so celebrated in history, a philosopher who entertained the bold and romantic project of founding, not a new system of philosophy merely, but a state based upon philosophical principles—a community of philosophers. This man was Pythagoras of Samos, who after a time fixed his residence in Crotona, in Lower Italy, an Achæan colony. Of this man's personal history not much authentic information can be gleaned. Tradition has reported much that is marvellous of his birth and history. "A fabulous *wonder-man*," as Fries expresses it. His birth supernatural, the son of Apollo, a divine glory wreathed his brow. As a mark of his divine origin he bore a golden thigh ; was seen at different places at the same time; wild beasts obeyed his call. He received the gift of recollection of his previous existence. He heard, what to our dull ears is inaudible, the harmony of the spheres. When he gave himself to meditation he discovered not only the nature of all beings, but at a glance of the eye took in ten or twenty ages of human history. "Shall we wonder," says Lewes, "that he was venerated as a god ? He who could so transcend all earthly struggles, and the great ambitions of the greatest men, as to live only for the sake of wisdom, was he not of a higher stamp than ordinary mortals ? Well might later historians picture him as clothed in robes of white, his head crowned with gold, his aspect grave, magisterial, and calm ; above the manifestation of any human joy, of any human sorrow; enwrapt in contemplation of the deeper mysteries of existence ; listening to music, and the hymns of Homer, Hesiod, and Thales; or listening to the harmony of the spheres. He was the first of mystics. And to a lively, talkative, quibbling, active, versatile people like the Greeks, what a grand phenomenon must this solemn, earnest, silent, meditative man have appeared."

There is great difficulty in ascertaining what the doctrines of this school were. He taught in secret, and each disciple carried out and modified the views of the teacher to suit his own turn of mind ; so that his disciples differ among themselves. Certain it is, however, that he founded an order, so to speak, somewhat as Loyola in after times founded the order of Jesuits ; the end of which association was at once scientific and moral, political and religious. The three hundred members of this order were of the noblest families in Crotona, the aristocratic families, and they were trained to self-knowledge, so that they should be fit to command the world. It was only after examination and probation that they were admitted to the society, and only by slow degrees and after a long novitiate, were they admitted to its higher honors. This novitiate of several years was passed in *silence,* hearing the instructions of others, but not themselves allowed to speak. For this class of disciples Pythagoras had one course of teaching, and for the initiated another, which latter was never fully divulged. Pythagoras differed from the Grecian spirit of the age in attaching importance to woman. His wife was a philosopher, and fifteen female disciples are numbered among his more distinguished pupils. How they managed to get through the many novitiate years of silence is still a mystery. The influence of Pythagoras and his fraternity in Crotona soon became unbounded; extended by branch societies to other Italian cities; supplanted existing politcal institutions; took the place of senates; excited suspicion and alarm by its rapid growth, its ambitious designs, its secrecy and mysticism—(perhaps the opposition of those, who found the rule of the order too severe for them, helped on the matter, as Fries suggests)—awakened first the fears, then the resentment of the people; involved a large portion of Italy in contest and convulsion, and was finally by a sort of general uprising broken up and scattered. Many of its adherents perished. Whether Pythagoras himself was a victim to the popular rage, or died a fugitive, is now uncertain. Some question even, whether the breaking up occurred before his death. So Fries. His fraternity, however, did not survive him. His philosophical system and sect may have continued longer, but his school died with himself, and his system and secret perished with his followers and immediate disciples. Hence it is that so little is known of his philosophy. The paucity of reliable writings, and the contradictory statements of his disciples, add to the difficulty.

This much is known, however, of his philosophical system. A proficient in *mathematics* and in *music,* he is struck with the beauty and simplicity of the general principles or primary laws of those sciences; meditates much on those two grand elements, number and time; perceives that everything in the universe is capable of being measured by these two elements, number and time; concludes that they must therefore be the first principles of things (Aristotle, Met. i. 5, xiv. 3; Cicero Acad. ii. 37; Sext. Emp. adv. Math. iv. 2), and carrying over in this way these prime elements into the sphere of philosophy, founds on this basis a system at once novel, beautiful, mystic, and ideal. Number is the prime element of all, the first principle of things. The essence of number is the *even-odd* as he calls it; that is the monad primitive and absolute, the absolute unity, containing in itself all other numbers and the elements of all things. This absolute unity is creator of itself, binds together the eternal duration of things, is deity; for deity provides for all, embraces all, and is one. Deity, then, is number. The grand problem of the universe and its supreme builder and disposer—the problem of things and of God himself is solved. To state the system a little more in detail, its essential process of thought is this: Among the phenomena of nature there is one and only one character which puts order and harmony among things, and determines their relations; which imparts to all existence the faculty of being intelligible and definite, and, in fine, to our intelligence itself the only means it has of knowing anything. This character is *number*. Owing to this, the world becomes orderly, harmonious, perfect; can call itself *Kosmos*—order, beauty—(which word he first applies to designate the world). What the nature is of this wonderful element, number, he cannot explain; but he can sing its praise, can incite to its study, as developed in geometry, astronomy, music; can trace its relations, and the ways in which it reveals itself.

This number is a creator, separate from matter; matter is passive—not living, as the Ionians have it. Here a *dual-*

ity: number on the one hand; matter subject to its wonderful operations on the other hand. Number produces, not the finite and limited only, but the *infinite* and undetermined. What in itself is not knowable brings into existence the unlimited being—the infinite one. The parent, the root, the germ of number—this mighty producer—is unity; and unity and duality, the one and the many, are the elements of all things; the one, the active or limiting; the other, the passive or limited principle (Sextus Emp. adv. Math. x. 261–2, 277; Diog. Laert. viii. 25; Plutarch de Plac. Phil. i. 3, 7). By means of this unity in multiplicity all things in the world harmonize completely, and there results the harmony of the spheres, analogous to earthly music, while the whole moves in agreeable proportion around a common central point, the central fire (Arist. de Cœlo ii. 9, 13; Sext. Emp. adv. Math. iv. 6, x. 283; Cicero de Nat. Deor. iii. 11; Arist. Met. i. 5).

Beside this subjective view of the universe, he seems also to have taken an *objective* view, thus: What unity is to intelligence, *such* is *light* to the *material* world, imparts life, illuminates, warms, fecundates, becomes the creator of the physical universe. Under the name of ether, it is the vital element of nature; the symbol, nay more, essence of Deity. His duality runs thus then: light, harmony, unity, on the one hand; darkness, disorder, plurality, on the other.

His idea of Deity seems to have been that of the invariable being that inhabits or dwells in the supreme unity, regarded as *manifest in the universe;* the spirit pervading it; the all-seeing light; the fire traversing creation and kindling up intelligences, minds, everywhere; represented by the sun or great central fire, the most perfect object in nature (so Tennemann and Butler), soul of the universe, from whom all souls proceed. Others, however, as Lewes, deny this view, and suppose that Pythagoras does not conceive of mind otherwise than as a *material* phenomenon, not as an infinite intelligence, merely a mathematical abstraction. But this does not well accord with the other parts of his system.*

The following table presents in contrast the various categories or primitive elements, to one or other of which all things in nature may be reduced. The limited and unlimited; the equal and unequal; the one and the many; the right and the left; male and female; that which rests and that which moves; the straight line, and the curve; light and dark; good and evil; the square, and the quadrilateral, not square; in all a decade; the essence of number. The fourth and the seventh also play a conspicuous part in the formation of things.

This general method of philosophy they apply to nature not only, but to the soul, to Deity, to morals, to everything. *Number* lies at the foundation of the whole. Thus soul (which is itself an emanation from and allied to the great central fire or light—he calls it a self-moving number—virtue is the harmony of the soul, its *unison*) is the harmony of body; justice is a number porportionately equal, etc. The scientific insight of Pythagoras, not much above that of his age, says Fries, and Aristotle suggests the same.

The world consists of ten great bodies or spheres, which revolve harmoniously around a common centre, the source to all of life and warmth. The sun is that centre, immovable, and worlds circle around it. So the disciples of Pythagoras taught, and such was probably the doctrine of Pythagoras himself. So Ueberweg. Pythagoras taught the

* For brilliant sketch of life and history of Pythagoras, see Lewes, vol. i. p. 15–20.

For the manner in which he came to regard *number* as the principle of all things, and to ground his system on that, see Butler, vol. i. p. 316–319, or series 1, lecture 6.

On the question whether P. makes numbers to be things or only *symbols* of things, see Lewes, i. 30.

existence of genii, and their apparition. Souls are preëxistent to the bodies which they inhabit, and survive those bodies, pass into other forms and dwell in other bodies by the law of animal generation. This doctrine seems to have been founded in the idea of retribution, justice after death. Life is a task, which we fulfil according to destiny. The soul is a monad self-moved. In its perfect and proper state it is unity, but it loses perfection, and becomes imperfect, by any movement or change. Imperfection he defines as departure from unity. Now in man the soul is not absolute unity, not therefore in absolute perfection. It has *three elements*, reason, intelligence, and desire (or *sensibility* as we should say), the two last in common with the brutes, the first characteristic of himself. The understanding has its seat in the brain; the sensibilities and passions in the heart. Each of these elements may become predominant, and as it does the man becomes eminently rational, or able, or *sensual*. Hence the doctrine of transmigration. As a modern writer has elegantly expressed it, "This soul, which can look before and after, can shrink and shrivel itself into an incapacity of contemplating aught but the present moment; of what depths of degeneracy it is capable! What a beast it may become! And if something lower than itself, why not something higher? And if something higher and lower, may there not be a law accurately determining its elevation and descent? Each soul has its peculiar evil tastes bringing it to the likeness of different creatures beneath itself; why may it not be under the necessity of abiding in the condition of that thing to which it had adapted and reduced itself?"

The rules of life and morals in the Pythagorean system are accordingly strict and ascetic;—temperance, moderation, fidelity, love, friendship, are insisted on. The morality of the system is severe and religious; daily self-examination is prescribed as a duty, the soul must be cultivated to all things excellent and true. Hence the importance of music and gymnastics in the training of children especially, who must by great care be educated to virtue. Suicide, however, is allowable. He compares this life to the Olympic games, where some seek honor and the crowns; others go for barter and gain; others, more noble, go to enjoy the spectacle and observe what passes. So we quit our native abode, the skies, come into the world, some seeking honor, some wealth, some power, etc.; a few study nature. These he calls philosophers, the noblest sort, the highest occupation of man.

CHAPTER III.

ELEATIC SCHOOL.

THIS school derives its name from Elea, a Greek colony of Lower Italy, the residence, in his later years, of Xenophanes, the founder of the school. It comprises among its distinguished members, Xenophanes, Parmenides, Zeno, and Empedocles. It covers a period of time from 100 to 150 years in extent, or from about the beginning or middle of the 6th to about the middle of the 5th century B.C.—550 or 600 to 450. It was, therefore, subsequent to the Ionian and, in part at least, to the Pythagorean school, and in some way may be regarded as the legitimate result and product of the latter. Its chief characteristic as a school was its purely rational and supra-sensible character—transcendental, as we should now term it—its utter disregard of the sensible, and attention to the supra-sensible.

Its origin—like that of all the preceding schools—Ionian.

§ 1.—XENOPHANES.

The 6th century B. C. was to Greece, and especially to her colonies, the era of liberty and thought, of commercial enterprise and activity, of science and of increasing wealth, beyond any that had preceded it. It was at this period that there arose in Ionia, fertile in great minds, a mind at once original and penetrating, animated with the genius of both the Ionian and the Pythagorean schools, yet coinciding with neither and opposed to both, destined to cast new light upon the problems of an intricate science, and to become the founder of a new school of philosophical thought, the first school indeed of *pure* metaphysics in Greece. Xenophanes was born at Colophon in Ionia. He flourished, according to Ritter, about the 60th Olympiad, or 540 B. C.; born 569 B. C., according to Ueberweg; but according to Cousin, he was born much earlier than that, —in the 40th Olympiad, or 620 B. C. As he lived to an advanced age, he may perhaps have been somewhat in years before he became known widely as a philosopher ; so that we suppose him, with Ritter, to have flourished at 540 or 550, and yet, with Cousin, to have been born at or near the beginning of that century.

He was contemporary with Anaximander and Pythagoras. Exiled from his country, he seems to have wandered for a time in Sicily, and subsequently, at the age of eighty, to have settled in Elea, in Lower Italy, a colony of Phocæans. This was an enterprising and active commercial city, not ill-fitted to become the centre of a school of science. Xenophanes was a poet. From his twenty-fifth to his ninety-second year he seems to have cultivated that peculiar species of poetical composition for which his native city was famous, the elegiac and rhapsodical. His philosophic thoughts are clothed in verse. He wrote epics, narrative and didactic. Opposed to the anthropomorphic representations of the earlier poets, especially Hesiod and Homer, he indulges in frequent and bitter denunciation of all such modes of expression. Plato, it may be remarked, afterward sympathized with him in this respect. A poor man, wandering for years from place to place, and supporting himself by the recital of his poems, he was nevertheless wealthy in his superior mental resources. He longed with insatiable desire to discover truth; as Tennyson has expressed it,

> "Yearning in desire
> To follow knowledge like a sinking star
> Beyond the utmost bound of human thought."

How finely expressive of this unsatisfied desire are these lines, which another Grecian poet, Timon the sillograph, puts into the mouth of Xenophanes.

> "Oh, that mine was the deep mind, prudent and looking to both sides;
> Long, alas, have I strayed, on the road of error beguiled.
> And am now hoary of years, yet exposed to doubt and distraction
> Of all kinds; for wherever I turn to consider,
> I am lost in the *one and all.*"

Xenophanes was, through a long and active life, a diligent inquirer after truth, and terminated that life, those long, anxious years, without having solved the great problem. Not to him was it given. He only learned how little he knew.

From this one stand-point, this nineteenth century since the advent of Him whom kings and prophets waited for but died without the sight, surrounded as we are by all the discoveries of science and all the light of revelation, it is easy to look back upon the path of such a mind struggling on unaided either by science or revelation; groping its way slowly and painfully in its fruitless search after truth, and congratulate ourselves that we are wiser and more fortunate; but for one I cannot, without a feeling of admiration and even of gratitude, regard the toilsome progress and earnest endeavors of such a mind—of those ancient thinkers, who broke out the path for all coming time, and by their unrewarded toil earned for us the riches of a better inheritance. How true is it—what Xenophanes himself has said—

> "Not from the first was all revealed by the gods unto mankind;
> Only in time and by long search can man find out the better."

The theology of Xenophanes. This, the principal thing in his philosophy. It was the doctrine of Xenophanes that men can know nothing with certainty respecting the gods. The anthropomorphic views of the Greeks he is never weary of ridiculing. If cattle could paint, horses would describe the gods as so many horses, and oxen as so many oxen.

> "Men foolishly think that gods are born like as men are,
> And have, too, a dress like their own and their voice and their figure;
> But if oxen and lions had hands, like ours, and fingers,
> Then would horses like unto horses, and oxen to oxen,
> Paint and fashion their god-forms, and give to them bodies
> Of like shape to their own, as they themselves, too, are fashioned."

Thus it is, he says, that the Ethiopians represent their deities as having flat noses and black faces, while the Thracians picture theirs with blue eyes and ruddy complexions.

What view, then, will Xenophanes take of the Deity? Surrounded with mysteries, and oppressed with doubts, how will he solve the great problem of existence? The physiological method of the Ionians, the mathematical theory of the Italian school, seemed to him neither of them to have solved the great problem, How came this great universe to be where and what it is? who and what is that invisible mysterious power or being that men call God? On this he pondered much, and reached at last a solution. Casting his eyes on the immensity of the heavens, he said that unity was God (Arist. Metaph. i. 5). The expression, God is a sphere, has also been attributed to him, though with doubtful authority. This has been differently explained by various critics. Some, as Cousin, Renouvier, and others, regard the expression as *metaphorical* merely, to denote the *perfection* of deity, an idea for which he could find no better expression or symbol than the sphere, a perfect figure complete in itself, equal throughout, and *one*. Ritter, and also Krug, however give it quite a different interpretation; suppose that by this expression, he intends to denote the entire unity of the material and the intellectual; the world and

God, as *one* and the same being, and made use of the sphere as a *symbol* of this identity. Lewes interprets it of the literal firmament: "Overarching him was the deep blue infinite vault, immovable, unchangeable, embracing him and all things; *that* his heart proclaimed to be God. As Thales had gazed abroad upon the sea, and felt that he was resting on its infinite bosom, so Xenophanes gazed above him at the sky, and felt that he was encompassed by it. Moreover, it was a great mystery, inviting, yet defying scrutiny. The sun and moon whirled to and fro through it, the stars were 'pinnacled dim in its intense inane.' The earth was constantly aspiring to it in shape of vapor, the souls of men were perpetually aspiring to it with vague yearnings. It was the centre of all existence. It was existence itself. It was the *One*, the immovable, in whose bosom the many were moved."

The view according to which the sphere is a mere symbol or metaphor to denote the perfection and unity of God, seems to me not only the far higher and nobler, but the one more accordant with the general spirit and tenor of the teachings of Xenophanes. Clearly enough, he holds the Deity, whether one with nature and the material world or not, to be self-existent, intelligent, eternal, one and not many, all-powerful, all-wise (Arist. de Xenoph. c. 3; Cic. Acad. ii. 37; Sext. Emp. Hyp. Pyrr. i. 225; iii. 218; Adv. Math. vii. 49, viii. 326; Diog. L. ix. 19). This being—such is his language—"sees all, hears all, one God alone; of gods and men the greatest, like mortals neither in figure nor mind, who without knowing fatigue directs all by the power of intelligence, all vision, all cognizance, all hearing." This deity is not begotten, for how can he be born of his equal? how of his unequal? If not born, he cannot *perish*, since he is independent, and by himself. He is negatively defined as being neither finite nor infinite; not finite, for one thing can be limited only by another, which implies plurality, but as the deity is *one*, there is no such limitation; not infinite, because *non-being* alone, as having neither beginning, middle, nor end, is infinite, but God is *being* and so not infinite. He is neither movable nor immovable, for the same reasons, one thing can only be moved by another, and God is one, not many, hence not movable; yet not immovable, for *non-being* alone is immovable. In a word, the Deity of Xenophanes is the one eternal being, self-equal, always the same, without beginning, without end, without *change.* Truly a grand conception for the unaided reason of any man to form of the Deity.

The leading features of the theology of Xenophanes seem to be these two: the importance which he attaches to the idea of Divine unity, the one all; the impossibility of forming adequate conceptions of such a being, of fully comprehending him, of defining him otherwise than by *negatives,* since we know what he is not rather than what he is. There was a tendency to scepticism in Xenophanes, as manifested in that portion of his theology just named. He doubted rather than assented; could not say positively that such things were so and so, but could only deny that they were so and so; was cautious in affirming, bold only in questioning. Nor was this manifest alone in his theology, where certainly it is a quality not out of place, but extended to all human knowledge. "He was the first," says Lewes, "who confessed the impotence of reason to compass the wide, exalted aims of philosophy. . . . He was a great, earnest spirit struggling after truth, and as he obtained a glimpse of her celestial countenance he proclaimed his discovery, how ever it might contradict what he had before announced. Long travel, various experience, examination of different systems, new and contradictory glimpses of the problem he was desirous of solving, produced in his mind a scepticism of a noble, somewhat touching sort, wholly unlike that of his successors. It was the combat of contradictory opinions in his mind, rather than disdain of knowledge. His faith was steady, his opinions vacillating. He had a profound conviction of the existence of an eternal, all-wise, infinite Being, but this belief he was unable to reduce to a consistent formula. There is a deep sadness in these verses:

"Certainly no mortal yet knew, and ne'er shall there be one,
Knowing both well, the gods, and the All, whose nature we treat of;
For when by chance he, at times, may utter the true and the perfect,
He wists not unconscious; for *error is spread over all things!*"

The great advance of philosophy under his auspices, thinks Ritter, is the recognition, more or less distinct in all his teachings, of the *opposition between pure truth* and its *sensible manifestation.* Yet we are not to conclude that he rejected all phenomena, all nature, as *semblance* merely, but only that he distrusted the knowledge thus obtained, sought something more certain and more valuable, sought through the sensible and through nature to get a glimpse of the eternal truth, and through the imperfect revelation which the material world affords, to reach the domain of pure, infinite, and unknown reality.

In his natural philosophy or cosmology, he admits the existence of the four elements as concerned in the production of the universe, viz., earth, air, fire, and water. He denies, strictly speaking, the *production* or *beginning* of all *being;* these elements are eternal, then, but by combination forms are produced, transitory, perishable, such as the earth, and the human race. Nothing can be produced out of nothing or non-being. Being, then, cannot begin to be. It must always have been. It may pass through various forms and modifications, however, and these are the manifold phenomena of nature. He holds that the petrifactions found in the strata of the earth, as in the mines and marble quarries, etc., show that the sea once covered the land, and and that land and water are probably changing places (So Hippolytus adv. Hereticos, i. 12).

§ 2.—Parmenides.

The doctrines advanced in the germ by Xenophanes, we find more fully developed in Parmenides. According to Ritter, who follows a statement of Plato, he must have been born somewhere about Olympiad 65, or 520 B.C. Commonly regarded as disciple of Xenophanes; may have been so in his youth. At least he derived his doctrines from him. He was of noble family; of wealth; in early life probably given to pleasure, from which he was diverted by Diochætes to the pursuits of calm philosophy. He took an active part in the political affairs of his native city, and framed for it a code of laws so wise and admirable that the citizens for a time yearly renewed an oath to abide forever by them. Plato and Aristotle make honorable mention of Parmenides and his doctrines as important in philosophy.

The chief peculiarity of his doctrine is this: His open war upon the evidence of sense, and his exaltation of *reason* above ideas derived from sense. The former gives only belief, opinion; the latter, truth and certainty (Arist. Met. i. 5; Sext. Emp. adv. Math. viii. 3; Diog. Laert. ix. 22). This doctrine was shadowed forth in Xenophanes, but not clearly laid down as the basis of a system.

The principal work of Parmenides is a poem entitled "Nature," which opens by a well-conceived allegory illustrative of the *soul's longing after truth.* Virgins, daughters of the sun, conduct the ardent poet to the midst of the realm of ether, to the gates of day, to the very depths of the divine secrets. There Dike, the goddess, dwells, who promises to reveal to him absolute truth, and also the uncertain opinions of mortals; these he is not to follow, not to be led by customary opinion. Opinion is *uncertain,* unreliable, follows the rash eye, and ear confused with ringing sounds, and tongue.

The centre or starting point of Parmenides' system is

not the notion of God, but that of being, in which, however, he means to include God. He starts with a more *general* idea than that of personal intelligence, or even intelligence of any kind, with that of *being* itself in its wide range. This is *unity* with him.

His fundamental position is this : "*All is, non-entity* is not;" *i. e.*, there is no such thing possible as non-entity. To affirm that *non entity is*, is a contradiction in terms. Mark the dialectic subtlety of this argument. "That which is not is inconceivable, unknowable, cannot be expressed in words." You cannot therefore affirm its existence. You can only think of it and speak of it as *not* being. Of course, then, nonentity is not, and of course, if so, then *Being is*. Syllogistically stated, the argument, if I understand it, would run thus: Either there is not being, or else being. Now there is not, and can not be, *not*-being; therefore there *is being*. From this point, the system moves on triumphantly to its conclusions. Being, thus established, of course is uncreated and unchangeable; has no beginning, no ending, no change of existence, no parts or differences, all being is one and the same thing, fills all space, limited only by itself.

"Whole and self-generate, unchangeable, illimitable,
Never was nor yet shall be its birth. All is already
One from eternity; what would you make its origin, and whence
Its increase? Not from what was not. . . .
For say what *need impelled it*
Sooner or later to commence its being, and from naught arise?"

(Fragments of Poem on Nature, in collection of Füllerborn, Arist. Met. i. 5. ii. 4; Phys. i. 2; Plutarch de Plac. Phil. i. 24; Sext. Emp. Hyp. Pyrr. iii. 65. adv. Math. x. 46.)

Being is, moreover, identical with unity. All being is one, not several and many. All is full of being. The relations of time and space are disregarded and set aside by this idea of being; merged in the idea of the *eternal unity* or *All*. The being thus established, then, is single, identical always with itself, neither is born, nor dies, indestructible, indivisible. Like a sphere, it is perfect, embraces all, yet has its own limits maintained by the force of necessity. This being has no motion, but only eternal rest. What seems to us change and motion is merely a delusive appearance. There is no such reality.

The all is identical with thought and intelligence ; for being is one ; and thought is being, since it exists, and nothing but being does exist. Thought and being, then, are one; *thought and knowledge* are identical. The fulness of all being is thought. The intellectual insight is only the expression of what is. (See Poem on Nature, verses 45, 46, 88–91.) Ritter supposes it certain that by being Parmenides understood that eternal essence which is the sole cause and ground of all things.

Ritter also considers this referring of all to the highest notion of pure metaphysics—that of being, as in itself a dialectic progress far beyond all preceding systems.

Parmenides did not reject all human opinions nor all evidence of the senses. He recognized all truth as one. But appearances were many and changeable, and beneath these lay veiled the divine truth and being, though concealed from man.

His view of man was a sad and gloomy one. He regarded him as a miserable and most imperfect being.

His theory of the earth was mechanical. Two opposite elements—light and darkness—mix and compose the world. From the mixture of fire and earth, water and air arise. The earth he places in the centre, spherical, rotating, surrounded by various *rings*. The upper one is of fire, the lower one of darkness. The earth lies midway between the two, and is therefore imperfect.

Souls are driven hither, into this dark, imperfect abode and state of being, by stern necessity. Thus they become separated from the universal being.

The seat of the soul is in the *stomach*, and the various

degrees of intelligence in different persons correspond to the variations of heat and cold in the body, or the elements of light and darkness.

The *warmer* persons are the more intelligent ones. Woman is in this respect more perfect than man, and was brought into existence in the sunny south. Man in the colder north.

§ 3.—Zeno of Elea.

Not to be confounded with Zeno the Stoic. One of the most distinguished of the ancient philosophers; great in action as well as in thought. Born in the 69th or, as some say, in the 71st Olympiad, in either case about 500 B. C., perhaps 496. The pupil and friend, and, as some say, the adopted son of Parmenides. Early life devoted to study and contemplation; learned to think more highly of intellectual pleasures than of wealth, or sensual gratifications, or political honors; yet not a misanthrope. Lived and labored for the good of his fellow-citizens and of his country, yet declined those honors with which they would have rewarded him. An ardent lover of his country. He lived at a period when Greece was everywhere awaking to consciousness of her political bondage, and rousing herself to throw off the Persian yoke and to found national institutions on liberty.

In this struggle Zeno shared; one of the bravest and most resolute spirits of the age. Implicated in a conspiracy against the tyrant of Elea, he was captured and put to the torture. Interrogated by Nearchus as to his accomplices, he throws the tyrant into great suspense and fear by naming *all the courtiers;* reproaches the spectators for consenting to be slaves to such a man, bites off his tongue and spits it in the tyrant's face, and raises the populace to such a pitch of excitement that they fall upon the tyrant and slay him. According to some accounts, Zeno was pounded to death in a huge mortar. Zeno seems to have been a peculiarly shrewd and acute thinker and reasoner, well fitted to trouble antagonists, to attack or defend ; not so well fitted to discover the solid foundations of truth. His distinctions are subtle, and often fallacious, and his arguments in some degree sophistic, yet always serious and earnest; not a quibbler, not a sophist.

Aristotle considers him the inventor of dialectics, inasmuch as he starts from acknowledged and received principles, and reasons onward from these to his conclusions. The system which Zeno maintains is essentially that of Parmenides. Xenophanes had originated it ; Parmenides had given it shape and precision ; Zeno defends it from attack, and manfully does battle for it against its adversaries. He is a skilful fighter, and the favorite weapon with him is the *reductio ad absurdum.** Plato has well defined the relation of Zeno to the Eleatic philosophy, when he says that the master established the existence of the one and the disciple proved the *non*-existence of the many. The doctrine of Parmenides reduced the universe to *unity*. Zeno shows that this is true by showing the opposite not to be possible, that *multiplicity* is not and cannot be true (Plato, Parmenides, p. 73–75 ; Phædrus, iii. 261; Simplicius ad Arist. Phys. 30). This he does by many arguments. He employs the mode of question and answer, on the dialogistic method, afterwards so skilfully used by Socrates. Zeno was the first to perceive the advantage of this method in polemic reasoning.

Like all the Eleatics, he goes strongly against the credibility of the phenomena of sense, and of the conceptions thus formed ; labors to show that all such conceptions, as ordinarily formed, are exceedingly doubtful and to be dis-

* For a more favorable view of Zeno, see Butler's Hist. Phil. i., 335–6. Butler supposes that Zeno argues as he does, merely to show that the theory of a real sensible world is open to as many objections as his opponents urge against the rationalists, that he was no idle and vain disputer, etc.

trusted; denies the *reality* of sensible appearances, however, rather than the appearances themselves, argues particularly against space, and motion in space, as being only delusions of sense.

The chief points of his reasoning against the supposed multiplicity of things are these three. 1, That, according to that theory, a thing must be like and yet unlike itself; 2, both one and many; 3, at rest and yet in motion. Under the first of these he instances, to show how deceptive are sensible phenomena, the case of a grain of wheat falling (Arist. Phys. vii. 5). Would it make a noise? No, replies Protagoras. Would a bushel? Yes. Is not a grain a certain definite part of a bushel? Yes. Ought it not, then, to make just such a part of the noise? Silence on the part of Protagoras; Zeno has him. What says anybody to this? Why, of course, that the senses are not sufficiently accurate to give information as to all things that are; *not* that they, so far as they go, are not reliable.

Under the second argument, he denies space itself, the conception of existence in space. If all that is, said he, must be in space, and if space is, then space itself must be in some other space, and that space again in some other, and so on *ad infinitum*. This is absurd. Therefore, space is not a reality (So Aristotle, Phys. iv. 3, 5; Simplic. in Phys. 130). What say we to that bright thought? Simply this space does not exist as a *substance*, an entity.

So far Zeno was in the right. But it does exist as a *conception* of the human mind, and a necessary law or mode of its thought. It is not set aside therefore by the above reasoning, which applies only to *substance*, or *material* entity.

Analogous to this is his subtle reasoning to show that, on the theory of multiplicity, every individual existence must be *infinitely great;* since made up of infinite parts, each one having an assignable magnitude of its own; yet *infinitely small*, also, since each part is infinitely small, and the multiplicity of infinitely small things can result only in the infinitely small. The third part of his reasoning, in which he argues against the *possibility of motion* (Arist. Phys. vi. 9, 14), is sustained by the following arguments:

1. If a body moves, before it can reach the end of the supposed distance over which it passes, it must first, of course, pass the middle point. If it has an inch to move, it must first reach the half-inch point before it reaches the whole distance; and before it can move that half-inch it must move to a point just half that distance, and so *ad infinitum*. Whatever be the distance to be accomplished, it must first get over half of it, before it can get over the whole. The consequence is, you can never get the thing to stir at all. There is no motion. Q. E. D.

2. The celebrated argument about the race of Achilles and the tortoise; the tortoise having the start of 1000 feet, but Achilles moving ten paces to one of the tortoise. Achilles can never overtake the tortoise, says Zeno; for while he travels the 1000 paces, tortoise makes 100; and while he is running these, tortoise makes 10 more, and so on *ad infinitum*. Philosophers from Aristotle down to Hobbes and John Stuart Mill, have puzzled themselves to point out just where the fallacy lies in this argument. That a fallacy is there, all agree, but just what it is, appears not quite so plain. It is a sufficient answer to say, with Mill and Hobbes and also with Aristotle, that time as well as space can be divided up in this way, and yet a finite time, say 5 minutes, may cover the whole transaction, just as a finite space, say 2,000 paces, covers the whole distance.

3. Motion and rest are one. For every object filling space rests in that space, and what we call motion is only the sum of the several spaces between the first and the last, and as the body is at rest in each one of these, so long as it is there, of course it is at rest all the way and all the while. So no *motion*. Q. E. D. Zeno takes essentially the same view of nature with Parmenides. Four elements,

the warm, the cold, the dry, the moist, and a moving force regulating all, viz., *necessity*. The soul is a compound, he said, of the four elements. The system tends strongly to scepticism, and results in it finally. He was not a Sophist, however, but only distinguished sharply between sense-knowledge and the higher knowledge of thought (So Fries and Tennemann). His doctrine of God is this. God is eternal and one, not composed of parts, hence uniform, and in figure spherical. Zeno is the founder and first teacher of logic (So Sext. Emp. adv. Math. vii. 7; Diog. Laert. ix. 25).

§ 4.—Empedocles

Born at Agrigentum in Sicily, a Dorian colony, about 84 Olymp. according to Ritter, *i. e.*, 444 B. C.; of wealthy family; commonly called a Pythagorean, but incorrectly; some resemblance between his doctrines and those of Pythagoras, but not essential; more properly Eleatic. Supposed in his early travels to have visited Italy and Athens. Fable attributes to him marvellous cures, control of tempests and of pestilence, and a death not according to the laws of nature. Evidently regarded by antiquity as a marvellous man and a wonder-worker; makes pretension to more than human knowledge, clothes himself in purple, cincture of brass, crown of gold, train of admiring worshippers; announces himself as immortal, the priest and favorite of the gods, himself in part divine. These pretensions, supported by really great skill as naturalist and philosopher, as well as medical practitioner, gave him unbounded control over the superstitious reverence of the age. He was even worshipped as a god, it would seem, on some occasions. Strictly ascetic in his habits and doctrines, however, so far from a selfish use of power and wealth, he seems to have despised all human distinctions and emoluments while possessing the highest, and refused to accept the supreme power offered him by his native city. Distinguished by his liberality, patriotism, intellectual endowments, he seems altogether a remarkable man. Death uncertain, probably suicidal; fabled to have perished in *Ætna.*

Principal work, that is known to be genuine, and of which fragments are still extant, the three books on "Nature," an epic poem, like the didactic verses of Parmenides. Adopted the poetic form probably as most elevated, and in keeping with the priestly and prophetic character. This of course would not recommend it to Aristotle, who, with little taste for the poetical and little appreciation for the mystic and ideal elements in philosophy, objects to this work, its entire absence of logical reasonings. The poem appeals, like all poems, to the gods and muses.

> "And thou, I beg, much mindful muse, white-armed virgin,
> Grant me to know whate'er befits the creature of a day."

It is only through the intellect, he continues, by means of the senses, that the truth can be arrived at; not by the senses, but only by the right reason can it be known, which (right reason) is partly human, partly divine. The work complains everywhere of the limited extent and uncertainty of human knowledge.

> "Swift fated and conscious how brief is life's pleasureless portion,
> Like the wind-driven smoke they are carried backward and forward,
> Each trusting to naught save what his experience vouches,
> On all sides disturbed: yet wishing to find out the whole truth.
> In vain; neither by eye nor ear perceptible to man,
> Nor to be grasped by mind: and thou, when thus thou hast wandered,
> Wilt find that no further reaches the knowledge of mortals."
>
> —RITTER'S VERSION.

This prominent ascription of human frailty and ignorance to the *fault of the senses* and generally to the imperfection of the *cognitive faculty* in man, is the peculiar philosophy of the Eleatic school, and fixes Empedocles among that class.

> "But consider each thing, with measure, according as it is evident,
> And have no more confidence in a sensation of sight than of hearing,

Or in the ear than in the manifestations of the tongue,
Or in all other things wherein the way for the thought
Is in the members. Withhold thy faith. Think only what is evident."
—RENOUVIER'S TRANSLATION.

Empedocles distinguishes between the divine and human knowledge the former is that of Deity, and is inexpressible, as is God himself. He inveighs against the common and unworthy notions of God entertained in mythology.

" Happy he who possesses the treasures of the thought divine,
Unhappy he who rests not satisfied with the shadowy conception which one has of the gods.
It is not possible to see him with the eyes nor to take him with the hands,
Which is the principal method of persuasion for the heart of man.
A human head serves not gracefully his members,
Two branches hang not from his shoulders,
Nor with feet—nor legs—nor having sexual members ;
But an understanding sacred, ineffable, exists
Which traverses the entire world with its rapid thoughts."
—RENOUVIER'S VERSION.

According to Ritter, he differs from the Eleatic in not making prominent the *negative* part of this doctrine, which represents God as *indivisible,* incorruptible, ingenerable, etc., out of space and time, not dwelling upon and seeking to find truth in the system of natural things.

Empedocles holds the oneness of all truth, like the other Eleatæ. It is a ball in its unity. It is a *sphere,* and hence the sphere has been regarded as the deity of Empedocles.

" Thus within the secret bosom of harmony firm-fixed
Is the sphere, well rounded, in glad rest calmly rejoicing."

This unity is the work of and is ruled by love ; is one with it. *Love* is the only true force ; has its seat in the centre, and pervades all ; the first cause which unites all together ; the *one,* the only ground of the universe ; the only entity. Thus he, with the other Eleatæ, makes the material principle and the active to be one and the same ;

not, like Anaxagoras, distinct, but as Parmenides, with whom the moving and the moved force are one, *i. e.*, fire.

The complete knowledge of this unity, this mundane whole, is indeed impossible. Yet to know this should be the great object of human endeavor.

> "Contemplate it in mind, nor sit with looks of amazement—
> Love, which to the frame of man connatural is deemed,
> Spring of their thoughts and deeds of love and kindly affection,
> Which they invoke by name of joy and Aphrodite.
> But it no eye has seen within the universe of things—
> No mortal eye."

That is, according to Ritter, the knowledge is necessarily imperfect, for man is a *part* of the whole, and cannot comprehend the whole; recognizing each element singly, but not all in their unity; the true unity is known only to itself.

The sphere plays an important part in the philosophy of Empedocles. Into it all things are combined by love, without difference or distinction; they lead there a happy life, replete with happiness and holiness.

"They know no God of war nor spirit of battles." Pure and bloodless sacrifices are there offered, and all is peace and joy and love.

But this perfect harmony is disturbed by the principle of hate, which comes in to break the unity and dissolve the spell; produces separation, emanation, plurality, beings; hence the sensible world and its phenomena, the world of movement and of separate beings. This movement of separation seems to be associated with *crime*, and to pertain to only a *portion* of the whole; the human imperfection and crime and misery are connected with it. Thus the following.

> "This is the law of fate, of the Gods, an olden enactment
> If with guilt or murder a *spirit* polluteth his members,
> Of those who have obtained an existence enduring through ages,
> Thrice ten thousand years must he wander apart from the blessed,
> Hence doomed to stray a fugitive from gods and an outcast,
> To raging strife submissive."

The restless, disturbed life of men and things in this world of strife and constant motion are strongly contrasted with the blissful life in the sphere. Everything in this world is spiritual, even material objects partake of reason and knowledge, the elements are influenced by hate and love. Having been separated and set in motion by hate, they are no longer at rest, they are in perpetual conflict, and hate all. Thus expressed is this unblessed life, this conflict of the mundane,

> "For the rage of the ethereal air seaward pursues it.
> Sea spits it back on earth's shores and earth up to the brightness
> Of the unwearied sun, who back to the eddies of ether
> Rejects it: each receives it from each; all equally hate it."

This principle of hate is, like that of love, *inherent* in things themselves; hence Aristotle objects that Empedocles leaves too much to chance. He seems however to have an idea of a higher principle, after all, uniting these two opposites, love and hate, viz., destiny, on which all depends. This separation and conflict is *unnatural.* Hence things strive, notwithstanding the inherent moving force of hate, to regain unity, rest, the sphere. This may be attained by purification, life of abstinence, avoiding the sources of impurity and of hate, care not to shed the blood of any living thing, entire consecration to a principle of love.

This perpetual restless movement of things gives rise to different shapes and configurations of the separate elements. They pass through changes continually; hence what is called his doctrine of metempsychosis. Man has been at one time a plant, a bird, fish, a maiden, etc., that is, the elementary parts of his body have passed through all these changes.

The pious soul, duly purified and absolved, and having expiated by the misery of its mundane being the former guilt, enjoys after death a god-like existence.

> "When, leaving this body, to the free ether thou comest
> A God undying thou shalt be, no longer a mortal."

Love tends to combine and organize harmoniously these

diverse and conflicting elements, and the world is under this influence gradually progressing to a higher and more perfect condition, toward unity and the sphere again, from the imperfect toward the perfect. Thus Empedocles sought to bring the existing evil to a good end.

He held to the existence of four elements: fire, air, sea, earth, out of which all organic existence is produced. Plants *first* produced by agency of fire and other elements, before day and night were separated. Plants possess feeling, desire, reason, knowledge. These all the works of love; to preside over the orderly composition of the element is the *work* of *love;* to *separate,* that of *hate.* The world of hate is wholly subordinate to the world of love; a minor affair, an exception to the general rule.

He holds that nothing can be *created* and nothing cease to be. Thus:

"Fools to whom is not vouchsafed far-reaching insight,
Who think aught can begin to be which formerly was not,
Or that aught which is can perish and utterly decay."

"Another truth I now unfold—no natural birth
Is there of mortal things, nor death's destruction final;
Nothing is there but a mingling and then separation of mingled,
Which are called a birth and death by ignorant mortals."

"First know, four are the roots of all, and elements of things,
Fire, and water, and Earth, and Ether's measureless expanse;
For thence is all that is, or was, or ever shall be."

Of these elements he regarded fire as the chief. Our knowledge of physical objects is through mechanical contact of bodies, certain effluxes from them passing off into corresponding pores in the recipient body; and these sense-impressions unite in the consciousness by means of the conflux of blood to the heart. Man's advantages and deficiencies are all owing to the ratio in which his blood is compounded, hence too the superior dexterity of certain members of the body. Man however partakes of a *divine* knowledge far superior to this sensuous. Hence he enjoins on man to contemplate *in his own mind the God, love. The distinguishing excellence of this Eleatic theory is its first attempt to correct sensible impressions by pure reason.* So Ritter. The resemblance of Hegel's theory to this of the Eleatic, and especially of Empedocles, may be traced also in Cousin. Fries traces a marked resemblance of the system of Empedocles to the Pythagorean; (for a general view of his system, see Arist. Met. i. 3, 4, ii. 4; Sext. Emp. adv. Math. vii. 121, ix. 620, x. 317; Diog. L. viii. 76).

CHAPTER IV.

THE SOPHISTS

APPEARED at a later period, and may be regarded as the natural result of the TIMES, not less than the *preceding schools of philosophers.* They have been greatly censured, especially by the Socratic and Platonic schools; yet accomplished an important mission in the progress of philosophy and the age.

§ 1.—THE CAUSES WHICH PRODUCED THIS SCHOOL AND MADE IT WHAT IT WAS.

I. The state of the country and the circumstances of the age were such as to lead naturally to the formation of such a school. The different states of Greece were coming into closer contact with each other. Mind was *quickened* by this. Trade brought men together; deeper interest and more general was felt in science and learning; these became more common property; demand for *teachers* increased; demand for information manifold and various: scientific thought, positive, tangible, practical information, took the place of mere ideal and speculative thought. The age became business-like, practical, stirring; men lost their faith in the quaint old mythologies and theories, and asked for something *knowable.*

The Sophists appeared and answered to this call—not *sophoi,* but *sophistai,* teachers of wisdom—men who knew a thing or two, and could let you into the secret forthwith. An appearance of wisdom where there *is* none, is Aristotle's idea of sophistry. A flippant, conceited, arrant position, not without considerable erudition and real learning, but specious rather than solid, communicative rather than reflective: men of action rather than investigation, men of show and outside appearance rather than of sound learning and real faith; men for the age, made to order, and who made knowledge and wisdom to order—men who philosophize for the sake of display or of gain, is Cicero's idea of them. The great need of the time was not so much to to know as to communicate what was known, the art of talking—and these men had it to perfection, they were *rhetores,* speakers, and could in easy lessons teach you how to hold forth eloquently upon any subject, whether it were one that you understood or not, nay, it was their boast that they could make the worse appear the better reason. Subtle, skilful in words, acute in rhetoric, detecting differences where there were none, and overlooking them where they really existed, it was their great art and profession to mystify and confuse, to persuade men that they were walking on their heads or flying in the air when they were all the while on their feet.

The age of faith and earnestness had gone, hollow pretence took the place of it. How different the thought of those men from that of the great, honest, earnest Ionians, Thales, Anaximander, etc., groping after the solution of their great problem, or rejoicing in the belief that they had found it. These men had no faith in anything; they were *sceptics,* downright atheists mostly; to doubt, disbelieve, prove the *contrary* from the impossibility of believing, ridicule you for having ever believed anything—this was their vocation.

They grew out of the preceding systems of philosophy not less than from the circumstances of the age. All these systems had been one-sided and imperfect. Ritter develops this idea with great justness. They had been exclusive, and, when pushed to their results, landed in absurdities. They were unsatisfactory attempts to grasp the true, the infinite, the unknown—but failures; and gradually the mind began, after so many vain attempts, to sink down in the conviction that nothing was knowable, and nothing attainable, nay, perhaps, nothing true even; began to lose confidence in all knowledge. This was precisely the sceptical tendency of the age, which resulted in, and gave birth to the Sophists as a sect. They were the full development and expression of this latent tendency, and did in time much to promote it.

Those earlier systems of philosophy also had themselves really done much to weaken the faith in the popular myths and superstitions of the age; had cultivated the spirit of inquiry, of scientific thought, before which, little by little, the popular faith in the gods, and stories pertaining to the gods, had melted away and dried up; and men were ready now to inquire further, Since these old traditions are not true; are even absurd, who will tell us what is true? Nay, is not the whole thing a humbug? With this, of course, not religious belief alone would be undermined, but *morality* and general honesty. Such was the case, and when the Sophists came upon the stage, and began to teach, that all things were about equally credible and equally useful and true; in other words, that nothing was so, and nothing was of any consequence in itself, save only for appearance sake and the gain to come of it; that virtue and religion and morality were creations of the state, fictions of the human mind, useful but unreal—they found ready listeners. They carried out the rationalistic and sceptical tendencies of the prevalent philosophy to its extreme. They showed the folly and utter failure of the preceding methods, and so prepared the way for a sounder and a wholly different philosophy. Hence they acted a most important part in the progress of thought. It was necessary that there should be Sophists, and it was time that they should be *then*. They were as essential to the establishment of a true wisdom and a true philosophy in the world, as night is to sunrise.*

§ 2.—THE DISTINGUISHING TENETS OF THE SCHOOL AND ITS PERSONAL HISTORY.

In general, as already intimated, the Sophists were *sceptics:* no faith in anything; none in truth, none in facts and the sensible world, none in man, none in God; hollow-hearted, of course—men of words not of things, dialectic, rhetorical, subtle, false. Maintained boldly and specifically these two leading positions: the *uncertainty of all particular truths* and, in fact, the *impossibility of all truth.*

The two leading names in the school are Protagoras and Gorgias. The first, born at Abdera about 485 or 486, died about 415 B. C. Common fame makes him a disciple of Democritus, but this is without evidence. Most accomplished of the Sophists; gives lessons in rhetoric in Athens and Sicily; gives lessons also in polity and citizenship. He proceeds always on the principle that of every proposition the contrary may be advanced and maintained, if one has the ability and skill to do it; and that of the two propositions, one is about as true and about as good as the other. "His doctrine tends to deny," says Ritter, "the possi-

* Lewes defends the Sophists against the usual charges, on the ground that the *state* would never have *tolerated* such teachings, and therefore they did not so teach, he infers. So Grote. But the evidence is too strong to be thus set aside. For general estimate of Sophists see Arist. de Soph. Elench. c. i; Cicero, Acad. ii. 23, 25; Xenophon, Memorabilia i. 6; Ueberweg, i. 73; Butler, Hist. Phil. vol. i. p. 340–345).

bility of anything objective being represented by thought, and consequently to make all thought a mere appearance."

According to him, *nothing is, in itself, by itself,* but only sustains a certain *relation* to some other thing. The relation is the only existence. *Man is the measure of all things* (Plato, Theaet. ii. 68; Diog. L. ix. 51; Arist. Met. x. 6; Sext. Emp. Hyp. Pyrr. i. 216–219), of *being* and of *non-being.* By which, says Ritter, he intended that to every one things *are* in the relation in which they appear, that to every one that presentation is true which he frames for himself. This of course destroys the universality of all propositions. Every thought is true for him who entertains it, and of course you cannot contradict any opinion or position whatsoever. Thought is only the relation of the thinker to the thing thought of, and the thinking subject, the soul itself, is only the sum of the different moments or acts of thinking. Of course this resolves all thought into mere sensation, and makes sensuous impressions the only realities; things are cold or hot, not at all in themselves, but only as they seem so to us. He denies of course, then, all science, and boldly attacks geometry even as false. There is no such thing as the circle and the straight line, nor is it true that the circle, as imagined, touches the tangent in only *one* point. He is said to have maintained the general opinion that everything is true of everything, no difference of true and false (Plato, Theaet. 89, 90, 102; Sext. Emp. Adv. Math. vii. 60; Cic. Acad. ii. 46; Diog. L. ix. 51, 53), and that nothing is one thing rather than another. Query, if so, then what becomes of his denial of geometrical propositions?—and why does he teach at all, if nothing is true?

While Protagoras was pushing the Ionian philosophy of sensationalism to its utmost extreme, Gorgias the Leontine, a still bolder and more shameless Sophist, carried the Eleatic doctrine also to the very farthest limit, and landed in absolute *nihilism.* He was, according to tradition, the disciple of Empedocles; flourished about 88th Olympiad, *i. e.,* 428

B. C. (born about 483, died about 375); famous as rhetorician; acquired wealth, died in old age; style florid, pompous, adorned, wordy, cold; principal strength lay in *antithesis;* boasted that he could speak extempore on any subject, and answer briefly or at length any question that might be put to him. As teacher of youth, he confined himself chiefly to oratory, and laughed at those who professed to teach virtue, of which he expressed his contempt. Wrote a work on *non-being.* These three positions (Sext. Emp. adv. Math. vii. 65–86; Arist. de Xenoph. Zeno and Gorgias, c. 5, 6): 1. Nothing is. 2. If anything is, it cannot be known. 3. If it can, it cannot be imparted to others. Argues thus in favor of the first position: Being is either that which is, or that which is not, or that which is and is not both at once; the two last are contradictions. Being then, is that which is. But this is impossible, for it must be, in that case, either produced or eternal; if the latter, then infinite, in which case it cannot exist in *another*, for the infinite admits of no superior; nor yet in itself, for that is to make it at once both substance and place; so then it cannot exist at all. If being be supposed, however, not eternal but produced, then it owes its birth either to being or to non-being not to *being,* for that is the very thing in question, and of course could not produce anything before it existed; not to non-being, for non-being cannot produce since it does not exist. Is being, then, at once begotten and eternal? No, for this is self-contradictory. Since then it is neither begotten nor eternal nor both together, evidently it is *not at all.* In other words, nothing exists, since neither being exists, nor non-being, nor yet both at once.

Second proposition. If something exists, it is incomprehensible. He shows that in order for being to be comprehended, thought must itself be *being,* else being could not be an *object* of thought, *i. e.,* be comprehended. If the object is white, the conception of it must be white also.

If, however, all thought is being, then everything which we think, (is *true*)—*exists*. Which is absurd. Therefore being is incomprehensible. Another argument, also. If that which we think, exists, then what does not exist cannot be thought, for the contrary of being is non-being, and if being is thought, then *non*-being should be not *thought*. But this is absurd. If there is such a thing as being, then, it is incomprehensible, that is, incapable of being thought.

Third position. Being, if it exists and can be known, is incommunicable. Words are not things, objects, but only signs to express them. What one *sees*, for instance, is not *audible*, and cannot be imparted to the *ear*. Discourse differs in its nature from other sensible things, and can no more indicate what is foreign to itself than things themselves can indicate each other's nature. The object begets the discourse, but the discourse expresses not the object. Nor can one hearer think the same as another, *for the same can not be at once in two different places.**

This of course assumes that the sensuously perceptible is the true, the standard; and that cognoscible truth is a matter of sensible experience. Here lies the fallacy of the whole. The reasoning of course strikes at the validity and reality of all intellectual knowledge. The contrast between sensation and reason is made use of to show the nothingness of the latter, just as Zeno had used it to show the futility of the former.

The dogmas of Protagoras and of Gorgias—all thought is knowledge, and no thought is knowledge—tend ultimately to the same thing, *i. e.*, that in thought is no recognition of real being, but only a representation of the *phenomenal*; that there is no objective reality corresponding to the conceptions of the mind. The doctrine of Protagoras and

* The distinction between the thought and the thing thought of, and also between the thought and the word which expresses that thought, is first brought to view in these three positions of Gorgias, as Tennemann and Krug have both remarked.

Gorgias as to God is that his existence very doubtful. Protagoras said he did not know whether the gods existed or not; the obscurity of the subject, and the shortness of his life prevented (Diog. L. ix. 51; Plato Theaet. 92; Sext. Emp. adv. Math. ix. 56, 57; Cic. de Nat. Deor. i. 12, 29).

The Sophists were of great use in philosophy. How?

They first called attention distinctly to the *subjective* phase of being—the mind itself; whereas only *objective* had been all the previous systems. They showed that nothing can be done till we settle the questions respecting the nature and origin of our own cognitions and impressions, draw the distinguishing line between sense and intellect more clearly than before; and called attention to that important distinction. They taught men to doubt, and so made them more cautious ultimately in philosophizing.

They showed how barren and worthless any and all philosophy, that recognizes not validity of moral distinctions, and how dangerous to the welfare of man and the state.

They prepared the way, in fine, for that star in the East, that was soon to arise upon the human mind—the doctrines, the life, the character of Socrates.

PERIOD SECOND.

SOCRATIC.

THE preceding period is properly but an introduction to this. The true philosophic method and spirit now begin. Preceding thinkers have but *prepared the way* for the rise and development of the true philosophy. At first, man is occupied chiefly with external nature, "the root and source," says Ritter, "of all intellectual life." He identifies himself with the universe around him, and his science is the science of universal nature. Thus the *Ionian* philosopher. This, however, does not long content him. He observes in himself what he finds nowhere else—the faculty of reason; evidently, the more he considers it, not a *physical* power, but one peculiar to himself. There is no longer, then, a complete agreement between himself and the powers of nature; his faith in this identity, in the agreement of the two, is shaken. The ethical and the physical begin to be distinguished. He can advance only by entering a new path, and recognizing the new elements, reason and morality. Otherwise he must make war upon this new principle and put down both reason and morals, making nature alone the arbiter. This the Sophists sought to do, "to show that reason is in fact nothing but a power of nature and that might makes right." This of course will never succeed for any time, for it is violence to the nature of man. It will open the way and create the demand for a new and better philosophy—that of reason,

4

that of morals. Thus, precisely, it was that the mind in its search for truth, and some positive science of itself, wondered and toiled in that first period already considered. Thus far precisely had it advanced up to the time of Socrates. A new era now opened on it, a new and golden age of philosophic inquiry. It was now to enter on a better path, pursue a better method, and arrive at better results.

General Character of this Period.—It is commonly regarded as emphatically *ethical,* in distinction from the preceding. In one sense it is so. That is, it brought distinctly forward that element which had no place in the sophistical and physical reasonings of the preceding period—the *moral.*

But it was not moral exclusively. It embraced a higher *range of thought;* and by dialectical investigation sought to give completeness and perfection to science by making it comprehend *both nature and reason.* This was the true characteristic of the Socratic philosophy. This perception of the unity of science, this comprehensive grasp of all knowledge as essentially *one,* this recognition of the human *consciousness* of *one's self* in thinking, is found in none of the earlier schools, and constitutes the peculiar character and value of this period.

CHAPTER I.

SOCRATES.

§ 1.—Life of Socrates.

It has been well remarked by Ritter, that his scientific influence is dependent very much on his individual life and character. The fact that his disciples recorded so many personal traits of the man, shows that he impressed them, not by his doctrines alone, but by his life, and that he stamped his *entire image* on their minds. He was not a philosopher alone, but a *man;* and it was the man, quite as much as the philosopher, that remained in the minds and hearts of those who had once seen and heard him.

He was the son of humble parents, Sophroniscus, a statuary, and Phænarete, a midwife; born about 469 B. C. and educated as an artist or statuary, with probably at first few literary advantages. Athens was, however, at that time the intellectual centre of Greece, and thither flocked all who had aught to communicate in letters, art, science, or philosophy. Socrates availed himself of these opportunities to cultivate the acquaintance of the most distinguished teachers of whatever science or art; took lessons in *music*, which through life he continued to cultivate; became proficient even in the physical sciences of astronomy and geography—to which, however, he allowed but a secondary rank and importance—and seems, in fact, to have neglected no branch of learning. It was the age of Pericles, and no Athenian youth, thirsting for knowledge, was denied.

Like Descartes, the founder of modern philosophy, Socrates was at one time a soldier. As such he distinguished himself for endurance of the hard life of the camp, and for personal bravery.

Plato has left us a fine description of the military life of Socrates. "At one time we" (Alcibiades and Socrates) "were fellow soldiers, and had our mess together in the camp before Potidæa. Socrates there overcame, not only me, but every one besides, in endurance of toils; when, as often happens in a campaign, we were reduced to few provisions, there were none who could sustain hunger like Socrates, and when we had plenty, he alone seemed to enjoy our military fare. He never drank much, willingly; but when he was compelled, he conquered all even in that to which he was least accustomed, and what is most astonishing, no person ever saw Socrates drunk, either then or at any other time. In the depth of winter—and the winters there are excessively rigid—he sustained calmly incredible hardships ; and among other things, while the frost was intolerably severe, and no one went out of their tents, or if they went out, wrapped themselves up carefully, and put fleeces under their feet, and bound their legs with hairy skins, Socrates went out only with the same cloak on that he usually wore, and walked barefoot upon the ice, more easily indeed than those who had sandalled themselves so delicately ; so that the soldiers thought he did it to mock their want of fortitude. . . . In one instance he was seen early in the morning standing in one place rapt in meditation, and as he seemed not to be able to unravel the subject of his thoughts, he still continued to stand as inquiring and discussing within himself ; and when noon came the soldiers observed him, and said to one another, 'Socrates has been standing there thinking ever since the morning.' At last some Ionians came to the spot, and, having supped, as it was summer, bringing their blankets, they lay down to sleep in the cool, they observed that Socrates continued to stand there the whole night, until morning, and that when the sun rose he saluted it with a prayer and departed."

The same writer has spoken of the appearance of Socrates on the battle-field at Delium, after the defeat of the Athenian forces, and while all was confusion and utter rout. He was on foot, heavily armed, and Alcibiades coming up on horseback, observed him walking, and darting his regards around "with a majestic composure, looking tranquilly both on his friends and on his enemies, so that it was evident to every one, even from afar, that whoever should venture to attack him, would encounter a desperate resistance." He departed in safety, for men hesitate to touch those who exhibit such a countenance as that of Socrates even in defeat.

His firmness and courage were equally conspicuous in the only instances in which he took part in political affairs. He could face not only death, but that which many a brave soldier has been unable to withstand—*public opinion.* He could defy the thirty tyrants, and defy an Athenian mob. The thirty ordered him, with four others, to arrest Leon of Salamis, a man who had the right of Athenian citizenship. It was an arbitrary proceeding. Socrates would do nothing of the kind. "Government, although it was so powerful," he says, "did not frighten me into doing anything unjust. . . The four went to Salamis and took Leon, but I went away home."

It is uncertain at what age Socrates engaged in the instruction of youth ; probably not until somewhat mature, as it was not till after many struggles in the earlier period of his life, that he arrived at anything like certainty and satisfaction in his own mind. He seems very gradually, and perhaps at first with no set purpose or plan of the sort, to have gathered about him the noble youth of Athens, who found his conversation instructive.

The personal appearance of Socrates must have been anything but prepossessing. Imagine a man past the freshness of youth, and the manly vigor of middle life ; of a countenance marked in every feature, but in every feature far from beautiful ; with eye-balls rotund and projecting, nose depressed and flattened, nostrils dilated and upturned, lips compressed, with not mere firmness but sharpness ; the cool critic and cruel satirist not to be mistaken in that whole *ensemble* of feature ; not mere firmness visible there, but keen irony and bitter sarcasm and scorn of the follies of the age, and quick insight into and contempt of the weaknesses and foibles of men—these enthroned there in that eye-brow and lip, looking into you with imperturbable coolness, and detecting at a glance your weaker and assailable points of character ; a figure by no means calculated to make amends for anything unprepossessing in the countenance ; a low, ungainly figure, rough and coarse in its whole contour ; a belly large and unwieldy, as if to make sure that no ideality of the brain and airy fancy should ever endanger the specific gravity of the general frame ; a dress coarse and simple in the extreme, and manners to correspond. Such is the founder of the ideal philosophy, the first true Grecian school, the first man of the age—perhaps of the world hitherto, in point of true greatness of soul and the highest wisdom,—such in personal appearance, according to the descriptions left us by both Xenophon and Plato. Imagine such a man as we have now drawn, coarsely attired, singular in demeanor, walking barefoot along the elegant marbles of the Grecian metropolis, stopping now and then for a time, lost in meditation and fixed to one spot regardless of the gay and fluttering crowds that passed him by, some with a laugh and some with stupid stare ; as unmindful he of the rare elegancies of the accomplished city, as the accomplished city was unmindful of the poor philosopher whom it distinguished not from the common Sophist of the day. Yet not without influence, not without respect, this man ; for, coarse and unmannerly though he be, awkward in form and figure, and scornful of the little elegancies of the capital, you see he goes not alone through the streets. Some of the first and most refined youth of Athens attend him ; have learned that those compressed and scornful lips speak golden words ; have come within the charmed circle of that strange power and influence, the like of which was perhaps never exerted by mortal man over his fellow men ; have learned with him to know themselves, and to despise what a foolish world most prizes and courts.

"It was impossible," says Lewes (Hist. Phil. vol. i. p. 133), "for Socrates to enter the market-place without at once becoming an object of attention. His ungainly figure, his moral character, and his bewitching tongue, excited and enchained curiosity. He became known to every citizen. Who had not listened to him ? Who had not enjoyed his inimitable irony ? Who had not seen him demolish the arrogance and pretension of some reputed wise man? Socrates must have been a terrible antagonist to all people who believed that they were wise because they could discourse fluently; and these were not few. He always declared that he knew nothing. When a man professed knowledge on any point, especially if admiring crowds gave testimony to that profession, Socrates was sure to step up to him, and professing ignorance, entreat to be taught. Charmed with so humble a listener, the teacher began. Interrogated, he very unsuspectingly assented to some very evident proposition; a conclusion from that, almost as evident, next received his assent; from that moment he was lost. With great power of logic, with much ingenious subtlety, and sometimes with daring sophistication, a web was formed from which he could not extricate himself. His own admissions were proved to lead to monstrous conclusions; these conclusions he repugned, but could not see where the gist of his error lay. The laughter of all bystanders bespoke his defeat. Before him was his adversary, imperturbably calm, apparently innocent of all attempt at making him ridiculous. Confused but not confuted, he left the spot, indignant with himself, but more indignant with the subtlety of his adversary."

If Socrates, however, sometimes employed the weapons of the Sophists, it was only to confute the Sophists themselves, or to destroy at once the arguments and the arrogance of some conceited opponent. He was himself no Sophist.

"He was a cool fellow, adding to his humor a perfect temper, and a knowledge of his man, be he whom he might whom he talked with, which laid the companion open to certain defeat in any debate, and in this debate he immoderately delighted. The young men are prodigiously fond of him, and invite him to their feasts, whither he goes for conversation. He can drink, too; has the strongest head in Athens; and after leaving the whole party under the table, goes away, as if nothing had happened, to begin new dialogues with somebody that is sober. In short, he was what our country people call *an old one.*" . . . One of the most remarkable traits of his mind was the tact and readiness with which he adapted himself to the mental condition of the listener. He knew that all useful instruction must begin with the perfect understanding of the wants and mental idiosyncrasies of the learner. He knew how to meet those whom he addressed.

He was withal a perfect Greek, devoted to Athens, which, after the military exploits of early life, he seems never to have quitted. He looked at all things, even at morals, from a patriotic stand-point. The state was first and chief in his thoughts.

In his domestic character he may not have been, and probably was not, a model; too absent-minded and wrapt in contemplation too profound, to be always sufficiently thoughtful of family matters, even had Xantippe been more amiable. His home was the state; his children were his disciples.

It was in the early part of the year 399 B. C., that Socrates, then seventy years old, was cited before the tribunal, and put upon his trial on the following charges, "Socrates is culpable because he recognizes not the gods which the city recognizes, but introduces other new divinities. He is culpable also because he corrupts the youth. Penalty, death." Schwegler supposes that his trial was not at first intended to be fatal, but only to humble his spirit and teach him the power of the people. Unquestionably the public mind was prejudiced against Socrates. He was a reprover and a reformer, a severe critic of men and manners. Many had felt the keenness of his sarcasm, and hated him for it. He was reputed by the multitude a Sophist. The mass had little in common with him. He saw through and ridiculed much that they held sacred; had views of his own in manners, morals, and religion; was wholly uninfluenced by authority; held up to scorn the foibles and follies of the age; was altogether a dangerous sort of man to that large and respectable class of worthies, to be found in every age, who are mainly interested in keeping all things substantially as they are.

Political prejudices came in also to render the man obnoxious to the prevailing faction. He had been the teacher, and was charged with being the adviser of Alcibiades, and even of Critias. Their parties and their policies were no longer in the ascendant. Democracy was rampant, reformers and aristocrats no longer in demand. In the eyes of the Athenian populace, Socrates was an aristocrat, as well as a reformer. His death was decided upon as a matter of state policy, and cloaked under the decent charge of impiety to the gods, and the corruption of youth. Aristophanes, the poet, had already, twenty years before, expressed the popular estimate of the man in holding him up to ridicule as a Sophist and a conceited buffoon.

It probably contributed not a little to his death that he appeared before his judges with such perfect coolness and indifference to his fate, never for a moment consenting to humble himself before them, or to employ any of the usual artifices to move their pity, scarcely even to plead in his own defence. He might have escaped had he taken a different course. He was far above that, however.

The bearing of Socrates on his trial was every way worthy of the man and the philosopher. Calm, self-possessed, fearless—a brave soul was on trial for the truth. What had it to fear? Socrates had been too long accustomed to penetrate with keen observant eye the hypocrisy, deceit, and conceit of men, to see through and through them, and tell them what he saw and what he thought, to stand in fear of any of them. We can readily believe that even an air of haughtiness and contempt might mark his demeanor on this occasion.

His whole bearing, especially his closing speech, affords one of the finest instances of the morally sublime. There was one present on whose mind it made a deep impression, and who afterwards reproduced in the "Apology" the words then uttered. It was Plato.

He begins by reminding his judges that he had not long to live in the natural course of events, and that had they waited a short time his death would have occurred without their agency. Perhaps they think he has been condemned because he could make no defence. On the contrary it would have been perfectly easy to have said what would have pleased them, and procured his acquittal. But he would not do it. Nothing unworthy of a free man would he say or do. Nor did he now regret the course he had taken. Far rather would he make the one defence and die, than the other and live. Death is not the greatest evil that can befall a man. "The difficulty, O Athenians, is not to escape from death, but from guilt; for guilt is swifter than death, and runs faster; and now I, being old and slow of foot, have been overtaken by death, the slower of the two, but my accusers, who are brisk and active, by guilt, the swifter. We separate; I, sentenced by you to death, they, having sentence passed on them by Truth, of guilt and injustice. I submit to my punishment, they to theirs.

"When my sons grow up, if they shall seem to desire and seek for riches, or any other end, in preference to virtue, punish them, O Athenians, by tormenting them as I tormented you. And if they are thought to be something, when they are really nothing, reproach them as I have reproached you, for not attending to what they ought and fancying themselves something when they are good for nothing."

How grand and impressive the closing words. "It is now time that we depart, I to die, you to live; but which has the better destiny is unknown to all but God."

He was condemned. The last day of his life was spent in conversation with his friends on the immortality of the soul, a conversation which forms the subject of Plato's Phædo.

As the time for drinking the fatal cup approached, his friends were deeply moved; even the officer who came to announce the fatal hour was in tears; but Socrates himself with perfect calmness takes the potion, lies down on his couch, draws about him, as Cæsar at the Capitol, his mantle, and falls asleep; leaving to his friends the bitterness of irrepressible sorrow, but to future ages and all coming time, the admiration of his heroic firmness, his commanding virtues, and his immortality of fame. "All is human in Socrates while he lives;" says Renouvier, "all reveals a God in his death" (Philosophie Ancienne).

§ 2.—Doctrines of Socrates.

Our sources of information as the doctrines of this great teacher are not altogether satisfactory. He left no writings. The "Memorabilia" by Xenophon, while of great value as biography, is of less value as to matters of doctrine; the question arising, whether the philosophy of Socrates was always correctly apprehended by the practical and military Xenophon. The writings of Plato, on the other hand, are not always available, for precisely an opposite reason. He was himself a philosopher, and it is difficult always to distinguish what is Platonic from what is purely Socratic in the dialogues. Aristotle, though scanty, is free from the above objection. Probably the most reliable method would be to compare, and critically examine, each of the three writers now named.

1. As to *the general course and drift of the Socratic philosophy* there can be no reasonable doubt. It was decidedly ethical. This tendency is explained by the previous neglect of morals as a science. The ethical element in philosophy, the higher nature in man, had been sadly overlooked. Philosophy had degenerated into sophistry, the very foundations of truth were undermined, the reality and even the possibility of all truth, of all certainty and science, had been denied. Scepticism was triumphant. Socrates saw

that the only way to save science itself from destruction was to lay hold of this strong eternal element of truth, this hitherto neglected element, the moral nature of man, that in him which was higher and nobler than the mere physical facts and laws of his being and of the material existences around him. Hence the predominance of the ethical in the teaching of Socrates. It was thus he lifted the eye of man to a sublimer height of wisdom and true science, while he secured the integrity of truth and the possibility of human knowledge from being utterly swept away by the flood of scepticism.

It has been supposed by some that Socrates neglected everything but ethics. Is this so? More probably he sought *to give universality and completeness to science,* and as physics were already assiduously cultivated, while ethical science had been greatly neglected, he would naturally devote his attention chiefly to the latter. His objections to physical science were rather against the *exclusive* pursuit of that department of knowledge, and still more against the confused and unscientific method in which such inquiries were, in that age, conducted. So he is represented by Plato. The physiology of his age, he complained, looked downward rather than upward, more to sensible than to divine things. It exalted the irrational above the rational. For physical science, properly conducted, he had no contempt. True, he objected to a profound acquaintance with mathematics. So did Plato also; and so in modern times have many distinguished philosophers. He sought to form in himself and others a manly, symmetrical, strong character, of universal comprehension, not limited in its range, not exclusive in its devotion to any one pursuit, or branch of science. This is the grand practical aim of his teaching. An exclusive devotion to any one department of knowledge, he regards as unworthy of a true man.

We are not to look upon Socrates, then, as merely a moralist. He saw that, in order to establish science against the attacks of the Sophists, it was necessary to begin anew, and lay a foundation which they could not overthrow. This he did. He directed his attention, therefore, not to this or that special science, but to science in general, its idea, its nature, its conditions, in a word, to *method.* "Man," said Protogoras, "is the measure of all things, and men differ. Things are only what they seem to us, and our conceptions vary; hence there is no such thing as absolute truth. "Man is the measure of all things," says Socrates; "but descend deeper into his personality, and you will find that underneath all varieties there is a ground of steady truth. Men differ, but men also agree. They differ as to what is fleeting and transitory: they agree as to what is abiding and eternal. Difference is the region of opinion; agreement, that of truth. Let us endeavor to penetrate that region."

When, accordingly, he affirms that his wisdom is simply the knowledge of his own ignorance, he means not merely to express a certain contempt for the self-esteem of those who were so wise in their own opinion; much less is it his intention to question the possibility of all certain knowledge; but rather to express strongly the limited range of the human faculties, the limited extent of all human knowledge, as compared with the unfathomable depth of truth. He attached great importance to that Delphic oracle "*Know thyself*"—the self-knowledge he sought being the knowledge of his own nature, the foundation of all true science.

Insomuch as all scientific thought is inseparably connected, Socrates attached importance to even trivial subjects, as not unworthy of careful investigation, since connected with all truth by means of whatever truth or certainty they contained. Every clear and certain thought every established fact, however trivial, is part, therefore, of the grand whole, and taken in connection with all others, forms the complete and magnificent structure of science. He was therefore much occupied with matters which others regarded as beneath their notice, thus fulfilling the prophecy of Parmenides, that the young Socrates, when mature, would despise nothing as unworthy of examination.

2. In what manner, now, did he seek to attain this comprehensive, universal knowledge? In other words, what was *the Socratic method?* Socrates, not content with discovering his own and human ignorance, sought to establish a true scientific method. This method was to consider everything in conformity to the genus to which it belonged, and by the definition of the genus to determine what the thing is in itself, or in its essence. The endeavor was *to apprehend in thought the essence of the thing;* and to accomplish this it depended on the definition of terms as the grand instrument. This is the very spirit and centre of the Platonic philosophy also; its root and form lie in the Socratic method now defined. So Aristotle affirms. There are two things, he says, which must in justice be attributed to Socrates; the inductive method of proof, and the general definition of ideas, both of which are among the first principles of philosophy (Met. xiii. 4; so also Xenophon, Mem. iv. 5, 12). That is, Socrates was the first to apply a right method to philosophic investigation, the first to point out the true path which later inquirers followed in the search for truth. Hence he has rightly been placed at the head of the genuine development of Greek philosophy. *To search out the* WHAT of everything, was the unceasing care of Socrates, says Xenophon (Mem. iv. 6, 1).

Tissot regards the so-called inductive method of Socrates as more properly analytic, a process of pure generalization. "What is called his induction is nothing else than this preliminary operation of grouping around an idea all those with which it might be confounded, so as the better to distinguish it from them, or to bring to notice what there is in common to them all, and so to rise to a higher generality. It is, then, a pure generalization" (Histoire de la Philosophie). Lewes also denied that the Socratic method was properly inductive, and regards it as merely a reasoning from analogy, a combination of analogous facts—a method quite opposed to that of the Novum Organum of Bacon. (Hist. Phil. vol. i. p. 151). Grote, on the contrary, in his admirable sketch of Socrates, points out the resemblance of the Socratic and Baconian methods in spirit and aim (Hist. Greece, vol. viii. p. 612). See also Archer Butler, Hist. Phil. i. 350). But whether the Socratic method be properly called induction, with Aristotle, or generalization, with Tissot, or reasoning from analogy, with Lewes, and whether it be or be not essentially Baconian in spirit and purpose, there can be little doubt as to what the chief peculiarity of that method really was. Socrates saw that to understand a thing in itself it is necessary to grasp its essential idea, to make sure of having seized definitely and exactly that idea; and this could be done only by sharply and accurately defining it. In order to this he compares and contrasts it with all similar ideas, notes the differences and resemblances, and having the idea thus clearly before the mind, he proceeds to analzye it, separating the individual and accidental from the essential, and thus gets at its true nature and essence, what it is in itself. The modern school of positive philosophy charges him with mistaking names for things, in this whole matter, definition of terms for description of the thing itself—the prime peculiarity and radical defect, it affirms, of the Platonic and Aristotelian schools as formed on the Socratic model. Thus Lewes (Hist. Phil. vol. i. p. 154). I cannot see the justice of this charge. It must be remembered that Socrates had special reference in this whole process of investigation, not to external nature, but to self-knowledge, the facts and phenomena of the mind; and it is difficult to see how in any other or better manner he could attain that clearness and definiteness so essential to all correct thinking, than that now described. How could he better apprehend, the precise nature of the idea of right, for example, or of truth, or justice—the precise nature of any mental state or operation—nay, for that matter, the nature of any external object as known to the sciences, than by that very process above described. Schwegler has well described the Socratic method (Hist. Phil. p. 65).

3. From this inquiry as to the method of Socrates we pass to the *general principles of the Socratic ethics.* The moral end of life is knowledge, the knowledge of the good, and of the Reason that rules over all. All virtue is intelligence, wisdom; and as wisdom embraces all the virtues, virtue may be called a science, (Aristotle, Nic. Eth. vi. 13). No act performed without a clear insight into its nature and tendency is morally good; no act performed with such insight is bad. There is no merit in the act unless intentionally performed as good, and for that reason.

From this identification of virtue with science follows the strange, and, as we should now call it, paradoxical opinion, that man always does what seems to him to be good and right; for he who knows a thing to be good will do it. He may mistake, may be ignorant of the greatest good, and so err; but it will be an error of judgment. Not knowingly, not voluntarily, does any man do wrong. Nay more, he who should knowingly do any evil thing were a better man than he who should do the same thing ignorantly. In other words, he who performs a wrong act, with clear insight into its nature and tendency, yet perceiving it to be on the whole a good thing for him to do, is wiser and more to be commended than he who acts blindly and without intelligence to guide him. Socrates could not conceive of a man's knowing the good, and not doing it. Hence Aristotle, very justly as it seems to us, censures him as not taking into account, in his estimate of human conduct, the sentiments an dpassions of our nature (Mag. Mor. i. 1, 5.

Socrates teaches clearly and strongly that virtue and happiness are inseparably united; that he only is happy who seeks the good of family, friends, and fatherland, and who learns to govern body and soul; in other words, true happiness involves the whole moral duty of man (Mem. ii. 1, § 19, iii. 9; iv. 2; i. 6). He held that temperance and moderation are preferable to sensual enjoyment, since the latter is merely the gratification of certain wants, of which the fewer, the better, and since it also destroys the true freedom of the soul. The true destiny and duty of man is to assimilate himself to the divine by emancipating himself from the dominion of his passions.

In a word, the drift of the Socratic ethics may be summed up in this general principle. The chief happiness of man consists in knowing the right and doing accordingly (Mem. iii. 9. 14; i. 5; iv. 4, 5, 6), the means to which are self-knowledge and self-control. Self-government is the foundation of all the virtues.

As to the question what is right and good, aside from general principles already indicated, Socrates gives no specific answer, but refers his disciples to the laws of the state as a legitimate expression of the general reason and the general will, sanctioned by the gods themselves, who are the founders of states. To these he would add the unwritten law, and also "that inner voice of Deity which speaks to every man's conscience, and in obedience to which his whole life and energies ought to be directed."

Schwegler and others have pronounced Socrates utilitarian in ethics, inasmuch as he appeals for proof of his prop ositions to the external advantages and benefits of virtue. But this is not so. He acknowledges, indeed, the benefits of virtue, but does not rest the obligation to virtue on that ground. The Sophists praise virtue for the sake of its advantages; Socrates for the sake of its own intrinsic worth. To be "καλοκάγαθος" is something desirable for its own sake; and therein lies the essence of every virtue. He taught that, of all the consequences of our conduct, its effects on our own spiritual nature are the most important (Mem. i. 6, 9; iv. 8, 6).

4. The *theology* of Socrates next demands our attention. Socrates nowhere, as reported to us, speculates upon the divine essence or even investigates it. Probably he considered it, as in fact it is, beyond human comprehension. He was, moreover, attached to the popular mythology and unwilling to overthrow it; hence cautious and prudent in his language. He maintains the omniscience, omnipotence, and omnipresence of the gods, and that they rule by the law of goodness. He counsels Aristodemus, with whom he holds an argument on the proof of the divine existence, if he would know the wisdom and the love of the gods, to render himself worthy of the communication of some of those divine secrets which are imparted only to those who adore and obey the Deity. "Then shalt thou, my Aristodemus, understand that there is a being whose eye pierceth throughout all nature, and whose ear is open to every sound; extended to all places, extending through all time, and whose bounty and care can know no other bound than those fixed by his own creation" (Mem. i. 4). He taught also that we ought not only to forbear what is impious and unjust before man, but even when alone ought to have regard to all our actions, "since the gods have their eyes always upon us, and none of our designs can be concealed from them" (Xenophon, Memorabilia, as above).

The Deity is to Socrates the supreme reason, the source of all things, the end of all human endeavors. But as the reason is one, deity must have been regarded by him as one, in distinction from the polytheism of the age. These various elements of the idea of a true God had perhaps all been separately maintained before, but not combined in one with such completeness and purity. "The doctrine of a truly intelligent deity," says Ritter, "without dualism, without either physical limitation, or pantheistic annihilation of individuality," had never been taught by any philosopher before Socrates (History of Ancient Philosophy). It has been a matter of much dispute what is to be understood by the *demon* of Socrates. The ancient and commonly received opinion, is that Socrates believed himself under the direction of a personal tutelar deity or guardian angel. This however he does not say, and probably does not mean ; "but only "δαιμόνιόν τι," *divinum quiddam*, as Cicero terms it, *a something divine.* He does not attempt to define it ; does not ascribe personality to it ; never calls it 'δαίμων ;' that is merely a blunder of the translators. He speaks of it now as a sign, now as a voice (Phædo, p. 242 ; Apol. Soc. p. 31), referring it however to a divine source (Xen. Mem. iv. 3, 12, 13). Schleiermacher supposes it a mere intuitive judgment, a presentiment, as, for example, of the issue of any undertaking. Others suppose it simply the voice of his own conscience. Schwegler thinks it cannot be explained on psychological grounds, but that there may possibly have been something magnetic about it—a state of ecstasy perhaps. Ritter thinks it was originally conscience that was meant, but that afterwards he fancied himself under the special guidance of heaven (See Butler, Hist. Anc. Phil. vol. i. p. 357, note by the editor).

The *immortality of the soul* was believed and taught by Socrates, though his doctrine is not wholly free from indecision and ambiguity. There must be another state of existence, in which man shall more successfully pursue the end of his being, and in which he shall be free from the present impediments ; else life were hardly to be preferred to death. The soul is, moreover, of a god-like nature, and therefore immortal. The future life is a condition of reward (See Cyrop. viii. 7 ; Mem. i. 4, § 8, 9 ; iv. 3, § 14 ; Phædo, c. 8).

The following passage (quoted also by Renouvier) from the Phædo of Plato, sets in clear light the Socratic doctrine of the immortality of the soul. It is in the conversation at the death of Socrates. "No man of sense will believe what the myths teach respecting another life ; but that a new sojourn, analogous to that which is promised us, awaits the soul truly immortal, is, it seems to me, what we may believe. It is necessary, then, that one should venture himself upon this thought, and delight himself with this hope. Let him take confidence in his soul; he who has renounced as foreign the pleasures of the body, he who has loved science, he who has adorned his soul with its true beauty—temperance, justice, strength, liberty, truth; and let him hold himself ready for departure from the world, against the hour when destiny shall call for him." Such, in brief, were the Socratic doctrines.

They are well summed up by Ritter (Hist. Phil. vol. i. p. 75, 76), as also by Tennemann, in his Manuel de l'Histoire de la Philosophie (see also Schwegler and Ueberweg).

As to the influence of Socrates on the subsequent course of human thought, what shall we say? "The great figure of this sage," says Renouvier, "rises not in the midst of myths, but pertains all entire to history; it *hovers over it.*" It is not too much to say that not merely the course of speculative thought, but the history of human progress in the world, from that day to this, the advancement of the human soul toward all that is noble and grand in its ideal, and its highest aspiration, had been far different had Socrates never lived. How noble the spirit that could breathe this prayer. "Give me the interior beauty of the soul." One may almost sympathize with Erasmus, who exclaims, "When I read some things of this sort concerning such men, I can scarcely refrain from saying, 'Sancte Socrate, ora pro nobis.'"

CHAPTER II.

IMMEDIATE SUCCESSORS OF SOCRATES.

§ 1.—The Cyrenaic School.

After the death of Socrates, his doctrines were held and promulgated under various modifications of several distinct schools or parties among his disciples. From the general doctrine of Socrates, that happiness is the chief end of man, arose two diverging systems. The one, starting from the sensibilities or desires, places happiness in pleasure—either that of the present moment and present act merely, ἡδονή, as Aristippus and the Cyrenaics; or the systematic pleasure, which looks to the future, and regards consequences, as Epicurus. The other system, starting from the reason rather than the senses and desires, grounds happiness in virtue: either that of action, as Xenophon and Plato; or that of negation and apathy to all pleasure, as the Cynics. Each of these schools presents a side of Socrates, according to the view that each took of that great master.

Among these stands prominent the *Cyrenaic.*

The head of this school was Aristippus, a disciple of Socrates, but regarded by the stricter Socratists as an unworthy pupil of the great master. His doctrines, though they diverged widely from those of Socrates, yet are based upon his principles; diverge from his stand-point.

Aristippus was born at Cyrene in Africa, a colony of note and power, but given to luxury. He was of illustrious and wealthy origin, and followed the pleasures which such a position and such an age placed in his way. He had heard of Socrates, however, and curious to know and hear the man, embarked for Athens and became a pupil of the great master, remaining with him till the death of the latter, 399 B. C.

He seems to have remained a man of pleasure, notwithstanding the teachings of Socrates on temperance, self-denial, etc.; kept himself aloof from no corrupting influences, but relied on his own self-possession and self-control to extricate him from all dangers and difficulties; frequented the society of disreputable persons; lived with Lais, a celebrated courtesan; was intimate with Dionysius the tyrant, and practically carried out the principle that a man ought to control circumstances, not to be controlled by them.

His starting point was Socratic. He began with the fundamental tenet of the Socratic school, that the chief aim and end of all human life and action is happiness. This, however, Socrates would place, not in the gratification of sensual desires and in irrational pleasures, but in self-knowledge, self-control, temperance, virtue, etc., as being the true and most exquisite as well as real source of happiness to man. On this point Aristippus begins to diverge. Happiness is the great aim of man (τὸ τέλος), but happiness is pleasure (ἡδονή). Pleasure is the good. Pain is the evil (Cicero de Finibus, ii. 6, 7, 13, 34; De Offic. iii. 33). Whatever contributes to pleasure is a good thing, as wisdom, virtue, friendship—good for that reason only (Diog. L. ii. 91, 93; Cic. Off. iii. 33); whatever interferes with it, an evil thing. In order to happiness, the mind must retain its independence, indeed, of all other and foreign influences; must not be enslaved by its passions, etc. But this independence may be secured not only in the Socratic method, by regulating and controlling one's pleasures, but also by banishing desire. Only as one is superior to hope and fear and desire, is he in the enjoyment of the highest pleasure (Diog. Laert. ii. 89, 90). Pleasure is good, but not the desire of pleasure; it is this that subjects the soul to hope and fear, and interferes with its enjoyment.

A man ought not, then, to desire anything which he is not at the moment in possession of, and the wise man will not. Such the doctrine; and the life and character of the man corresponded. He was of a serene, happy temperament: never allowed himself to want what he did not possess, manifested perfect indifference to all good things which were not within his reach, gave himself up with ready assent to whatever circumstances happened to surround him, lived for the present, neither regretting the past nor caring for the future; for the present alone is ours, the past gone, the future uncertain. His maxim seems to have been, Be content with such things as you have, and by no means fret thyself on any account. An easy, good-natured soul he must have been, and an easy time he must have had of it. Of course there could have been no great and elevated idea of what man might become or what he ought to be, no high moral purpose, no moral unity of life and purpose.

The school of Aristippus regarded pleasure and pain as something positive; pleasure was not merely the gratification of a want, not merely the removal of pain, nor was pain the absence of a pleasure merely, but both were emotions, or *motions* of the soul; the absence of both is a state of rest or sleep, as it were. As to their idea of virtue, it was this: all actions in themselves are morally indifferent, the only question being as to its result, pleasure or pain. They agreed with the Sophists that no action is in itself either good or evil, but only as established and regulated by law and custom (Diog. Laertus, ii. 98. 99). Yet they maintained the general expediency of doing that which is just, on the ground that *injustice will not pay*. Whatever is a means to pleasure, that is *virtue* in the estimation of this school.

Pleasure, pain, and entire indifference, or absence of either, are the three states of the mind, analogous to gentle motion, violent motion, and rest, or to a gentle breeze, a tempest, and a sea-calm. Pleasure is the sensation produced by gentle motion, pain, that produced by violent motion. In order to the highest enjoyment of pleasure, *self-control* is necessary, and this art of controlling pleasure is to be acquired only by knowledge and culture. The pleasure of the moment is not the highest goal.

Reason is the regulating principle, the chief element of virtue, which teaches how to avoid what might interfere with the pursuit of true pleasure. They did not limit pleasure to the bodily gratifications merely, but took into account the pleasures of the mind, and the spiritual part of man, though the former they held to be the stronger of the two (Diog. Laert. ii. 89, 90).

Aristotle reproaches Aristippus with having neglected all mathematical learning on the ground that it does not treat of the *good* and the *evil*, the only things worth knowing. Yet the Cyrenaic school seems to have cultivated logic, and even to some extent physics. Aristippus taught his doctrines to his daughter, Arete, who instructed her son, Aristippus junior. He also taught Antipater, who became one of the leaders of the school. Theodorus, the the pupil of the younger Aristippus, was another prominent teacher in the school. It is doubtful if Aristippus the elder ever taught public, or published his doctrines. His disciples carried out the system to its farthest divergence from the Socratic ground. Theodorus, according to Sextus Empiricus (adv. Math. vii.), *held the entire subjectivity of our knowledge;* things are sweet, bitter, etc., not in themselves but merely as they so seem to us; we know nothing but *our own sensations;* hence there *is out of us no criterion of truth;* the *changes, successions,* of our own feeling are all that we are conscious of, all that we know (Diog. Laert. ii. 92; Cic. Acad. ii. 46, 142). This is carrying out the doctrine of Aristippus, who, according to the same authority, held that we knew our sensations, but not the occasion or source of them, *i. e.*, not the qualities of bodies which produce them.

§ 2.—The Cynic School.

The chief of this school was Antisthenes, of Thracian descent by the mother; pupil in earlier life of Gorgias the Sophist, but subsequently pupil of Socrates, at an age when his moral and philosophical opinions were already somewhat matured. From this and other causes he seems to have but partially understood the Socratic system, viewing it in a one-sided light. He was by nature a one-sided man, for nature produces; such a man of narrow views, and of coarse *illiberal; stern,* moreover, as such men are apt to be, harsh, censorious, yet conceited withal, placing undue estimate upon his own superior powers, and cherishing a vain desire of the admiration of others. Hence his love of *exaggeration.* It was not till after the death of Socrates that he opened a school of his own in the Cynosarges (whence the term Cynic), a gymnasium for the Athenians of foreign extraction. By his descent he was excluded from all participation in politics. He was poor, moreover, and he gloried in both these things, as sources of *independence.* He was above the world, that was so far above him. Assuming the mendicant's staff and wallet, negligent of attire, coarse and slovenly in appearance, he walked his round as proud a man, as scornful, as self-sufficient, as unamiable and uncomfortable a character as one could find in all Athens—a genuine radical reformer, ready to quarrel with society and with anybody that came in his way. The age was one of increasing luxury and civilization. Athens was fast coming to be a pleasure-loving city. Antisthenes, in the true spirit of *an anti,* set himself *against* all this. He must forsooth bring men back to the primitive simplicity in dress, manners, etc. So, like a wise fool, but a true *anti,* as he was, he goes over to the opposite extreme, and seeks to correct an amiable fault, a pardonable sin, by committing himself an unpardonable one. Here you have the *cynic,* the man Antisthenes, as contemporaries have drawn him, and as his own life and doctrines show him—true type of a class of men to be found in every progressive age, and of a spirit which never has been, perhaps never will be, quite extinct in this world.

Annoyed at the little success with which his school met, he broke up the concern and *drove away* the few scholars that lingered about his doors; for an *original* character, however unamiable, will always have some *followers* and admirers. One only remained, Diogenes of Sinope, too much like his master to *be* driven away; so a compromise was effected, and the two kindred spirits remained in company, like master like pupil, till the death of the former. Which was the more *unlikely* character it would hard to say.

The doctrines of Antisthenes seem to be little more than this one idea—stern, determined resistance to all luxury and effeminacy, absolute resistance to all indulgence and all pleasure. In this was *virtue*. This was *morals*. The very name of pleasure seems to have filled his righteous soul with horror. "Pain, labor, even injury, is a good. Pleasure, on the contrary, an evil." "I had rather go mad than experience pleasure;" so Diogenes Laertius (vi. 3) makes him say. Poor man, he had his choice; pleasure certainly he could have had but little experience of; *mad* he certainly did go. He formed a theory on the subject, in which he endeavors to maintain that there is *no such thing* in fact as pleasure, what we call pleasure being only the limitation of pain.

It is possible to put a more favorable construction, however, upon this doctrine, by supposing that he meant by pleasure only sensual gratification, while by labor and pain he intended those manly struggles by which the soul attains true intellectual wealth, and pleasure, and freedom, and becomes great in action. If this were his meaning, it is easy to see how he was merely carrying out, though intemperately and to extremes, the true Socratic doctrine of temperance and self-denial.

According to this view, the philosophy of this school amounts simply to this principle: Live in the simplest and most natural way, in order, like the Deity, who wants nothing, to lead the happiest life of which man is capable. Thus Socrates said: "To want nothing is God-like; to want the least possible is most nearly to resemble God" (Xen. Mem. i. 6, 10).

Virtue, according to Antisthenes, is the true supreme good (Diog. L. vi. 103, 104); everything which stands between it and vice is indifferent, such things as wealth, poverty, honor, birth, and the like, matters of no moment. Virtue consists in action, and must have reason for its basis and ground-work, its true root and essence. "*Man must have reason or a halter*," is his pointed and bitter expression. What is this virtue? An insight into the good; something which he cannot further explain than that.

His system was a purely selfish and morose one. He isolates man entirely within himself, makes him sufficient for himself. Affection, love of kindred, are of no moral worth; civil institutions are contemptible; love of country, ridiculous. Marriage has no further value or sacredness than as it relates to the propagation of the species. Insolent, proud, overbearing, shameless men, were the sages of this school.

As to other matters, Antisthenes held that the Socratic method of arriving at truth by definitions is not of much use, since the essence of a thing cannot be expressed in or learned by a definition, but only by intuition (Aristotle, Met. v. 29; viii. 3).

Science he cultivated to some extent. He wrote a work on physics; and shows in his writings, which are numerous, a good acquaintance with logic. In his old age, and increasing moroseness, he seems to have regretted his own literary labors, speaks depreciatingly of science, and comes to the conclusion that nothing is of use but virtue, not even the ability to read and write.

Socrates well understood the man, and thus keenly rebuked his pride. "I see your vanity, Antisthenes, peering through the holes in your cloak." The cloak was his only garment. Being told that many persons praised him, he said, "Have I done anything wrong then, that I am praised?"

Diogenes of Sinope, he of the tub, is the natural result and termination of this system. This man outraged all decency; filthy in person, vulgar and degraded in habits and manners. When Plato on one occasion gave an entertainment, Diogenes burst in, uninvited, and stamping on the carpets with dirty feet exclaimed, "Thus I trample on the pride of Plato!" "With greater pride!" was the admirable rejoinder. He died at ninety, of eating a raw neat's foot!

§ 3.—Megaric School.

Most of the disciples of Socrates, after his death, retired to Megari, to escape the popular excitement against the friends of the illustrious martyr. This was the abode of Euclid, one of the oldest of the disciples of Socrates (Diog. Laert. ii. 106); and about him naturally clustered the outlawed band. After a time the little society, no longer held together by the common bond, the influence of the great master, and differing among themselves in many things, broke up; a few only remaining with Euclid, who thus became the leader of a school, called, from the place, the Megaric.

It is related of this man that so great was his admiration of Socrates, and his desire to profit by his instructions, that disregarding the law which forbade any citizen of Megari from visiting Athens on pain of death—such was the feud between the two cities—he used to travel the distance, twenty miles, on foot, by night, in order to escape detection, and was rewarded by an interview with the great master; after which, in like manner he returned, meditating on the truths he had heard. Knowledge thus hardly acquired we may well suppose to have been of value to him.

He seems to have been present at the death of Socrates (Phædo, p. 59).

Though a disciple of Socrates, Euclid seems to have been partial to the *Eleatic* system and to have made that the basis on which he erected his philosophical structure. He is represented as mild and conciliating in disposition, moderate in character and conduct, but fond of subtle disputation and sophistic distinctions. His doctrines were Eleatic, modified by the Socratic. They partook of the moral element and the scientific cast of the latter school. "*The one*" can be known only by reason, not by the senses, and is *unalterable.* This only one is "the good," known under other names as, reason, intelligence, wisdom, God, etc. By this "one," they seem not to have intended an ontological unity, a being, so much as an abstract conception—being in general. The distinctive character of true morality, as of true being, lies in its oneness, unity, or identity.

The system assumes a strongly negative character. In refuting an opponent, Euclid does not attack the premises but drives right at the conclusion. Of course his method is indirect, nor does he admit the validity of definitions, nor even of comparisons; for these must be either of like to *like* or to *unlike;* in the first case, it were better to speak of the object itself; in the latter, comparison must mislead. Sophisms and fallacies play a conspicuous part in the later history of this school, employed as convenient instruments of refuting opponents and of showing the vain pretensions of superficial thinkers.

Several of these fallacies are ascribed particularly to

Eubulides, though not invented by him, but by the Sophists, as, *e. g.*, the somewhat noted sophisms termed the Liar, the Sorites, the Horn, the Bald-head, etc. These were employed, perhaps, merely to show the necessity of care and skill in the employment of even scientific terms, perhaps as means of posing arrogant pretenders, probably however with the further and laudable purpose of casting a doubt upon all acquired knowledge—for it was a maxim with the Sophists that to learn what we do not know is impossible. Thus the sophism of the *liar*, which is thus stated by Cicero. If you say that you lie and say truly, you lie ; but you say that you lie, and you speak the truth ; you lie therefore. Another of the sophisms has reference to the fact that you may meet a disguised person without recognizing him, in which case, though you know the person, ever so well, yet you do not know him.

Diodorus Chronos seems to have figured somewhat conspicuously in this method of reasoning. His favorite doctrine was that nothing is possible, except that which is necessary. This, as Aristotle says, leads naturally to the denial of all motion and generation ; it attacks the contingent, the visible phenomenal order of things, making against the senses and all sense, and knowledge. His arguments to show that motion is impossible are quite ingenious. For instance he contends that if a body consists of several parts, the motion must begin with one and be communicated to the others. Suppose, then, two out of three parts to be already set in motion, but not as yet the third ; we must conclude that the body as a whole is in motion, since the greater part of it is so ; the moved portions preponderate ; suppose now another, a fourth part, be added, which is unmoved ; the body still moves, for the *one* part last added to the body which was moving cannot destroy the preponderance of the moved parts, it is only one to three, the body moves, then, that is the whole four ; add on now to your heart's content, you get by and by a body of ten thousand parts, only two of which are actually in motion yet the whole body is so. Is this absurd? then it is impossible to show that a body is in motion in its preponderating parts, and of course, then, impossible to show that in its *totality* it moves, since the majority of parts must move before the *whole* can stir.

By a little artifice he demonstrates the impossibility of change, as shown in case of a wall. If that wall is ever to *cease* to be a wall, it must be either while the stones of it are together, or when they have been separated, but while they are together the wall continues, after they have been separated the wall does not cease to be, for it is then already in pieces and has no further change to undergo. When did it cease, then, in the name of reason? Never, and never will, is the implied answer; your senses altogether mystify and deceive you in this whole matter of material existences and the changes to which they appear to be subject.

Stilpo was a later disciple of this Megaric school, and a philosopher of some note. But his doctrines present nothing of special importance in distinction from those of the school generally.

CHAPTER III.

PLATO.

In treating of the philosophy of this most distinguished disciple of Socrates, it will be convenient to speak first of his life and character; second, of his method; third, of his psychology; fourth, of his theology; fifth, of his ethics and politics; sixth and lastly, of his physics. Abundant materials are at hand for such investigation; first of all, his own philosophic writings, chiefly dialogues, then commentaries almost innumerable on these by scholars and critics of all ages since Plato's day, and of almost all nations of the civilized world. On no one writer of antiquity, perhaps, has so much been written by subsequent writers as on Plato. Many of these writers, it must be confessed, had but a a limited knowledge of the original works, for of all ancient authors, Plato is probably *the most* difficult to be intelligently read and the least likely to be completely and thoroughly perused.

§ 1.—Life and Character of Plato.*

Born about 429 B. C., about the time of the Peloponnesian war and of the death of Pericles; a most active and brilliant period of Grecian history. His family was of noble descent, connected on the maternal side with Solon. His real name was *Aristocles,* surnamed Plato, or the broad-browed (Diog. Laert. 3. 4). Fable relates that he was the child of Apollo, and his mother a virgin (Plutarch, Symposium viii. 1). However that may be, he was unquestionably connected with the most illustrious families of Athens, and hence had many opportunities for superior education and for a career as a statesman had he chosen; but from this he was deterred by weakness of voice, which unfitted him for public speaking, and also by his turn of mind. He seems to have divided his early efforts and enthusiam between poetry and philosophy. Wrote epics, lyrics, etc., not so much, as Ritter well conjectures, because of any true poetic genius, but because of a vague longing to *express* that which was in him, the reflections of his own mind, coupled with a profound study of the creations of earlier genius. It was not till he became acquainted with Socrates, in his twentieth year, that his mind took altogether a philosophical direction, and he abandoned poetry (Val. Max. 1. 6. Ælian. Var. Hist. 10, 21). From this time till the death of Socrates he remained with the

* Tenneman's Life of Plato; Biblioth. der Alten Lit.; Vit. Plat.; Ritter, Hist. Phil.

great master, a disciple not of him alone, however, but of all ancient philosophy. After the death of Socrates, tradition makes Plato travel and reside for many years in foreign countries, in Egypt, Phœnicia, Babylonia, Assyria, etc. To Egypt he probably did go; perhaps to other countries. "Whilst studious youth," says Valerius Maximus, "were crowding to Athens from every quarter in search of Plato for their master, that philosopher was wandering along the winding banks of the Nile, or the vast plains of a barbarous country, himself a disciple to the old men of Egypt."

On his return, he opened a school for gratuitous instruction in his favorite science. The place was one fitted rather for the poet or the artist than the severe dialectician. The beautiful grove of Academus, in the highly wrought description of Lewes, "was planted with lofty plane-trees, and adorned with temples and statues; a gentle stream rolled through it, with

> "A sound as of a hidden brook
> In the leafy month of June,
> Which to the sleeping woods all night
> Singeth a quiet tune."

It was a delicious retreat, "for contemplation framed. The longing thoughts of posterity have often hovered round it and made it the centre of mingled associations. Poets have sung of it. Philosophers have sighed for it."

Nor did the beauties and graces pertain entirely to the place where the exercises were conducted, for whatever poetry there may have been in the grove, the lectures and discussions of the Academy proper, while of the highest order of thought and requiring hard thinking in the hearer, yet were clothed in the most poetic and imaginative diction. Such was the renown of the master that there was no lack of hearers and disciples. His school was frequented by many of the higher classes. His pupils were among the most distinguished. Women even, it is said, attended his teachings. They were probably of that class which, at that period of Grecian history, combined the highest mental cultivation and the highest personal accomplishments with not the strictest ideas of virtue.

Plato visited Sicily in his fortieth year, to see Ætna. There he saw, however, the tyrant Dionysius, whom he so offended by his plainness of speech that the monarch sought the life of the philosopher, and the latter escaped death only to be sold as a slave. He was purchased by a Cyrenian, who immediately set him free. Without prosecuting further his studies upon volcanoes, tyrants, and other Sicilian curiosities, Plato seems to have made the best of his way home and contented himself thenceforth for the most part with the safer investigations of the Academy. Twice, however, afterwards he visited Syracuse, to confer with Dionysius the Second. Actively employed in philosophical composition, death overtook him in a peaceful and tranquil old age, 346 B. C., æt. 83.

Against the character of Plato malice has found little to say or insinuate. His enemies reproach him, but without ground (Diog. L. iii. 26). He seems to have been eminently a moral, blameless, just man, given chiefly to abstraction and severe thought; little to pleasure, little to the practical matters of life. He has been accused of *plagiarism!* What will become of the rest of us, if a mind as rich as Plato's is liable to this charge? He is accused of haughty and overweening self-esteem. Not unlikely. Where was ever the truly great and noble mind, towering above its compeers and all its time, that was not somehow self-conscious of superiority. He attacked, it is true, with some bitterness, the philosophical opinions of certain contemporary teachers, but not till they had as violently assailed him. It is said that his school was not, like that of Socrates, aimed at the salvation of the country, through reformation of the manners and morals of the age, but that it neglected this high aim. True, Plato did not, like Socrates, make himself a martyr to virtue; nor did he so directly and resolutely assail the vices of the age. He probably saw the inevitable drift of things, and that it would be useless to think of renovating a country and an age so corrupt. But he did present to the mind a high and noble aim, and sought to elevate those within his reach and sphere to a loftier style of thinking, feeling, and acting. His school was doubtless one of culture and refinement as compared with the Socratic. In place of the pristine severity, there was ornament, splendor of thought and diction, a true refinement, and severely cultivated but exquisite taste. That it was lacking in the sterner and more essential qualities of excellence has never been shown.

"Plato," says Lewes, "was intensely melancholy. That great broad brow, which gave him his surname, was wrinkled and sombre. Those brawny shoulders were bent with thought, as only those of thinkers are bent. A smile was the utmost that ever played over his lips; he never laughed. 'As sad as Plato,' became a phrase with the comic dramatists. He had many admirers; scarcely any friends. In Plato, the thinker predominated over the man. That great expansive intellect had so fixed itself upon the absorbing questions of philosophy, that it had scarcely any sympathy left for other matters. Hence his constant reprobation of poets. . . He had a feeling not unallied to contempt for them, because he saw in them some resemblance to the Sophists—an indifference to truth and a preference for the arts of expression. . . His soul panted for truth. Poets, at the best, he held to be only inspired madmen, unconscious of what fell from their lips. . . There is something unpleasant in Plato's character, which finds its echo in his works. He was a great, but not an amiable man. His works are great, but lamentably deficient. His ethics are the ethics of a logician, not of a large-souled man familiar with and sympathizing with the complexities of life; they are suited only to an impossible state of humanity."

This is, perhaps, a severe judgment of Plato's character; but it contains an element of truth. Plato may very probably have been but a poor companion and friend. He was too much absorded in his own contemplations. He was too far *above* all his contemporaries. He was, not unlikely, a sad and melancholy man; for what great soul is not so? Like the wind, like the ocean, the great soul murmurs to to itself a low, sad, mighty strain, heedless of passing incidents. If Plato had little in common with humanity, it was because humanity was so far below him.

What, now, was the effect and influence of this man upon his time and the world? "The influence of Plato," says Ritter (Hist. Phil.), "must be estimated not so much by its effect upon his contemporaries, as upon posterity and ourselves. This influence has been wrought principally by his writings. It rarely happens that a great thinker is rightly and fully understood by those who receive his inspirations directly from his own lips; time is requisite for a due and rightful appreciation of their import. *All posterity gathers around him as his scholars, in the same manner as he had applied himself to all antiquity as his teacher.* As to Plato, the ancients have, with great care and often in an envious spirit, explored the sources from which he might have derived the system of his philosophy, or his artifice of language. We are told by his great disciple Aristotle that he had diligently studied the doctrines of Heraclitus, Pythagoras, and Socrates; he might have added of Parmenides and Anaxagoras, for of Plato it may justly be said that he reduced into a beautiful whole the scattered results of the earlier Greek philosophies, reconciling their seeming differences and conflicting tendencies. From this fountain, as well as from the abundant sources of his own good powers, flowed the rich elements of his philosophy. In fact, where we compare the barrenness of the earlier philosophers with the fertility of Plato, that love, which Plato knows so well how to inspire in us, warms almost to veneration : so rich, so varied, and so abundant are his observations, and so profound his knowledge of man and the world !"

§ 2.—METHOD OF PLATO.

Was he a sceptic or a dogmatist ? Was he a mere expounder of Socratic doctrines, or himself the founder of a school ? As to the first of these questions, the ancients are divided, some regarding him as a sceptic, others as a positive teacher. Cicero says, "Plato affirms nothing, but, after producing many arguments, and examining a question on every side, leaves it undetermined." This is true, doubtless, of some of the writings of Plato, those which are intended as mere exercises of dialectic skill, but by no means of his more important dialogues. *Plato was no sceptic.* Yet he doubtless did attach more importance to *the method* of investigating truth than to the results of that investigation ; doubted the certainty of those results, and of his own knowledge as regards the higher elements and objects of thought ; expressed himself usually with reserve as to the definite objects of knowledge ; sought truth without professing to have arrived at certain apprehension of it. In all this he followed Socrates. But he was not a mere expounder of the Socratic doctrine. He enlarged the boundaries of the Socratic philosophy, and added to it new elements and instruments of great power. He brought into the sphere of philosophical investigation whatever was truly valuable in the researches and results of preceding thinkers, gathering from the Pythagorean, the Eleatic, even the ancient Ionian, valuable and needful materials for the symmetrical and complete structure of the temple of truth. He was not so much a creator as a composer ; a critic, an eclectic, rather than a dogmatist ; an architect and skilful builder of materials already elaborated. "He was," says Lewes, "the culminating point of Greek philosophy."

What, then, was the *Platonic method?* Socrates had relied on induction and definition. Definition was with him the basis of all science. To know what a thing is, you must also know what it is not. But in arriving at his definitions Socrates proceeded by a purely inductive or analogical process. Plato gave exactness and a scientific form to this part of the process of investigating truth, by adding the new and more efficient instruments of analysis and synthesis. Analysis, the decomposition of a thing into its component parts, the study of those parts, the idea of the whole thus acquired, the seeing the one in the many, —this process Plato was the first to introduce into science. (The process of this dialectical procedure is described in Phædrus, 265 *seq.*). Would you know what virtue is? Resolve the term into all the separate virtues, build up all these again into one, and you have virtue; you know what it means, you have a definition of it or a knowledge of its *essence* (Rep. vii. 534). The definitions of Plato relate to general and abstract ideas, for these alone are capable of definition; these alone are permanent, while the individual thing is transitory, phenomenal, not the subject of science at all. Science has nothing to do with individuals, but only with *general terms,* or *classes, abstract ideas.* These, according to Plato, stand for the only *real existences,* the only proper objects of science.

Plato is generally represented to have been a Realist and not a Nominalist. He gives to his general terms, as Socrates did not, a distinct and separate existence," says Aristotle, and called them ideas. This, however, is strenuously denied by Butler (Anc. Phil. ii. 16. *seq.*). Lewes has well stated in brief the summary of the Platonic method. "His great dogma was the necessity of an untiring investigation into general terms (or abstract ideas). He did not look on life with the temporary interest of a passing inhabitant of the world. He looked on it as an immortal soul longing to be released from its earthly prison, and striving to catch by anticipation some faint glimpses of that region of eternal truth where it would some day rest. The fleeting phenomena of this world he knew were nothing more. But he was too wise to overlook them. Fleeting and imperfect as they were, they were the indications of that eternal Truth for which he longed, footmarks on the perilous journey, and guides unto the wished-for goal. Long before him, wise and meditative men perceived that sense-knowledge would only be knowledge of phenomena; that everything men call existence was but a perpetual flux—a something which, always *becoming,* never *was;* that the reports which our senses made of these things partook of the same fleeting and uncertain character. He could not, therefore, put his trust in them; he could not believe that Time was anything more than the wavering image of Eternity.

"But he was not a sceptic. These transitory phenomena were not true existences; but they were *images* of true existences. Interrogate them; classify them; discover what qualities they have in common; discover that which is invariable, necessary, amidst all that is variable, contingent; discover The One in The Many, and you have penetrated the secret of Existence" (Hist. Phil. i. 210, 11).

§ 3.—Plato's Division of Philosophy.

Before treating of psychology in particular, it is necessary first to inquire into Plato's general view of philosophy, and his division of it.

Philosophy Plato divides into Logic, Physics, and Ethics (so Cic. Acad. Post. i. 5, 19; Sext. Emp. adv. Math. vii. 16), as comprising the various departments of human knowledge. There is among the many different sciences one, whose office is that of *regulator* of the others, to determine the value of each special science. This, *the science of all other sciences,* he terms *dialectic,* or logic. It embraces all, gives unity to all, and no particular science is of any further value than as it contributes to advance the soul in this all-comprehensive science. Mathematics, astronomy, etc., are like sportsmen who seize whatever prey comes to hand, without even the ability to make any use of it. Dialectic teaches the true use and value of all such acquisitions. It is the "self-consciousness of the reason, the conviction it has of itself. This first gives to life its intellectual energy, by affording a definite end to whatever the soul enters upon and accomplishes, while it contemplates the supreme truth, the true good of the soul, of all things." This perfect science is difficult to attain, indeed can never be fully attained by man, for everything in him is perpetual change, his very science is fluctuating and never the same; imperfect therefore. The object of the one true science is *eternal* truth, the unchangeable, unborn, imperishable ; that which *is*, that which we call God, and which is possible, *knowable*, only to God. Nevertheless this absolute and perfect science, though above human reach, is yet the true ideal at which the soul of man should ever aim; the province and privilege of the rational and truly intelligent mind. This, then, is the basis of the Platonic idea of true science or pure philosophy, viz., that science which from its high vantage ground overlooks and reviews all others; embraces all others within itself; determines the value and true end of each—the science which is "cognizant of all notions in their respective differences and affinities, and whose object is being in general"; the science which orders and disposes all things, can discourse of all things, presides over every thought and every utterance, *real* only as existing in Deity, but the *grand ideal* of the *excellence and endeavor*—divine philosophy. He refuses the name of science to all other arts and branches of knowledge, however accurate, as mathematics and its application to music and astronomy, in comparison with this ideal, this one grand *true* science of them all.

In order to reach toward this, a feeling of desire is needful, a consciousness of our own ignorance. Curiosity comes in also, and a feeling of wonder Plato calls the first step toward philosophy; wonder, that is, at the uncertainty of our present knowledge and the vagueness even of right opinions.

No mental tendency or development, in his view, was legitimate and right which did not contain in itself the germ of this lofty ideal, of this science *par excellence;* this highest development of human consciousness.

Plato distinguishes between opinion and *science.* Right opinion is a *transition* to philosophy, but is not itself science. Even mathematical science, geometry, astronomy, music, in so far as grounded on abstract truth, and so immutable, are only so many *means* of forming the soul to philosophy; helps and necessary steps to it (Rep. vii. 526, vi. 510); they are more certain than mere opinion, right opinion, *intermediate* between it and philosophy (Rep. vii. 533). But they are not themselves philosophy; for they proceed upon the assumption of certain primary notions, and give no account of *principles*—a method quite unscientific; they employ, moreover, visible figures for illustration, yet do not really treat of them, but only of what the mind alone perceives. Hence Plato refuses them the name of science, and calls them *διάνοια,* cognition, something clearer than opinion, but less clear than science.

To this one lofty and only real science Plato applies the term dialectic, meaning by it the true and pure philosophy. By dialectic, the ancients usually meant the same thing as logic in its widest signification.

Plato makes a similar use of it. Dialectic, or logic, being with him (Soph. p. 253; Phædrus, 266) essentially the art of right thinking and right speaking, language and thought being identical, except that the latter is a dialogue in the soul without sound, the former is vocal or uttered. His logic, then, is the science of *thought* and *being* (Philebus, p. 57), in so far as these are *eternal* and *immutable.*

Combining with this physics and ethics, two subordinate sciences, philosophy is complete.

§ 4.—Plato's Psychology.

We are ready now to proceed with the inquiry as to Plato's psychology. The soul, according to Plato, is of a twofold nature, or rather we have two souls, the rational and the sensitive; the latter regards phenomena, the former deals with and is percipient of the *noumena*, dwells in the region of pure *ideas* (Phædo, 25; Phædr. p. 247). Each completes the other, and both together make the complete soul. Sensation is the result of the union of the soul with the body, the sentient and the sensible—the union of the *same* with the *other*. Beside sense and reason there is a third principle, as bond of union to the two, *i. e.*, the spirit or active principle, emotion; this is inferior to reason but superior to sense. These three potentates rule the soul—appetite, spirit, reason—like the three divisions of plant, animal, and man in nature. The soul has existence in a previous state (Meno, p. 81), is indeed an eternal, imperishable existence (Phædrus, p. 245; Tim. p. 41; Phædo, 62–107). In that previous state it dwells in the region of celestial truth, travels with the gods, beholds and is conversant with real existences, self-existences, not mere phenomena.* If, however, it fail of reaching the necessary height and perceiving these realities, if its wings are clogged and weighed down by vice, it loses its primitive state, loses its wings, falls to the earth, enters and animates some corporeal body, and the person thus animated becomes a lover of wisdom and beauty, or a monarch, or statesman, or artist, or poet, or sophist, or prophet and religious teacher, according to the nature and rank of the preëxistent soul. They who conduct wisely in these different circumstances will next time obtain a more eligible lot. The soul never

* On this supposition of preëxistence, see beautiful passage in Butler (Anc. Phil. vol. ii. p. 229 *seq.*).

regains its pristine state, in less than 10,000 years; its wings requiring that time for growth. At the end of its first mortal life, it is judged, sentenced, and either sent for punishment under the earth, or rewarded in heaven. At the end of a thousand years it is called back, to choose by lot a new life. This time it may pass into the body of a woman, a bird, a beast, or a fish, according to its intelligence and virtue, or the soul of a beast, if once human, may now pass again into the human body. Thus it changes each thousandth year, till the decade is complete and its pristine state regained, if it ever is to be. The souls, however, of those who diligently seek wisdom and philosophy with sincerity, if they thrice successively choose this kind of life, in the three thousandth year regain their wings and are off. The soul in its mundane existence has many ideas of a higher and purer order than those of sense, ideas of things according to their kinds which are the combination of many perceptions into one by the reason. These ideas are reminiscences of its former state, when it was with the gods and beheld self-existent truth (Phædo, 74, 5; Phædrus, 249). This differs widely from *sense-knowledge*. Sense-knowledge is vague and uncertain: it is the knowledge of that which is never permanent and certain, but always in a flux, always *becoming*, never *being*. Were it not for our recollections of our previous state, the soul would apprehend only the *becoming*, the changeable, the sense-world, never the real and the true. "It is as if in our youth," says Lewes, "we had listened to some mighty orator whose printed speech we are reading in old age. That printed page how poor and faint a copy of that thrilling eloquence! And yet that printed page in some dim way recalls those tones, recalls that face, and stirs us somewhat as we then were stirred. Long years and many avocations have somewhat effaced the impression he first made, but the printed words serve faintly to recall it. Thus it is with our immortal souls. They have sojourned in that celestial region where the voice of truth rings clearly, where the aspect of truth is unveiled, undimmed. They are now sojourning in this fleeting, flowing river of life. Stung with resistless longings for the skies, and solaced only by the reminiscences of that former state, which these fleeting, broken, incoherent images of ideas awaken in them." *

What say we, now, of this doctrine; the soul's *preëxistence,* its reminiscence of that former knowledge? Beautiful it certainly is, nay more, sublime. It explains some things not otherwise resolvable. But is it true? Not more improbable *a priori* than its future existence after death, says Archer Butler. Who *knows* but it may be true? Who will say positively it is not? What is soul? Whence comes it? Who can tell?

§ 5.—The Platonic "Ideas."

In order to understand Plato's system it is necessary to know what he meant by the term so much employed, so fundamental to his philosophy, yet so much disputed, and after all so uncertain in its meaning—the term *Idea.*† Whatever it means, it lies at the basis of the Platonic philosophy, and even gives it its most appropriate name—the *Ideal* philosophy. Greek philosophy and Greek art, it has been well said, were eminently objective; their tendency was to transform the mind's conceptions into perceptions; to project its ideas out of itself, and then to look at them as images, as entities. This is characteristic of Plato's philosophy. He was, in this sense at least, a Realist. Our general conceptions were, with him, the images or representatives of eternal realities; our abstract universal notions, notions of *man* as a genus distinct from all individual men; of virtue in general, apart from the specific virtues—these

* Vol. i. p. 222.

† For a clear and admirable statement of the Platonic doctrine of Ideas, see Butler's Hist. Phil. ii. p. 112, 113.

genera, these universals—were with him not mere conceptions of the mind but represent real existences, entities; which entities he call *Ideas*. Not only were these "Ideas" existences, but the only real existences, the *noumena*, of which all individual things were the *phenomena*.

"Thus the object of Plato," says Butler, "was to trace all that was offered by the senses throughout this wondrous world down to its root in a deeper and invisible world." It is in these ideas that science seeks to seize the *essence* of things, to exhibit what everything is, in and by itself, or absolutely. These ideas are themselves unchangeable, always maintaining one and the same character. All else that exists beside ideas has reality only so far as it *participates* in them. It is by participation in these ideas, that things are what they are, for all is formed out of ideas, and numbers are to them as copies to originals. The word is not limited to species and genera and similar abstract and universal terms, but comprehends *every sort of true being*, not merely the most perfect, the beautiful, the good, etc., but the base and vicious even. There are ideas, also, of the one and the many, the great and the small, health and strength, speed and slowness; of unity, of the sphere by itself, the circle by itself, of individual and sensible things, a bed, a table, etc. (Repub. x. 596). Nay, the ideas of bed, table, etc., were first formed by the Creator, first *existed*, before man *copied* the idea by making the sensible table, etc., the shadow, as it were, of the reality. The *qualities* of things are also ideas, and so likewise actions and activities; a color, a sound, etc. (Cratyl. 423), even a name; finally the soul itself is an idea. To use his own words, an idea may be attributed to whatever as a plurality may be indicated by the same name (Rep. x. 596; so Arist. Met. xiii. 3). The extent to which the term is thus applied is explicable, if one consider that in Plato's view there is nothing which is not comprehended in the range of true science as its legitimate object, while at the same time science deals only with the fixed and immutable; of course, then, something fixed and immutable pertains to all, even the most changing and sensible things, and that something is its idea—the prototype of its existence. Thus only, universal science becomes possible. Here the question arises, since ideas comprise all reality, and truth, all real existence, what becomes of the sensible, how comes it to be, and of what value is it? The transition from the ideal to the sensible is the most difficult point in the whole Platonic philosophy, the point least *clear*, most doubtful and ambigious.

The sensible, according to Plato, is a *compound* of the "*Idea*" with the "*Other*," or "*non-being*" (Tim. p. 35)—a combination of different ideas to form one essence, for it is the nature of the sensible to comprise *opposites* within it, as the beautiful and the ugly, the great and the little, etc., as confusedly presented by the sensuous perception. This sensible world, however, is not a mere conception, but has reality in a sort, because it *participates* mysteriously in the nature of ideas. The relation of the sensible to the ideal is, however, merely that of *resemblance* (Rep. x. 597). The idea is the true measure or standard of the sensible. Plato in one place speaks of God as creating these ideas or prototypes of sensible things, in another place as creating the sensible after the pattern of these ideas already and eternally existing.

The close resemblance of the Platonic theory of ideas to the Pythagorean doctrine of *number* is noticed by Aristotle (Met. i. 12,13).

As an example or illustration of what Plato means by ideas, W. A. Butler (Ancient Phil. vol. ii. pp. 116–118) instances the law of causality. Our senses perceive the *changes* that are going on in the external world, but it is only by the faculty of reason that we perceive the necessity of a *cause* to produce that change. Thus every change brings the reason of man into contact with an "*Idea*," and that idea is independent of the mind that conceives it;

eternal. In like manner in all the phenomena of the world the "idea" of the *God* is revealed; the idea—partially developed it is true, but yet manifest—of absolute perfection. And so throughout, as the phenomena of sense cannot be explained without calling to our aid something *beyond* sense, so in the eternal world exists a *reason* for every phenomenon of sense, a reason antecedent to the sensible phenomenon. And these *reasons*, or general principles, are the "ideas" of Plato. Nor are these reasons, or laws, or ideas, to be regarded as identical with being or the conceptions of God. He is as far above them as they above sense.

§ 6.—Plato's Theology.

These ideas all stand related to each other; the less included in the greater, rising rank on rank above each other, and it is the business of science to trace each idea up to its higher and still higher sources, till the last is reached. And what is the last, the supreme, the grand idea that comprehends under it and in itself contains all others? What is this great supreme idea? It is God, the grand ultimate of all existence and reality. A perfect knowledge and comprehension of this being is impossible to man. No one general term will express the idea of God, or the good, as Plato interchangeably expresses it, but under these three terms it may be exhibited; viz., BEAUTY, PROPORTION, AND TRUTH. God is the supreme object of science (Rep. vi. 505) and the sum of ideas; as all variable phenomena proceed from and suppose an invariable essence, so the essence of all ideas and essences is in the last analysis to be found in the idea of the good (Rep. vii. 517), or God; the pattern after which all is fashioned and to which all things tend; God is the really beautiful and good. Man can strive after the beautiful and the good, and so participate in it, become assimilated to the divine. God is ever the same, for the more *perfect* anything is, the less liable to be changed by another; hence Deity, as the most perfect, is incapable of being thus changed. Still less can he change himself, for nothing good voluntarily becomes *worse.* Yet, being perfect, there is no change possible except for the worse. He changes not, therefore. Pleasure and pain are alien from him, yet his existence is eternally blissful, since participating in the good. All sensuous conditions of time and space are of course inapplicable to the Deity of Plato. He is omnipresent and omnipotent, and provides for all things, alike the great, and the little without which the great cannot be. *He wills good to all so far as each is capable of receiving it.* He unites in himself all wisdom and virtue. Hence God is *reason* (Phileb. 22). But wisdom and reason exist not without a spirit. A sovereign soul and sovereign reason belong to him. Such is the God of Plato, in comparison with whom man is worthless and contemptible. Yet Schwegler (Hist. Phil. p. 96) questions whether with Plato God is a *personal* being.

§ 7.—Plato's Ethics.

As Plato includes *Theology* under *Dialectic* or *Philosophy,* so his Ethics comprise not only *Morals* but *Politics.* It will conduce to clearness, however, to consider the two separately. The basis of ethics, with Plato, is not the idea of *obligation* or duty, the idea of the right, on which in our own view all morals rest, but the idea of human perfectibility, as attained by the right regulation of the conduct. Hence the close connection of ethics with dialectics, the latter furnishing the knowledge of the good, the true, the perfect, by which alone man can rightly govern his conduct. This is the distinguishing feature of the Platonic system of ethics, it being based, not on the idea of obligation, but of man's *capacity for self-improvement,* and its consequent intimate connection with science or knowledge. Indeed, in this latter point, Plato only carries out the Socratic doctrine, that virtue is knowledge,—that the two ideas are inseparable, no one is willingly or voluntarily evil, only from ignorance does any man do evil; but not voluntarily is any one subject to ignorance, since every volition aims at the good; only from ignorance does the soul ever yield itself to the baser desires, following the *apparent* good, mistaking it for the real. Where science is, then, there is the knowledge of the true and the good, and so there is morality. The mistaking of evil for good is an involuntary fault, a want of *art;* the virtuous man is the skilful and successful artist, who knows how to accomplish the right and the wrong. The vicious, *i. e.,* ignorant, man is a *bungling* artist. This is a grand defect in Plato's system. It sets aside the influence of the passions as a moving and disturbing force, and makes virtue a mere matter of intellect. It makes every man do *as well as he knows how,* and even excuses his ignorance, since that, too, was involuntary. Is this a true picture of human nature? Whose consciousness does not say no? Who will not say with Ovid, "Video meliora, proboque, deteriora sequor"; with Euripides, "I *know* that what I am about to do is evil, but desire is stronger than my deliberations"; with Paul, "that which I do I *allow* not, or approve not," Rom. vii. 15.

As to the idea of *pleasure,* what part does it play in the Platonic ethics? The Sophists had taught that the *good consists* in pleasure. Plato refutes this error, yet does not deny that it is a good thing. It does not consist, according to Plato, simply in the negation of pain, as the Cynics maintained, but is a feeling of fitness and harmony in man's composite nature. Pleasure is of different species or kinds. There is that which is preceded by pain, as in case of hunger and thirst and other bodily desires, where the sensation of a *want* or pain precedes the gratification. This species of corporeal pleasure has its source in the *want.* There is another sort of pleasure which arises from painless desires, *e. g.,* sight of beautiful colors, forms, etc., perception of agreeable odors, tunes, and purely intellectual pleasures. These are the simple and pure, while the former sort are impure or mixed pleasures. *True* enjoyment consists in those pure delights which mingle not with pain ; that which the rational nature feels in the possession of truth and goodness.

Virtue, according to Plato, is of fourfold character. The soul is of *threefold* nature : reason, spirit, and sense ; each of these three has its appropriate virtue (Rep. iv. 441); that of reason is *knowledge of the good*, or wisdom ; that of the spirit, *courage ;* that of the desires, *temperance.* There is a fourth, however, whose office it is to regulate the others and secure their due proportion and harmony, that is, *justice.* By means of this, each faculty of the soul without interference performs its due functions and produces within the man complete and perfect order and harmony. Hence the just man alone can live in harmony with himself or with others. *Weakness* is the natural result of injustice ; *strength*, of justice. The just man alone is at one with himself ; the unjust is not one but a compound of many disjointed parts ; no strength in such a man.

Happiness, says Plato, consists *in the possession of the good and the beautiful* (Sympos. 202, 204) ; or, as he elsewhere expresses it, in the possession of *justice and wisdom* (Gorgias, 508), or in the possession of moral beauty and goodness (Gorgias, 470). In the Euthyphron, Plato takes ground expressly against the doctrine, that the *moral qualities of actions are dependent on the will of the supreme being.* In the language of Butler (Hist. Phil. vol. ii. p. 145, 146), "his whole philosophy of ideas as related to God is a structure raised to fortify the elementary principles of the eternal law of right against the irruptions of this degrading tenet." In the mind of Plato the nature of goodness is coëternal with God himself, not produced by him, nor dependent on him ; but he governs himself in all his acts according to these eternal relations of things, and makes his work conform to that perfect model. "Plato has, indeed, with his usual metaphysical accuracy, seen that the eternal laws of Right are in some mysterious bond (altogether beyond our conception), entwined with the divine nature, and he accordingly represents them as contained by him in his own divine reason; but nevertheless he maintains their substantial distinctness from the personal activity or volition of God, and their relation to him, not in the bond of cause and effect, but, to express eternal truths by sensible analogies, in that of model or examplar. They are coëxistent, they may even be pronounced coincident; but they are not consequential, resultant, inferior. . . God is related to the eternal ideas, as an architect is related to the model by which he labors."

As to the relation of the divine being to the good and evil that are in the world, there is a fine passage in the Laws (x. p. 903–4), in which the position is taken that the goodness of God is the final cause and law of creation and that everything is arranged with a view to the greatest good, while at the same time he has left to the disposition of our own wills the causes on which our distinctive characters depend, "The King of the world, having known all this, conceived, in the general distribution, the system which he considered simplest and best, *to the end that good might have the upper hand and evil be undermost in the universe.* It is with this view to the whole, that he has constructed his arrangement of the positions that each individual, according to his distinctive character, is to occupy,—at the same time that he has left to the disposal of our own wills the causes on which these distinctive characters shall depend; "*for men are what they make themselves to be*" (Quoted by Butler—whose translation I follow—Hist. Phil. vol. ii. p. 159–60).

§ 8.—Plato's Politics.

With Plato, the individual is subordinate to the state. This is the grand characteristic of his political system. The distinction of individuality is an unavoidable *imperfection* of a state, as also the difference of sex, temperament, character, etc.—distinctions to be, as far as possible, merged and lost sight of in the polity of the state. The state is a unity, composed of individual parts indeed, but the parts are of no consequence except as constituent of the whole; are not to come up with an importance of their own. To the good of the state all these individual distinctions are to be sacrificed. The state is everything. In this he only carried out with great vigor the spirit of the earlier Greeks. Accordingly, the right of property is to be given up, or is allowed only to the baser order of the community, viz., tradesmen and mechanics. Property belongs not to the citizen but to the state. In like manner, children are the property, not of the parents but of the state; nay, parentage is to be unknown. A community of wives is to exist. The domestic and family relations are to be ignored. The increase of the race is to be provided for on the same principles as farmers provide for the increase and improvement of stock. Women are to be selected for marriage with special reference to this, and to be assorted to the men, not indiscriminately, but with special reference to the temperament and character of each—the mild of one sex with the violent of the other, and the reverse. Yet no man is to have wife or children of his own. The state is to provide nurses for the early education of the children, and the state is also, at a proper age, to assign each to his proper rank or office or profession, according to his capacity and talent. Woman is to share with man the toils of war and agriculture, and the few that are fitted to do it may share with him also in the pursuits of philosophy and government. The sick and the aged, as no longer useful, are to be abandoned.

The duty of education lying thus in the state, the arts, music, poetry, dancing, etc., are under its exclusive control. Education is twofold: that of the *body, gymnastics,* and that of the *soul, music;* the former, all training of the physical man, not for its own sake but for the benefit of the soul; the latter, including the fine arts, grammar, the arts of the muses, the sciences. These latter, however, subject to restrictive laws, by which he would counteract the prevailing tendency to effeminacy and luxury in the arts, substituting the simplicity and gravity of the olden time. Poetry, *dramatic* and *epic,* he proscribes, as striving to imitate the passions and emotions, and so dangerous; but lyric poetry, under due care and authority of the elders, is to be allowed as a branch of culture, so it be decent and grave, abstaining from all seductive ornament, and singing devoutly the praises of gods and heroes. As to this, Plato was a regular *puritan.* Not even John Calvin looked with a colder and more philosophic eye on the fine arts, nor stout old John Knox on Queen Mary's music and dancing.

The best form of administration he regards as the monarchical, or power vested supremely in one rather than in the many. He is no friend to democracy. Very few are endowed with the capacity for governing the state. One truly intelligent mind is alone competent for this. But he must be intelligent, knowing the good, a philosopher; not till kings are philosophers will the state be well governed.

As to different classes of society, the state is to be divided, as the individual soul, into three orders. Corresponding to the reason is to be, in the state, the sovereign power; corresponding to the spirit, the next order in rank, assisting the sovereign; parallel to the appetite, a third class, ministering to the bodily wants of man; the *ruler,* the *warrior,* the *craftsman.* This last order, including merchants and mechanics, and workmen generally, he considers as of little consequence except as necessary for the support of the other classes. They are left to train themselves; are a sort of serfs; nay, these manual and mechanic arts should as far as possible be confined to slaves, not citizens. Slavery, as an institution of nature, he maintains. The warrior class is vastly more important. From this, the sovereign is to be chosen. Hence the whole class is to be most carefully trained and educated in gymnastics and music (as above explained), and so made fit for the art and office of government. The prosperity of the state depends on its care and faithfulness in this matter of educating its future rulers. Such is the model state of Plato, as developed particularly in the two dialogues, "the Republic" and "the Laws." A strange admixture, you will say, of aristocracy, despotism, Fourierism, Puritanism, and the most thorough-going inhumanity. It is, indeed, a strange compound, but viewed as a whole, with all its defects, it excites our admiration, as an idea of government at once consistent, symmetrical, comprehensive, grand, and far-reaching in its general view, and altogether beyond and above the ideas of his age. Ueberweg (i. 131) regards it as an advance on all Hellenic forms and ideas of government, and an anticipation of the Hierarchy of the Middle Ages—the philosophers of the former being replaced by the priests in the latter. Plato indeed admits that it is a model not to be fully realized on earth, a perfect standard that can only be approximated.

§ 9.—Plato's Physics.

Plato denies to physical inquiries all pretension to true science, since they deal with the indeterminate and ever-changing,—with material forms,—and the knowledge thus derived cannot be therefore itself precise and permanent. The fundamental idea in his theory of physics is that of *becoming;* all nature is in a state of inchoation, it is always becoming, never is; nothing fixed and determinate about it; hence nothing positively certain can be known or laid down respecting it (So Tim. p. 28). Matter or, as he calls it, the absolutely indeterminate, and which he does not distinguish from space, is the *receptacle*, the mother of all things, it is eternal, coëxistent with Deity (Timæus, *passim;* Cicero Acad. ii. 37, 118). It is *without form*, without an idea, without any primal property, unless it be that of a certain disorderly motion. Matter, then, is simply the condition of all natural existence, becomes orderly and animate only by the formative energy of ideas, of the good, of Deity, operating on it, giving it form, figure, fashion, order, beauty.

Plato conceives of *matter*, *space*, and *time* as not real existences. Matter is the *substratum* of *sensible qualities*, a conception of the mind, a fine abstraction (Timæus, p. 49–51). Space is a mere *condition* of the sensible (Timæus, p. 49 *seq.*). Matter is eternal; did not originate in time. Time is merely *relative* to the phenomenal world, created with it, and to end with it, if there be any end; closely resembling the doctrine of Kant respecting time (Krit. der Rein. Vern. i. Theil. § 4). The Epicurean view is analogous in some respects. They held the sense-world to be real, but time to be a mental conception; Plato holds both the sense-world and time to be equally unreal, the copies of the supersensible realities (See Butler, Anc. Phil. vol. ii. p. 173, 174). The reality is *eternity*, of which time is the *moving image*. "The Creator," says Plato (Tim. p. 37), "determined to create a moving image of eternity, and in disposing the heavens, he framed of this eternity, reposing in its own unchangeable unity, an eternal *image* (αἰώνιον εἰκόνα), moving according to numerical succession, which image he called time."

The world as it stands, is it from eternity, or had it a beginning? The latter. It is visible, tangible, corporeal; that is, it is sensible, and the sensible is not eternal but produced (Tim. p. 28).

It must have a cause then, rational and intelligent;

the father and fashioner of it. The operations of this cause proceed according to an idea or pattern, and that pattern is not itself an imperfect and perishable one, but eternal and immutable, for the world is the most beautiful of the works of God, the best of causes, and is made after his own resemblance and likeness (Tim. p. 29; Arist. Metaph. i. vi. 2). But God, reflecting, perceived that, to be the best, the world must not be irrational; and that to be rational it must have a soul. He therefore made it an intelligent, rational, *ensouled,* and living being. This soul of the world is the medium of connection between the eternal, immutable nature of reason and the changeable, divisible nature of corporeal things, God uniting "*the other*" with "*the like*" (Timæus, p. 35). The world, then, is an animate and rational being, and as it is modelled after a perfect idea, itself the image of the supreme idea, it is of necessity a unity; there is but one world. It is perfect, moreover, subject neither to age nor dissolution; indestructible, save by the power that formed it; yet even this divine work is limited, for whatever is produced must decay, has its periods of decay and reproduction, has already experienced several successive revolutions, both by fire and water—which few of the race of men alone survived; not to be destroyed, however, but to commence again a new era and a new existence. Its periods are determined by a perfect number. This periodic decay, this limitation of its existing forms, is closely connected in his system with the existence of moral evil, a fact which Plato finds it as difficult as any other and all other reasoners satisfactorily to explain. It cannot be from God, this he is sure of (Repub. ii. 379). His view on this point closely resembles the ancient Manichæan doctrine of two opposing principles, the good and the evil; the latter inherent in matter or the corporeal. He calls this latter principle, in one place, the *evil soul* of the world (De Leg. x. 896; see also Polit. p. 268). Evil subsists only for the souls that are enshrouded in corporeal and mortal forms. The ground of its existence is that the body united with the reason or soul, disturbs its action, the mortal is impelled by its sensual desires. Hence the desires are classed by Plato among the passive states, and even diseases of the soul. Physical evil exists as a consequence of the moral, and the gods are, in some sense, its authors; that is, so far as it contributes to good results.

The world in order to its perfection, and to containing in itself all animals, must comprise every possible figure; hence it is *spherical,* the most perfect and symmetrical of forms. As living, it has *motion,* and this, too, is the most perfect of motions, the circular. The body of the world, as that of man, exists only for the soul of it, which is diffused through the whole, yet has its chief seat in the centre, whence the action extends to the utmost heaven, which it draws about itself as a vesture. The four elements are the forms through which the becoming, or nature, necessarily passes in space, so many modes of the corporeal. These are necessary modes, since without fire nothing can be seen; without the solid, or earth, nothing can be felt, and the corporeal *must* be visible and tangible. God necessarily, then, composed the world of fire and earth. But two things cannot cohere without a third, and if bodies are to have volume as well as surface (that is, to have four connected surfaces), there must be two connecting media, two more elements, water and air. The five regular bodies or figures correspond to these four elements (the pyramid to fire; the cube to earth; the octahedron to air; the icosahedron to water, while the dodecahedron—equivalent to the cube—corresponds to the shape of the world and comprises all the elements). The entire sum of vitality is divided into seven parts, according to the harmonic numbers in the octave. By this, Ritter supposes he intended the seven planets of the ancients, in accordance with the Pythagorean doctrine. The external regularity of phenomena, the principle of beauty, the health and strength of all living things, result from this determinate order and harmonical composition of things according to numbers and figure. To make the world as like the eternal prototype as possible, God gave it, since he could not make it eternal, the property of measured time, the *moving image* of eternity. The sun, moon, and five planets were created to determine and watch over the numbers of time. Plato supposes a double revolution of the mundane bodies: the outer circle, the sphere of the fixed stars, whose movement is from left to right; the inner, comprising the seven planets, moving from right to left, less perfect motion than the former. The former is the motion of "*the same*"; the latter, of "*the other*," or of matter; the former, revolution round its own centre, moving ever in the same space, *after the pattern of true reason;* the latter, the movement of *the other*, or of matter, progression in a straight line. These stellar bodies are also living beings, more or less perfect according to the regularity of their movements, composed principally of fire, to look as resplendent and beautiful as possible, and spherical in form, similar to the shape of *the All.* Plato calls them divine beings, a race of heavenly gods, yet distinguished from the *eternal* God, since created and visible. The Earth is first and oldest of all the fixed stars, its place in the centre of the universe, where it spreads itself around the mundane axis, balanced by its own equilibrium, the guardian and artificer of night and day. It is uncertain whether he supposed the earth to be at rest in the centre of the universe, or to move round the axis of the world.

Beside these immortal gods, or fire bodies, the stars, three species of mortal creatures were formed to inhabit the earth, the water, and the air. The Supreme God himself could not make these, since they would have been like and equal to the gods, consequently he committed the work of their creation to the subordinate deities, reserving the right to communicate to these creatures whatever in their nature was to be immortal. A like number of these mortal creatures is assigned to each of the stars. The male man was the first birth of all mortal creatures, and after a fixed period, known only to the gods, did the female and all other animals issue from this mortal form.

As soon as the world, that vast animal, began to move, live, and think, God looked upon his work and was glad. In this account of the Platonic system of the universe, one cannot but be struck with the close resemblance in several points between his theory and the account given in Genesis of the creation of the world. The earth in the centre—first and chief of all—sun, moon and stars moving round it and subordinate in rank; the latter bodies created and moving to measured periods of time for the convenience of the former. Man first created, the eldest born of time; woman from him; Deity beholding his finished work and rejoicing. Had Plato read Moses? Had he caught fragments of floating tradition? Or were these the ideas that would most naturally commend themselves as probable to a deeply thinking and penetrating mind? The latter is, I think, the true solution. Such is the Platonic system of the world, the soul, the universe (see p. 225–253).

The influence of Plato on the subsequent thinking of the world has been perhaps even greater than that of Aristotle. At present it is on the increase. One cause for this, as Butler suggests, "is doubtless to be found *in the attractive and affectionate tone,* in the high and consoling doctrine, with which from the depth of antiquity Plato still addresses every elevated spirit. Wearied with the daily nothingness of a life which mocks with the illusion of happiness that retreats as we approach it, it is wonderfully soothing to speak, across the chasm of ages, with one who could thus distinctively perceive in the nature of his own reason, the promise of an eternal heritage above and beyond the visionary scene of earthly life" (Anc. Phil. ii. 11).

Another cause of this influence seems to me to lie in the peculiar charm of Plato's poetic and highly imaginative style, of which the same writer just quoted has so well said, "The 'Homerus Philosophorum,' as Cicero calls him, loves to see everything flush with the colors of pure and solemn poetry; standing forever in front of the changeless and eternal, his spirit is filled with the exceeding awfulness of the presence; and when he would speak, his thoughts swell into the strong rapture of a hymn" (Anc. Phil. ii. 215).

CHAPTER IV.

ARISTOTLE.

THE great master mind of antiquity. Less lofty and imaginative than Plato, less ideal, less grand; but with a keener insight, a more sharp and subtle penetration, a more thoroughly scientific spirit; of wider erudition and vaster learning, content to deal with facts and phenomena, but content with nothing short of a thorough comprehension and complete mastery and scientific arrangement of these; a mind that has left its impress more thoroughly on all succeeding time and all succeeding progress of the race, than any one mind, beside, that was ever created. Plato has had and will always have his admirers. But to Aristotle men go, even at this day, for *information*. Is there a parallel instance in all antiquity? Professor Agassiz says of him,* "Aristotle knew more of certain kinds of animals and their general relations than is known now. For instance, he never confounded sharks and skates with ordinary fishes, while all modern naturalists would put them in one and the same class. Strange to say, I have studied the Selacians on the South American coast by the light of Aristotle's

* Agassiz' lecture at Cambridge.

researches upon them in the Mediterranean Sea, made by him more than 2,000 years ago. I can fairly add that the knowledge of Aristotle on these topics is so far ahead of the current information recorded in modern works of natural history that his statements can only be understood by one who has made a special study of these animals. The community evidently shared his knowledge, for he refers to text-books of natural history which must, from the details he gives about them, have been superior to those we have now. You may seek in vain in the anatomical atlases of Wagner or Carus for information about the structure of the reproductive apparatus of Selacians, to which Aristotle alludes as contained in the text-books of anatomists and belonging to the current knowledge of the time. My aim is to give you in this course a comprehensive though very condensed sketch of zoological science in our own day and generation, attempting to do what Aristotle did in his zoology. I wish I could handle my subject with the same mastery."

I can best present what you will wish to know of Aristotle by sketching first his life, next the leading outlines, briefly, of his philosophy in general, and then discussing more particularly the chief divisions of that philosophy, under the several heads of Logic, Physics, and Ethics.

§ 1.—Life of Aristotle.

Born at Stagira in Thrace (hence called Stagirite), 383 B. C. His father, a distinguished physician, friend of Amyntas, king of Macedonia, descended from Esculapius, left many works on medicine and natural history. This gave a bias to the intellectual development and pursuits of Aristotle, a tendency to physical investigations which is strongly characteristic of him through life. Aristotle was a great naturalist. At early age lost both parents; carefully instructed in physical science by Proxenus. Tradition makes him a wild and not very economical youth;

obliged when the patrimony was expended to resort to arms, in which career he is said to have distinguished himself chiefly for that species of valor which is commonly called discretion and consists in keeping one's self in reserve for more important occasions. This I take to be a malicious slant, however, at philosophers in general. Better authenticated accounts make the youth, at the early age of sixteen, become a disciple of Plato at Athens, where he continued for twenty years, during which time he was most assiduously studying, not the system of Plato merely but all the works of the earlier philosophers, and indeed of all Grecian literature. He seems to have been impelled by a restless and insatiable desire for knowledge—a desire which no acquisitions could satisfy and no attainments quench. Plato calls him the *reader*. Aristotle's wonderful extent of information in almost all the branches of natural science may doubtless be attributed to these diligent years of investigation and research in early life. Among other branches of knowledge, he was a proficient in medical science and, according to tradition, always uncertain, practised medicine in Athens.

It is frequently asserted that Aristotle quarrelled with his great teacher, and was guilty of signal ingratitude and want of due respect toward him. Of this, however, there is, I think, no sufficient evidence. Plato may have disliked the caustic and severe spirit of his pupil, his keen and unsparing criticisms of all preceding systems and teachers; he may have disliked his manners and life. But there is no evidence that the former friendship had given place to mutual enmity. Aristotle does indeed attack with unsparing severity many of the doctrines of Plato; but this he was certainly at liberty to do, as one to whom truth was of more consequence than even the authority of a great name. It must be confessed, however, that he seems on the whole to have become widely and perhaps unnecessarily estranged from the Platonic views, and to have assailed those views often with a bitterness that was needless and unbecoming. On the death of Plato, Aristotle left Athens, and resorted to the court of Hermeas, tyrant of Atarneus, a former pupil, it is reported, of Plato and Aristotle, at Athens. After the death of Hermeas, Aristotle, out of gratitude to his deceased friend and patron, marries his sister Pythias, left destitute by her brother's death. Shortly after, he is called by Philip to take charge of the education of his son Alexander, then three years old. He enjoyed the highest confidence of Philip, and also of the youthful prince. Stagira, his native town, was for his sake restored, and a gymnasium built there for his lectures. Aristotle did not accompany Alexander, as often reported, on his Asiatic expedition, but parted from him at the commencement of the Macedonian war and returned to Athens, where he opened a school. He taught in the Lyceum, walking up and down the shady avenues with his disciples, whence called *peripatetic;* taught not philosophy alone but all useful sciences (Diog. Laert. v. 3; Cic. de Orat. iii. 35), especially rhetoric. Two sorts of pupils: in the morning, those who discussed with him the profound questions of philosophy, and in the evening more general and preparatory instruction; the first called acroatic, the latter exoterical, investigations. Spent thirteen years in these pursuits at Athens, during which time composed many of his ablest works, and pursued his extensive investigations in natural history. After the death of his friend and patron Alexander, under whose displeasure he had latterly fallen in consequence of too free remarks on the habits and character of that monarch (Diog. L. v. 10; Plut. Vit. Alex. 55), Aristotle fled from Athens, to escape a fate similar to that of Socrates; and died soon after at Chalcis, æt. 63. His works still extant are numerous, while at the same time many of his most valuable treatises are supposed to be lost.

His general character as a philosopher is well drawn by

Ritter in the following paragraph (Hist. Phil. vol. iii.): "In his works, on the other hand, we see him the calm, sober inquirer, who does not, like Plato, pursue a lofty ideal, but keeps carefully in view the proximately practical, and is not easily misled into any extravagance of language or of thought. His principal object is to examine truth in all her aspects, never to step beyond the probable, and to bring his philosophical system in unison with the general opinions of men as supported and confirmed by common sense, observation, and experience. . . . Generally a wise moderation characterizes his views of science and of life. The love of scientific pursuits was the predominant feature of his character. . . Moreover, in Aristotle we have the cold inquirer and little more. Rarely, if ever, does he step aside to consider the bond which connects the science of the universal and of nature with the human intellect and will. Consequently his works have more of that *impressiveness* which constitutes the principal charm of Plato's writings. In the intimate contemplation of the soul's activity he is neither so profound nor so natural as in the observation of the forms and shapes in which outward nature reveals herself. In whatever degree this neglect of all that moves and excites the mind may have contributed to the simplicity of his works and the rigor with which the intellectual view is carried out, they have suffered in warmth and earnestness of style. . . Aristotle, even if his mind were not totally alien from every poetical element, was unable to combine the sober results of science with a lively imagination. Hence his deficiency in large coördination of matter; hence the necessity of his frequent repetitions; hence, notwithstanding the occasional purity and clearness of his style, his ordinary exposition is rude, abrupt even in details, which renders it difficult to seize the connection of his ideas, and which seldom attains to perfect transparency of thought. At times the perusal of his works creates a suspicion that he had formed an aversion to and intentionally avoided every grace of style, consequently he is always serious, at times cutting and even bitter, generally brief, though occasionally on unimportant topics he becomes diffuse from an incapacity to seize his own meaning. With Aristotle, erudition has taken the place of art. He is the first philosopher in whom this is noticeable, and assuredly he contributed no little to establish that estimate of the preëminence of mere learning which was entertained by the later writers of Greece." Ritter further adds that we must look upon this "as the sign of incipient decay. For in the freshness of its youth the Greek mind loved art more than learning." He admits, however, that Aristotle is not chiefly to blame for this, since he only follows the tendency of the age, and allows that in his conclusions Aristotle is more vigorous and decisive, and in his expressions more precise, than either Socrates or Plato.

§ 2.—General View of Aristotle's Philosophy as a System.

It seems to have been his aim to collect, compare, digest the multiplied opinions and views of all past time in all the wide domain of science, and from the mass extract and set forth in scientific form whatever was there contained of truth and value. This was a magnificent plan, and diligently and strictly was it carried out. Plato, it has been well remarked, flourished at a period when the "Athenians were for the most part content to be merely spectators of events," and had leisure to reflect upon the springs of human conduct. His philosophy accordingly, is mainly directed to the inner, and has little application to the outward and actual. But the course of events was now changing.

The Greek mind began to look out of itself. Important revolutions were now commencing in history. Greece, as a nation, was about to lose its high and independent position. But it was also to become the teacher of nations, and, while the sceptre of national dominion passed out of its hands, it was to wield that mightier sceptre of intellectual ascendency over the minds of men. Greek letters and Greek philosophy were to become the predominant culture of other and great nations. What shall better prepare the way for this than that some capacious and great mind should arise and lay out for itself the bold scheme, to grasp in one comprehensive and complete view the whole product hitherto of Greek thought and science, arrange, collate, reduce to scientific form, and then, if anything were wanting, by diligent investigation of nature and her phenomena, add that to the already existing material. Such a mind was Aristotle's. Such a plan, such a work was his; and faithfully he wrought it out. "This," says Ritter, "this exactly, is the signature of great minds, to be almost perfect representatives of whatever is peculiar and characteristic in their age." It will be perceived, then, that the aim and labors of this great workman were twofold: to seize and set forth scientifically the results of past efforts and previous thinking, and also to present in complete and compendious form the objects and laws of the external world as the sphere of man's activity; *facts*, and the philosophy of facts; the "*what is*," and the "*why it is*." Of these, he looked on the latter as even the more important. With Plato, he regarded a knowledge of the *first grounds* of things as the most perfect science. These two aims seem to be very seldom combined in the labors and plans of any one mind. It is usually the work and delight of one man to investigate and collect facts and phenomena; of another, to inquire into the first causes and grounds of these phenomena, and set forth the laws and philosophy, according to which it must needs be so and so. It is a striking peculiarity of Aristotle that he proceeds cautiously, is never rash in his conclusions, limits his own assertions and conclusions, goes no farther with any confidence than phenomena will bear him, is undecided and hesitates the moment facts are wanting on which to rest with certainty, does not hazard an assertion then; "we must wait," he says, "for further phenomena, for phenomena are more to be trusted than the conclusions of the reason." What more truly philosophical remark did Lord Bacon or Sir Isaac Newton ever utter?

Aristotle's general view and definition of philosophy would seem to be this: the science of the ultimate grounds of all being; the science, whose object and aim it is, by purely scientific reasoning, to ascertain the grounds on which all science rests. This view distinguishes philosophy from every species of action and all the arts of life; for these do not, like the former, regard the eternal and immutable, but respect the changing circumstances of life.

"All science," says Aristotle, "must set out from something already known—in a word, must have its *first principles* or grounds, *ἀρχαί*, which are not themselves *science*, but the result of *immediate cognition* (Anal. Post. i. 1; Eth. Nic. v. 3), which he distinguishes from strict science, though he calls it a *certainty*. Who does not perceive in this the very doctrine and almost the very language of Reid, Stuart, and others, who claim for their philosophy a basis of *first* principles, and style it accordingly the philosophy of common sense. The very term, *ἀρχαί*, first principles, is the very expression employed by Dr. Reid.

Aristotle divides philosophy generally into the theoretical and the practical (according to Diog. L. v. 28; so also Metaph. vi. 1), including under the former, metaphysics, physics, and mathematics (Metaph. x. 7), under the latter, or the practical, ethics and politics (Nic. Eth. l. 1, x. 10; Rhet. i. 2), the former, whatever pertains to right thinking, the latter, to right acting. The more general, the Platonic division of philosophy into logic or metaphysics, physics, and ethics (Cicero de Fin. v. 4, ascribes to him this division, and some of Aristotle's works, as Topica i. 14; Anal.

Post. i. 33, indicate the same), seems, however, best to suit his general system. What we term metaphysics, what Plato called dialectic, and the ancients usually logic, Aristotle calls the "*first philosophy.*" "There is a science," he says, "which occupies itself with the principles of every other science, investigates the nature of that which all other sciences assume. It is, then, the science of the universal; has to do with *being as being*. This is the *first philosophy. Physics* would be the first and only philosophy, if there were no other substance than physical. But if there be another, existing neither in matter nor motion, the ground of all entity, then there is a science lying back of physics. There is such a substance, the ground and cause of all being—even God. The first philosophy is, then, essentially a theology; but it includes also the consideration of all existence, so far *forth as* existence, independently of any special mode in which it exists. Being, as distinct from matter—this is the object and sphere of the first philosophy, that is, of *absolute* philosophy. Physics, on the other hand, treats of being, not *as being*, but as participating in motion, while mathematics treats of it as permanent, indeed, but not as separable from matter. Physics and ethics cannot, from their nature, then, admit of the same certainty as the first philosophy. Ethics, he grants, will not admit of strict demonstration, but, as conversant about what generally happens, its reasonings start from phenomena, and can reach only probable conclusions. Physics are equally uncertain; for nature is inconstant as well as opinion, and so in this case also we must look only for probable, not for certain, conclusions. Aristotle employs the term dialectic, not as Plato, but with reference to such objects as admit only of *probable* conclusions.

With Aristotle, as with Plato, the science of the good is that which holds the first place above all others. This falls, however, under the first philosophy, or metaphysics.*

* The relation of the logic proper of Aristotle, or the Analytica,

Next follows physics, as the *second* philosophy. In the last place comes ethics, science of the practical or of human nature, which Aristotle, however, designates by the term politics, rather than ethics. Of all these, it is only that which investigates *first principles* that *strictly* deserves the name of philosophy.

§ 3.—Aristotle's Logic.

The first thing which attracts our attention on looking over this department of the Aristotelian philosophy is the frequent reference to the so called categories. These are nothing more than the several genera under which the various forms of thought and being—of whatever is—may be included, and to which they may all be reduced. He enumerates ten of these, without, however, professing to give a complete enumeration. These are essence, magnitude, quality, relation, the where, the when, position, habit, action, passion. These were afterwards reduced to eight (Anal. Post. i. 22 ; Phys. v. 4; Met. v. 7). Whatever is affirmed or thought of things falls under some one of these heads, supposing the enumeration to be complete.

With Aristotle, as with Plato, language holds an important place as the manifestation of thought, and he directs his inquiries specially to the investigation of the forms of language, as the true way of arriving at a knowledge of thought and being (Met. v. 7). He begins with the simplest element of it, the *word.* This is neither *true,*

to the other divisions of his philosophy, is not very clear. It is not to be confounded with the first philosophy, the science of the ultimate ground of things, to which the name logic, in the wider sense of that term, is sometimes given. Logic proper is not included under either of these three divisions, Metaphysics, Physics, or Ethics, but is regarded as *preparatory* to them all. As to the logic proper, it has been remarked by Kant that only in two points has the logic of the moderns advanced beyond that of Aristotle, *i. e.*, the fourth figure, and the hypothetical and disjunctive syllogism. It may be seriously questioned whether either of these is any true addition to the science.

nor false; cannot be; becomes so only when united with other events in a *proposition.* The true and the false can be expressed only by the union or separation of *subject* and *predicate,* indeed being and non-being are nothing else than this. Combining subject and predicate, or the thought of one thing with that of another, we have the proposition; and the proof is true or false necessarily, since it expresses a relation of one thing or thought to another, which relation may or may not be true—*must* be either true or false. The simple enunciative proposition is here intended. This is of two kinds, affirmative or negative; mutually opposed, and when asserted of one and the same thing in one and the same sense, *contradictory* of each other. Propositions are either universal or particular, and here again admit of opposition to each other. This principle of contradiction is with Aristotle the groundwork of reasoning, the highest principle on which all demonstration is founded. You can find no *reason* of this principle; it is a first truth, that is, the affirmative and the negative, the particular and the universal, cannot both be true at once of the same thing in the same sense.

Aristotle finds it necessary here to confute those who maintain the falsity of every idea predicable of thought and of being, on the ground that the *sensible,* which comprises all thought and being, is not worthy of reliance: in sensation the same object appears differently to different persons, is susceptible of opposite changes, and consequently nothing can with truth be affirmed of it. Aristotle replies that *sensation* is *not to be confounded with mere conception,* that *every perception is true as regards its proper object,* as to its immediate declaration. Its testimony is not opposite to itself, nor conflicting with itself, at one and the same time; and when there is doubt at any time as to it, the doubt is not as to what the immediate perception is, but as to whether it corresponds to reality. Sensation, he further argues, is an operation of the sentient person, exists not of itself independently of the sentient being. There is something distinct from it which *produces* it, is *the ground* of it, and so prior to it of course, and even if *sensation itself be false, this something which is the ground of it must exist, and exist as true quite independently of all sensation.*

Our knowledge Aristotle, with Plato, holds to be relative; but things themselves are not mere relations. There is a *substance,* a primary to which relations appertain, a first ground and substratum of which all else is predicated. *Not all* things, then, can be reduced to mere sensations. Aristotle also combats the notion of the Eleatics and Heraclitus, who held that all things are *equally* true. Even those who had this view, he says, must admit that there is such a thing as false opinion (else why do they argue or affirm), and if all assertions are equally true, then distinctions of good and evil are annihilated, and those who speak of what is as they think are really speaking of what is not.

Aristotle next proceeds to examine the laws of right reasoning, as regards especially the use and value of the *syllogism.* He speaks only of the first three figures of the syllogism, and regards the first of these only as perfect, *i. e.,* both *universal* and *affirmative,* while the others may be reduced to this. Aristotle makes two sorts of syllogisms, the demonstrative and the inductive; the latter sets out from the consideration of particulars already known and so reaches a general conclusion, the former sets out from some general and admitted principle, and reasons to a particular conclusion. Of these the former deals with what is best known to us, but still is *uncertain,* since all phenomena are changeable. The latter is more certain and valuable.

These two are the only strictly scientific procedures.

§ 4.—Metaphysics of Aristotle.

There are four essential principles common to all realities. These are *matter, form, moving cause,* and *end or final cause* (Met. i. 3). And first, of *matter.* Of all external existence, possessing such and such qualities and presenting such and such appearances, there must be back of all these qualities and appearances, some primary substance, the basis of all this *becoming*, the ground of it all, capable of receiving all possible determinations, yet in itself indeterminate, imperceptible even, and unknowable. This is *matter*. It is to all determinate things what the wood is to the table, or the marble to the statue. *Form*, or essence, is matter become knowable and perceptible, having received some determination, having become this or that which the senses can recognize. It is whatever a thing is *actually*, not brass in the abstract, mere material without figure or any determinable quality, but a brazen statue of such and such dimensions and proportions. With Aristotle, *form* takes the place of the "Ideas" of Plato.

The Platonic theory of ideas as actual existences or essences, Aristotle rejects, as inconsistent with physical and even with ethical science, as confounding the grounds of all things, and so at variance with truth and with phenomena, assimilating things that differ widely, as the perishable and the imperishable, the sensible and the eternal—these all resting, according to that theory, on one and the same ground, having one and the same essence, *i. e.*, the *idea;* whereas there must be different grounds for things so different. The only essence, according to Aristotle, is that of the individual (Metaph. i. 9, vii, 13, xiii. 9 ; see also, De Anima, iii. 4. 8).

Aristotle admits the idea and existence of infinity. The infinite exists, but not as the actual, for that is always *finite;* it exists as *potential*, and consists in this, that it is always possible to take more and more in addition and subtraction, and so on forever. In and by itself it is *inconceivable*, however, and, like matter, is a ground of things ; itself, like matter, ingenerate and imperishable.

These investigations as to matter lead to similar inquiries as to the nature of *motion*. How does matter pass into form, the potential become the actual? By *motion*, of course. Motion is the passage from the potential to the actual (Phys. iii. 1). Now the potential does not, of itself, possess the power to become actual. *Motion* does not result *from it* therefore, but from something out of it. Matter cannot move *itself*. There must be out of it some already existing actual substance, as a *moving cause* (Metaph. ix. 8; De Gen. An. ii. 1). Motion, moreover, is without beginning; has always been; else, prior to all motion, the movable and the mover must *have come into being*. This would itself be motion, and that prior to all motion, which is absurd; hence motion is eternal. That is, the movable, the moving cause, and the motion, are all without beginning. The same thing follows also from the infinity of *time*. Time cannot be conceived without a *now*. A *now* is the point intermediate between past and future; every now implies a past, and as this is true of every moment, every now, it is therefore impossible to conceive of the *beginning* of time. Time, however, is only a particular kind or determination of *motion*. If one is without beginning the other is.

As there is a moving cause, so there is also a final cause; the former indicates the *source* or origin of the motion, the latter the *end* or *design* of it. Every *becoming*, all motion, has some design, some end. This tends to the consideration of final causes, which Aristotle regards as the highest problem of philosophy. In answer to the question, Wherein consists the end of all becoming? Aristotle replies, *Good* is the final end, also Being; all change or becoming is for the sake of Being or Essence, which is better than non-being. (He distinguishes two kinds of activities: that which has its end in itself, and that which has not; as seeing, knowing, life, etc., are complete in themselves, while to *learn*, to be convalescent, and so generally anything not yet complete, are activities looking to some end out of themselves. The former he calls *energies*, the latter *motions*.

There are, then, *four causes* of phenomena; the material,

the formal, the moving, and the final (Phys. ii. 1, 3, 7; Met. i. iii, xi. iv. 5, v. 2, 4, vii. 4), not acting independently of each other, but coöperating in every sensible object, distinct only as the object is regarded from these several points of view. This he illustrates from analogy. A house or statue, in order to be built, must have an art or artist as moving cause; an end, the proposed work; a form or thought—logos—after which it is fashioned; some *material*, of which it is built. So also in nature the same four causes.

The existence of a self-moving cause, as a separate self-subsisting essence, is a very important feature of the Aristotelian metaphysics. He arrives at this position in the following manner. If there is anything imperishable, there must be also an imperishable substance as the *ground* of what is imperishable. But time and motion are imperishable. Therefore there *is* an imperishable substance as their *ground*. Moreover, phenomena would otherwise be inexplicable if there were not a *necessary* mover, one whose essence consists in activity and motion, else he might at some time not have moved, and then motion were not eternal. Argument of *Clark* anticipated completely in this. This cause is itself unmoved, since always working in the same manner. It is *one*, since a single eternal unmoved cause is sufficient to account for all phenomena; *one*, for *another* reason also. Motion is permanent and eternal; what is permanent is one, and proceeds from a *single* cause. Still another argument for the same. The eternal mover, being all activity and not mere potentiality is, by the very notion thus formed, devoid of matter (Metaph. xii. 6, 7), but *matter* is the *ground* of *multiplicity*, hence the eternal mover, not participating in matter, cannot be resolved into diverse individual beings; must be *one*. This cause or being is free from all constraint; is a necessary being, *i. e.*, cannot be otherwise than it is, immutable, ever-existing, therefore not to be compassed by, or contained in time—

nor yet in space, for it is without parts and indivisible, and so has not extended magnitude. It is not sensible but conceivable by the understanding alone ; hence is itself understanding, or reason, or mind. Thought is the mode of its activity, the highest and most blessed form of life (Met. xii. 7). It is the essence of things, the best, the end of things. It is the fulness of entity, the fulness of felicity—happy, not by the accession of external good, but by the felicity and perfection of its own nature. Its activity is its life. In it the knowing and the knower are one. In the Metaphysics (xii. 7), we have, as Schwegler appropriately terms it, an almost devout sketch of the ever-blessed Deity. Such is the sublime yet strictly scientific view of the Supreme Being in the philosophy of Aristotle.* Different quite from the Platonic. With Plato, God was the supreme unity, far transcending all human conceptions, above reason and above science. Aristotle is more definite, less mythical, discards all figures of speech in such a connection, lays down everything in definite, exact, scientific statement. Yet is cautious and reverent, aware of the sublime height which he was endeavoring to scale. The God of Aristotle is not indeed above all comprehension of science, for then it would be only an imaginary God ; but he is above all that pertains to the human ; above all *virtue* even, for virtue is a human quality ; morality is not to be ascribed to Deity, who is far above all such conceptions (p. 260). From this elevated view of the supreme he seems to us to descend when he proposes the question, whether the moving cause has its seat in the centre or circumference of the moved world, and concludes that it is in the latter, since the latter moves more rapidly, and is therefore nearer the source of motion.

Ritter well remarks, in comparing the Aristotelian with the Platonic doctrine of the supreme, that in either and

* In the De Nat. Deorum (ii. 37) Cicero gives, from the dialogue concerning philosophy, a fine passage of Aristotle, in which he presents an argument of a more popular sort, drawn from the divine works.

in every possible theory of the system of the universe, "*a principle of necessity* gradually and as it were imperceptibly takes its place alongside of the divine or intellectual power." There must be a limitation somewhere. The difference between these two systems is that Aristotle does not, like Plato, ascribe the imperfection and evil of the world to the *nature* of things, but at once and without explanation of the evil, admits the coëxistence of matter and of becoming, such as it is, good or bad, with God from eternity. God, then, is not to be held responsible for the fact of evil. Neither is he the *absolute creator* of matter. He is limited in this. He bestows on things, not their potentiality to be—that is inherent in matter—but only their actuality, and even this in the sense merely of permitting these various forms to arise. "Aristotle," says Ritter, "was the first of the Socratists to reconcile the idea of life with that entity—so gave a wide extension to the domain of philosophy."

§ 5.—Aristotle's Physics.

Aristotle conceives of nature as an opposite to reason and to art. It has in itself the ground of motion and rest, whereas works of reason and art have not. This idea lies at the basis of his physical speculations. Nature is in itself a principle of motion and rest in that to which it pertains—an inward force or energy which sets things in motion or at rest, according to their nature. Like God, it performs nothing without an end; avoids all infinity; is not omnipotent. It is both form and matter. It is that which works in all things, and is the ground of their existence and development—the universal mundane force. As there is eternal motion—the life of all things—in the world, so also a life-giving heat pervades it, and in some sense a *soul*. The world is a sort of living being; for though some things are lifeless, and have not power to move themselves, yet even these possess the principle of universal nature, while living things enjoy a special moving force. All phenomena are derived from this inner force of nature. Hence the physiology of Aristotle is *dynamical.* All becoming has an end in view, God and nature do nothing without a purpose (De Cœlo i., 4), and the most important problem in physiology is to *determine* the ends which phenomena are designed to accomplish. Nature always pursues the good, but is limited by the nature of its means, and so often produces the imperfect ; is an artist working with a sort of *unconscious* impulse, not self-conscious ; it is easier for it to produce the bad than the good ; it is rarely, and only with painful effort and many trials that it reaches excellence. Whatever does not fall in with the general laws of nature and attain the general and designed end, he calls a defórmity and abortion. Thus the female is a deformity and not equal to the male, and all inferior orders of animals are deformities, judged by the same standard, the male man. This seems to have been the type at which nature aimed, and whatever falls below it is a failure. The soul is the end for which the body exists, and is the essence of it ; just as the several organs have some special end, so the body is for the sake of the soul.

As to *motion,* this is the condition of all nature ; for there is no rest possible except where motion is also possible. Motion, as already said, he defines to be the passage from the potential to the actual, a middle term between the two. It must belong to what is continuous, therefore, and must presuppose space and time. This calls up the notion of the infinite and its relation to space, time, and motion. Infinity of time has its ground in infinity of motion, and this again in infinity of space ; which latter does not consist in the infinite extension of corporeal body, for that is limited by surface and cannot be infinitely extended. The world, as corporeal and special, is *limited* therefore, in magnitude, and so not infinite. Every *whole,* every *complete* thing, has an *end* and *limit.* The infinite is *imperfect,* and *nature has a horror of it as such.*

Infinity of space, therefore, consists not in unlimited corporeal extension; in what, then? in *infinite divisibility* which pertains to space and all that is special. Now motion proceeds through the infinite parts of space, and hence is itself infinite, being equally continuous with special magnitude. But what is space? This is a question which puzzled Aristotle as much as it does us. It is neither matter nor form; of that he is sure. It is that which contains all things (Phys. iv. 4). He seems to have taken an *objective* and physical view of it. It is something which admits of division into particular spheres, each with some special faculty of its own. The proper place of the earth is in water; of water, in the air; of air, in ether, while the ether is in heaven, which last is the *Ultima Thule*—nothing beyond. Hence Aristotle speaks of *above* and *below*, the *right* and the *left*, *before* and *behind*, etc., as relations not referring to man only, but pertaining to nature itself. Space is full of contents, *no vacuum*. And what now is time? Had there been no motion this question had never been asked, for without motion, without change and the perception of change, time would not have existed for us. *If the present did not differ from the past, there would be no time.* Time must either be change, *i. e.*, motion itself, or some accident of it. But it is not motion itself, for motion is something moving in space, which is not true of time. It can only be an accident, then, of motion. We become conscious of time only by designating motion as earlier and later. In order to have a clear idea of time, we must in like manner distinguish two parts of time, as before and after, separated by an *intermediate* Now (Phys. iv. 11). Consequently *time is the number of motion, the more or less of it*, the *measure* of it. But is it not the measure of *rest*, too, as well as of motion? Yes, incidentally, but rest is only the *privation* of motion and is therefore measured by the same standard. This intermediate Now is the indispensable condition of time, for it is the *limit* between the past and the future, holds them together, is to it what the point is to space. Through it, time becomes continuous and infinitely divisible, like space and motion; but the now itself is indivisible and in *it nothing can either move or rest.* Time could not be without a soul, for it is the number of motion, but there can be no number without *one who numbers,* and only the human soul is capable of numbering. This is of course a *subjective* view. Time does not with him consist in the revolution of the heavens, though this revolution, being uniform and well known, is best adapted to be the measure of motion.

The motion of nature is uniform, continuous, and infinite. But as the space of the world is *finite,* how can infinite motion go on in it? Not in a *straight line,* of course, for the end would by and by be reached: only a circular motion answers the conditions of the case, a motion in circle and a motion always in *one direction,* returning into itself, uniting the beginning and the end, thus perpetual and unbroken, and proceeding through all time. Such is then the motion of the world. The world is a *sphere* which is a perfect figure, a complete whole, and can receive no accessions, and, as the world is itself a complete whole, it must therefore be of that figure. Now the parts at the centre of course have but an imperfect motion, those at the circumference partake of the perfect revolution of the circle. Heaven is at the circumference, fit abode for the gods as nearer the source of motion. Earth at the centre, far away from the perfect motion and the prime-mover, given over to imperfection. As to Heaven, Aristotle with due modesty acknowledges our incapacity to know much, yet holds it desirable to investigate that which is of all things most worthy of regard. The stars he thinks are passionless beings, more divine than man, who have reached the highest end of their existence. The Heaven has a soul and possesses in itself the cause of its motion, else inferior even to man. Its movements, unlike men's, require no repose. Its motion is from left to right, since that is the better. The heaven is divided into two parts, the upper the place of fixed stars, the lower, of the planets, sun, and moon. The upper receives its motion directly from the prime mover; the planets, influenced by the motion of the fixed stars, move in contrary directions and in oblique orbits. The earth is in the centre of the universe. There are four sensible elements, derived from the contrarieties of sensible qualities, which may be reduced to four, viz., the warm and cold, the dry and moist. These combining, the warm and dry constitute *fire;* the warm and moist, *air;* the moist and cold, *water;* the cold and dry, earth. These are the only possible combinations, and therefore there are these *four* elements. All living beings are composed of these four elements. *All nature* is in fact *endowed with life,* in his view; even the lifeless elements are organic parts of an animated whole, and are in some sense animated.

There is regular transition and progressive advance from the lower to the higher in all forms of life, from the element to the plant, thence to the animal, and thence upward to man. As life is, with Aristotle, only spontaneous nutrition, growth, and decay, and as the soul is the energy (entelechy) or power of every organic living body, so even the plant has life and also a soul; yet plants have no sensation, for they have no central seat of life, no internal principle capable of receiving the forms or impressions of the sensible.

Beside the four elements that enter into all forms of life, there is a fifth equally universal, that of ether, the first in rank, extending from the stars to the moon (Meteor. i. 3; De Cœlo, i. 3), the source of the vital heat, which all living beings possess, though in different degrees. Those creatures that have the most of this vital warmth are noblest; those that have the least are the inferior. Such are plants and aquatic animals.

All animals have sensation, as necessary for the perception of their good, and therefore pleasure and pain, necessary consequences of sensation. All have not voluntary motion. Touch and taste are the most needful senses, and so possessed by all; sight and hearing are useful chiefly to the *sagacious* and self-moving animals. There can be but five senses, for no sensuous organism for more than five is discoverable, the *media* through which the senses reach *distant* objects are incapable of transmitting any other impressions than those of sight, hearing, and smell. These five senses are referred to the four elements: taste and touch to earth, smell to fire, hearing to air, sight to water. The brain is not the seat of sensation, says Aristotle, neither the blood, which serves for aliment, but the *heart*, which is also the seat of motion as well as sensation, and in which all the activities of animal life meet and centre. Each sense requires a medium through which the sensation may be conveyed to the prime sentient. The flesh is such a medium, and all the perceptions of the several senses are transmitted by means of it, and meet together in a common or principal sense, the heart, which is cognizant of them all. The brain is intended solely as a counterpart to the heart, cold to temper the warmth of the latter.

As regards *psychology*. The soul is the reunion of all the activities of the body. The hand has its end and design, which is its proper action, so every member, so the whole body also; and the design of the whole, its perfect action, is the soul. The soul is the first energy, or entelechy, then, of the organized body. It is not to be conceived as extended magnitude, for thought has not parts; neither as in space, or capable of motion; it is above all natural generation and all corporeal existence, itself the cause and principle of body, both as essential, as final, and as moving cause. The soul possesses these several faculties: the nutritive, which is alone the property of the plant; the sensitive, which animals possess; the locomotive, belonging to the higher classes of animals; the *rational*, peculiar to man. Each of these, as named in its order, may exist independently of those that are higher, *e. g.*, the nutritive without the sensitive, etc. Man combines the whole. The heart, as already stated, is the *common* sense, which takes cognizance of all the others. It also has another office, to perceive certain sensuous representations not perceived by the other senses, viz., motion, time, number, etc. Sensation he defines as a motion of the soul through the body (De Somn. i. 185), and distinguishes between sensation and the object sensed (De Anima, ii. 5, iii. 1, 16 ; Met. ix. 3). From sensation are evolved imagination, memory, and recollection. Imagination (as Hobbes afterwards taught), is a weaker sensation, explained by the motion which sensation leaves behind in the soul, and which continues awhile : memory combines with the sensation a perception of having had the same before, and so is the faculty of those animals only which have the perception of *time*. Recollection, the voluntary search for the past occurrence, is peculiar to man alone, memory pertains to brutes.

Aristotle rejects the doctrine of Plato as to the origin of ideas—that they originally subsist in the mind, brought over from previous existence and awakened to reminiscence by sensation. He regards it absurd to suppose that we knew all along certain things without knowing that we knew them until the moment of sensation and reminiscence. He rejects, accordingly, the Platonic doctrine of ideas as a source of knowledge, and he traces the origin of all our knowledge to sensuous perception or observation and experience (Met, i. 1 ; Anal. Pr. i. 30 ; Anal. Pos. i. 18 ; De Anima, iii. 5 ; Diog. L. v. 29 ; Cic. Acad. i. 9), which, however, he makes the *ground of a higher knowledge* not confined to phenomena, but acquainting us with principles that are non-sensuous, and of which intellect alone takes cognizance. Still the two are intimately allied. That which the intellect alone grasps exists, not in and by itself but only in the *sensible*, can only be known in the sensible, and in that sensation one could know nothing : not merely perception of external objects, but memory and imagination come through some previous sensation. But without the imagination presenting some definite image to the mind, something conceived and definitely present before our minds, we cannot *think ;* so that all intellectual activity is due primarily to sensation. The *sensuous presentation* is prior in time to the *rational intelligence,* and the necessary condition of it. The latter is the product of maturer age, the former exists in childhood.

It is evident that Aristotle relies much on *experience* as a source of knowledge, but yet not *wholly.* In this he is often misunderstood and misrepresented. *Mere* experience, he admits, is not *science.* Men of mere experience he calls lifeless instruments working without knowing what they accomplish. Mere collectors of facts, they know only that things are so and so, without inquiring why they are as they are. There is then a higher faculty than experience—the reason, or rational faculty of the soul—which stands related to the sensible, much as the soul is related to the body. This faculty is not dependent on the senses ; is impassive, incorporeal ; has no bodily form ; is of gradual growth in the individual ; exists at first as a mere *potentiality,* not as an actuality ; a blank tablet, on which as yet no inscription is entered. How is it awakened to action ? how written upon ? not by sense or experience, though these are the prior and necessary conditions of its activity ; but by the divine and internal reason, the supreme intelligence, acting on and awakening the individual reason to action. Science is the result.

Yet so intimately allied are the reason and the sense that, though pure science is the product of reason alone, still *Induction* is the basis of all science, and complete knowledge the result only of complete experience.

Sensation is accompanied with pleasure or pain, and these are always followed by desire, and so result in voluntary motion. Conception, or thought also, as well as sensation, leads to voluntary motion; for a certain degree of warmth attends thought, and thereby produces a motion in the body, slight at first but greater as it removes from the starting point. Reason or the rational conception and sensation both stand in the same relation to desire. Both may produce desire, by presenting some good capable of being attained. Sensation is often erroneous in its conclusions, however, while reason is not so. So that sometimes we desire real good, at others only apparent good. These rational and sensuous desires are often in conflict, and the soul is ruled now by one, now by the other. In either case, however, we act freely, and are therefore *responsible.* It lies in our power to follow the reason, and so we are the authors of our own virtue and vice; else it were idle to exhort man to virtue or punish him for crime.*

As regards the immortality of the soul, the doctrine of Aristotle is by no means clear. The soul is the first *entelechy* of the body, the perfect flower and blossom of it, that for which the body exists. It is the possession alike of plant, animal, and man. The former, the plant-soul, possesses the principle of nutrition; the second, the animal-soul, has not only this, but in addition, the principle of sensation and voluntary motion; the man possesses, in addition to all these, *reason.* Now this latter element of the human soul is impersonal and eternal; not the soul itself as a conscious existence, a personal being, but only the impersonal reason. That is the only immortality I can find in Aristotle (See Butler, vol. ii. p. 389–391).

* The Aristotelian psychology, or doctrine of the soul, is most fully developed in the three books, *περὶ ψυχῆς*, or De Anima, of which Butler gives an excellent analysis in the second volume of his Ancient Philosophy. See also Ueberweg and Schwegler.

§ 6.—Ethics of Aristotle.

The term politics he employs to designate what we usually denote by ethics, comprising whatever has for its object human good, whether in the family, the state, or the individual. Hence a three-fold division of the subject: into *ethics*, which investigates what is for the moral good of the individual, and which is the basis of the whole science; *economics*, the right management of the family; *politics* in a stricter sense, or the offices of the state.

In general, it may be observed that Aristotle does not, in his ethical investigations, take so high a ground as Plato. The latter connected with all his inquiries on this subject, the consideration of the highest possible good, absolute good in itself, the *divine* element, while Aristotle limits himself to that which is *practicable for man* (Eth. Nic. i. 2.)

Morality, according to Aristotle, grows out of many natural endowments. He is, by *nature*, a social and political creature. Nothing, indeed, which is contrary to nature, can be either morally beautiful or morally good. Nature has implanted in man an impulse to action and desire, and this is the spring of all our actions. So that the basis of all moral acts is some natural disposition. In this he diverges from Socrates, who made reason the basis of morality. Aristotle makes the πάθη, the disposition and affections of the soul, the basis of moral conduct. First, there arises an irrational impulse to good. Reason afterwards comes in with its sanction. The child may act right from impulse merely—instinctively. This is not *virtue*, however. Not till, at a mature age, reason is developed, does virtue come into play. Socrates overlooked that part of our nature which brings us under the influence of *sentiment* and *habit*, and the very important part which these principles perform in our moral procedure; hence, the idea that man can transgress only involuntarily, and of course irresponsibly. True, Aristotle says, all men pursue what seems, or appears good, and cannot control entirely their own conceptions of the good, but then men have power by their moral conduct over their imaginations and conceptions. While as yet the moral character is in part only formed, it is under their control. It is only by their actions that men acquire virtue or vice. As when one throws a stone, after it has gone forth from his hand he has no power over it indeed; but while it is yet in his hand he gives it force and direction, and has full control of its movements. Hence, men are responsible for their conduct. It is in their power. Even those who sin ignorantly should be punished for that ignorance, provided they *could* have known. Aristotle insists much on the *practice* of virtue, as essential to the true knowledge of it. The *habit* of virtue must precede the practical knowledge of it. It is not a thing to be learned, as Socrates taught, at least in any other way than by practice. It is by three things, then, that man attains virtue, viz. *nature, habit,* and *reason.*

The passive states of soul, or passions, desire, anger, fear, love, truth, envy, etc., give rise to conduct which is, in Aristotle's view, contrasted with the moral. These feelings are neither virtuous or vicious in themselves, do not make one good or bad, are undesigned on our part, and man is irresponsible for them. Only it is necessary that there should be observed the right measure and medium of them. Immoderation in them becomes a fault. How we are to know and attain the right measure in all cases, is left somewhat in the dark.

The *first and last object of man's endeavors* should be to *realize the good and the beautiful.* The practical good is that which is performed for its own sake alone.

Aristotle attaches a higher value to pleasure than Plato and Socrates had done. Pleasure is not always happiness, he admits; some are *evil* pleasures. But yet he goes not with those who decry all pleasure as unworthy of man, and as intrinsically bad. The real tendency of pleasure he pronounces to be good. Pleasure is not with him, as with Plato, a mere transient state ; it is itself an *end*, an energy ; not a mere inactive enjoyment, but inseparably combined with the soul's activity (Eth. Nic. x. 4). The pleasure which he recommends, is a rational self-love, desiring good for itself, but not to the injury of others, held within due limits, and subject to the control of reason. It is a pleasure which is ready to sacrifice anything and all things for some great and noble end ; for, says Aristotle, "It is better to live gloriously for a year than for many years as the common herd ; better to perform one great and glorious deed than many trifling acts."

What, then, IS *virtue?* It is the acting, not from instinct, impulse, and passion, but the doing of the good and the beautiful, consciously and intentionally. It is not a mere capacity of the soul, but a disposition acquired by practice—a habit of the soul. The right standard of it varies always with circumstances. What is right for one, is not for another, necessarily. It is the due medium between the *too much* and the *too little*. All virtues are inseparably connected with each other ; and there are, in fact, as many virtues or species of virtue, as there are of passions of the soul. Each virtue is the *mean between two vices*. He makes a general division, however, into the moral and the intellectual virtues, the desires to good, and the intelligence or reason governing the desires.

The aim of all moral action is happiness—*εὐδαιμονία, τὸ εὖ ζῆν* or *εὖ πράττειν,* right living, or well-doing ; and this only comes from doing the particular work which pertains to man as man (Eth. Nic. i. 6, x. 7). Man's peculiar work consists in a life of action controlled by reason, an honorable and a virtuous activity (Eth. Nic. ii. 5) ; and in this, accordingly, lies his highest happiness (i. 6, x. 7).

The ethical virtues are courage, temperance, liberality, love of honor, mildness, truthfulness, urbanity, friendship, justice (ii. 7).

Courage is the mean between fearing and daring, between the fool-hardy man and the coward (ii. 7, iii. 10). He only is truly courageous, who is not afraid to die honorably, and who is ready to face danger and death for the sake of the morally beautiful (Eth. Nic. iii. 9, 10).

Temperance is the mean in regard to pleasures and pains—the mean between intemperance and insensibility (ii. 7, iii. 14). Liberality is the proper mean in giving and receiving—between prodigality and stinginess (ii. 7, iv. 1). Mildness is the proper mean as regard desire of revenge or anger (ii. 7, iv. 11). Truthfulness regards veracity in speech and action ; friendship has regard to the social relations ; urbanity to the rendering ourselves agreeable to others (ii. 7, iv. 12–14). Justice, in the general sense, is the exercise of all virtue toward others (v. 5), the giving of every man his own or his rightful due. Regarded more specifically, it is of two kinds, *distributive* and *commutative*, the former relating to the distribution of honors or property according to the merit of the individual, the latter exacting equality in wares, in the medium of exchange. Aristotle limits justice solely to the civil relations of life. It is the mean between doing and suffering injustice. He distinguishes between what is naturally just, and what is legally so in the state. Natural law is better than positive law, equity than legal justice.

Aristotle gives few precepts for the conduct of practical life. It has been justly objected to his system that it leaves ultimately everything in doubt ; that it directs us to pursue a just medium, but tells us not how to determine what a just medium is. The explanation of this is that Aristotle did not look upon ethics as a distinct branch of philosophy, but only as incidental to politics as dependent on man's relation to family and to country. As to *friendship*, Aristotle has some fine thoughts (Nic. Eth. viii. 9). Friendship may be based on the agreeable, the useful, or the good. The latter is the noblest. Friendship is not indeed a virtue, but virtue cannot exist without it. Society is indispensable to man, he cannot live alone, but to live with others he must be virtuous. There can be no love without return ; still the loving is better than the being loved, for to love is an energy of the soul. Love is possible only among the good, who only are capable of a true self-love, since they only have attuned their souls to harmony and concord. Love and concord are the bonds of political society, and there is a very close affinity between love and justice. The end of love and friendship is the social and civil state.

As to the *family* : the family consists in the society of husband, wife, and children, and the communion of property. As to the property, Aristotle thinks that the most valuable possession is *man*, the slave ; and therefore that this is a necessary element in the family economy. Like Plato, he regarded slavery as a natural dispensation. Nature determines the end of all her creatures, and of man the destination is to govern or be governed. Some have intelligence to design and foresee, these she intends for masters ; others have bodily strength to labor, these are meant for slaves, for whom it is better to be governed than to govern, having not reason enough for that. If such, mistaking their calling refuse to serve, they may be forcibly seized. The slave is the absolute property of his master, and has no rights against him. Still he should be treated kindly and well. The child until of age is in like manner wholly under the father's control, though not a slave, yet not his own governor. The father is the rightful king of the house (Pol. i. 12). The rule in the family belongs to the man as better than the woman, yet the woman is not to serve like a slave. Her duties are within the house, man's without, and where she is obliged to do the latter, it is proof of a degenerate race of men, unfit to be masters. Yet she ought to be subject to her husband, "for though she has a will of her own, still it is but weak." It would seem from this last remark that Aristotle's experience in this line must have been somewhat different from that of Socrates. The latter, while thoroughly convinced that woman has a will of her own, would hardly have added, that it was a will deficient in strength.

Out of the family, a community arises, a company of families forming a society, and several such communities of families forming a state, that is, a sufficient number of such families to be able to provide within their own limits the necessaries of life. The state arises, then, out of the weakness of separate communities; out of considerations of utility. Its object is not, however, merely to provide the necessaries of life, but to secure good order and the general welfare. The end of the state is *good living* (εὖ ζῆν), the virtue and happiness of the citizens (Pol. vii. 8). Its citizens must be men of virtue, then. Not merely living in the same country together, makes men citizens, and forms them into a state; for the *brutes* do that, yet are no citizens. They only are citizens, who by a just constitution enjoy rights, authority, and law. A state can only subsist between freemen and equals. Aristotle is decidedly *conservative* in his views; averse to political change. The duty of the citizen is to *maintain the constitution under which he happens to be born and live.*

There must be different classes in the state: cultivators of the soil and mechanics are needful to provide the necessaries of existence; soldiers to fight; rich men to defray expenses; priests to do the religious; and judges to do the civil services. Unlike Plato, he does *not* advocate a community of property, for these reasons: that such a plan would diminish the care of property; nobody takes such care of the public property as of his own; and also it would destroy the *virtues* of *liberality* and modest demeanor toward others. The better way, he thinks, is to *make property personal,* but *the benefit of it common by insuring right sentiments among the people.*

Nor would he have a community of wives and children; such a plan is against the very notion of a state, as growing out of the union of families. The true object of the statesman should be, to prevent both extremes—luxury and indigence. "It is much more important to make wants equal than property."

Of the different forms of government, Aristotle regards a monarchy as best, as being most favorable to virtue; aristocracy next; democracy least of all. *Tyranny* is the very worst. In this view, he shows the current of his age and nation. What is to be done, he asks, with a man far superior to all others for political wisdom? put him to death; banish him; let the mass and rude herd rule over him? No, he is a lion among hares; let them submit to his rule. But he may be a vicious king. To avoid the danger from this source, let the monarchy be limited in its powers; the king having more power than any other one, but less than the whole together.

The political power varies with the various pursuits of a people. Agricultural and pastoral nations suitable for republics, being occupied with their own concerns, and not disposed to change, or greedy of offices and honors. Handicraft-men and hired laborers make the worst kind of democracy. Riches tend to oligarchy. A flat country will be likely to be democratic, a hilly one aristocratic. The best form of constitution, not theoretically, but *practically*, is that where the middle classes preponderate over both the rich and the poor, and have the supremacy.

It is advisable that laborers should be a distinct class from the military and sovereign, as their pursuits are degrading. Those who are engaged in producing the necessaries of life should be a lower grade or caste of citizens, if not slaves.

The first and great end of legislation should be the *virtuous character* and *conduct* of the citizens. Politicians, however, look more to what is expedient, he says, than *to what is good and beautiful,* more to war than to peace. Their object is to *enlarge the territory,* rather than *to render the state just and wise.* This is a mistaken policy. *Whatever is not at the same time just* is *impolitic ;* and it *is a wrong precept,* he says, which bids *men be gentle only* to *friends* and *savage* to *enemies.* Noble sentiments these, for an age like that ! It is an erroneous opinion, he affirms, that a state must be at war in order to its own activity and prosperity. A state ought to possess within itself enough to keep it active continually. "War exists *only for the sake of peace,* and *unquiet for the sake of quiet.*" The virtue of a state consists not in the *bravery* of its citizens exclusively, but in their justice, moderation, and wisdom. These four virtues ought to be the paramount object in the efforts of the legislature. In order to train the citizens to these virtues, education becomes indispensable, and must be under the control of the state. The state should care most of all for this (Pol. viii. 1). The state should commence its care of the individual at birth, should direct and control marriage with a view to the physical perfection of the race ; a deformed child ought not to be reared, and the number of children should be limited. To secure this, abortion is allowable, but not infanticide. Education is to begin at birth, and have regard first to the body, through that it must influence the desires, and through these the reason. Till the age of seven, the child is to be brought up at the father's house, and this period is to be devoted chiefly to the training and rearing the bodily frame. It must be inured to hardships, not to luxuries and ease. Children must be kept as much as possible from the company of slaves, and especially from everything immoral in word or act.

Before five, they should be taught nothing to tax the mind ; education should not be mental until after that age ; from five to seven they may be shown what they are subsequently to learn. Two other periods of education follow this : from seven to puberty, and from that to twenty-one. During all this time, education is to be public and controlled by the state. As to the means of education, and precepts for it, Aristotle is deficient. He simply informs us that four means are usually employed : grammar, design, gymnastics, and music.

Such is a brief outline of the philosophy of Aristotle, as comprised under the different departments of Logic, Physics, and Ethics or Politics.

In review of the whole, we are struck with this one feature of his system, the magnitude of the plan and design which he marked out for himself to accomplish ; with the general thoroughness and completeness also of his execution and detail. We are struck also with this general characteristic of the man as a philosopher, viz., his want of an *ideal,* his preëminent fidelity to the *real, tangible, possible, practical.* In this respect, how widely does he differ from Plato.* He is scientific rather than imaginative and lofty. Yet he is theoretical, quite as much as practical. His philosophy† has been that of the schools,

* As to the agreement or disagreement of Aristotle with Plato, it is sufficient to say that while in some important matters they agree, in others equally important they widely differ, *e.g.*, as to the doctrine of "ideas," the nature, and previous existence of the soul, the nature of virtue, the nature and value of happiness ; in a word, as to psychology and ethics, to say nothing of other matters, the two writers differ essentially, so that we can hardly accept as true the statement of Cicero and the philosophers of the New Academy, that Plato and Aristotle agree in substance, and differ only in terms (see Cic. Acad. i. 4 ; De Fin. iv. 2, v. 3 ; De Leg. i. 13).

† Beside those already mentioned, the following references may be given as authority for the foregoing statements :

For the Aristotelian Ethics in general, (Eth. Nic. i., iii. 1–8, vi., vii. 12–15, x. ; Mag. Moral. i. 1–20, ii. 7, 8, 10 ; Eth. Eud. i., ii., vii. 14, 15 ; Diog. L. v. 30, 31 ; Cic. de. Fin. v. 4, *seq.*).

For the doctrine of Aristotle respecting Natural Theology, the following general references : (Phys. ii. 6, vii. 1–3, viii. 1–9 ; Metaph.

rather than of the nations. Still, in its general influence on the world, on all countries and all ages, for more than 2,000 years, it has no superior, no rival. Accuse Aristotle, and all antiquity rises up as his pupil in his defence.

xii. 1, 2, 6–10; De Cœlo, 3, 4, 9; Nic. Eth. x. 8. 9; Cic. de Nat. Deor. i. 13, ii. 37).

For the Psychology of Aristotle, the following: (De Anima, i. 1–5, 7–9, ii. 1–3, 5, 6, 12, iii. 2; Eth. Nic. i. 13, vi. 2; Cic. Tusc. i. 10; Diog. L. v. 32–34).

PERIOD THIRD.

POST-SOCRATIC.

GENERAL VIEWS.

WITH Aristotle the Socratic period terminates. After his death certain disciples of his school taught his doctrines with some modification. *Theophrastus,* his immediate successor, and *Strato* are the most celebrated of these. The tendency of the school was more and more to sensationalism; to observation and experience and study of nature, and consequently, finally ran out into materialism with the later disciples, and especially with Strato, who so far deviated from the ground of Aristotle, yet following the general drift of that system, as to deny the immateriality and immortality of the soul and the being of God, as first cause and distinct from nature itself. The influence of the school and system diminished in proportion as it reached these results, and gave way to other systems called up in part by the spirit and tendency of the Aristotelian views.

Before we proceed to speak of the several schools that sprang up subsequently to the Aristotelian, it is well to notice the state of Greek society, and especially of Athens, at this period, since philosophy was greatly modified by it. Aristotle had survived the fall of Grecian independence. The liberties of Athens were at the mercy of a foreign power, and after the death of Alexander, its political importance and its independence were finally destroyed, and its degradation became complete. The Athenian mind consoled itself for the loss of political distinction and prosperity by a still greater abandonment to voluptuous gratifications of every kind, and the city became as noted for its luxury and refinement and manifold pleasures, as it had been and still was for its intellectual culture. A general corruption of morals had already become prevalent; the pleasures of the table were immoderately pursued; cooks were in as great demand as philosophers, and in fact both were considered indispensable. A life of pleasure was perhaps nowhere and at no time made so systematic a study and business as at Athens at this period. Hence it became the favorite residence of the tyrant Demetrius, to whom the Athenians paid worship as to a God, and to whose courtesans altars were erected in the temple of the chaste goddess Minerva. Against this corruption Stoicism set itself with scowling bitterness and asceticism; while the lighter philosophy and the lighter comedy fell in with the current and relished the spirit of the times. That was a strange mingling of intellectual culture with the refinements of luxury; of philosophy with the most open and systematic voluptuousness, the like of which is nowhere else to be found in history. Never in the palmiest days of Athens, had philosophy and its teachers been in higher honor and repute. Women of pleasure frequented the halls where the profoundest questions of intellectual science were discussed, and tyrants neglected their thrones to take part in these discussions.

It was impossible, of course, that philosophy should escape the degrading influence of such manners and such an age. The stern spirit of Socrates, of Plato, of Aristotle, no longer ruled in the schools. That spirit, so profound, so calm, so earnest, so little akin to the merely sensual, so lofty and divine, had passed away, and in place of it reigned a flippant, superficial scepticism on the one hand, and on the other, a philosophy as easy and sensuous as the age which gave it birth—the Sceptics and the Epicureans.

CHAPTER I.

THE SCEPTICS.

THE most noted teachers of this school were Pyrrho of Elis and Timon of Athens; the former a pupil of Democritus, the latter a noted author and poet. The general tenet, or *ground view*, of this class of philosophers was that *virtue and happiness are one and the same.* Three things, they say, are to be considered by him who would live happily: 1. What things are in themselves; 2. His relation to them; 3. Consequences of that relation.

As to the first: All things are indifferent, and as to truth uncertain; neither our senses nor our opinions are to be relied on. All that you can say of anything is, that whatever is affirmed of it, the opposite may just as well be affirmed, and with equal truth. Nothing is certain, nothing true, nothing beautiful or the reverse, nothing just or unjust (Diog. L. ix. 61, 62, 105; Cic. Acad. ii. 42; De Fin. ii. 11, 13, iii. 3. 4., iv. 16; De Offic. 1). Against the reliability of sensation they argued that the sensations of men are not always the same; things appear sour or sweet, straight or crooked, according to circumstances; to one person the one, to another the other, and even at different times differently to the same person. A strong sensation and a weak one give us perception of altogether different qualities in the same object.

To the second question, then, the answer is obvious. Everything is doubtful; no positive assertion can be hazarded. "We do not know certainly anything." "I assert nothing, not even that I do not assert anything."

As to the third point, consequences, the answer is, Entire indifference to things in general, and a total apathy, are the true and just consequences of this relation (Cic. de Fin. as above, and De Offic.; Diog. L. ix. 66–68; Sext. Emp. adv. Math. iii. 2; Hyp. Pyrrh. i. 25). Things being thus, it is not worth while for us to go out of our way for anything. The sage will take things as they come, and troubles himself about nothing. He will be a tranquil man; happy because without agitation, and without opinion, almost without humanity. There is no difference even, nothing to choose, between sickness and health. Life itself is not of any great value, for death is the end of all disturbance, and insures that tranquillity which so many things in life tend to disturb. In practice, however, these philosophers were obliged to contradict their theory, and conform to the state of things about them; could not be indifferent to all things, nor totally inactive; were obliged to choose, and to act, but did it under a protest of necessity, and contented themselves with the moderation of those desires and passions which they could not wholly suppress.

CHAPTER II.

THE EPICUREANS.

THE philosopher from whom this noted sect takes its name was born at Athens or Samos, it is doubtful which, 341 B. C., of Athenian parents. His father was a teacher of grammar, and his mother of magic. The youth was of inquiring spirit, and early began to develop the philosophic tendency. So early as his thirteenth year he puzzled his teacher with a question which showed the bent of the boy's mind. A passage of Hesiod was repeated to him which speaks of all things arising out of Chaos: "And from what did Chaos arise?" The teacher extricated himself from this unexpected difficulty, as well as he could, by referring the troublesome pupil to philosophy for an answer. To philosophy he went, studied this and studied that, but got nowhere an answer to his question; but instead of that plenty of new questions to be settled. His views in general, however, were drawn from Democritus and the earlier philosophers. After various changes and vicissitudes, he opened a school for philosophy at Mytilene, and afterward at Lampsacus, in which places he resided nearly five years. In his thirty-sixth year he came to Athens, opened a school, and continued it till his death, 270 B. C., at the age of 71. When his reputation was established, he left the resorts of the other philosophers and set up as an independent teacher in a villa and garden of his own. Here, surrounded with friends, he passed a life of ease and pleasure, devoted to philosophy and tranquillity. He wrote more works than even Aristotle, but by no means so profound. The Epicureans are as noted for their friendship to each other, as the Pythagoreans. In a time of need they contributed to each other's support. No very strict or sombre views of life prevailed in the garden of Epicurus. Men of pleasure patronized the new philosophy, so congenial to their tastes, and daughters of pleasure were constant attendants upon its teachings. Yet the moral character of Epicurus is said to have been far removed from that general corruption of the time, in even the natural tendency of his own doctrines. "*Men are always better or worse than their opinions*," said a profound observer of human nature.

What was the real tendency of those teachings is matter of doubt. There are not wanting reasons to suppose that the common opinion regarding the Epicurean school is quite incorrect; that the looseness of morals so often charged upon its disciples, and the pleasure-loving and sensuous character of its teachings, are not justly attributed to this system, but are unfounded calumnies arising, in part, out of mistaken notions respecting that system, and in part out of the malice of the rival and antipale sect of the Stoics, who were not slow in charging all manner of evil upon a sect so totally at variance with themselves as to all the great principles of philosophy. Certain it is, that Epicurus not only led a strictly temperate life himself, and enjoined it upon his followers, but the essential principles of the system make moderation in all sensible enjoyments an indispensable requisite to true happiness. There can be no doubt, however, that the philosophy of the garden was of a character to be readily abused and perverted by evil minds, and that it could be made, and was made, to tolerate vice and justify unsound opinion and unsound practice.

Nothing, certainly, could be more unlike the severe doctrines of Plato and Aristotle. The school of Epicurus set out from an entirely different conception of what philosophy is and should be. With them philosophy is no longer the art of truth, the science of the true and the good ; but the art of life, the science of the useful, the science of the means of happiness. Hence ethics is the chief philosophy (Diog. L. x. 24–31 ; Sext. Emp. adv. Math. xi. 169). Science as such, Epicurus disregards, as contributing nothing to happiness. All logical discussions especially he despised as useless. Physics were subordinate also, and ethics are the main philosophy with him. The supreme good is happiness, the satisfaction of all our natural desires (Diog. L. x. 131–139 ; Cic. Fin. i. 9, 11). Pleasure is the principal constituent of happiness. Not man only, but all animals instinctively pursue pleasure and avoid pain. Men ought to do deliberately what animals do by instinct. Every pleasure is a good in itself, but compared with other pleasure may be an evil. Pleasure ought not to be pursued, then, for its own sake, but with reference to the general happiness of life, and so some pleasures should be avoided as occasioning future grief and pain. No pleasure is *per se* to be rejected, but some must be sacrificed on account of consequences (Diog. L. x. 141). Even pain is to be endured at times, for the sake of the good to come from it. It is not the happiness of the moment that is to be regarded, but that of the whole existence. In this he differs from the Cyrenaics, who looked only at the present enjoyment. Like Aristotle, too, he makes happiness and virtue to be inseparably connected;—a life of true pleasure *must be a virtuous* life (Diog. L. x. 132). Epicurus, moreover, places the highest pleasure, not in *corporeal* gratifications, but in mental, since the former pass away in the moment of their existence, but the latter endure and are for the past and the future, as well as the present.

This mental pleasure arises from some past corporeal pleasure remembered afterwards, or from some like pleasure anticipated in the future. At least so Cicero represents him (De. Fin. i. 7, 17, ii. 30). But this is doubtful. That the senses are the chief inlet of happiness, he doubtless did teach. The strictest temperance is enjoined, however, in order to the full enjoyment of even the pleasures of the senses. Epicurus lived plainly, dispensed with all luxuries; is averse to costly pleasures as injurious, is content with little; give him barley bread, and water from the spring, and he will rival Jupiter in happiness. He would not limit man to the fewest possible enjoyments, but rather *multiply* those enjoyments; but he must be able to *live upon little,* in order to this. Contentedness with a little he regards as a great good, and *makes wealth consist,* not IN GREAT POSSESSIONS, but in SMALL WANTS.

As to *pain:* it cannot be dispensed with altogether, and the only alternative is to make as little of it as possible, and to *ignore* it as far as may be. He regards pleasure as greatly predominant over pain, even in periods of lingering sickness. Everything which is not pain is put to the account of pleasure; and the truest pleasure is the repose of the soul, freedom from agitation and mental disturbance.

When everything else fails, death is at least the end of all misery, and so ought not to be feared. "For while we live death is not, and when death is we are not; when it is we feel it not, for it is the end of all feeling" (Diog. L. x. 124; Lucret. iii. 842, *seq.*).

It is but a meagre philosophy indeed, that can console us under misfortune, not by the promise of some great gain and future good, but only by holding out the expectation of a final and irremediable loss; not by the hope of immortality, but only of that dreary blank which ends our pains only by ending our pleasures. Still we see in this philosophy only a prevalent form of that scepticism which was the natural growth of the times, and, in some sense, the natural result of preceding systems of doctrine, rather than the peculiar characteristic of this philosopher or of his school. He divides philosophy into Canonics or Logic, Physics, and Ethics (Diog. L. x. 29). Logic merely introductory to Physics (Diog. L. x. 30; Cic. Acad. ii. 30; De Fin. i. 7). With respect to *sensation*. Every sensation is *true*, says Epicurus, for it is a motion produced in the mind by something else, to which nothing can be added, and from which nothing can be taken away. *But what the sensible is* which produces the sensation is another question; *that* we do *not learn* in sensation itself. Sensation is to be carefully distinguished from its exciting cause, and also from the opinions and conclusions of our own minds respecting them. This was the doctrine of Aristotle also—likewise of Reid and the Scotch school, you will say. Precisely, I reply. There is nothing absolutely new under the sun. The newest thing is at least two thousand years old.

By sensations, says Epicurus, we know not things themselves, but only certain accidents of things, certain qualities. Yet the sensations have some resemblance to the external objects (see pp. 161, 167; Diog. L. x. 31. *seq.;* Sext. Emp. adv. Math. vii. 203; Cic. Acad. ii. 25, 32). Beside sensation,

Epicurus makes conception a criterion of truth, *i. e.*, the recollection of many previous phenomena produced by sensuous impressions from without. Memory takes its place beside sensation, then, even in cognition. All investigation remounts to such conception based on memory; all general thoughts resolve into sensations or the remembrance of them. All conceptions are, like all sensations, *true.* Error is possible in opinion formed upon sensation, but not in sensation itself, *e. g.*, a distant tower seems round—coming nearer we find it to be square; however, the first sensation was true; *i. e.*, it *seems* round, but our *opinion* was wrong, *i. e.*, it is not round in reality, as we thought it to be (Diog. L. x. 33 *seq.;* Sext. Emp. adv. Math. vii. 211. *seq.;* Cic. Acad. as above; also De Nat. Deor. i. 16, 17, 20). In all investigation *words* in their primary significations are the main elements to be regarded. Dialectic, or the art of syllogistic reasoning, he rejects. Cicero complains of his logic as deficient in many respects (De Fin. i. 7, 22). Mathematics also he rejects (Cic. de Fin. vii. 21, 71). In physiology Epicurus adopts the atomic theory of Democritus. The atoms are infinite in number, moving in an infinite vacuum, and from eternity precipitated downward. These atoms, colliding with and repelling each other, produce a rebounding motion. They combine together and form worlds *ad libitum.* No need of any external ordering and producing power on this theory. No need of gods to do what is done as well without. It is not true, he says, that in physics, every regularly occurring phenomenon is brought about by some *law,* for the same thing may have at one time one cause, at another, another, and every possible cause may be admitted as a sufficient explanation of any natural event.

The soul is corporeal in a sort, as is indeed, everything except *vacuum,* a space (Diog. L. x. 67). As it animates the whole body, it must be *diffused through the whole,* of course (modern Scotch again). It is invisible, but suffers many changes, consists of round and smooth atoms, which *move easily* (Diog. x. 63). He compares it to a breath united to a certain degree of warmth. In death these atoms are scattered, and we no longer exist (Diog. L. x. 64; Lucret. iii. 418). The soul has four activities; gives rise to motion, to repose, to warmth, to sensation, each produced by a distinct element in the composition of the soul—motion by breath, repose by air, warmth by fire, etc. Body and soul are mutally dependent, neither existing without the other. The soul, being composite, admits of decomposition when the body, which is its protection and covering, is dissolved. Sensation is produced by the emanation from all bodies of certain effluxes or corporeal images which enter through the organs of sense, and in that way we get our conceptions. All sensations and perceptions are true, because they correspond to these images. This is also the doctrine of Democritus. The theology of Epicurus is obscure. The Stoics call him an atheist (Cic. Nat. Deor. i. 30–44). He admits the existence of gods of human form, but free from human imperfections and wants, given to supreme repose, troubling not themselves or mortals with any disposition to interfere in human affairs. The world is too imperfect to be their work—nor it is consistent with their repose and dignity to create such a world (Diog. L. x. 39, 76, 77; Cic. Nat. Deor. i. 9–16). Much of the popular belief in gods he regards as superstition. Such is a brief outline of the philosophy of this somewhat distinguished, and, we must confess, much calumniated sect.

CHAPTER III.

THE STOICS.

THE degeneracy of the times, the general corruption of morals, the softness and effeminacy of Epicureanism, the indifference of scepticism, the fading out of the earlier Greek earnestness of character and energy of soul, the waning national courage and patriotism and spirit—these influences combined cast a deep shadow over the period of Grecian history as connected with Grecian philosophy which is now passing under our review. But these influences, though widely prevalent and almost universal, were not altogether unresisted. There did arise in certain Greek minds a feeling of indignant resentment at the general spirit of the age and irresistible current of events. By the law of opposites, there arose a sect antagonistic to all this, planting itself firmly on the opposite extreme, and battling to the last, on the field of acknowledged defeat, against influences and opinions which were destined to prevail over all opposition.

Such a sect were the Stoics, who considered themselves followers of Socrates. The leader of these, Zeno of Citium, a small city in the island of Cyprus. He was born about 350 B. C. His father was a merchant, and he himself (Diog. L. vii. 1, 2, 5) was early engaged in mercantile pursuits ; but in after years, losing his all by shipwreck on a voyage to Athens, he betook himself in that city to philosophy, to which his mind had already received a bias while yet in earlier youth, from the perusal of some writings of the Socratic teachers, especially Xenophon's Memorabilia and Plato's Apology (Diog. L. vii. 3). The life of a Cynic fell in with the circumstances and feelings of a shipwrecked and penniless voyager, and he sought the instructions of that school ; not fully satisfied there, he became subsequently a pupil of the Megarean philosophy, and afterward of the Academy. Twenty years were spent in these studies. There was a place in Athens where poets had, in palmier days, been accustomed to convene for the purpose of reciting their inspirations—the Variegated Porch. It now stood empty. There Zeno opened a school in philosophy, 310 B. C., and seems to have gathered around him many disciples. It was not looked upon with favor by the community, who regarded it as a sort of continuation of the Cynic sect, and it had few converts among the wealthier classes, but was frequented mostly by the poor. Over this school Zeno presided fifty-eight years, (Diog. L. vii. 28, citing Apollonius), and at last put an end to his own life. Temperate, frugal, abstemious, living upon a spare and meagre diet, he enjoyed the reputation, not only of severe morality and strict virtue, but of remarkable integrity, so much so that Athens intrusted to him the keys of her gates, and at his death erected (Diog. L. vii. 6) a tomb and a monument of brass in his honor, bearing for inscription the simple but high eulogium that his life had been accordant with his teaching. A few fragments only of his works have come down to us. His successors were Cleanthes, of Assus in Troas ; of poor parentage, a boxer in early life (Diog. L. vii. 168), working at night as a common laborer that he might study by day, attaching himself to the doctrines of Zeno, and faithfully retaining them in their purity ; finally, like his master, ending his own existence ;—and after him Chrysippus, a native of Cilicia, 282–209 B. C.; likewise of poor extraction, but remarkable for quickness of apprehension and great sagacity, a bitter opponent of the Epicurean system and of the new Academy, a diligent cultivator of all branches of science, and a voluminous writer above all the great names of antiquity. His works amounted to 705 ! (Diog. L. vii. 180), not one of which, however, has come down to posterity, and which, as might be well conceived, were not remarkable for clearness or elegance, for care of composition or grace of style. It was his custom to produce five hundred lines a day.

§ 1.—General View of the Stoic Philosophy.

With regard to the philosophical views of the Stoics, it may be observed, in general, that the systems of Plato and Aristotle were not, on the whole, sufficiently simple and natural in their method; were too cumbrous and complicated to satisfy fully the wants of inquiring minds, especially at a period not remarkable for patient investigation or profound thought. Some simpler and more direct solution of the great problems of human inquiry was demanded. The Stoical system grew out of that demand, in part, and set itself in a straightforward way to solve the difficulties and satisfy the doubts of the human mind on the most abstruse and important as well as difficult subjects. It takes decidedly a practical and common sense view of things; bases itself in part on that sound common sense which governs men in practical life; appeals to the current opinions and prevailing views of men; connects itself intimately with the practical duties of life; combats the notion that a life of solitude and contemplation is best for the sage; demands a life of activity and virtue; makes philosophy in part to consist in the practice of virtue—that only useful art. Science and virtue are thus intimately blended. A life of virtue is a life of true science, as both Socrates and Plato had taught. Wisdom is the science of divine and human things, and philosophy is the pursuit of wisdom. As this relates to thought, to knowledge and to practice, so accordingly they divide philosophy into physics, ethics, and logic (Diog. L. vii. 39, 40, *seq.;* Plut. de Plac. Phil. i. 1; Cic. Acad. i. 10, 11). They make the two last subordinate to the first, and logic especially so—the handmaiden of the other sciences, the shell of the egg—while ethics are the white, and physics the yolk. Plato and Aristotle would make logic or dialectic the yolk, and physics the shell. It is to be noticed, however, that in this deviation they followed the already existing tendency of the times, to make logic rather the *organum* of philosophy than philosophy itself, while, on the other hand, they transferred to physics many of the inquiries which had hitherto fallen under the department of logic. The *cognition of the Divine* is, in fact, declared to be the great object of physics. Under logic, they include grammar and rhetoric. They are in fact the founders of grammar, and inventors of the terms which designate the different parts of speech. Under physics, they treat of whatever is most sublime and divine, and discuss mythology, and pagan superstition even; while the domain of ethics is enlarged by practical rules of life and treatises on duty and propriety. We shall do best to consider separately these several divisions of their philosophy.

§ 2.—Logic of the Stoics.

Discarding as already obsolete the theories of Plato and Aristotle as to the source of ideas, they set out with a theory on the whole simple and perspicuous. Under the term (φαντασία), fantasy, or conception, they include the contents of the *consciousness* both of man and brute; the representation of the sensible, and the notion of the non-sensible—representation by a present object, and also that which has the semblance only of being thus caused. Corresponding to the representation (which is a passive affection of the soul, and supposes some active object, external, as its producing cause), there is also something capable of being represented, some φάνταστόν for every φαντασία, and this active cause, this φανταστόν, is some external object, which, by means of the senses, produces an impression on the soul (Sext. Emp. adv. Math. vii. 244, 227. *seq.;* Diog. L. vii. 49–54; Cic. Acad. i. 11, ii. 6, 24). The soul is originally (as others had previously taught), a blank tablet, unwritten, but ready to be written on. Sensation writes on it (Plutarch. de Placit. Phil. iv. 11), thence memory, and as the result of memory, analogous sensations, experience. So far, they agreed with Aristotle. But they went further, and derived from sensation not mere knowledge of phenomena, but also intellectual thought, thus coinciding here with the Epicureans. Science is a firm conviction, or any system of such convictions, incapable of being shaken by argument. The *reciprocal action* of outward *objects* and of the *faculties* of the soul gives rise to cognition and sensation. Assent of the mind is subjective and voluntary; and yet sensuous impressions may *constrain* it. The idea in the soul produced by an outward object is a passive affection, but *reveals* its *cause*, just as light shows not only itself, but the objects which it illumines. This manifestation of objects by sense, they say, leads at once and of necessity to the judgment that such objects have real existence.* But how are we to distinguish the false from the true, since all are not equally credible and veritable? Since all knowledge results from sensation ultimately, and there is no higher faculty to sit in judgment on the representations of sense, evidently the only criterion of truth must be found in these representations themselves. This seems to have been the *distinctness* of the sensuous impressions. But how can the representation express what is in the *object?* Answer: It is a sort of copy of that object, formed in the soul like the impression of the soul left on wax. Chrysippus, however, objects to this view on the ground that many ideas may exist in the soul at one time, just as many sounds in the air, which could not be on the above supposition. His explanation is simply this, that an idea is a *modification* of the soul by some outward object; further than this, the matter is inexplicable (Sext. Emp. adv. Math. vii. 228). With the Stoics ideas are merely conceptions, *have no existence* out of our minds (Plut. de

* The doctrine of Reid and the Scottish School.

Plac. Phil. i. 10). In this they differed from Plato. They distinguished two kinds of the true—the sensible, and the intelligible.

They distinguished also between the *true* and *truth*. Truth is in essence corporeal, as is all true substance, while the true is incorporeal. The number of categories with them was four: (*a*) the substrate, lying at the foundation—the ground of things; (*b*) that which has a quality; (*c*) that which has some general relation; (*d*) that which has some particular relation, as the terms father and son, right and left, relations which change with change of circumstances. To these four categories the four parts of speech correspond, the article, noun, verb, and conjunction. The Stoics were *nominalists*.

§ 3.—Their Physics.

The Stoics regarded everything as material or corporeal, following out the tendency of the Aristotelian system in this; hence physics were of so much importance in their philosophy. They derived their views on this subject, however, mostly from Heraclitus and the earlier, or pre-Socratic philosophers. Of *incorporeal* things there are four kinds: vacuum, place, time, the inexpressible. Body with them is not simply *the extended in three directions*, but something, moreover, which is active or passive. Virtue and vice, the thoughts and dispositions and faculties of the soul, and faculties of the body, the seasons, day and night—all such things are bodies; *whatever has a property*, and even *properties themselves*, are bodies. They do not accordingly distinguish between a thing and its *properties*. The property is with them the body itself. The *passive*, as a ground of things, is matter without property or quality. The *active is God in matter* (Diog. L. vii. 134; Seneca Epist. lxv. 2; Cic. Acad. i. 11; De Nat. Deor. i. 14, ii. 8, 9). Matter is the primary subject, and universal essence, yet inseparable from the active force. The *world is simply the substance or matter of God.* If the universe were to pass away, both matter and God would remain. The dissolution of heaven and earth is merely the resumption of all into himself again by Deity, from whom they first proceeded. The divine Spirit, as also the human, is conceived by them as a *force* inherent in matter, rather than as a *nous* or intelligence subsisting apart. God and matter are *one.* Viewed in one aspect, as passive, it is matter; in another, as active, it is God. They regard God also as the universal reason, pervading all as the soul does the body, governing all, providing for all, wise, source of natural law, punishing the evil, rewarding the good, perfect, and conscious of felicity. This soul of the world is destiny, moreover; and is associated by the Stoics with the idea of *vital heat* in the body—the breath, the artistic fire, the ether (Cic. de Nat. Deor. ii. 9), also called spirit, πνεῦμα (ii. 14, Diog. L. vii. 139). He is distinct from the world in a subordinate sense, as producer, fashioner, disposer of it, according to the universal law of reason (Cic. de Nat. Deor., as above, 9, 14, 22; Diog. L. vii. 134, 147–156, *seq.*), as the active and passive are different, as soul and body are different, yet one life, unity of being. This development of soul or active force, as *fire* in the world, etc., proceeds through certain fixed gradations and periods and finally returns into itself or God, and closes with a grand conflagration (Cic. de Nat. Deor. ii. 46; Plut. de Stoic. Repugn. 41; Diog. L. vii. 142). It is a period in the divine life, having its beginning and end. In the world evil will always exist, but in the final conflagration will cease. The development of things and worlds is one which will continue in successive formations, precisely like the preceding ones; all returns, comes round again by the same old laws as before.

As to the existence of evil. God wills not war, disease, etc., but they come in *consequence* of the good which he does will. Moral evil, which is real evil, is necessary for the perfection of the world. God wills it not; for law never sanctions its own infraction; but he wills that of which evil is the necessary consequence. Without evil, good could not be; so that it is neither possible nor expedient to get rid of it altogether. Nothing can exist without its contrary, as Heraclitus taught; not even good without evil. If there were no such thing as injustice, there could be no justice; nor courage without cowardice, nor truth if there were no falsehood, etc.

With respect to inferior deities, the Stoics defended the popular superstitions and beliefs against the current scepticism of the day.

The world, as being the work of God, must needs be beautiful, for the divine act is not to realize the useful only, but the beautiful also. Variety, multiplicity, diversity, is the rule of beauty. Hence the wonderful diversity of nature, who, in all her works, never repeats herself. The individual in the Stoic philosophy exists for the *universal;* brutes for the service of man; plants and inferior animals for brutes; man for the *gods;* the gods for society, for the whole, for each other.

The four elements are derived originally from the primary fire, which, condensed, becomes air, which further condensed, water; which, still by condensation, becomes earth, but by rarefaction and evaporation goes back to air again, and so finally becomes fire. This process is set in operation by precipitation, which, commencing at the centre, extinguishes the adjacent fire, but the surrounding fire combats it, and by the contending fires the universe is founded. Of these elements, earth is in the centre, water at circumference, air next, and highest is fire, which embraces and surrounds the whole.

All individual objects are compositions of these elements. Inanimate objects have but one property, and that oneness of quality is what binds them together; plants and animals, many, and are held together, the former by their "nature," the latter by their soul. Individual souls, being a part of the mundane soul, are not immortal strictly, but will subsist after death, till the final conflagration, when absorbed into the divine (Diog. L. vii. 157). Chrysippus taught that only the wise and good would survive death. The human soul is a breath inborn, pervading the whole body (Diog. L. vii. 159), a fiery spirit (Cic. de Nat. Deor. iii. 14 ; Tusc. Quæst. i. 9). There is a ruling principle in the soul, which directs and governs it, the subject or *ego,* the reason or intelligence, the seat of which is in the heart. There are eight parts of the soul : the ruling portion in the heart, five operating in the organs of sense, one in the organ of voice, one in the organs of generation (Plut. de Plac. Phil. iv. 4 ; Diog. L. vii. 157, *seq.*). Every appetite, desire, lust, is an *opinion,* knowledge incompletely developed. The soul is not *capriciously* moved, not by chance, but by motives; though sometimes the motive which strikes the balance is unperceived. By the freedom of the soul, they understand the assent which it gives to certain ideas, not arbitrarily but according to its nature ; still, in so acting, we go according to destiny, a universal fate, just as a stone, rolling down hill, receives its first impulse from without, but the course depends afterward on its weight and figure. The liberty of things is simply the law of their nature ; but the law of individual nature is dependent on the nature of all.

§ 4.—Their Ethics.

Nature is the ground of right ; yet, as God and nature are one, the divine reason is the ground of right (Diog. L. vii. 88, 89, *seq.;* Tusc. Quæst. iv. 13, 15; De Off. i. 5 ; Fin. iii. 7, 9, 15, 18) ; and physics is the ground of ethics, according to the Stoical philosophy. A virtuous life is a life conformable to nature (Diog. L. vii. 87), or in harmony with one's self, as Zeno expresses it. All virtue is founded in *instinct,* a certain natural propensity of the soul. This instinct in man is developed according to the reason, and in this differs from that of brutes. It is the assent which he gives to a particular representation, or the idea of good determining him to action. Follow nature, then, is their ultimate principle of ethics. A life agreeable to nature is one in which all the elements of the individual life are in perfect harmony (Diog. L. vii. 87–89; Cic. de Fin. iii. 6, 7; Acad. i. 10. ii. 45). The *model* for this is that *animal* state, or state of nature as we say, in which, as yet, life is not spoiled by custom, law, habit, etc. Pleasure was of no account with the Stoics, not the end of nature, without moral value, a mere passive state of soul. The morality of a deed lies not in the outward act, but in the volition; consequences, works, are not to be regarded; *virtue* alone is good; he who has it wants nothing, though destitute of all things. Still, health, wealth, etc., though not *good*, and without real value, nevertheless (by a *refined distinction*), are *preferable* to other things, as sickness, poverty, etc., and so the sage may choose them of the two, when he can (Diog. L. vii. 101–107; Cic. de Fin. iii. 3, 15, 16; Sext. Emp. adv. Math. ix. 59–67, 73, 77). Self-preservation is the instinct of nature, and so due regard must be paid to life, health, etc., as well as to knowledge of things. These objects are "the *first things according to nature*" of the Stoics; opposed to which are disease, weakness, deformity, etc. Self-love, or love of existence, is, then, the foundation of moral action. There is a period in life when reason awakens and takes command of the soul and all its impulses. If under this guidance, the soul is wholly good; if without it, wholly evil. There is no medium. Four things indispensable to virtue: knowledge of good and evil, temperance, fortitude, justice. Man cannot wrong himself, nor other animals, for they exist only for his good. The perfection of humanity is a state of *apathy*—freedom from the emotions, of which the chief forms are desire, fear, joy, sorrow; complete mastery of these, so as not to be governed by them (Cic. Tusc. iii. 9, iv. 9; Acad. i. 10, ii. 47; De

Fin. iii. 7, 10). There is a difference between the *merely befitting*, and *duty*, which is the *befitting according to reason*—the act of walking may be befitting, though not a duty unless some moral end in view; or *perfect* and *imperfect* duties. The sage is superior to law and custom ; like Zeus himself, his own law. So long as the motive is not selfish or voluptuous, he may do almost anything : *lying, suicide, prostitution ;* entire disregard for customs of society are allowable, with that limitation only. The sage is one who cannot err, and whom reason never fails—a character, in fact, nowhere to be found. Such, in brief, are Stoic ethics and philosophy.

§ 5.—General Estimate of the System.

In forming a general estimate of the system which has now passed under review, it is impossible to deny it a very high, possibly the very highest, place among the ethical systems of ancient philosophy. As a system of pure and elevated morals, it has perhaps no superior among them all ; yet its defects are by no means to be overlooked. The very elevation of its standard, the very loftiness of its ideal, rendered it, in a measure, ill suited to the ordinary conditions of humanity. As has been well remarked by Lecky, in his History of European Morals (vol. i. p. 204–5) : "A moral system, to govern society, must accommodate itself to common character and mingled motives. It must be capable of influencing natures that can never rise to an heroic level. But Stoicism was simply a school of heroes. It recognized no gradations of virtue or vice. It condemned all emotions, all spontaneity, all mingled motives, all the principles, feelings, and influences, upon which the virtue of common men mainly depends. It was capable of acting only on moral natures that were strung to the highest tension, and it was therefore naturally rejected by the multitude." The principle of self-approbation, the essential inherent dignity of man, constitute the centra-idea of the system. A life of virtue is to be pursued, because such a life alone is consistent with this self-approbation, and this inherent dignity. Of sin, in the Christian sense, and of repentance for sin, it has no idea. It would deter men from evil by appeals to their pride and self-respect. These are its highest motives, its prevailing influences. The *emotional* part of our nature—and this is one of the most serious defects of the Stoic system—it discourages, and seeks in every way to repress. All feeling, sensibility, emotion, the joys and sorrows that agitate the human heart, it regards as unworthy the true man. There must be no tears over our own losses, no sympathy with the bereavements of others; but calm and lofty indifference to the gifts of fortune and all human ills. It would train us to self-reliance and complete self-control, as the goal of human endeavor, the ideal of human excellence. And if at length the burdens and the ills of life are such as can no longer be borne, one method of escape is always in our power, we have but to put forth our hand, write *finis*, and close the volume.

Yet I know not where to find, even among Christian writers, loftier sentiments than abound in the writings of the later Stoics. The excellence of virtue, for its own sake and not merely for the advantages it brings; of virtue concealed from the world, and known only to the peaceful soul that in obscurity and silence cherishes and adores it; the greatness of a soul calm and self-reliant under all the storms of adversity, the duty of uncomplaining submission to the Divine will—these and the like virtues are even more earnestly and beautifully set forth in the pages of Epictetus and Seneca, of Marcus Aurelius and Antoninus Pius, than in those of the Christian fathers. "Nothing for opinion, all for conscience," says Seneca (De Vit. Beat. c. xx.); "He who wishes his virtue to be blazed abroad is not laboring for virtue, but for fame" (Ep. cxiii). A great man is none the less great, when he lies vanquished and prostrate in the dust (Cons. ad Helv. xiii.). "Never forget," says Marcus Aurelius, "that it is possible to be at once a divine man, yet a man unknown to all the world" (Marc. Aur. vii. 67). "To ask to be paid for virtue, is as if the eye demanded a recompense for seeing, or the feet for walking" (ix. 42). Nor is virtue to be sought merely for its advantages. "*Non dux, sed comes, voluptas,*" says Seneca; "pleasure is not to be our leader, but our comdanion;" and again "*Voluptas non est merces, nec causa virtutis, sed accessio;*" "pleasure is not the reward nor the cause of virtue, but its incidental acquisition" (De Vit. Beat. c. viii. ix.). "Misfortunes, and losses, and calamity, disappear before virtue as the taper before the sun" (Seneca Ep. lxvi.). In the Stoic theology, the soul of man is but "a detached fragment of the Deity"; hence its best impulses and efforts are of divine origin or inspiration. "Nothing is closed to God," said Seneca. "He is present in our conscience. He intervenes in our thoughts" (Ep. lxxxiii.). "I tell thee, Lucilius, a sacred spirit dwells within us, the observer and the guardian of our good and evil deeds. . . . No man is good without God" (Ep. xii.).

To the allotments of Providence the Stoic philosophy enjoins an unquestioning and uncomplaining submission. "To fear, to grieve, to be angry, is to be a deserter," says Marcus Aurelius. "Remember you are but an actor," says Epictetus, "acting whatever part the Master has ordained. It may be short, or it may be long. If he wishes you to represent a poor man, do so heartily; if a cripple, or a magistrate, or a private man, in each case act your part with honor" Ench. (xvii.). Never say of anything that you have lost it, but that you have restored it; your wife and child die—you have restored them; your farm is taken from you—that also is restored. It is seized by an impious man. What is it to you, by whose instrumentality he who gave it reclaims it" (Epict. Ench. xi.). "God does not keep a good man in prosperity," says Seneca; "He tries, He strengthens him, He prepares him for Himself" (De Prov. i). As we listen to such sentiments, it is difficult to persuade ourselves that they are the precepts of a pagan philosophy, and not the meditations of some devout monk of the middle ages.

CHAPTER IV.

THE NEW ACADEMY.

We are approaching the close of the history of Greek philosophy. The great systems, of which we have already spoken, stand forth as the almost complete embodiment of that history. Nothing worthy of the name of a system is added to them afterward, but only such modifications of them are made as would adapt them to the tendencies and habits of thought which characterized the times. The New Academy, as it was termed, somewhat later than the foundation of the Epicurean and Stoic schools in its origin, presents the principal of these modifications of earlier systems. As the name indicates, it was a school attaching itself to the Platonic system in its main features, while it modified the views and widely departed from the earlier spirit of that system.

§ 1.—Founder of the School.

The author of this new school was Arcesilaus of Pitane, born 315 B. C.; at first given to oratory, afterward to philosophy, under Theophrastus and Polemo, also the sceptic Pyrrho. He seems to have considered himself a good Platonist; like Plato manifests great respect for the *earlier* philosophers. Into the Academy he introduces the old Socratic method of teaching by dialogue. He is highly praised for his smooth, ready, and flowing eloquence; did not commit his doctrines to writing. His views, learned mostly from works of his opponents. According to the statements of these persons, a perfect scepticism would seem to be the main result of his speculations. He knows nothing ; not even his own ignorance, which even Socrates admitted that he knew. He denied the certainty, both of intellectual and sensuous knowledge (Cic. de Orat. iii. 18, 67). He attacks vigorously the Stoics, who were his chief opponents. With Plato, he appeals to the uncertainty of the senses, which declare opposite things of the same object, and cannot reveal the true nature of things. He sets forth the mutual inconsistencies and contradictions of the different philosophic systems. Still his scepticism assumes a practical direction. Men should study, not works of art, etc., but their own lives and conduct, which are the most instructive objects of science.

Hence nothing is known for certainty of the real existence and nature of things ; our *knowledge* falls of course into the domain of the probable, and we do well to suspend our judgment (Cic. Acad. Quæst. ii. 24, i. 12 ; Sext. Emp. adv. Math. vii. 150, 154, 108). In the pursuit of good we must be guided by probabilities. In this, the New Academy differs from the Sceptics, who made the end of life to be the attainment of a perfect equanimity, and the difference of good and bad to be the result of convention, not of nature. The New Academy, on the contrary, allowed the sage to conform more nearly to the customs of society, observe its decencies and proprieties, without mortifying entirely his natural passions and desires, or bursting away entirely from the bonds and restraints of civilized life. Arcesilaus is said to have been rather inclined even to luxury, and, as the story goes, killed himself at seventy-five by hard drinking.

§ 2.—His Successor.

His only distinguished successor was Carneades of Cyrene ; born 213 B. C.; carefully instructed in the principles of the New Academy, and also in those of the Stoics.

Learned in the history of philosophy, he seems to have labored mostly to refute the positions of all the systems of philosophy, but chiefly the Stoical. His reputation rests chiefly on his refutation of the latter. "Had there never been a Chrysippus, I never should have been what I am." Noted for his eloquence, on account of which he was chosen one of the ambassadors to Rome on a certain occasion, where he enchanted multitudes, chiefly young men, by his powers of oratory. He discoursed one day—when Cato, the stern, stoic Roman, was present—on justice: setting forth in such lofty tones its praise, that the old Roman grimly smiled. Next day, however, he showed the falsity of all his preceding arguments, and Cato's brow grew dark. So much was the stout old Roman troubled that he persuaded the Senate to dismiss the Grecians with all despatch, lest the youth of Rome should be hopelessly corrupted. He generally presented both sides of every question, insomuch that his most trusty pupil admitted he could never discover what was, on any subject, the real opinion of his master.

He attacks the doctrine of the Stoics respecting the being and nature of God, and their defence of the popular superstitions and mythologies; he shows the folly of ascribing human form to the Deity (Cic. de Nat. Deor. iii. 12; Sext. adv. Math. ix. 138, 140). He also attacks the Stoic doctrine of necessity versus free-will. Practical life he regarded as an art. He takes a nobler view of humanity than Aristippus, but less noble than the Stoics. Justice is, according to him, a mere civil institution, not a *natural* one (Cic. Repub. iii. 15, 24), since not identical everywhere, but varying in different states and at different times in the same state—hence not a virtue, for virtue is one and invariable. Prudence and justice are often at variance; often imprudent, for states to be just. Justice has its source in the weakness of man, who, in order to protect himself from injury, abstains from inflicting it on others.

The sovereign good is "enjoyment of the gifts of nature," "union of virtue and happiness," and the like ambiguous expressions (Cic. Tusc. v. 30, 84). It is impossible to find any criterion of truth. If any, it must be either in sensation, conception, or reason. But reason deals only with objects first presented to it through conception, and this latter only with objects of sense; so that all comes back to sensation, which is notoriously untrustworthy, and carries false tidings, like an unfaithful messenger. Still even as to this scepticism he is sceptical; does not affirm positively, but doubts, questions, denies. His theory of probability is somewhat noticeable. There is no certainty of anything, only probability (Cic. Acad. Quæst. ii. 24, i. 12; Sext. Emp. adv. Math. vii. 150, 154, 408). We choose between opposite courses of conduct, not by blind impulse or necessity, but according to higher or lower degrees of probability. Every idea has two relations: one to the object, one to the subject, or the mind that conceives it. In the first case it is true or false, as it agrees or not with the object, and this we can never know. In the latter relation it *appears* true or not true; that is, it is *probable* or *improbable;* and it is of importance to determine which, for our conduct proceeds on this principle. An idea is probable, according as it proceeds from a perception which is invariable and unquestioned; and if, on thorough examination, nothing be found to contradict it. Carneades recommends the study of philosophy as the best and only road to oratory.

§. 3—Subsequent Fortunes of the School.

Carneades was the last distinguished name of the New Academy. It began, after him, to decline and fall into disrepute. Philosophy, both with the Academy and the Porch, became less profound, more erudite, more artistical, more popular, more sceptical. This tendency shows the degradation of the science and of the age. The differences between the Academy and the Porch became less clearly defined, and a sort of eclecticism grew up, and semi-conciliation and agreement between the two, the Stoics growing more mild, and also more sceptical, as time passed on. Efforts were indeed made to restore the Academy again to its pristine purity, to bring it back to the doctrines of Plato and Aristotle, but with little other than merely temporary success. Antiochus, pupil of Philo, is noted for his labors to this end. Meanwhile, alongside of the Academy and the Porch, the Epicurean philosophy now became almost obsolete, and the Aristotelian became quite so, dragged out a feeble existence represented by here and there a disciple. And so we reach the close of that period and movement which, commencing with Socrates, shed such lustre on the *Greek*—nay more, on the human mind. It is with melancholy interest that we take leave of Grecian philosophy ; that we see it gradually losing its hold on the mind, as corruption and decay become more and more prevalent, until finally its brilliant light, which Socrates and Plato kindled, and Aristotle with a master's hand had trimmed and nourished, dwindles before our eyes into a dim and solitary taper, and finally goes out in darkness on a nation no longer worthy of his beams.

What was the result, now, of all these profound investigations from Thales downward ? "Scepticism," says Lewes. "Centuries of thought had not advanced the mind one step nearer to a solution of the problem with which, child-like, it began ; it *began with a child-like question ;* it *ended* with an *aged doubt.*" "Was then all this labor in vain ? Were these long, laborious years all wasted ? Were those splendid minds all useless ? No ! Human endeavor is seldom without fruit. Those centuries of speculation were not useless. They were the education of the human race. They taught man's mind this truth at least : The infinite cannot be known by the finite ; man can only know phenomena." To this view, eloquent as it is, we should somewhat demur ; for Lewes is himself a sceptic as to the possibility of any solid results in philosophy. We would not take so sad and sombre and despairing a view of the labors of these old Grecians. They are the germ of modern philosophy, the seeds of things, the dawn of a brighter, higher day, that shines on us; our eyes behold what these old kings and prophets of the mental world desired to see, but died without the sight. Let us not forget our debt of gratitude to these first inquirers, these patient thinkers, these ancient masters.

CHAPTER V.

THE GREEK PHILOSOPHY AMONG THE ROMANS.

It remains only to notice the effect of Greek philosophy upon foreign nations; and of these I shall select only the Roman, as the one most directly and favorably influenced by the Greek mind, and the one with whose history and literary remains the student of the present day is most interested. The Romans, while they conquered Greece, were in turn conquered by it; the vassal became the master, and the master, conscious of inferiority, submitted to willing bondage; became the *pupil* and sat at the feet of the slave, to learn of him the secret of that higher power which intellect wields over mere brute force. The literature and philosophy of Greece held the Roman mind in complete and willing subjection. Even stern old Cato, who sent off the Grecian ambassadors, applied himself in his old age to learning the Greek language. Such men as Scipio Africanus and Caius Lælius and L. Furius were not only patrons of Grecian learning, but maintained friendly and intimate intercourse with the scholars and philosophers of Greece. Eminent lawyers became the disciples of Panætius, the Stoic and Platonic philosopher. But no one of Rome's distinguished men gave himself up with more hearty relish, perhaps, to Grecian erudition and philosophy, than Cicero. At the outset, Epicurean doctrines gained a popularity in Rome, and found numerous advocates. Subsequently and in the time of Cicero, the New Academy, then in its brightest phase, became more generally the prevalent philosophy of the Romans. The Peripatetic doctrines also found adherents when Sylla brought home the works of Aristotle. On the whole, the Epicurean, the Stoic, and New Academy were the chief schools and favorite systems at Rome. The practical turn of the Roman mind led them to look with more favor on these schools, as being practical rather than speculative systems, as Tennemann suggests. The old Academy, however, had such adherents as Lucullus, M. Brutus, and Varro, who nevertheless mingled much of the Stoical philosophy with the Platonic. The same thing is more or less true of all those Roman disciples of Greek philosophy; they were really eclectics in good measure, no one more so than Cicero; and while they believed themselves to belong to this or that particular school, unconsciously or purposely mingled with that the views of other sects, and especially the prevalent Stoical doctrines.

The Stoics gained to their cause most of the learned legists and teachers of jurisprudence. Q. Mutius Scævola, C. Aquillius Gallus, and L. Lucilius Balbus, distinguished compeers of Cicero, were Stoics. So was Servius Sulpicius, and, still another, the younger Cato, who contributed more than any other to the glory of this school among the Romans. At a later period, Seneca, Epictetus, and M. Aurelius Antoninus shed honor on this philosophy by their writings. On the other hand, Pomponius Atticus, the bosom friend of Cicero, and C. Cassius, the conspirator against Cæsar, were Epicureans; while as authors, the Epicurean school could boast Lucretius, the poet, and the sparkling Horace. It was principally, however, by the labors of Cicero, that philosophy became domesticated in the Latin tongue. He claims for himself the merit of being the first to earn for the Latin language the same reputation in philosophy as the Greek had acquired. A glance at the philosophical views of Cicero must suffice for the whole. Early educated in the philosophy of Greece, he owed to Grecian training whatever he had of intellectual culture.* His fame rests, not so much on his political life as on his oratorical efforts and philosophical writings. To philosophy, when the ship of state foundered, he again devotes himself, in his later years, as a last and only resource. His philosophic writings are clear, elegant, popular in cast; never original, but noble in sentiment. He professes to follow the New Academy, yet is something of a Stoic and much a Sceptic. A sober scepticism is the philosophy accordant with his mind. He was eclectic, however, and strictly confined to neither of the three prevalent schools. To the Epicureans, in fact, he was decidedly and unhesitatingly opposed. He wrote for the people, and combined eloquence with philosophy, and especially gives his philosophy a practical turn. As to the great problems discussed by the schools, he either does not thoroughly comprehend them, or thinks them of less difficulty and less importance than they really are, for he passes vaguely and superficially over most of them. With regard to morals, he is clear and earnest; as to physics most uncertain and wavering. He maintains eloquently the doctrines respecting God and the human soul, but yet wavers between belief and doubt as to the popular religion. He takes lofty views of

* Cicero studied philosophy at Athens and at Rhodes. He heard the Epicurean, the Academic, and the Stoic teachers. In later life, he turned again to the study of philosophy, as a resource from the ills of the state; as he touchingly says (Tusc. v. 2), while in the early period of life, our inclination and love of acquisition compelled us to the study of philosophy, so, as a resort from these great calamities, we fly again, tempest-tossed, to the same peaceful harbor from which we wandered forth.

humanity, of virtue as superior to pleasure, of the dignity of human nature, and the excellence of reason; strongly advocates free will. In natural theology, Cicero is clear and decided against the fortuitous or accidental origin of the present well-ordered system of things. As well throw up the letters of the alphabet and expect them to assume, in falling, the shape of the Annals of Ennius (De Nat. Deor. ii. 37). He attaches importance to those opinions and beliefs in matters of theology in which different nations and ages agree (Tusc. i. 13), especially the doctrines of a superintending Providence and the immortality of the soul (Tusc. i. 1. 2, *seq.* 49). He is lofty and eloquent in praise of disinterested virtue (De Fin. ii. 4, v. 22), and the dignity of the human mind (Tusc. i. 24, *seq.*; De Leg. i. 7, *seq.*); of a life devoted not to self alone, but to country and friends (De Offic. i. 7; De Fin. ii. 14); and of philosophy as the guide of life (Tusc. v. 2; Acad. i. 2; De Off. ii. 2).

He defines the morally good—*honestum,* as that which is praiseworthy, *per se:* the τὸ καλόν of the Greeks (De Fin. ii. 14; De Offic. i. 4), and is inclined, with the Stoics, to regard virtue as of itself alone capable of securing happiness—all else being of little worth in comparison with it (De Fin. v. 32; De Offic. iii. 3).

On the whole, we agree with Ritter, that while the philosophical writings of Cicero have had not much influence on, or been much valued by, profounder thinkers, they are the foundation of not only Roman philosophy, but of that of the later church; have had great influence on the opinions of the middle ages, and of the subsequent literature, and have tended powerfully, in a word, to the general enlightenment of mankind.

While disposed to be something of a sceptic in physics, Cicero takes refuge, in matters of practical and ethical moment, in the certainty of our moral consciousness, the universal consent of nations, and those intuitive conceptions which nature has implanted within us. These are to him a satisfactory ground of conviction and confidence, and he does not wish them disturbed by the cavils and questions of the mere sceptic, to whom nothing is sacred, nothing certain. In theology, he would eliminate whatever is mythical and unworthy of belief, but retain as sacred the great truths and beliefs in which all ages and people agree, specially the grand doctrines of a superintending providence, and of immortality. Still he holds even these beliefs not without some hesitation and question.

Virtue—the *honestum*, the τὸ καλον, is instrinsically and *per se* a good; good for its own sake; and is of itself sufficient to secure happiness—though he comes with some hesitation to this position of the Stoics. In common with the Stoics he rejects the πάθη—perturbations, as he calls them—the passions or disturbing forces and impulses of our nature, as unworthy of us, and to be suppressed.

Cicero's highest ideal of government is one embracing the monarchical, aristocratic, and democratic elements. He regards the mass of men as unfit for freedom and self-government. He would allow the practice of consulting auguries, and similar superstitions, in deference to the prevailing popular belief. It is when he comes upon those great moral truths which the consciousness of man affirms, that Cicero rises to his highest and most eloquent utterances.

The character of Cicero is well drawn by Ritter in the following paragraph: "With the nicest knowledge of men and things, without which no orator can be great, he combined a fine sense of justice and benevolence, love for his friends, who remained true to him through the various changes of his fortunes; unwearying diligence, and a shrewd and comprehensive forecast of future events, and the inevitable consequences of the present position of affairs. To be as great as he was brilliant in political life, he only wanted that perfect enthusiasm which is engendered in the mind by confidence in its own resources, and resolute firmness in the moment of action. This, however, is what indeed at all times is most difficult to attain to, but especially in such circumstances and in such an age as that of Cicero, when feeling as he did the clearest conviction that the fortunes of the state were hopeless, such bold resolution could only have been purchased by a calm spirit of self-denial, which was hardly to be expected of the soft and yielding mind of Cicero. We cannot therefore wonder if we see him often wavering, often hesitating and dissatisfied with himself, unable either to encourage hope or to banish fear, ashamed of his unworthy position and ambiguous policy, and yet unable to follow out his own plans of honorable action. His character and career as a politician," Ritter proceeds to remark, "closely accord with the part which he played as a philosopher. The same qualities which procured him splendor in the political world, made him also a brilliant champion and disseminator of philosophic labors; the same defects which, as a statesman, deprived him of the highest praise, also prevented him from being truly great in philosophy. Moreover, all his philosophical labors were mainly dependent on his political life" (Hist. Phil.).

CHAPTER VI.

THE JEWISH-ALEXANDRIAN PHILOSOPHY; AND THE SUBSEQUENT NEO-PLATONISM.

§ 1.—Jewish-Alexandrian Philosophy.

About the beginning of the Christian era, or even earlier, there arose in the East a school of philosophy, mainly theosophic, or theologic, blending the doctrines of of Plato with the Jewish theology—the result, in part, of the general yearning after some more direct and satisfactory knowledge of God than the preceding systems of speculative thought had been able to attain. Such a desire seems to have been very generally felt in the closing period of the ancient, or pre-Christian world. The result of so many systems, and so many ages of patient thought and investigation, was what?—a heartless scepticism. To this had come the brilliant speculations of the greatest thinkers—scepticism—eclecticism. Not satisfied with this result, men turned with restless longing to the systems of Oriental theosophy, to see what, perchance, might be learned in that quarter of the great problems of human thought and human destiny. Chief among these religious systems of the East in practical influence on the Grecian mind was the Jewish theology, as presented in the Hebrew Scriptures, and which, as blended with the lofty idealism of Plato, formed the philosophy known as the Jewish Hellenic, or Jewish-Alexandrian system. In common with the Neo-Platonists, of whom they were in fact the precursors, these philosophers opposed the divine to the earthly, contemning the material and the sensible, holding the descent of the soul from a superior world into the body, requiring an ascetic emancipation of the soul from the bondage of sense, and believing in a divine revelation to man in the state of enthusiasm.

Germs of this philosophy may be seen, though hardly the philosophy itself, in the Septuagint translation of the Hebrew Scriptures; as also in the Second Book of Maccabees, and in the Book of Wisdom (Ueberweg, vol. i. p. 226). Aristobulus, 160 B. C., finds in the Pentateuch the source of much that was taught by Grecian poets and philosophers. He personifies the wisdom of God as an intermediate essence between God and the world, preëxistent before the heavens and the earth. God himself is invisible to the eye of sense not only, but to the eye of the soul. The *nous*, or reason, alone perceives him. It is the divine power or force that governs the world, and not God himself, who is above and beyond all mundane

9*

affairs. The light, which was created on the first day, is symbolic of the wisdom which illuminates all things, and which Solomon, in the Book of Proverbs, has described as existing with God before the Creation. The whole order of the world rests on the number seven.

But it is in Philo the Jew, that the system now under discussion finds its first clear and complete exponent. Philo, whose home was at Alexandria, was descended from an illustrious family, according to Josephus (Antiq. xviii. 8); a sacerdotal one, according to Eusebius (Hist. Eccl. ii. 4). His brother was superintendent of the Alexandrian library. Philo went as ambassador to Rome in 40 A. D., then an old man; so that he was probably born some twenty-five or thirty years B. C. Philo interprets the Scriptures allegorically. His theology is a blending of Platonism and Judaism (Ueberweg, 229). God is the τὸ ὄν, the only true existence, above all knowledge and all virtue; above even the idea of "the good," with which Plato identifies him. He is one and simple, the only free nature, without suffering, grief, or fear; present everywhere by his power though not in his essence. He is the place of the world, for he encompasses and contains all things.

In creating the world, God employs certain ministering agencies or potencies, the chief of which is "the logos," God's wisdom, or son, through whom he creates the world. As the plan of an edifice lies in the mind of the master builder, so the world of ideas lies from eternity in the mind of the logos. He is the mediator between God and man. To imitate God, to become like him, and dwell in him, is the highest duty, as it is the highest blessedness, of man. All other knowledge is valuable only as a preparation for the knowledge of God. The highest aim of philosophy is this knowledge.

The logos doctrine of Philo, while closely resembling that of the gospel of John, in many respects, differs from it, *toto cœlo*, in this respect: that Philo, with his view of the essential baseness and impurity of matter, cannot conceive of the logos as incarnate in the person of Christ, which is the distinctive feature of the Johannean doctrine of the logos.

§ 2.—New Platonism.

The golden age of Grecian philosophy had already passed before the Christian era. Its great names and its illustrious systems were remembered as traditions of a former time. With the advent of Christianity, a new era was ushered in; a new light arose upon the world. Yet not wholly had the speculative spirit and tendency died out. As late as the third and fourth centuries of the Christian era, an effort was made, and with some success, to revive the ancient philosophy—a last and almost despairing attempt, as Schwegler well characterizes it, of the ancient mind, at a philosophy which should solve the great problems of speculative inquiry. The closing period of Grecian philosophy was a revival of Platonism, *Neo-Platonism*, as it was called. Its chief teachers were Plotinus, a pupil of Ammonius Saccas (an Alexandrian philosopher of the third century, founder of the *Neo Platonic* school); born at Lycopolis in Egypt, in 204 A. D., teacher at Rome from 244 to 268, died in Campania, in 269; and Porphyry, his disciple, born in Syria in 232 or 233, educated at Tyre, pupil for a time of Longinus, afterward of Plotinus at Rom where he lived and taught from 262 till his death, about 304 A. D., a clear and vigorous writer, author of several treatises, mainly expositions of the writings of Plato and Aristotle, and of the system of Plotinus. Iamblichus, disciple of Porphyry, a native of Chalcis, in Cœle-Syria, and Proclus, born at Constantinople about 411, disciple of Plutarch at Athens, were also eminent as Neo-Platonists.

The latter was the most distinguished of the later Neo-Platonists, and taught with much success at Athens, where he died 485 A. D. He collected the whole body of transmitted philosophy, arrayed it in systematic form, and added what he deemed wanting to its completeness. The doctrines of Plotinus and the Neo-Platonists continued to be taught at Athens, till the final closing of the school, by order of the Emperor Justinian, in 529, who interdicted the further teaching of philosophy at Athens.

The practical tendency of the school was to mysticism. Magic, sorcery, divine illumination, ability to foresee the future, were claimed and professed. The scepticism of the previous and closing period of Grecian philosophic thought, led to unrest, and a vague yearning for something which should better satisfy the craving of the mind for solid and tangible reality. Christianity supplied this want. Neo-Platonism sought to do it, in another way, by mystical absorption into Deity. God, say the Neo-Platonists, is the primal essence, or first principle, the One, the Good, the First; not itself the *νοῦς*—the reason, nor yet *νοητόν*, to be known by the reason, but infinitely exalted above that. Superior to all being, to all thinking and willing and energy, this primordial principle needs nothing, desires nothing. Neither life, nor being, nor action, can be predicated of it. It can neither be expressed, nor thought. The world is the emanation or effluence of this first principle. As the sun radiates light, as fire emits heat, so this principle sends forth from itself that which is eternal—the reason, *νοῦς*, its own image. From this again emanates the world soul, from which in turn the material, sensible world proceeds—the transcript of the former, as that was the image and emanation of the *νοῦς*. Individual souls, like the world-soul, partake both of the rational and the sensible, having their proper home in the rational world, from which they came, and to which all their aspirations should ever tend. By means of virtue, and that immediate intuition of God which is the soul's prerogative, it may become mystically one with him, and thus return to him. The system, especially as developed by Plotinus, is manifestly a modification of the Platonic doctrine of ideas, from which it does not essentially differ, though not in all respects the same. Iamblichus seems to have derived his doctrines, however, rather from Pythagoras than Plato; while the later Neo-Platonists, as represented by Proclus, diverge yet more widely from the doctrine of Plotinus, as to the order of creation, or emanation from the primordial unity—a multitude of unities being supposed to proceed from this first principle, instead of the νοῦς, or reason, of Plotinus; from which unities again proceed a triad of creative and formative essences. The soul is in its very nature eternal, occupies a middle rank between the sensuous and the divine, and is endowed with freedom of will. Matter, in itself, is neither good nor evil.

PART II.

MODERN PHILOSOPHY.

CHAPTER I.

INTRODUCTORY.

THE SCHOLASTIC PHILOSOPHY OF THE MIDDLE AGES.

WE have traced, in the previous pages, the progress of speculative thought, from its rise among the early Greeks of the Ionian and Pythagorean schools, through its meridian of Platonic splendor, to its decline and final disappearance with the Neo-Platonism of the first Christian centuries. The philosophy of the church fathers of the early centuries, was more properly a *theology* than a philosophy, and has its place, therefore, in the history of church doctrine, rather than in the history of speculative thought. As such, it is fully treated by ecclesiastical historians. It cannot, however, be denied, that the theology of the early church was very largely modified—whether for good or ill, may possibly admit of question—by the philosophy of the preceding Grecian schools, more especially by the Platonic and Neo-Platonic doctrines, and to some extent by the philosophy of Aristotle. This is specially the case with Justin Martyr—150 A. D.—a disciple of the Stoic and Platonic philosophy before he became a Christian, and who ascribes whatever of truth is contained in the writings of

Grecian philosophers and poets to the influence of the divine *logos*, present in them, and in all men, partially, but revealed in his complete fulness only in Christ. Socrates, Heraclitus, and others of the Greeks, living in communion with the logos, and inciting men to a better knowledge of the true God, Justin regards as Christians, though they may not have been so called. Much of the theology of Plato he regards as in reality borrowed from the Jewish Scriptures. Even Tertullian, A. D. 160, who, in his opposition to the philosophic tendency, goes so far as to adopt the irrational proposition "*Credo quia absurdum,*" still held many opinions in common with the Stoics, and highly esteemed the writings of Seneca.

Clement of Alexandria and Origen—185–254 A. D.—show very clearly, in their writings, the influence of the Grecian philosophy, especially that of Plato, whose doctrine of preëxistence was held by Origen. Clement, like Justin, held the Grecian philosophers, as well as the wise men of other times and nations, to have been under the guidance of the divine logos, and philosophy itself as a guide to righteousness (Strom. vii. 2, i. 5, vi. 5).

Among the Latin fathers, Augustine—354–430—carries the Platonic spirit into the discussion of Christian doctrine; and even anticipates Descartes in placing as the immovable foundation of all our knowledge *the consciousness of our own mental processes* (Soliloquia, ii. 1). The very doubt implies the existence of the doubter. The same principle is maintained in several of his most important treatises, as in the De Vera Religione (72, 73), and in the De Trinitate (x. 14, xiv. 7). As with Plato, the idea of the good, or God, is the highest of ideas and the most complete form of being, comprehending in itself all others and crowning all; so with Augustine, God is the *summa essentia,* eternal and unchangeable. The soul is immaterial and immortal; possesses the faculties of memory, intellect, and will, under which latter term the passions and sensibilities are included; and partakes of immortality by virtue of its union with the eternal reason and the divine life —a sentiment closely analogous to the arguments of Plato in the Republic and in the Phædo.

If, as already stated, the philosophy of the early church fathers may more properly be called a theology, and relegated as such to the department of ecclesiastic or dogmatic history, so on the other hand the Scholastic philosophy, so called, of the Middle Ages, may be characterized in brief as philosophy made subservient to theology. Scholasticism was, in a word, philosophy subordinated to the doctrines of the church, and made to do service in their behalf, as the handmaid of religion. Some indeed, as Scotus Erigena, maintained the essential identity of religion and philosophy, and sought to bring the doctrines of the church into harmony with reason and philosophy. Still in the main, and by far the larger number of the Scholastics, the dogmas of the church were held as above the reach of speculation, and when there was any conflict, real or seeming, between the two, philosophy must give way to faith. The doctrine of the church, and not reason, was held to be the standard. Johannes Scotus, or Erigena—about 800 A. D., is the earliest Scholastic philosopher of note. He was born and educated in Ireland, then called Scotia Major; whence the epithet Scotus by which he is designated. He was subsequently called to Paris, and placed at the head of the court school. His conceptions are decidedly Platonic, or Neo-Platonic and mystic. With him true philosophy and true religion are one; and the authority of the church fathers is hardly surpassed by that of Scripture itself. God, the creating and uncreated being, alone has real subsistence; he alone truly is. He is the essence of all things, the beginning and end of all (De Div. Nat. i. 3, 12). Among created natures are some which themselves have creative power; viz., *ideas*, which are the archetypes or prototypes of things, the first causes of individual existences. These ideas are contained in the divine wisdom or word, *i. e.*, the Son; and the influence of the Holy Ghost, or divine love, causes these ideas to develop into the external forms of nature (De Div. Nat. ii. 19). The creation from nothing is out of God's own incomprehensible essence (iii. 19); a procession through the primordial causes into the world of visible creatures; and this procession is an eternal act (iii. 17). God is the substance of all finite things; our life is God's life in us (i. 10). God descends to the finite, not in the act of incarnation alone, but in all created existence. All things ultimately return to God, and repose in him (ii. 2). This view of God as the universal substance, the one existence, the all in all, it need hardly be remarked, is so clearly analogous to that of Spinoza, that it might almost be pronounced identical with it. The doctrine of ideas as creative powers residing in the divine being is manifestly of Platonic origin.

Nominalism, in distinct opposition to realism, first appears in the latter part of the eleventh century. According to this theory, genera and species are to be regarded as only collections of individuals, possessing the same characteristics and called by the same name; having no real existence therefore, the only real existence being the individuals which constitute the class or collection. And in like manner all general or universal terms are to be regarded as names or terms only, and not, as Plato taught, real existences. One of the most famous, though not indeed the first who advocated this doctrine was *Roscellinus*, a native of Brittany, in the latter part of the eleventh century, a distinguished teacher, one of whose pupils was the youthful Abelard. He applied the doctrine of nominalism to the church dogma of the trinity, and so became involved in controversy with the ecclesiastical authorities, thus bringing nominalism itself into disrepute. If, said his opponents, only individuals have real existence, then the three persons of the Trinity are three individuals or three Gods; that, or else they have no existence. This Roscellinus admits; but is compelled by the Council of Soissons, in 1092, to retract. He still adhered, however, to the principle of nominalism. This principle was revived and more successfully advocated in the fourteenth century by William of Occam. The doctrine of Roscellinus was vigorously opposed by *Anselm* and also by *Abelard*, both philosophers of note.

Anselm, born 1033, at Aosta in Piedmont, prior of a convent in Normandy in 1063, Archbishop of Canterbury, England, from 1093 till his death in 1109, was a bold and earnest champion of the church and its dogmas. The creed was to be the final test and absolute standard of truth, and no questions asked. *Credo,* UT *intelligam,* was his motto. His fundamental principle is that knowledge must rest on faith, and that in matters of faith the authority of the church is supreme. Yet he seeks to establish on rational grounds the essential doctrines of the Christian faith, as the Divine Existence, the Trinity, the Incarnation, and Atonement. The latter he regards as satisfaction to the divine justice. With Anselm, goodness, truth, virtue, et cetera possess *real existence,* independent of individual beings, and not merely immanent in the latter. On this realistic basis he builds a proof of the divine existence, on the ground that all merely relative good implies an absolute good, a *summum bonum,* and that is God.

The celebrated argument for the divine existence drawn from the conception of God as the most perfect being, and as therefore possessing necessary existence, can hardly be pronounced logical. True, the attribute of necessary existence may pertain to the most perfect being, as conceived by our minds. But do we know that such a being really exists? If so, then he possesses this attribute. In other words, *if there is* such a being, then he exists in this particular manner, to wit, by necessity of his nature. But the question of his real existence remains undecided (See

Ueberweg, Hist. Phil. vol. i. p. 384). The validity of the argument was called in question at the time by Gaunilo, a monk, and has been much debated since.

The nominalistic doctrine of Roscellinus was also opposed by *Abelard,* born 1074 in Nantes, in France, a pupil of Roscellinus. He taught at Paris from 1102 to 1136, and died at the priory of St. Marcel in 1142. He is justly regarded as the father of the Scholastic philosophy of the Middle Ages, and is chiefly distinguished for his rigorous application of dialectic or logic to theological reasoning. He tends, it may be said, to rationalism, rather than the opposite extreme of credulity, in matters of religious belief. In the main a nominalist, he still avoids the extreme view of that doctrine as well as of realism. The universal exists, he would say, not in words as such, but with reference to their significations or *conceptions.* These conceptions existed in the divine mind before the creation of the external objects to which they relate. In opposition to the "credo *ut* intelligam" of Anselm, he holds that rational insight must precede and prepare the way for faith. Like Augustine, he takes a monotheistic, in opposition to a tritheistic view of the trinity, as held by Roscellinus. He affirms the *generic unity* of the three divine persons; whereas Roscellinus maintained the independent existence of each, as three beings, *tres substantiæ.* Abelard on the contrary likens the three persons to the three parts of a syllogism, together constituting one syllogism (Introd. ad Theol. ii. p. 1078). In ethics, he maintains the doctrine that the morality of an act consists in the intention, and that actions as such are indifferent. Sin is, properly speaking, a *voluntary* error. The propensity to evil which we inherit is not itself sin. Only the consenting to evil is sin; only that which is in conflict with our own moral consciousness. In these respects the views of Abelard were far in advance of the theology and philosophy of his age.

In the later period of Scholastic philosophy, the doctrines of Aristotle became predominant as the approved method of explaining the doctrines of the church. So with Alexander of Hales, who died 1245, and Albertus Magnus, a Dominican monk of the same century, educated at Paris and Padua, teacher at Paris and Cologne, and from 1260 to 1262, bishop of Ravensburg; called "the Great" from his extensive erudition. He was the first to reproduce in systematic order the whole philosophy of Aristotle, in a series of commentaries and expositions, modifying the system to suit the ecclesiastical dogmas. But though an Aristotelian, still Platonism exerted no little influence over his mind. His knowledge of Aristotle seems to have been mainly through the channel of Latin translations, from the Arabian commentators and from the Greek. He teaches that not only the *nous* of Aristotle is distinct from the body, and immortal, but also with it the inferior mental faculties. He held the freedom of the will as the basis of moral action; and viewed the doctrine of the Trinity as one not to be treated by rational and philosophic theology.

Thomas Aquinas, born 1225, near Aquino, in the territory of Naples; educated in the convent of Monte Casino; a monk of the Dominican order; pupil of Albert the Great; became teacher of theology and philosophy at Cologne, Paris, Naples; died 1274.

He brought the Scholastic philosophy to its highest development, uniting the Aristotelian doctrines to those of the orthodox church. He wrote commentaries on Aristotle, and treatises of theology, of which the Summa Theologiæ is one of the most noted. With him, as with Aristotle, the supreme end of life is knowledge, especially the knowledge of God. He is a realist in the Aristotelian sense. The universal exists in the individual, not independently; only by the mental process of abstraction is it separated from the individual. In the Divine mind also, the universal exists, as the thought of God, before He creates. But not independently do ideas exist, either in the Divine mind or elsewhere.

Aquinas reaches the proof of the Divine existence by the *a posteriori* method. The chain of causes cannot be infinite. The order of the world shows an orderer. The world is not eternal; yet its non-eternity does not admit of demonstration. The soul, including the intellect with its various faculties, is immaterial; for it thinks not the individual merely but the universal. It is not preëxistent; and has no innate conceptions. The will depends on the understanding. What seems good is willed. The necessity which thus accrues is not the necessity of compulsion, but is true freedom. We have the power of choice, and yielding ourselves to one or another class of ideas it is in our power to control our own decisions and shape our characters. Yet in order to right action we need divine help. In the division of the virtues into ethical and dianœtic, Aquinas follows Aristotle, adding however to the philosophical the theölogical virtues, faith, love, and hope. The good is good, not *because* God commands it, but *he commands it because it is good;* a distinction of highest importance in ethical science.

Another distinguished Scholastic teacher was Johannes Duns Scotus, born in Dunston, Northumberland, or in Dun in the north of Ireland, it is uncertain which; a monk of the Franciscan order; a teacher first at Oxford, afterward at Paris, and Cologne, where he died in 1308, at the age of thirty-four. He was an opponent of Thomas Aquinas and his system, and became the founder of a school in theology and philosophy which bore his name. His position is rather that of a critic than a dogmatist, assailing the weak points of other systems, rather than establishing positions of his own. Philosophy is with him only the submissive and unquestioning handmaid of theology. That which the church teaches is to be received with implicit trust; the arguments by which these teachings and dogmas are enforced, the proofs drawn from reason and philosophy to sustain these doctrines, may be called in question, and should be viewed with distrust. Indeed, the principal doctrines of religion cannot be demonstrated to be true on rational grounds, but must be received by faith as matters of divine revelation. Not only the doctrine of the Trinity, the Incarnation and Atonement, and other like dogmas of the Christian faith, but also the Creation from nothing, and the immortality of the soul, are beyond the power of reason to establish, but can only be rendered more or less probable aside from revelation. Still there is no necessary antagonism between faith and reason. His position is not unlike that of Kant in respect to these matters. Rejecting much of the reasoning employed to prove the existence of God and the immortality of the soul, he bases the evidence of these truths on the moral nature of man (compare Ueberweg, vol. i. p. 459).

The *authority of the church* is, however, with Duns Scotus, as not with Kant, the final court of appeal. While in the main an Aristotelian, Duns Scotus is by no means a blind follower of the great Stagirite, but sits also at the feet of the Platonic and Neo-Platonic philosophy. His notions respecting matter and form are of this source. As regards the human will, it is not determined by the understanding, but is free and self-determining, and this power of self-determination is the ground of the merit which attaches to right conduct. The will, not the intellect, is the grand moving agent in the realm of the human soul. "*Voluntas est superior intellectu,*" is with him a fundamental proposition in psychology. In common with Thomas Aquinas, Scotus rejects the theory of innate knowledge. Unlike him, he makes the arbitrary will of Deity the ground of right. The good is good, simply because He commands it.

Contemporary or nearly so with the distinguished teachers last mentioned, were *Roger Bacon*, 1214–1244, and *Raymond Lully*, 1234–1315, both names of honor in the realm of letters and philosophy. *William of Occam* followed; born in the county of Surrey, England; of the Franciscan order; pupil of Duns Scotus; afterward teacher at Paris; died in 1347. A stout opponent of the doctrine of realism, he is regarded as the renewer of nominalism. Universals are a mere conception of the human mind; only the individual is real. He carried, even farther than Duns Scotus, the destructive criticism which calls in question or rejects the arguments from reason in defence of the doctrines of religion. He even denies that there are *any* theological doctrines that can be established by reason alone, aside from revelation and church authority.

In the 14th and 15th centuries, Platonism was revived by the mystics of Germany, under the lead of Eckhart of Strasburg (1250), a Dominican, who taught at Paris, was called to Rome and advanced to high honors, and afterward appointed Vicar-General of Saxony and Bohemia. His doctrines awakened opposition; he was brought before the tribunal of the Inquisition at Cologne; appealed to the Pope, by whom a bull was issued condemning a large number of his doctrines; but before the publication of the same, Eckhart died, 1329. The psychology of Eckhart was in the main that of Thomas Aquinas and of Augustine. In theology his fundamental principle seems to be the idea of the equality in essence of the soul with God. So far from rejecting the aid of reason, in establishing matters of faith, as preceding teachers had done, he maintains the absolute supremacy of reason. It is by theoretical knowledge that we become partakers of the divine knowledge. The highest function of the reason is, however, an immediate intuition of truth and of God, as Plato and the Neo-Platonists had taught. The will is made, by Eckhart, subordinate to the faculty of knowledge, precisely the opposite of the doctrine of Scotus. Knowledge is a union of subject with object. The Absolute, or Deity, is without personality, and is distinguished from God, who is contained in the former—the Godhead and God being thus regarded as distinct. The Godhead is above all understanding and comprehension, and cannot be revealed. God acts, and can reveal himself. The eternal Godhead, as the beginning and end of all things, remains in eternal obscurity. The one Divine nature, in the act or process of self-knowledge, develops into a Trinity of persons. The subject in this process is the Father; the object, or the Divine nature thus contemplated, is the Son, and the delight and love awakened by this contemplation is the Spirit—a theory of the Trinity which has been received in Germany in more recent times. The whole system savors strongly of mysticism and fanciful speculation; but the object of Eckhart and his followers was doubtless to present the doctrines of religion, and also of the schools, in such a way as to touch and impress the hearts of the people. And in this they seem to have succeeded.

CHAPTER II.

BACON AND THE INDUCTIVE SYSTEM.

THE Scholastic philosophy, however powerful in its time, could not always hold in subjection the human mind. Its servile submission to the authority of the Catholic Church as a tribunal and court of appeal above reason; its elaborate and ingenious word-quibbling, to which the whole science of dialectic had in its hands become degraded, could not always endure. Men were beginning to detect the cheat, to inquire for truth, to demand some fruit of all this immense erudition of doctors "seraphic," doctors "subtile," and doctors "invincible." Men were beginning to think for themselves independently of ecclesiastical dictation and the authority of the fathers.

At this juncture arose one whose writings were destined to create a revolution in science and philosophy, and turn the thoughts of men into new channels of investigation. And while his own researches lay chiefly in the domain of physical science, as the field then most neglected and most needing to be cultivated, yet his method was one which applied equally to the whole realm of knowledge and his plan, vast and far-reaching, embraced the whole. It would be an imperfect and incorrect survey of the history of speculative thought, which should omit the name of Francis Bacon, or fail to assign him a place as the illustrious precursor of that reformation in philosophy, hardly less remarkable than the religious reformation which followed.

Francis Bacon was born, January 22, 1561, at York House, in the Strand, London, of honorable parentage. He was the youngest son of Sir Nicholas Bacon, Lord Keeper of the Seals, who held that office, with rank of Chancellor, for twenty years under Elizabeth. His mother was a daughter of Sir Antony Coke, known as a linguist of some repute. Born at a time when the arts and sciences were beginning to be more generally and more thoroughly cultivated, and endowed by nature with rare gifts, he has been well described by one of his biographers as "an original genius, formed not to receive implicit notions of thinking and reasoning from what was admitted and taught before him ; but to prescribe laws himself, in the empire of learning, to his own and succeeding ages." * He was educated at Cambridge under Whitgift, afterward Archbishop of Canterbury, having entered Trinity College in his twelfth year. His progress was so rapid, that before he was sixteen he had already "run through the whole circle of the liberal arts as they were then taught ;" and had begun even then to perceive the unsatisfactory nature of the

* Life of Lord Bacon prefixed to his Works. English edition. 5 vols., folio. 1778.

philosophy then prevalent. While yet quite young indeed' Queen Elizabeth, discerning the genius of the boy, took delight in plying him with questions, and was so much pleased with the readiness and manliness of his replies hat she used to call him playfully her young Lord Keeper.

Having been left with but small inheritance at the death of his father, he devoted himself to the study of law as a profession, in which he soon rose to eminence. He was appointed by Elizabeth her counsel extraordinary, but owing to the secret opposition of his kinsman Cecil, secretary of state, he was not at first raised to any office of emolument. Essex, however, was his friend, and conferred on him a fine estate. In 1605, two years after the death of Elizabeth, Bacon published his great work, "The Advancement of Learning," the aim of which was to survey the whole extent of the intellectual realm, both those fields which had been cultivated, and those which had not, and to ascertain, if possible, what might be done to improve and complete the one and to supply the want of the other. This work he afterward translated into Latin. How closely the aim and purport of this work resembles that which Aristotle in like manner laid out for himself, the student of history need hardly be reminded.

After the accession of James, the fortunes of Bacon, notwithstanding the enmity of Sir Edward Coke, attorney-general, and of Cecil, steadily improved. In 1607 he was made solicitor-general, and in 1613, attorney-general. In 1617 he was intrusted with the keeping of the seals, and in 1619 was promoted to the dignity of Lord High Chancellor; a post to which he had long aspired as the height of his ambition. Shortly after he was created Baron of Verulam, a title which he afterward exchanged for that of Viscount St. Albans.

Though now possessing a liberal income, he seems to have been negligent of financial matters and destitute of economy. His dependents squandered his fortune; and thus the foundation was laid for subsequent troubles which led ultimately to his ruin.

But neither the weight and pressure of public business, nor the dazzling honors of his position, could divert a mind like his from the true end of his life, the study of philosophy. Already in 1610 he had published his second great work, "The Wisdom of the Ancients." In 1620, the year following his appointment as Lord High Chancellor, his "Novum Organum" appeared, the second part of the "Instauratio Magna"; a work which he had been engaged for twelve years in elaborating and polishing (Life of B. prefixed to London edition of his works, 1778, vol. i. p. 23); according to others, thirty years. Rawley speaks of having seen twelve autographs of the work "wrought up and improved year by year, till it reached the shape in which it was published (Hallam—Literature of Europe, vol. iii. p. 38). And Bacon himself, in his dedication of the work to King James, says that he had "been about some such work near thirty years, so as I made no haste. And the reason why I have published it now, specially being imperfect, is, to speak plainly, because I number my days and would have it saved." (Works, as above, vol. iii. p. 584). He seems to have written with an eye to the future, for he assures his majesty, "I account your favor may be to this work as much as an hundred years time; for I am persuaded the work will gain upon men's minds in ages, but your gracing it may make it take hold more swiftly."

The close of Bacon's career was far less brilliant and commanding than his course had been. His sun was destined to go down under a cloud. He was accused of receiving bribes in his official capacity, nor was the charge perhaps wholly without foundation. That he had ever allowed himself to be influenced in his decisions by presents thus received there is no evidence, nor that in receiving such gifts he had done more than was the custom of the time. The government of James was notoriously corrupt; and that monarch, compelled by pressure of public sentiment to sacrifice either his Lord Chancellor or his favorite minister Buckingham, the author of all the troubles, preferred to give up Bacon as a scapegoat in order to save himself and the guilty favorite. He would not even allow Lord Bacon to be present at his own trial before parliament, lest he might too successfully defend himself, promising his royal word that if he would remain silent he would screen him from punishment and reward him with favor. The sentence was severe, the noble Lord Chancellor, full of years and honors, was rudely stripped of all his dignities and offices, condemned to inprisonment, and heavily fined. The king partially redeemed his pledge, by restoring him to liberty after short imprisonment, and remitting his fine, but permitted his faithful servant to pass the remainder of his days in penury, obscurity, and disgrace. He died in 1626, about five years after his dishonor, at the age of sixty-six, and was buried in the church of St. Nicholas, near St. Alban's.

Although, as already intimated, the researches of Bacon were more particularly directed to the department of physical science, as then demanding investigation, because most in the back-ground, still his plan embraced the whole realm of philosophy, and his principle was applicable to mental and moral, no less than physical science. That principle was the *inductive method of observation and experience,* as the only valid basis of conclusions and ground of true science. In this he set himself in opposition to the Scholastic philosophy, then, and for a long time previously, in vogue which, relying chiefly on the deductive or syllogistic method of reasoning, and employing itself for the most part in fruitless discussions relating often to the meaning of words, had shown itself for ages barren of useful result, and had in all this widely departed from the spirit of Aristotle, while yet claiming to be the method and philosophy of that great master. This whole method of the schools Bacon resolutely and vigorously assails, and in so doing considers himself as opposing Aristotle. How far the Baconian or inductive method really differs from that of Aristotle himself, may admit of question; that it differs *toto cœlo* from that of Aristotle, as represented by the schoolmen of the middle ages, there can be no question. His merit as a philosopher lies chiefly in having called back the human mind from the wrong direction in which it had so long been seeking knowledge, and setting it on a new path of investigation. This, rather than any brilliant discoveries made by himself in science, constitutes his great merit and achievement. Yet this, in itself, has revolutionized the thinking of the world. We cannot agree with Schwegler, that "strictly speaking, we can allow no *content* to the Baconian Philosophy" (Hist. Phil. p. 167). The method is itself a content of inestimable value. The progress of science, the rapid advance of the human mind in every department of useful knowledge for the two hundred and fifty years since the publication of that method, is its content; and surely it is a sufficient one. In physical science at least, though not perhaps in the realm of speculative thought, in the outer if not in the inner and spiritual world, to Bacon belongs the honor, now generally accorded to him, of being the father of modern philosophy.

The chief work on which his fame as a philosopher will ever rest is the "Novum Organum," the second part of his "Instauratio Magna." The object of this was to furnish the world a better mode of investigation of truth, that is, a better logic than the so-called Aristotelian, or syllogistic method; a logic of which the aim should be not to supply arguments for controversy, but to investigate nature, and, by observation and the complete induction of particulars, arrive at truth. It was designed to be, as he expresses it, "the science of a better and more perfect use of reason in the investigation of things, and of the true aids of the understanding." In its present shape it is rather a summary of topics, or theses, which it was his intention to treat more fully, than a complete and final statement; and of the nine topics of which he proposes to speak in the second book, we have only the first, the other eight not being discussed at all. He lays out the programme as follows. "And so we will speak in the first place of prerogative instances; secondly, of the aids of induction; thirdly, of the rectification of induction; fourthly, of varying the investigation according to the nature of the subject; fifthly, of prerogative natures as regards investigation, or of what shall be first inquired into, and what afterward; sixthly, of the limits of inquiry, or the synopsis of all natures in the world; seventhly, on the application to practice, or concerning what is in relation to man; eighthly, on the preparations for inquiry; and lastly, on the scale, ascending and descending, of axioms" (Lib. ii. Aphor. xxi.). Of these the first only is taken up; the rest are wanting.

The Novum Organum, as we have it, is in two books, both consisting of aphorisms, or detached sentences. The first book contains, among other things, an enumeration or classification of the various illusions or fallacies which deceive the mind—*idola,* as he calls them—"idola et notiones falsæ, quæ intellectum humanum jam occuparunt" (Aphorism xxxviii. lib. i.). These are *idola tribus,* illusions or fallacies of the race, such as pertain to human nature itself; "fundata in ipsâ naturâ humanâ, atque in ipsâ tribu, seu gente hominum" (Aph. xli.); *idola specus,* fallacies of the individual man; *idola fori,* fallacies arising from the intercourse of man with his fellows, and especially from the use of words; *idola theatri,* fallacies arising from false systems of philosophy and incorrect rules of reasoning—"ex diversis dogmatibus philosophiarum, ac etiam ex perversis legibus demonstrationum" (Lib. i. Aphor. xliv.).

The second book contains the new logic or rules for

the interpretation of nature after the inductive method; consisting mainly of the prerogative instances above mentioned—"*prærogativæ instantiarum*" (Lib. ii. Aphor. xxi.), or the phenomena to which our inquiries should be specially directed in the study of nature.

The prominence given by Bacon to natural philosophy, or natural science, in his whole discussion of the inductive method, and the fact that all his illustrations are drawn from that source, have led to the question whether he really intended to include the realm of mind, as well as external nature, among the objects to which the logic of induction is applicable. He has himself decided this matter. "One may doubt, not to say object, whether it is natural philosophy alone that we speak of perfecting by our method, or other sciences as well—logic, ethics, politics. But we certainly intend what has been said as applicable to all; and as the common logic which governs by syllogism pertains not only to natural but to all sciences, so also our own, which proceeds by induction embraces all" (Lib. i. Aphor. cxxvii.).

The Novum Organum constitutes, as already stated, the second part of the Instauratio Magna, of which the treatise on the advancement of learning, "De Dignitate et Augmentis Scientiarum," in nine books, forms the first part. The third part of this grand design is entitled, "Preparation (parasceue) for history, natural and experimental; or a description of natural and experimental history, such as may suffice and be in order for the basis and foundation of true philosophy" (Insta. Mag., pars tertia) This is rather a survey and outline of the vast field to be explored than an actual exploration of it; a sketch or chart of what is to be done in this department of knowledge. A field so vast it was not for any one mind, however comprehensive, to explore. He gives a catalogue of one hundred and thirty particular histories, which are necessary to the completion of this part of his grand work;

as, for instance, a history of the celestial bodies, of the configuration of the heavens, of comets, of meteors, of lightnings, of winds, of clouds, of rain, hail, snow, etc., etc., including in the list a history of the natures and powers of numbers and of figures (Works, vol. iv. p. 397–400). A few of these he has himself sketched, as illustrations or samples of the proper method of inquiry; as, for example, a treatise on the history of winds, one on the history of life and death, another on sound and hearing.

The fourth part of his great work is entitled "Scala Intellectus, sive Filum Labyrinthi"—of which only the opening pages were ever completed.

A fifth part was contemplated, which should furnish a specimen of the new philosophy after the inductive method, or as he calls it, "Anticipationes Philosophiæ Secundæ." A perfect system of philosophy according to the inductive method, forming a sixth part, would be necessary fully to complete the grand design of this Instauratio Magna; but this Bacon had never expected to accomplish. "To perfect this last part," he says, "is above our powers and beyond our hopes. We may, as we trust, make no despicable beginnings: The destinies of the human race must complete it" (Distributio Operis, Works, vol. iv. p. 13). "Such," in the beautiful language of Hallam, "was the temple which Bacon saw in vision before him: the stately front and decorated pediments, in all their breadth of light and harmony of proportion; while long vistas of receding columns and glimpses of internal splendor revealed a glory that it was not permitted him to comprehend" (Literature of Europe, vol. iii. p. 37).

In the above sketch of his great work, the "Instauratio Magna," I have spoken more at length of the "Novum Organum," as the more important of the several portions which compose the grand whole, that in which the spirit of the Baconian system is more distinctively and fully expressed. The treatise De Augmentis is by no means, however, to be overlooked. In this, Bacon divides human learning into history, poetry, and philosophy, according to the several faculties of the mind involved, viz., memory, imagination, and reason. By poetry he understands fictitious narrative only. Philosophy relates to God, to nature, and to man. Natural philosophy he divides into speculative and practical; the former again into physics and metaphysics, the former having to do with material and efficient causes, the latter with formal and final causes. Philosophy, as it relates to man, is concerned with the intellectual and moral faculties, and comprises the sciences of logic and ethics, as related to the human reason, and the human will, respectively. These sciences cover a wider territory, however, than it is usual now to assign them. The former—logic—contains whatever pertains to the human intellect: the art of inventing, judging, retaining and delivering the conceptions of the mind." The latter—ethics—comprises whatever relates to the sensibilities and the will. "Altera decreta, altera actiones progignit." The main division of moral science is into the nature of good, and the rules by which the will may be conformed to that which is good, which latter he calls "the Georgics of the mind." The essence of good he makes to consist in seeking the good of the whole, rather than of the individual.

The mind of Bacon, far as it towers above that of the race, is not without its individual blemishes. He is no mathematician, and knows little of geometry. The pure mathematics he depreciates. He would have mathematics and logic "to be the serving-maids of physical philosophy." His fondness for metaphor and analogies sometimes carries him to excess in that direction. His phraseology is sometimes affected, his style obscure, and his arguments fanciful. In the laying out of his work he proposes more than he has achieved, or could possibly achieve. These things are often said of him, and these things are true of him. These defects may have impaired, as Brucker supposes, the influence of his writings upon the public mind. By philosophers and men of science, especially on the continent, he was at once appreciated. Richelieu speaks of him in the highest terms. Gassendi was an ardent admirer. The De Augmentis was published in France the year after its publication in England, and was translated into French a few years after. Three editions of that work, and three of the Novum Organum appeared in Holland within forty years of their first appearance in England. Leibnitz and Puffendorf are loud in his praise, as the reviver of true philosophy. Bayle calls him one of the greatest men of his age. It was not till near the close of the seventeenth century, however, that he began to be specially honored in Great Britain, and even then it was chiefly by natural philosophers that his works were studied. Hallam even ventures the suggestion "that more have read Lord Bacon within these thirty years than in the two preceding centuries"; and that the fashion of referring to brilliant passages of his works, "at least in books designed for the general reader, is not much older than the close of the last century" (Lit. Eur., vol. iii. p. 73).

Referring to the fact that in the Novum Organum not a single example is given from moral philosophy, and only a single one from mental science or logic, the same writer very justly remarks, "we must constantly remember that the philosophy of Bacon was left exceedingly incomplete. Many lives would not have sufficed for what he had planned, and he gave only the leisure hours of his own. It is evident that he had turned his thoughts to physical philosophy rather for an exercise of his reasoning faculties, and out of his insatiable thirst for knowledge, than from any peculiar aptitude for their subjects, much less any advantage of opportunity for their cultivation. He was more eminently the philosopher of human, than of general nature. Hence he is exact as well as profound in all his reflections on civil life and mankind; while his conjectures in natural philosophy, though often very acute, are apt to wander far from the truth, in consequence of his defective acquaintance with the phenomena of nature. His "Centuries of Natural History" give abundant proof of this. He is, in all these inquiries, like one doubtfully, and by degrees, making out a distant prospect, but often deceived by the haze. And if we compare what may be found in the sixth, seventh, and eighth books De Augmentis, in the Essays, the History of Henry VII., and the various short treatises contained in his works on moral and political wisdom, and on human nature, from experience of which all such wisdom is drawn, with the Rhetoric, Ethics, and Politics of Aristotle, or with the historians most celebrated for their deep insight into civil society and human character—with Thucydides, Tacitus, Philip De Comines, Machiavel, Davila, Hume—we shall, I think, find that one man may almost be compared with all of these together" (Literature of Europe, vol. iii. p. 66).

Perhaps it is not too much to say with Dugald Stewart, that "in the whole history of letters, no other individual can be mentioned whose exertions have had so indisputable an effect in forwarding the intellectual progress of mankind" (Life of Reid, sec. 2; quoted also by Hallam).

It is not without emotion that we read in the last will of this great but unfortunate man, these touching words: "First, I bequeath my soul and body into the hands of God by the blessed oblation of my Saviour; the one at the time of my dissolution, the other at the time of my resurrection. For my burial I desire it may be in St. Michael's Church, near St. Albans: there was my mother buried. . . . . . . For my name and memory, I leave it to men's charitable speeches, and to foreign nations, and the next ages" (Works, vol. iii. p. 677).

CHAPTER III.

RENÉ DESCARTES.

In order rightly to estimate the man to whom, more than any other, belongs the honor of being the founder of modern philosophy, we must know something of the *age* to which he belonged, something of the *man* personally, something of his *system*, something of the *impress* and *effect* of the man and his system on other minds and ages.

§ 1.—The Age.

The close of the sixteenth century, and the beginning of the seventeenth, were a transition period in the history of philosophy and the progress of human thought. The philosophy of Aristotle, which, in one form or another, for two thousand years had held sway over the minds of men, keeping its throne and state amid all the commotions and changes of empire, itself unshaken and undisturbed by the rise and fall of nations, was now in its decadence, fast losing its hold upon the mind of the age. Through the whole sixteenth century, in fact, this process had been going on. Nothing in the history of mind is more remarkable than this prevalence, for so long a period, of the Scholastic philosophy. "For more than five centuries," says a somewhat too ardent eulogist of Descartes, "this philosopher—*i. e.*, Aristotle—attacked, proscribed, adored, excommunicated; always victor, dictated to the nations what they should believe." "From the age of Aristotle to that of Descartes, I perceive a desert of two thousand years, where original thought loses itself, as a river which perishes in the sands, or hides itself in the earth, and reappears, a thousand leagues away, under new skies and in another land."* If these state-

* Eloge, par Thomas.

ments of the French eulogist are somewhat too bold and sweeping, as I must concede they are, they have nevertheless a basis of truth.

At the period of which we speak, the Scholastic philosophy, however, had lost its primal vigor, and was fast falling to decay. Men had come to distrust and disbelieve it, while as yet they had nothing better to accept in its stead. It stood like some old edifice of a former age, its glory dimmed, its columns fallen and shattered, but majestic in its ruin. There needed some one to clear away the rubbish, and lay the foundation of a newer and a better structure. The first principles of human knowledge were to be readjusted. A right method of investigation was needed; a right field. In both respects men had been led astray; seeking neither for the right things, nor in the right manner. The nations, waking from their long slumber, felt the need of an instructor. Something indeed had already been done in the way of discovery; the light was already dawning. Copernicus had announced the true theory of the earth's motion; Tycho Brahe and Kepler had given definitions in the science of astromony, and enlarged its domain; the telescope, by which, it has been eloquently said, man touches the extremities of creation, was already invented; and Galileo, going forth on voyages of discovery, had brought back strange tidings. Sufficient had been done, enough had been disclosed, to awaken and stimulate the minds of men. The materials were at hand for the most successful research, but the principle of order was wanting, the law and the lawgiver, to reduce to form and method the discordant elements.

Such, in brief, was the state of human learning at the close of the sixteenth century. In the language of Morell; "There needed some master mind, who should be daring enough to trample upon the sacredness of ancient and established authority, acute enough to show the true objects of all philosophy, and powerful enough to furnish a new organum, and dig, as it were, a new channel, in which the philosophic spirit of the world should flow." Such a mind arose; two such, Bacon and Descartes, and after them, in the domain of human knowledge and philosophy, all things became new.

§. 2.—The Man.

Born in 1596, of honorable parentage, in Touraine in France; his father, counsellor to the parliament of Brittany, his mother, the daughter of the Lieutenant-General of Poitiers; a feeble and sickly child, giving promise of no long life; while yet a boy, noted for the liveliness of his imagination, and a peculiar inquisitiveness of mind, always seeking to know the causes of things, so that before he was yet nine years old he had acquired the title of the little philosopher. At the school of the Jesuits, where he was placed at the age of eight years, he showed a marked fondness for poetry and mathematics, which latter alone, of all the sciences, gave him entire satisfaction, as furnishing the evidence of its own assertions. At sixteen he finished his studies at the school, having learned not to think much of his own attainments, or those of his teachers. "The result, ordinarily," says one of his biographers, "of one's first studies, is to imagine that one knows everything. Descartes was already so far advanced as to see that he knew nothing." We next find him at Paris, seeking in the gay and pleasure-loving city, occupation for his eager and restless mind. Breakingly off presently from these follies and dissipations, he shuts himself in entire seclusion in an obscure section of the city, and devotes himself exclusively for two years to the study of geometry, no one of his former companions knowing of his whereabouts. For the next twelve years we find him travelling in foreign parts, visiting, in the careful observation of men, the principal countries of Europe, spending often not a few months but years in one country before passing to another, sometimes bearing arms, and serving as common soldier, always passing much time in seclusion and careful thought on the topics suggested by his observation of men and of nature. All this while, his mind was passing through those painful processes of doubt and struggle which laid the foundation of his own future system of philosophy. It was during this time also that he made those scientific observations among the Alps, which constituted in fact the material of his subsequent work on natural philosophy. At the age of thirty-three, he fixes his permanent residence in Holland, choosing that in preference to his native land, principally from the desire of escaping public notice and enjoying that solitude so congenial to his spirit and so favorable to his studies. Intrusting his secret to a single friend, who alone knew his place of abode, changing often his residence as it became known, hiding himself now in the throng of some large town or city, now in the seclusion of some obscure hamlet, now in some building, that stood solitary in the fields or on the sea-shore, everywhere he sought retirement and gave himself to profound thought.

At the age of forty-one appeared his first work, scientific in its character, with an introductory treatise on the method of arriving at certainty in the investigation of truth ; in other words, the famous "Discourse on Method," which laid the foundation of his fame and also of modern philosophy. Four years later appeared his second great work, entitled "The Meditations," the most strictly philosophical of all his works. His "Principia Philosophiæ" appeared in 1644, three years later, and is a complete system of Natural Philosophy. The work on the Passions, or Psychology, as we should now term it, followed five years later, and is the last of his principal works.

Some of these productions, especially the "Meditations," involved him in controversy with the principal theologians of the time, and these discussions, extending through a considerable part of his subsequent life, form not the least interesting part of his published writings.

These works gave him precisely what he did not wish, great celebrity. Previously to the publication of the treatise on the Passions, he was invited to the court of France, not so much, as it appeared, from a desire to profit by his wisdom, as from curiosity to see so distinguished a man. "I perceived," says he, in his peculiarly artless way, "that they wished to have me in France, a little as the great lords like to have in their menagerie an elephant, or a lion, or some rare animal." Among those who sought the acquaintance of Descartes, were those, however, who were prompted by higher motives than mere curiosity; among them two of the most illustrious women of the age, Elizabeth of Bohemia, daughter of the Elector Palatine, who preferred the honor of being the friend and pupil of Descartes to that of being Queen of Poland; and Christina of Sweden, who invited him to her capital, sent one of her admirals to conduct him thither, received him with great distinction, and in order to receive his instructions in philosophy, undisturbed by the cares of state, fixed upon the hour of five o'clock A. M., in the depths of a northern winter. Determined to retain him at all events in her dominions, she was about to bestow upon him the title of nobility and extensive lands, but a monarch more imperious demanded the man, and after a residence of only four months in Sweden, Descartes was attacked by a fatal malady, and died in 1650. It was her wish to have interred him among the kings, and to have erected a splendid mausoleum to his memory, but Descartes was a Catholic, and the rules of that church forbade his interment in other than a Catholic cemetery. Years afterward his remains were transferred to France, and interred with great pomp in the church of St. Geneviève.

Whatever honors were conferred on Descartes at the courts of princes, his own family seem not to have regarded him with any feeling of pride or veneration—ashamed to have had in their ancient and aristocratic family one who was known under the vulgar title of philosopher. It was not until his became the first name in France, that they began to appreciate his merit.

The personal character of Descartes was unexceptionable. No one can study his life and writings, and not feel that he was a sincere lover of virtue and truth, and carried his philosophy into practice. He early laid down for his own practical guidance, while tossed on the uncertain sea of doubt and conjecture as to all speculative truth, the following rules: 1. To obey the laws and customs of his country. 2. To adhere with constancy to a given course, and be not easily turned aside from any proposed measure, as those who, lost in the woods, wander round and round, instead of striking out a straight path, and keeping to that be it right or wrong. 3. To take the side always of the moderate opinions, because, in morals, that which is extreme is almost always wrong. 4. To labor to overcome himself rather than fortune, because one's desires are more easily changed than the order of the world, and nothing is in our own power but our thoughts. By these principles he regulated his life. He seems to have had admirable self-control. When one commits an offence against me, says he, I strive to elevate my soul so high that the offence shall not come anywhere near me. Reputation he both scorned and shunned, as inimical to the two most valuable possessions of the philosopher—liberty and leisure. The line of Ovid was his motto: "Sad the death of him who dies well known to others, to himself unknown." The modesty of Descartes was conspicuous; yet no man better knew how much men are influenced by other considerations than those of intrinsic merit. In dedicating his great work, the "Meditations," to the Doctors of the Sorbonne, he thus beautifully apologizes for what might otherwise seem an ambitious thing: "I wished to avail myself of authority, because *Truth is so little a thing when she is alone.*"

§ 3.—The System.

The peculiar features of the Cartesian philosophy may best be learned by an examination or analysis of his two principal works, of a strictly philosophical nature, "The Method" and "The Meditations," which contain the main principles of his system. The Method opens with an account of the mental process by which he came to doubt of many things commonly received. It is an exceedingly interesting narrative of the struggles of a noble mind, reaching after truth with a determined earnestness which no difficulties could overcome or turn back from its purpose. Having learned in the schools whatever others had learned, and, not content with that, having run through all the books most curious and rare on which he could lay his hands, and finding to his surprise so little certainty and so much doubt about all the matters thus investigated, that in philosophy, for example, which had been cultivated by the best minds for ages, there was not yet to be found one thing which was not disputed, while other sciences, deriving their principles from philosophy, could of course be no more solid and reliable than the foundations on which they were built, he comes to doubt of almost everything—to doubt if there be any such thing as positive truth and certainty, in the whole circle of human knowledge, and to regard whatever is only probable, as very likely false. He casts about him to find some way of discovering and separating the true from the false, the certain from the doubtful in this mingling of truth and error. The careful manner in which geometricians proceed leads him to question whether, with a *like process,* he might not arrive at *like results* in other departments of knowledge; might not in them also reach clear and certain convictions of truth. Such a method of procedure he resolves to adopt: 1, never to take anything for true, which he does not *know* to be so, which does not present itself so clearly to his mind that he shall never have occasion to call it in question; 2, to break up every difficulty into its constituent parts for examination: 3, to begin with the things most simple and easy to know, and proceed gradually to the more difficult and complex; and finally to make so complete a survey as to be sure that nothing has escaped him. Applying these rules, he begins by pulling down and tearing away *ad libitum* whatever he thought himself already to have known, calling in question all preconceived opinions however venerable and sacred, not indeed as the sceptics who doubt for *for the sake* of doubting, but only in order to arrive by this means at some certainty of knowledge and faith. At the outset, and at a single stroke, all the impressions made through the senses are discarded, for these are often found to be erroneous. So also are his own mental convictions and judgments; for the things which he thinks, and sees, and does, in his waking moments, he not unfrequently thinks, and sees, and does, in his sleep; and how can he know that they are any more real in the one case than the other? But granting all this, that the evidence of the senses, and even his own mental impressions and convictions, are unreliable, one thing is and must be unquestionably true, that is, he *certainly thinks* that these things are thus and thus, they *seem to him* so and so; and from this it follows that he *himself exists;* for even if the thing thought be called in question, it is impossible to deny that there is a thinker; the very doubt implies a doubter. Hence the famous proposition, the starting point and first principle of the Cartesian philosophy, viz., COGITO, ERGO SUM.

It is, however, not of himself as a natural or bodily substance, but only as a thinker, that he is thus made certain; in other words, of the spiritual existence, the soul in distinction from the body. But among his thoughts he finds one unlike others—the thought, that is, of an absolutely perfect and infinite being. Whence comes that thought, and what of it? Not from himself, surely, for there is nothing in himself corresponding to such an idea, and the greater cannot proceed from the less, nor something from nothing. There must be some reality, some being containing in himself all those perfections of which his own inferior mind is able to form the idea ; else he would never have had the idea of such a being more perfect than himself. That being, perfect and infinite, is God.

These two things established, these two grand corner-stones fairly laid—his own existence as a spiritual being, and the existence of an infinite and perfect Intelligence, from whom his own spiritual being and power of thought proceed—the way is ready to build on this foundation the solid structure of human knowledge ; and on this basis, in the Cartesian philosophy, everything is made to rest. All certainty depends on these two grand principles : There is a *me ;* a thinking, feeling, spiritually active, in other words, *conscious* being ; there is also a Being, infinite and perfect, as I am not, the source of the me and of all its powers, who, as perfect, cannot be himself a *deceiver,* nor have made me to be always deceived. The veracity of our faculties is thus established, and the way is open to a certain knowledge of whatever lies within the grasp or compass of those faculties. Such is substantially, and in brief, the famous method of Descartes.

The same plan is substantially followed in the "Meditations," the direct object of which work is to elaborate more fully and carefully the argument for the existence of the soul as a spiritual and immortal reality, and of God as the infinite and absolutely perfect being.

As before, he begins with doubting. Knowledge comes through the channel of the senses, and these have often deceived him. He seems to himself to be at the present moment seated before the fire, in his dressing robe, with papers in his hands, yet how often has he in sleep really thought he was thus seated and occupied, when really he was in his bed. Since he has so often been mistaken as to the reality of such impressions, how is he to know what to depend upon? Is there, then, nothing certain? The exact sciences must surely be exceptions, for whether he be awake or asleep it is equally certain that 3 and 2 make 5, and that the square has only four sides. But what if, according to an idea he has long entertained, some being were his creator, and in making him to be what he is, what if this creator had so constituted him that he should always come to a false conclusion whenever he adds 3 and 2, or numbers the sides of a square? Is he too good for that? Then why does he permit him ever to be deceived, as he often is? Suppose, then, that there is in fact no such thing as light, sound, extension, figure, etc., but all such impressions are only a deception and illusion practised upon men by some deceitful and powerful being—granting all this, still one thing is certain, there is and must be such a being as himself; for whether he really sees, hears, touches the external object, or not, it certainly seems to him that he does, he thinks he does; and this necessarily involves the existence of the nature or being that so thinks.

He then proceeds, as before, to establish the certainty of the divine existence. Upon analyzing and classifying the various ideas which he finds in his mind, he perceives one, the objective reality of which is so far superior to anything in himself, that he clearly cannot be the source of it, it cannot have originated in his own mind—and that is the idea of a being infinite, eternal, all-powerful, all-knowing, all-creating. These qualities are so excellent, so far beyond anything which he finds in himself, that it seems impossible that the idea of such a being could have originated with himself; for how could the finite originate the infinite? It is not simply the negative of the finite, for he has in some sense a clearer and more positive conception of the infinite than of the finite. How does he know the finite and imperfect, and that he himself is so, except as he has in the mind the idea of a being more perfect than himself?

It is from this idea of the infinite then, that the idea of the finite is derived, and not the reverse. Whence, then, this idea, and how comes the mind to form it? Not through the senses, for there is no external manifestation of any object corresponding to this idea; nor is it wrought in the mind's own laboratory, a fiction of the brain, for he cannot in his own thoughts add anything to, or subtract anything from it. It is then, a fixed, immutable idea. It must have been created with the mind itself, *"the mark of the workman impressed on his work."* There is a fine passage occurring at the close of this demonstration of the being of a God, which brings out the religious spirit of the man in distinction from the mere philosopher, "But before I press on to the consideration of other truths, I wish here to pause a little, while in the contemplation of God himself, to think over leisurely with myself his marvellous attributes, and to consider, admire, adore, the incomparable beauty of this immense luminary, so far as the force of my mind, which is dazzled thereby, may be able to bear it. For as faith assures us that the sovereign felicity of another life consists only in the contemplation of the Divine majesty, so from the like contemplation now, though far less perfect, we perceive ourselves deriving the greatest pleasure of which we are capable in this life.

In the meditation which follows, Descartes gives still another form of argument for the divine existence, derived from the same source, the nature of the idea which the human mind forms of the divine being. He finds that he cannot separate the idea of actual existence from the idea which he forms of God; cannot think of him as not existing; can no more separate in thought the actual existence from the essence of the divine being, than he can separate in thought from the essence of a triangle the fact that its three angles are equal to two right angles, or from the idea of a mountain the idea of a corresponding valley. Not that the conception of a triangle, or of a mountain and valley, necessarily involves the existence of these objects—that is not the argument, as Morell seems to suppose. Descartes distinctly disclaims this idea. "From the fact that I cannot think of a mountain without a valley, it does not follow that anywhere a mountain and a valley exist, but only that mountain and valley, whether they exist or not, are not able to be dissociated from each other; and so from the fact that I cannot think of God except as existing, it follows that existence is inseparable from God, and thence that he really exists; . . . for it is not in my power to think of God without existence, that is to say, of the *most perfect* being without the *chief* and *highest perfection of all.*" The only question respecting the validity of this reasoning is, does it necessarily follow that God exists, *because we cannot conceive* of him as non-existent? Granting the premises that whatever pertains necessarily to the *idea*, pertains also to the *corresponding reality, if there be one*, it is *certain* that there is in any given case a reality corresponding to our conceptions? The most perfect being conceivable would be one possessing a certain attribute, *a* or *x*; I cannot conceive of the being as without that attribute; but *is there* such a being? This previous question remains unanswered, as it seems to me. Some of the most acute minds, however, have conceded the validity of the above argument.

Whatever may be thought of the methods of reasoning now presented, certain it is that the author makes high claim for them. In his prefatory epistle he says: "I dare even propose them for most certain and most evident propositions. I will add, even, that they are such that I do not suppose any way lies open to the human mind by which better ones can ever be found." He believes them "to equal, or even surpass in certainty the demonstrations of geometry." He is well aware, however, that they are of such a nature as to be understood and appreciated by but few; and for this reason he wrote the Meditations in

Latin, and not in French and in a form to be generally read, lest feeble minds might think it was meant for them. He counsels no one to read the work who is not willing to meditate seriously and intently with him, and who cannot detach the mind from all the associations of sense; and the number of such persons he knows to be very small indeed.

Of the system as developed in the works now analyzed, the following are evidently the characteristic features:

1. The *starting point* of the whole system, the *basis* of all belief and certainty, is *doubt*. Doubt everything. It is only when, in this way, you at last reach something which cannot be doubted, that you strike the real and only solid foundations of rational belief.

2. The mind itself is the field of observation. The appeal is much to *consciousness* throughout. This is the stand point, the meridian line in all the observations. This is where the anchor first holds as we drive before the storm on the sea of doubt and uncertainty, "Cogito, ergo sum." Even the knowledge of God, on which all other knowledge depends, is sought and found in the soul itself. Instead of going out of himself to find God, Descartes descends into himself and brings up God out of the depths of his own existence; finds there the maker's name stamped on his innermost works.

3. This fact once established, that there is an infinite and perfect being, and the certainty of our knowledge, the veracity of our faculties, is guaranteed; for an infinite and perfect being cannot be false, would not so constitute his creatures that they should be always deceived. We may therefore rely upon the testimony of our senses and the veracity of our faculties generally, and so we reach a sure and permanent basis of all knowledge.

§ 4.—The Effect.

What impress was left by this man and his system on his own and the succeeding ages? A question not easy to answer. This, however, seems to be plain. To this man belongs the honor, now generally conceded to him by discerning minds, of being the founder of modern philosophy. To the Method and the Meditations of Descartes, as the starting point, may be traced back both the Scotch and the German philosophy. It was he who led the way. It was he who first ventured to strike out a new path in philosophy. Bacon had done this in physics. Descartes did the same in metaphysics. Bacon went forth into the outer world, observed, explored, classified. Descartes, with equal penetration, passed at once into the inner world, that little but wonderful kingdom, the soul of man, a world which Bacon seems never really to have explored, and began his investigations there. He was the first to discover and plant himself firmly on the true foundation of metaphysical science, the principle that the *human consciousness* is the true starting of all investigation, and an analysis of the facts of consciousness the only true method of scientific inquiry. No philosopher before Descartes had built a system on these principles, or explicitly announced them as such; but once announced they commended themselves to every thinker and put a new phase not upon psychology alone, but upon all science.

The tendency of the Baconian philosophy was doubtless to materialism. It built up a whole fabric of science on the observation of external things. It overlooked the internal. It ran out into the sensationalism of Hobbes and Locke, and finally into the downright materialism of the school of Hartley and Priestley in England, and Condillac in France. The tendency of Cartesianism, on the other hand, was plainly to idealism, as subsequently developed in Spinoza and Malebranche. The outer world was nothing until the inner world had first been explored as the basis on which all knowledge of the outer might rest. It exalted the idea of the infinite so far above the finite, as to throw the latter quite out of sight. God, the eternal, the infinite, the supreme, arose ever before it as the only object worthy of human thought, and on this wonderful vision it fixed its eye, until, dimmed by that brightness, it could see nothing else. Even eternal and necessary truths resolved themselves ultimately into the will of God. God was all and in all. The result in those who came after, and carried out the inherent tendencies of the system, was pantheism.

No small part of the life and writings of Descartes was devoted to natural science. If in this he was prone to go beyond the facts into the region of theory and speculation, in his anxiety to reach some explanation, some law regulating the observed facts, and if subsequent discoveries have proved his theories, however brilliant, not always correct, his system, however grand and imposing, not always the true philosophy of nature, it must still be conceded that he was greatly in advance of his age, even in those matters where to us he seems chiefly to have erred, and that no man did more by his investigations and reflections to promote the progress of physical science and to hasten its subsequently more complete development, than René Descartes. One would entirely mistake, who should think of him as devoting his life and studies to metaphysical pursuits. With him the metaphysics were merely the foundation on which to construct a system of physics; and in this he builded better than he knew, for while in the progress and subsequent development of science, the superstructure which Descartes erected no longer remains, the foundation stands the only true and solid basis of a sound philosophy. Nor are the studies of Descartes of little value in natural science, as Morell seems to suppose. No one has investigated more diligently, or stated more correctly the general phenomena of nature than Descartes.

The nature and properties of light, the nature, laws, and movements of the atmosphere, were well understood by him, and for a century at least these branches of science remained essentially where he left them. It was to the observations of Descartes that Pascal was indebted for the idea of the experiment by which he demonstrated what Galileo and Torricelli had taught respecting the weight of the atmosphere. It was Descartes who first correctly and fully explained the law by which the rainbow flings its arch over the troubled sky and presides in beauty over the retreating march of the tempest. He carried the science of mechanics to a perfection it had not before attained. He took up the telescope where Galileo had left it, developed the theory and perfected the mechanism of the instrument, and made of it a new thing. A treatise on music, composed at the age of twenty-two, passed after his death into many languages. With a view to understand the structure of the human frame, he devoted himself for some years to the study of anatomy and chemistry; and the work published after his death, which embodied the result of these labors, ranks among his best productions.

It was in mathematics, however, that Descartes made the greatest advance, and stood preëminent, the foremost man of his time. He first greatly simplified the science of algebra, reducing the number of signs, and introducing the method of representing by letters the forms of quantities; and having perfected this instrument, applied the algebraic process to geometry, which no one had dreamed of uniting with it, and thus gave more progress to that science than had been made in it for centuries. The analysis of Descartes, it has been justly said, has been the instrument of all the great discoveries of the Moderns.

From this brief survey it will appear how wide was the field of Descartes' investigations, and how little he deserves to be regarded as merely a metaphysician. One can pardon the enthusiasm of his countryman and eulogist,

Thomas, when he affirms that "it was the fortune of Descartes to be able to approach no science which did not immediately assume a new aspect."

Like most discoverers of truth, however, Descartes was too far in advance of his age to be fully appreciated by it. Commencing with most sciences, as geometry for example, where others had left off, there were few who could follow him in his rapid march. In one of his letters, so full of childlike simplicity, we find him computing how many geometricians in Europe will be likely to understand him, viz., three or four in France, two in Holland, and two in Spain. Descartes has been often compared with Bacon. "If," says Thomas, "we seek among the great men of the Moderns some with whom to compare him, we find three, *Bacon, Leibnitz,* and *Newton.* Bacon ran over the whole surface of human knowledge, sat in judgment on past ages, and ran on into the future; but he indicated more great things than he executed. He raised the scaffold of an immense edifice, and left to others the work of putting together the edifice itself. *Leibnitz* was whatever he chose to be. He carried into philosophy a great loftiness of mind; but his metaphysical systems seem designed to astonish and crush men down, rather than enlighten them." Newton, he goes on to say, following as he did Galileo, Kepler, Huygens, Bacon, and Descartes, profited by the labors of others, aud owes to them in part what he became. Descartes "deserves to be placed beside Newton, for he created a part of Newton, while he was created only by himself." "Time has destroyed the opinions of Descartes, but his glory remains. He is like those kings dethroned, who, among the ruins even of their empire, seem born to command the world."

The works on which I have chiefly relied in the preparation of the above, are the collected works of Descartes, in Latin, published in Amsterdam in 1656, and the French edition of his works, edited by Cousin, and published in Paris in 1824.

CHAPTER IV.

SPINOZA.

In 1632, there was born in Amsterdam a Jew, one Spinoza, whose writings and whose name have been now for two centuries the admiration of half the reflecting world and the terror of the other half; whose influence has been felt over all Europe, and feared farther than it has been felt; who has been branded, now as an atheist, and now as a pantheist, and not unfrequently as both; whose calm, fearless mind shrunk from no difficulties and no consequences, but moved straight and steadily onward with its inexorable logic, its geometrical precision, its terrible self-reliance, to the investigation of the profoundest problems of philosophy and to conclusions from which a mind less honest and fearless, and less conscious of its own integrity and its own strength, would have shrunk back at once and forever. It is pleasant to be reminded that this strange and profound thinker was once a boy like the rest of the world, in those busy Dutch streets of the olden times, watching the ships—wondering at many things.

He was a feeble and sickly lad; but for this all the more thoughtful and studious. The energy which nature intended at that early period of life to be expended in muscular activity and athletic sports, sought in him another direction, mounted to the brain, quickened the intellect, and instead of passing off in the more usual form of leap-frog and other boyish amusements, set the lad upon thinking, observing, reflecting, questioning, and opened to him that broad and wonderful field of thought—the mysteries and problems of his own conscious being.

The parents of Spinoza were humble and honest people, merchants of Amsterdam, whither they had fled from the persecutions encountered by the Jews in Spain. The boy was at first destined to a commercial life, but such was his unusual fondness for study, and the remarkable development of his intellect, that his parents altered their purpose, and determined to give him a rabbinical education. Accordingly the Old Testament and the Talmud became his principal studies, and such was his proficiency in these as to excite the highest hopes of the great rabbi, Saul Levi Morteira, his instructor. But alas, a cloud oft obscures the brightest morning. It was soon discovered, most unfortunately, that this promising lad was not a little disposed to think for himself—possessed one of those inquiring, penetrating, restless minds, so much the terror of mere parchment and ritual expounders, which are never content with mere facts and statements, but are ever prying into the reasons, and demanding the why and wherefore of things. The great rabbi had trouble enough with his hopeful pupil. Difficulties were started, questions were put, from which all good rabbis, great and small, piously shrunk back. What does the boy mean? Will he not believe the Talmud and the tradition? What right has he to ask questions, and to have thoughts and opinions of his own in such matters? They threaten the youth. He coolly defies their rage. He shall be excommunicated. Very well. Excommmunicate if you like. I anticipate your kind intentions by voluntarily withdrawing from your community; and so, with bitter sarcasm, he turns on his heel and walks out of their ranks to return no more. Foiled in this attempt, they offer him a pension of a thousand florins, to be silent and retain some nominal connection with their body. He is indignant at the bribe. His life is next attempted. An assassin aims at his breast a deadly blow, but misses his mark. Nothing remains but to execute the sentence of excommunication. The day arrives. A vast concourse assembles. Black candles are lighted—the books of the Law are opened. The chanter sounds aloud, in solemn tones, the fearful curse, and is answered back by the notes of the trumpet. The black candles are reversed, and melt drop by drop into a tub of blood. The fearful and final anathema is pronounced, the lights are plunged into the blood, and in that sudden and solemn darkness the assembly, filled with fear and sorrow, shout Amen. And so poor Spinoza gets his first degree—the only one they ever gave him.

Having now fairly finished his Talmudic education, Spinoza, cast upon his own resources, finds a friend and patron, Van den Ende, a physician in Amsterdam and teacher of philology, from whose fair and accomplished daughter, Spinoza takes lessons in Latin and in love. He seems to have succeeded better in the former branch of study than the latter. The lady prefers a young Hamburg merchant to a penniless excommunicated Jew ; and Spinoza, disappointed in love, betakes himself more vigorously to his Latin. It was a happy day for him when the writings of Descartes fell into his hands. He read them with avidity. They were precisely that food and sustenance for the eager mind reaching after truth, which he had long needed. Here he found instruction, light, rest. He stood now upon a sure basis, and felt that he could mark out for himself, at last, a definite object and pursuit in life. He is poor but independent. He knows a trade, and can support himself by his own labor ; and content with little, master of his own time and pursuits, can devote himself to reflection and study. And this he does. By polishing glasses for optical instruments, which he does with a skill that attracts the notice of Leibnitz, he earns a competence, and still reserves his best moments for philosophy. How moderate were his wants, and how simple his style of fare, may be judged from the fact that a dish of soup, which cost three half pence, and a pot of beer, costing three farthings more, sufficed often for the day's provisions. As to clothing, he said it was not good sense to put a precious envelope on things of little or no value. Yet this same man, supporting himself by his own labor, and living upon four pence a day that he might gain the more time for study, is charged, among other things, with Epicureanism. If this is Epicureanism, may the disciples of that school never be wanting. So little desire for gold had Spinoza, that one of his friends, one day, having offered him a present of 2,000 florins, he resolutely refused it, on the ground that so much wealth would divert him from his studies. He prevented this same friend, the generous and wealthy De Vries, from leaving him a handsome legacy in his will—actually made him alter the will already drawn up, and finally consented to receive from the heirs, a pension of 300 florins only, instead of 500 which they urged upon him. The talents of Spinoza, and his growing reputation, alarmed his enemies, who finally stirred up the magistrates to banish him, in a sort, from Amsterdam, as a dangerous person to the peace and public morals. So upon exile, half voluntary, half compulsory, he leaves his native city, and retiring to Rhynsburg, and afterward to the Hague, devotes himself with new assiduity and zeal to his favorite studies. So wholly absorbed was he in these pursuits, and so fond of solitude, that sometimes for months together he hardly quitted his cabinet. Here he had all he desired : profound peace, long leisure, the few books that he valued—and they were very few, for, like all other truly great and original minds, he read little and thought much—and a few friends who listened to him ; here he studied, he thought, he philosophized, to his heart's content. It was in this retreat that he published his first work, an exposition of Descartes' philosophy, which by its clearness and masterly comprehension of the system of that great man, at once attracted great attention. The Prince of Condé invites him now to France, the retreat of letters and science at this time ; but having no disposition to dedicate his next work to Louis XIV., which would in that case be expected of him, he declines the offer, and prefers to keep on living in solitude at a few pence a day. The Elector Palatine also invites him to Heidelberg, to the chair of philosophy; but this, too, he declines, on the ground that the state religion might cramp somewhat his liberty of independent thought, and also on the ground that the duties of instruction would necessarily demand time which he could ill spare from his studies.

His death occurred in 1677, at the age of forty-four. Feeble in constitution, and never, in the course of life, enjoying good health, his system was doubtless enfeebled by his absorbing devotion to study (continued from ten at night till three in the morning), his solitary mode of life, his abstemiousness, his too arduous labors. "He was a calm, brave man," says one of his biographers. "He could confront disease and death as he had confronted poverty and persecution. Bravery of the highest kind distinguished him through life, and was not likely to fail him on the quitting it, and yet beneath that calm, cold stoicism, there was a childlike gayety springing from a warm and sympathizing heart. His character was made up of generous simplicity and heroic forbearance."

"His humor and his manners," says Damiron, "were in perfect harmony with his vocation. He was neither melancholy nor gay, but calm, mild and moderate; affable, and compassionate, and, what is perhaps more remarkable, full of tolerance and respect for the belief of others." "His figure," says another, "has an air of recollection and meditation; his eye announces an immovable courage, his mouth betrays an agreeable modesty, a slight tinge of sadness seems to cast a shadow over all his traits." Such was Spinoza in habits, character, and life.

The principal works of Spinoza are the "Principles of the Philosophy of Descartes," published 1664, and the "Cogitata Metaphysica," in the same year, and the "Théologie Politique," six years after. It was not until after his death, however, that his most important treatises were published, viz., the Ethics, the Politics, and the treatise on the improvement of the understanding ("De Emendatione Intellectus)." It is in these posthumous works that his system can best be learned, for in these only is his doctrine fully developed. His earlier treatises were designed rather to prepare the way for his own peculiar doctrines, than as a full expression of them.

The style of Spinoza is peculiarly concise, severe, logical; setting forth in the plainest manner, with fewest words, and little ornament or elegance, just the simple thought that was to be expressed—that and nothing more; but that in a way not to be mistaken. As a reasoner and metaphysician he is marked by the boldness with which he states, and *follows out to their legitimate conclusions,* whatever positions he assumes, never shrinking from any unpleasant or even apparently absurd consequences. He handles his themes with the air and bearing of a master, who thoroughly understands himself and the instrument on which he plays; and touches the keys, not with a trembling and hesitating hand, but with a positiveness and boldness and certainty, and yet with a precision which awaken the admiration of the observer. He never seems to ask himself, Is such a conclusion reasonable? but simply, Does it justly and necessarily follow from my premises? He marks out his path; fixes the direction and aim of his movements, and having decided upon this, steadily pursues that path, and that direction, and that object, come what will. If a precipice lies in his way, he walks deliberately on and deliberately over, with the most resolute determination, the most utter disregard of results.

This process, though admirable in many respects, is not always and altogether safe for a finite and limited mind. One ought to have a clearer and more complete survey of the whole field of thought at the outset, than any finite mind can ever have, in order rightly to choose a path and direction that shall in no event be deviated from in the least degree. Omniscience might work in that way. Yet, to omniscience what need of reasoning at all ? Spinoza was led to this method of reasoning by his mathematical propensities. Accustomed to start in geometry with principles whose truth is beyond question, and then to follow out step by step a process of reasoning based upon those principles, to a conclusion perfectly inevitable and certain, he demanded a like method and certainty in all reasoning on abstract truth ; was not satisfied with anything less ; applied to metaphysics a method strictly applicable only to mathematics, and felt as little responsibility for the conclusions thus reached as for the result of a demonstration in Euclid. It was this that led him astray in his reasonings. He forgot that with respect to ideas of time, space, spirit, good, evil, and other abstract and purely metaphysical ideas, it is impossible either to lay down at the outset premises that shall be as certain and definite, or to reason as positively and as surely from those premises as we can about the points, and lines, and ratios of mathematical science. This, if I mistake, not, is the key of his entire mistake, the grand secret of his total aberration.

Another peculiarity of his method is, that he invariably pursues the *a priori* process, begins with *ontology*, with being in general, and reasons downward to particulars. The "Cogitata Metaphysica," *e. g.*, is divided into two parts, the first of which treats of being, the second of God and the soul. Under the first he discusses *existence*, essence, the real, the necessary, the contingent, time and duration, the one, the true, etc. From these purely ontological heights he descends to treat, in the second part, of the nature of God ; and so, by this high avenue of approach, he comes at length to consider the human soul. Spinoza was throughout, in all his tendencies and all his writings, a pure ontologist.

But it is time to lay before you more exactly the outlines of his system. In general it may be said that Spinoza starts from the position and ground principles of Descartes, and rigorously carries out those principles to their extreme. He is a Cartesian, differing only in minor points as he proceeds, and in the conclusions at which he arrives by logically carrying out the main principles of the system. Dugald Stuart is hardly correct in affirming that Spinoza agreed with Descartes in little else than his physical principles, and that no two philosophers ever differed more widely in their metaphysical and theological tenets. In their philosophy they mainly agreed. In their results and conclusions they differed, and for the reason stated. The system of Spinoza may perhaps best be viewed as developed in the "Ethics," his most elaborate and complete work. This is in five parts : of which the first treats of God, the second of the soul, the third of the affections, the fourth and fifth of servitude and liberty. The arrangement and treatment are strictly mathematical. It begins with definitions and axioms. Then follow propositions based upon these. Damiron says of this treatise that, with the exception of the prefaces and Scolia, in which the author resigns himself to the use of common speech, there is from beginning to end but one massive and compact argument, in which there is not a thought, not a phrase, not a word, which is not closely connected with the whole on which it depends.

Among the definitions with which the work opens, the following are the more important. *Substance* is defined to be that which is, in itself, and is conceived by itself. *Attribute* is that which is conceived of substance as constituting its essence. *Mode* is an accident or affection of substance. God is the being absolutely infinite, or the substance consisting of infinite attributes, each expressing his infinite and eternal essence. A thing is free which exists by the sole necessity of its nature, and by itself alone is determined to action.

To these definitions he strictly adheres in his whole treatise. Several axioms follow these definitions. Among which these : 1. Everything which is, is in itself, or in some other thing. 2. That which cannot be conceived through another, *per aliud,* must he conceived *per se.* 3. From a given determinate cause, the effect necessarily follows ; and, *vice versa,* no determinate cause, no effect. 4. The knowledge of an effect depends on the knowledge of the cause, and includes it. 5. Things having nothing in common with each other cannot be understood by means of each other, *i. e.,* the conception of one does not include that of the other. 6. A true idea must agree with its original nature. 7. Whatever can be clearly conceived as non-existing does not in its essence involve existence.

From these follow certain propositions. 1. Substance is prior in nature to its accidents. 2. Two substances having different attributes have nothing in common with each other. This follows from the definition of substance as a thing conceived in and through itself. 3. Of things which have nothing in common, one cannot be the *cause* of the other. The demonstration is, that having nothing in common they cannot (Axiom 5th) be conceived by means of each other, and so (accordingly to Axiom 4th) one cannot be the cause of the other.

Prop. IV. Two or more distinct things can be distinguished only by the diversity of their attributes or of their modes. V. It is impossible that there should be two or more substances of the same nature or of the same attribute. For they could not be distinguished from each other. Hence VI. *One substance cannot be created by another substance ;* since there cannot be two substances with the same attributes, and so having nothing in common one cannot (Prop. 3d) be the cause of the other. It follows from this, by corollary, that substance cannot be created by anything else, since there is nothing in nature but substance and its modes. Hence VII. It pertains to the nature of substance to exist ; or it is the cause of itself. VIII. All substance is necessarily infinite ; for if finite it must be so (Definition

2d) by virtue of another substance of the same attribute—which is impossible (Prop. 5th). The result of this chain of reasoning is this. *There is only one substance, and that is infinite. God is that infinite substance.* Whatever exists, exists in him. He is the one being of which all things are but the manifestations; he the sole substance; everything else a mode of that substance. He is the efficient universal cause of all things, not indeed transitively but immanently, and his attributes are eternal and infinite. They are two in number: extension and thought. These two attributes he regards as the one objective, the other subjective; extension is visible thought. Thought is invisible extension. God is the identity of the two, that is, the substance in which both unite; the root from which both spring—as man is the identity or ground of union of soul and body. Everything is a mode of God's extension; every thought, wish, feeling, a mode of his thought. God is the only existence, though there are many existing things; the only substance, though many powers—the one and all. Such, in outline, is his system.

It will be perceived that these conclusions follow inevitably from the definitions and axioms laid down at the outset, and as these are essentially Cartesian, it is impossible for a disciple of that school, however he may shrink from the conclusions, to escape them. Once within the current and vortex of this irresistible geometrical reasoning and there is no escape. Tissot hesitates not to say that this system is one of the strongest and most admirable conceptions of the human mind, viewed merely as a system of ontological reasoning, a hypothetical system, towering aloft with a majestic grandeur. He thinks it impossible for the ancient metaphysics to overthrow this system. It can be done, he thinks, only by admitting, with Kant, that the ontological conceptions of pure reason, the categories of substance, mode, cause, effect, etc., have no real and objective value apart from the sphere of experience. However that may be, it is doubtless true, as Tissot admits, that nothing is more easily overthrown than a system logically and closely reasoned out from given principles, provided you can attack and show the falsity of those principles. And this is precisely what can be done in the present case. The system is entirely built on principles that will not stand the test of critical examination. We have but to attack these, and the building falls. Examine any one of the fundamental positions of this curious, and in many respects, wonderful fabric of human reason, you will perceive its falsity. Substance, says Spinoza, is *that which is, in, and by, itself.* True, we say, of some substance, but not all; of uncreated substance, and that only; true only of *Deity.* Spinoza in this postulate begs the whole question, assumes that there are not, and cannot be, any other than *self-existent* substances. Neither is it true that substance is infinite, indivisible, unique. This again is applicable only to that class of substances which is self-existent—to the Deity. We *deny* that this class or definition *exhausts* the idea of substance.

It is not true that things can be distinguished only by the diversity of their attributes. We distinguish them in other ways; by circumstances extrinsic and accidental to the things themselves; by place; by number; nay, by the different degrees in which the same attributes may be possessed by each. Hence it is not true that there cannot be two substances possessing the same attribute, on the ground of its being impossible to distinguish them, for no such impossibility exists. And if there may be two substances of the same attribute, then it is not true that one substance may not be the cause of another; for the two have something in common. There may be, then, a diversity of substances, created and uncreated, finite and infinite. God is not, in a word, the unique and only substance. The system falls the moment you attack the definition of substance on which the whole is built.

It is hardly necessary to remark that Spinoza is a fatalist. The will of Deity is the mainspring of all motion and volition; literally, and not metaphorically, we do live and move and have our being in him. Our thoughts and passions are only the movements of the eternal mind. That mind acts according to the laws of its own nature; acts, without constraint; is the only free cause. But in what sense free? Only with the liberty of *necessity*, not of choice. All things, he says, flow on necessarily; always, by the same necessity, follow; just as from the nature of the triangle it follows, from eternity to eternity, that the three angles are equal to two right angles: wherefore the omnipotence of God was, in act, from eternity, and will to eternity remain in the same actuality. Nothing is contingent, he holds, since everything is determined, to act and to be, by the necessity of its nature. This is fatalism surely; but, as Damiron well remarks, it is fatalism arising from excess of theism, rather than want of it.

Was Spinoza then an atheist? Never a man further from it. How is he an atheist, who sees everywhere and everything God and God only. It is not without reason that Schleiermacher calls him the *God-intoxicated* man. Was he a pantheist? Most surely, in *one sense* of that term. There are two sorts of pantheism, it has been well said. The one brings God down to nature, and annihilates him in it; sees no other God, no higher being, than the universe. This is true and proper pantheism. The other, which passes for the same thing but is widely diverse from it, carries nature up to God, and loses sight of it, annihilates it in him. This was Spinoza's pantheism. In this sense alone was he a pantheist.

Cousin pays the following very just, though glowing tribute to this philosopher:

"Far from being an atheist, of which he is accused, Spinoza possesses so strongly the sentiment of God that he loses the sentiment of man. This temporary and limited existence, everything that is finite, seems to him unworthy of the name of existence, and for him there is no true being but the eternal being. This book, bristling as it is, in the manner of the times, with geometrical formulæ, so dry and so repulsive in its style, is at foundation a mystic hymn, a transport, a yearning of the soul toward him who alone can legitimately say : I am that I am. . . .

"His life was the symbol of his system. Adoring the eternal, ever in the presence of the infinite, he disdained this passing world; he knew neither pleasure, nor action, nor glory, for he did not suspect his own. Young, he desired to know love; but he knew it not, because he did not inspire it. Poor and suffering, his life was spent in waiting for and meditating upon death. He lived in a suburb of the city, where, gaining as a polisher of glass, the little bread and milk necessary for his subsistence; hated, repudiated by the men of his communion, suspected by all others; detested by all the clergy of Europe, whom he wished to subject to the state; escaping persecutions and outrages only by concealment; humble and silent; of a gentleness and patience that were proof to everything; passing along in this world without wishing to stop in it, never dreaming of producing any effect upon it or of leaving any trace upon it—Spinoza was an Indian mouni, a Persian soufi, an enthusiastic monk; the author whom this pretended atheist most resembles, is the unknown author of the 'Imitation of Jesus Christ'" (**Cousin, "Fragments Philosophiques, article Spinoza"**).

CHAPTER V.

MALEBRANCHE.

CONTEMPORARY with Spinoza, and at the head in some respects of the literati of France, yet very little known as an author, and still less as a man, is Nicholas Malebranche. Born at Paris 1638 ; a weak and sickly child, afflicted with curvature of the spine ; on this account, like Spinoza, less attracted to the pursuits and pleasures of the external world, he was all the more a philosopher ; of good family, of hereditary wealth and rank, one of his uncles having been viceroy of Canada, he was carefully educated under the eye of the mother, who seems to have had some considerable share in forming his youthful tastes for the investigation of profound and hidden truths. Studied philosophy at the College de la Marche, and theology at the Sorbonne. Destined to an ecclesiastical life, he refused a canonicate at Notre Dame, and connected himself with the Oratoire, a religious order distinguished for its devotion to St. Augustine and its attachment to Descartes. The masters under whom he was at first placed in this order sought to interest him in history and philosophy, but to no purpose, his mind found nothing congenial in these pursuits. One day, however, as he was passing down the rue St. Jacques, a bookseller put into his hands Descartes' treatise on man. He had heard much said of Descartes, but had never read him. With what charm, with what mental agitation and transport, does the young ecclesiastic peruse these pages. It was not the Discourse on Method, it was not the Meditations, it was not even the Philosophy, but only the Physiology of that great author, says the writer to whom I am indebted for this incident ; but it was his spirit, his reasoning, his manner of procedure, his way of philosophizing; and scarcely had Malebranche opened the book before he was captivated and profoundly moved, so much so that he was obliged to pause in his reading on account of the palpitation of the heart which was induced by his emotion. This was the beginning of his true career as a philosopher. He found in Descartes that which met the profound want of his intellectual nature; that which he had never met before. From this moment his career as a thinker was decided. Without cessation or relaxation or any turning aside to other pursuits, he devotes himself thenceforward to one grand pursuit, the only one that seemed to him to be worthy the name of true science.

The age was favorable for this man and his pursuits. Descartes was in the ascendant. One who should profoundly comprehend and clearly unfold his system, would be sure of approbation and success. In literature the great roll of illustrious authorship was nearly complete in France. Pascal, Bossuet, and Fénelon, had written prose. Corneille, Molière, Racine, La Fontaine, and Boileau, had handled the lyre. In style, the most perfect models were before our young aspirant, nor did he fall behind these models. Combining in himself the peculiar qualities of Pascal, Bossuet and Fénelon, the liveliness and force of the first, the loftiness and grand simplicity of the second, the peculiar grace of the last, his style is in many respects superior to that of any one of these singly, and it is not without reason that he is styled the *Plato* of Cartesianism. His thoughts are always lofty, his observations acute, his method luminous, his style attractive, his spirit earnest, truthful and sincere."

His first work, the "Search for Truth" ("Recherche de Verite"), was published in 1674, and met with the most flattering success. Subsequently, he published, chiefly by way of defending the principles of that treatise, and showing their consistency with the dogmas of the church, the "Christian Conversations," and "Christian Meditations," and the treatise on "Nature and Grace." It was on a copy of this, which was sent him by the author, that Bossuet wrote the words of St. Augustine—*Pulchra ; nova ; falsa.*

In 1684, appeared his "Treatise on Morals," and in the next year the "Reflections Theologic and Philosophic." In 1688, his work on metaphysics appeared. Beside these, he published, at various times, several minor works. Beside these publications, he wrote much in the way of correspondence, in an age when men conversed much, and corresponded little. His letters, on important subjects, and addressed chiefly to distinguished persons, amount to more than 500. In addition to these he devoted much thought to physics and mathematics, and there are in the possession of the Academy of Sciences, many parcels of papers by him on this class of subjects. He was chiefly devoted to speculative studies. History, and the studies of mere erudition had no charm for him. He read little, and erased from his writings all that which, however valuable in other respects, advanced no information. "An insect," says Fontenelle, "interested him more than all Greek and Roman history, and he had as little regard for that species of philosophy which consists only in learning the views of different philosophers."

Had he read more, and been better acquainted with the history of philosophy, we cannot help thinking he would have philosophized better.

In his mind and in his works, religion is ever in the first place ; philosophy is her handmaid. The two are closely and inseparably united, in his view, and ought never to be put asunder. "Religion is the true philosophy ; not that of pagans *indeed*, nor of those who discourse *before the truth has discoursed to them.*"

Reason is not however to be *subjected* to *faith.* The reason of which he speaks is "infallible, immutable, incorruptible ; ought ever to be mistress. God himself follows her. Evidence, intelligence, is better than faith, for faith will pass away, but intelligence will eternally abide; faith is a great good, but it is because she conducts to intelligence." In this he differs *toto cœlo* from Spinoza, who divorces completely religion from philosophy, assigning to each a distinct and separate sphere. In the one, we see the mystic; in the other the rationalist.

His death occurred October 13, 1715—hastened, it is said, by an interview and somewhat animated discussion with Berkeley, who, passing through Paris, called on him a few days previous to his decease.

Such was Malebranche, as a man and as regards the leading events of his life; one of the three great names that have adorned at once the Cartesian philosophy and the seventeenth century—trio illustrious: Spinoza, Malebranche, Leibnitz.

Let us first take a bird's-eye view of his philosophy as a whole; and then examine with more care its separate features, as we shall find them developed in his principal works.

The general outline of his system may be thus given. He was a Cartesian in his principles and tendencies. The characteristic feature of his philosophy is the consistent carrying out and making prominent what in Descartes had lurked as only a tendency, a germ not fully developed, viz., the merging and losing sight of the finite in the infinite, of the human soul in God; of all second causes in the great first cause, in the infinite; the making God to be everything, and man nothing.

In carrying out this view he makes but two kinds of existence in the world: body and spirit; the qualities of the former, extension and mobility; of the latter understanding and will. Neither body nor spirit can act of itself, however, without the immediate will and power of the great first cause; neither matter on mind, nor mind on matter. Hence as the ideas of all things exist in God, we see all things in him, in him live, move, have our being. What then, the use of matter at all? To this he can give no answer, but that it has pleased God to make a material world, and *this* he knows from *revelation only*. Gen. i. is all that stands between him and blank, complete *idealism*.

Such in mere outline is his system. Let us look at it more closely as developed in his principal works, "The Inquiry after Truth" and the "Ethics."

The design of the former work is to point out the errors derived from the senses, imagination, understanding, propensities, and passions, and also the causes and remedies of the same.

It is divided into six books. The first points out the errors of sense, and in so doing strikes at the root of the evidence for a material world. It begins by an analysis or classification of the powers of the mind. The soul is indivisible, yet of two parts: one passive, the mind or understanding; the other, passive and active both at once, *i. e.*, the will. The understanding has for its modifications, or faculties as we should say, sense, imagination, and pure intellect. The will has, for its modifications, the inclinations and passions. Such is his general map of the country to be explored.

He speaks next of the nature of error. It consists of false judgment, of which the cause is the *will;* the occasion, the understanding; and the prime reason, the fall of man. The remedy accordingly is, not to yield assent, except to propositions so evidently true that we cannot reasonably do otherwise; and also careful abstinence, penitence, self-denial as to pleasures of sense.

He specifies as errors of *sense*, our mistaking certain sensations as those of color, savor, etc., for qualities of bodies, whereas they are only impressions or sensations of our own , whence he concludes it may be so with our notions of figure and motion, since there is no necessary connection between the idea in the mind and the existence of the thing represented by that idea. The reason why men do not at once perceive that those are mere modifications of the soul, is that they have not a clear idea of the soul. There are several things to be distinguished in sensation : 1, action of external objects on the body ; 2, passion of the organ affected ; 3, passion of the soul consequent on that of the organ ; 4, judgment that what the soul perceives is out of itself and in the organ. It is because of not distinguishing these several things, that we fall into so many errors as to sensible qualities.

Next, as to errors of *imagination.* He defines imagination to be, at bottom, only a *feeble* and *languishing sensation ;* with this difference, however—sensation acts from without inward, imagination from within outward—to produce the excitement of the nerves. "Imagination is that power which the soul has of forming images of objects, by producing a change in the fibres of that part of the brain which may be called the principal ; and to imagine is to judge that the thing thus imaged or imagined is not *within* but *without ;* or that the object which is in view is an absent object." The cause of the nervous excitement aforesaid is the flow of animal spirits.

The errors of the imagination consist in bestowing on the imagined objects a reality and a place in time and space, which do not belong to them. Men of study and erudition, he says, are peculiarly liable to errors of the imagination. They are liable to confound novelty with error, to think that all new things are false, and to mistake antiquity for truth, as if all ancient things were true things. They are liable also to the opposite error—a passion for novelty, a desire to be inventors of new systems ; flattering themselves *that in saying what has never been said, they shall not want admirers.*

The author in the next book treats of errors of the understanding. The mind, or pure intellect, *has for its essence, thought ; and for the character of that essence, limitation.* It is *a thought limited.* Whence follows a twofold consequence. 1. It cannot perfectly know the infinite. 2. It cannot even know many things at once. If, not aware of this, mistaking its own capacity and sphere it thinks to comprehend the infinite, or to embrace that which surpasses it, it falls into error and confusion.

In this connection he takes occasion to define and describe what he calls ideas. "I believe," he says, "all the world agrees that we perceive not external objects *in themselves*. We see the sun, the stars, and a great variety of objects without us, and it is not to be supposed that the soul leaves the body and goes, so to speak, promenading through the skies to contemplate there all these objects. It sees them not in and by themselves, and the immediate object of our mind, when it sees the sun, for example, is not the sun itself, but something which is intimately united to our soul ; and it is this which I call *idea*. So by idea I understand here nothing else than that which is the immediate object, or the nearest thing to the mind when it perceives some object, that is to say, that which touches and modifies the mind in the perception which it has of an object."

Whence come these ideas ? From the mind itself, by its own power ? Or, if not by its own power, at least by virtue of its qualities, which are likewise the very qualities of things, and which to see in it, will be to see the things themselves ? Or come they from objects, as species, which detach themselves, and reach the mind through the channel of sense ? Are they produced in the mind by Deity, in the beginning, and once for all ; or else each time that it thinks of the objects ? Or, finally, united to a being all perfect and containing in himself all intelligible perfections, the models of all beings, are they simply manifest and present to the mind as *the representation in God*, of all that which it is possible to know ? The last supposition, he concludes to be the true solution of the problem ; and for these reasons : It is necessary to conclude that God has in his own mind these ideas of all existences ; else he could not create those existences. But God is intimately united to our spirits by his presence. He is the place of spirits, just as, in one sense, space is the place of bodies. Hence the possibility of seeing in God all the works of God, provided he chooses to discover them to us. He does choose to do so, and for these reasons: 1. He does all things in the simplest possible manner, and the simplest way in this case is to make us see in him all things by means of the ideas which represent them. 2. Because this places created minds in entire dependence on his power.

The conclusion is that we see, in fact, nothing but God, or that which is in God, and that, if we saw not God in some way we should not see anything. He is the intelligible world, or the place of spirits, just as the material world is the place of bodies; it is from his power that they receive all their modifications, and in his wisdom that they find all their ideas; and as his power and his wisdom are only himself, we believe with Saint Paul that he is not far from every one of us, and that in him we live and move and have our being. Such is the celebrated theory of vision in God. It is a sufficient spell with which to dissolve and sweep away this magnificent cloud palace of the fancy, to deny that there is any such thing as an *idea*, in the sense now given; that our ideas are in fact anything but modifications of our own minds; that they *represent* objects at all, in fact. Our choice is between this and that thoroughgoing idealism which resolves all things into God, with Spinoza and Malebranche, or into nothing, with Hume and Hegel.

Malebranche next discusses the *inclinations*, or, as he calls them, the natural movements of the mind. These are to mind what motion is to material things—imparting variety and life. These inclinations are only continual impressions of God on us, and correspond of course to the ends which he has in view in all his actions. These ends are: first, himself; secondly, the preservation and care of his creatures. To these ends our inclinations also relate; and thus deduced, we have first, the love of good in general, or of God ; whence spring two other inclinations : the love of self, and the love of others. The love of self, again, is twofold : the love of being or of greatness, *i. e.*, virtue, knowledge, wealth, honor, reputation ; and then the love of *well*-being, or pleasure. The latter is a good, notwithstanding the stoical views to the contrary ; at least partakes of the character of a good. All these, however, are frequent sources of error to the human mind, as he proceeds to show. Next he treats of the passions and errors thence arising. *Passions* differ from *inclinations* in this, he holds : the latter to the soul as their object, the former to the body. Passions are impressions of God on us, which dispose us to love our body and seek its welfare. Inclinations are impressions leading to the love, not of body but of soul, as God, ourselves, our neighbors, etc.,

In all our passions there is a certain judgment of the relation of objects to us, accompanied with a certain movement of soul corresponding thereto, as joy, sadness, desire. He notices particularly, in this connection, the characteristic feature of all our passions, viz., a certain satisfaction which we take in being thus affected : the consent of the mind to, and its delight in being thus affected, even when the passions are in themselves not of an agreeable nature. Even in the emotion of grief or of anger we take pleasure. The errors to which passion leads are next pointed out : all summed up in this general one—they lead not to our true good, but to that of the body merely ; but the body is not us ; its good is not our true good—that is God only, and union with God, which is truth.

In the last book, the author treats of method, and gives various rules and observations on right reasoning. He takes the ground that all the forces of nature are only the will of God in operation, and that what we call natural causes are not in fact true causes at all, but only, as he elsewhere expresses the same thing, occasional ones—causes only in name; "all that can be said is that they have the power to do what God does by means of them, or rather that they are for him only the occasions of producing effects in consequence of laws which he has made for the sake of executing his designs in a uniform and constant manner." "There is no relation of causality between a body and a mind, much less between a mind and a body; there is none indeed between one body and another, or one mind and another. Neither body nor mind, then, are causes of anything—they are only the occasions. Everything which happens must have a cause, however. What can it be but God?" * (This is the very root and substance of the school of modern theology, named from Emmons).

Such is the outline and general contents of this celebrated treatise, which contains, perhaps, the fullest development of the philosophy of Malebranche.

It will not be necessary, after this somewhat full analysis, to go with any minuteness into the examination of other works of the author. Sufficient to say that, as regards moral philosophy, in common with all Cartesians, he makes the will synonymous with desire or love; to will is to love, and even liberty itself is but a form of love. His treatise on ethics consists of two parts: the one treats of virtue, the other of duty. Virtue is the *love of order*. There is but one order, and so but one virtue, or love of order. Order is the relation of ideas among themselves, and as God is the seat and substance of ideas and their relation, the love of order is the love of God, and of those whom God would have us love, *i. e.*, our fellow-men. But this love must be *free, dominant, habitual.* Virtue is thus at once *science* and *obedience.*

He accounts for the existence of evil in the universe as follows: "God desires positively the perfection of his work, and wishes only *indirectly* the imperfection that pre-

* These extracts are from another work, the "Christian Meditations," but the same views are maintained in the "Inquiry after Truth."

sents itself; he does the good and permits the evil, because it is for the sake of the good that he has established natural laws, and it is, on the contrary, only *in consequence* of these natural laws that evil comes. He does the good, because he wishes his work should be perfect; he does the evil, not because positively and directly he wishes to do it, but because he wishes that his manner of acting should be simple and regular;" closely resembling the modern theory of evil as *incidental* to the best possible system; indeed is it not, substantially, the very same theory? "Malebranche," says Mackintosh, "is perhaps the first philosopher who has precisely laid down, and rigidly adhered to the great principle, *that virtue consists in pure intentions and dispositions of mind*, without which, actions, however conformable to rules, are not truly moral; a truth of the highest importance, which, in the theological form, may be said to have been the main principle of the first Protestant reformers. The ground of piety, according to him, is the conformity of the attributes of God to those moral qualities which we irresistibly love and reverence. "Sovereign princes," says he, "have no right to use their authority without reason. Even God has no such miserable right" (Hist. Eth. Phil. p. 128). This of course presupposes the existence of moral distinctions, and makes those distinctions, in fact, independent of Deity. We are bound to love God, because his character conforms to such and such moral qualities of which we form a conception, and which we admire. Were he otherwise, we were not bound to love him. There are such things as right and justice and goodness, and there are ideas of them in our minds. God conforms to these ideas, possesses those attributes, therefore we are bound to love him.

Such, in brief, the system of Malebranche. How much to choose between it and Spinoza's, as a system? Not much, as Cousin says. By the doctrine of occasional causes, Malebranche takes away the efficacy of the human will, and destroys human liberty and personality; while by his theory of ideas and vision in God, he destroys all evidence of the existence, all possibility of the independent reality of external things; thus both the soul and the mind are absorbed in God. What is this but the pantheism and absolute *unity* of Spinoza?

CHAPTER VI.

LEIBNITZ.

On the third of July, 1646, was born at Leipsic one of the most remarkable men of the seventeenth century—one of those great minds that seem destined by Providence to take in at one glance all that has been previously made known to man, to comprehend within the limits of one little life the collective wisdom of past centuries, and not content with that, having quickly reached the bound and farthest limit of human wisdom yet attained, to overleap that line and push onward into regions hitherto unexplored and dwell among yet undiscovered truths. Such minds there are, one or two such in a century perhaps; two such, at least, in the century named—Newton was one, such another was Newton's great rival and contemporary, Leibnitz. Of the two, Newton's was perhaps the stronger mind, Leibnitz's the more active and ready. Newton was the more cool, cautious, patient thinker. Leibnitz the more ardent explorer, the more general, comprehensive scholar, the greater genius; Newton adhered more closely to the one pursuit in which he was destined to make the most brilliant discoveries. Leibnitz, conscious of no special superiority in any one department of science, and confined to no one either by nature or choice, ranged at will the whole field of human knowledge, gathered rare flowers wherever he wandered, and enriched with new discoveries whatever region he explored. Like Newton master of mathematical science, and like him far in advance of all other men in it, unlike him he was master also of law and jurisprudence, as far outstripping the ablest proficients in these sciences as he outstripped the ablest mathematicians of Europe ; unlike him he gave himself also to history, and enriched that science with some of the most profound and erudite treatises of which that age could boast ; unlike him he was master also of philosophy in the true sense of that term, and created an era in the philosophical speculations of more than one country in Europe. Nor was he less a theologian than a philosopher, and in whatever department of human knowledge we follow him, whether as mathematician, jurist, historian, philosopher, or theologian, we find him in each and all proficient, a master, enlarging the borders and widening the fields of whatever science he investigates ; so that of him it may with truth be said, *whatever he touched he adorned.* Nor was Europe unaware of his greatness—or ungrateful for his services. He was loaded with honors and rewards, pensions and decorations. Foreign courts and princes vied with each other to do him homage. In the earlier part of his literary career, while yet not so widely known to fame, he attracted the notice of Baron Von Boineburg—by whom he was recommended to the Elector of Mayence, and by whose favor he was appointed Electoral Counsellor and Chancellor of Justice. Afterward he found a friend and patron in the Duke of Brunswick, who bestowed on him a pension, with leave of foreign residence. After the death of that nobleman, he was appointed historiographer to the family and spent some years in collecting materials abroad, for that work. The Elector of Brandenburg, afterward Frederick I. of Prussia, seeks his advice and aid in establishing the Royal Academy of Sciences at Berlin, and appoints him its first president. From the Emperor Charles VI. he receives the dignities of Aulic Counsellor and of Baron, with a pension of 2,000 florins. Even the Czar Peter of Russia avails himself of the advice of so wise a man respecting the improvement of his vast empire, and in return confers on him a pension of 1,000 roubles. Evidently then, we are not to think of this Leibnitz as one of those retired and quiet men who in obscurity and poverty work out, unknown to fame while living and honored only when dead, the great problems of philosophy. He stands in a very different relation to the men and events of this busy world. Seldom indeed has man of letters and science been more honored or more widely known while living than Leibnitz. The reason of the phenomenon is, he was a man of universal genius, of varied and vast attainments—a speculator and philosopher, but not a speculative philosopher merely; a thinker and theorist, but not a theorist merely; not an impracticable man, but a man in contact with other men, with the age—a man whose attainments, vast as they were, were all available and of use to mankind, of use in action and for the present time, and therefore nations and kings gladly availed themselves of his labors.

In reading, Leibnitz devoured everything — nothing came amiss, nothing escaped him. His mental activity was almost without a parallel. He spent days and nights in succession in the most severe mental exertions, interrupted with only now and then an hour or two of sleep, which he frequently took in his chair. Nor was his memory inferior to his mental activity. What he once fairly grasped was thenceforth *his*, and forever his. Time rolled its successive waves upon the firm shore of that tenacious mind, not as with other men to weaken and wash out little by little the acquisitions of former years, but rather to deepen and consolidate the impression already made upon it. In his old age we hear him, in the intervals of toil, repeating whole books of Virgil. His career as an author commenced in early life, and continued till the late evening of his days. He had already published a mathematical treatise, a dissertation on philosophy, and several legal treatises, at the age of twenty. At sixty-four he gives to the world his celebrated work on theology. Five years after, at the age of sixty-nine, he publishes his essay on the Human Understanding. These last were the fruits of his latest and most mature thoughts. He dies the year following (November 14, 1716), at the age of seventy. A life of such severe and continued mental labor, embracing fifty years of active authorship, is quite unusual, and constitutes not the least remarkable feature in the history of this rare man. In his habits he was frugal and temperate ; in appearance a thin, spare man, of medium height, with an habitual stoop of the shoulders, of firm health, of pleasing countenance and animated, lively manner of address, simple and easy in his manners. His hair, in early life black, was soon turned white by toil, but his eyes continued strong and capable of service to the last. His style of living was simple in the extreme, and his enemies charged him with avarice. Of his domestic affairs he was totally negligent, and was never married. His monument—in form a Grecian temple—bears the simple inscription, *Ossa Leibnitii.*

Such was the man—what now his philosophy ? A follower in general, as you know, of Descartes, yet not a blind follower of any system or any master. A Cartesian in the main, and as regards the school in which he received his training and first impulse ; a Cartesian as to his general principles ; yet it were hard to say, so fully did he breathe his own spirit into that system and so widely modify it, whether he were more indebted to Cartesianism or Cartesianism to him. Withal, unlike the founder of that system, he was almost as much a *Platonist* as Cartesian. Of Grecian philosophy, and specially of the wisdom of Plato, he drank early and copious draughts, nor did his study and his admiration of that philosophy fall off as he advanced in years. He was a Cartesian, yet he possessed one advantage which Descartes did not—that of coming after Descartes, of coming forward at a period when the system of that great master had attained its development, and had produced its legitimate fruits; when its ultimate tendencies, as shown in Spinoza and Malebranche, were obvious; when its renowned antagonists, and especially Locke, were vigorously assailing it in its weakest points and striving to build the edifice of speculative truth on another foundation. Hence we are not surprised to learn that a mind so sagacious and comprehensive as Leibnitz received the system of Descartes only with essential modification, and remodelled after the designs of his own creative genius.

We have no systematic development of the philosophy of Leibnitz—no complete exposition of his system; yet in his occasional treatises lie the germs of much of the future philosophy of Germany and indeed of Europe and the age. "The mind of Leibnitz," says Morell, "was cast in a gigantic mould, and formed by nature to tower above the rest of the world around him. By virtue of this it was, that like all great minds he cast his shadow before him, and gave more pregnant suggestions in some of his cursory writings than most other men could do in the combined and systematic labor of their whole life."

At the basis of the Leibnitzian philosophy, we find this general fundamental principle: that, in philosophy, as in other sciences, there are certain grand first truths, necessary truths, not to be learned from experience, but grounded in the soul itself, and resting on principles and proofs quite independent of the testimony of sense. Upon this foundation rests whatever is peculiar to his system. Herein of course lies the fundamental difference between him and Locke. There is nothing in the understanding which was not first in the sense, says Locke. Nothing *but the understanding itself*, says Leibnitz, the very power and faculty of forming ideas; this surely is not derived from sense and experience, this, *at least,* though not ideas themselves, must be innate, and thence spring those necessary truths, those laws of the understanding, that are the primary sources and elements of human knowledge.

Hence he stands midway between Locke and Descartes, rejecting the *innate ideas* of the latter, and rejecting also the *sensational origin* of all our ideas as maintained by the former. This is the ground subsequently maintained and systematically defended by Kant and his followers in Germany, by Cousin and the eclectic idealists in France, and now very generally regarded as the true ground with respect to the origin of our knowledge; *viz.*, that, while much of our knowledge is doubtless derived from sense, while ideas are not, strictly speaking, innate, nevertheless there are certain necessary first truths, or laws of thought and of the human mind, not derived from experience, but bedded in the framework of the soul itself, integral in its nature and constitution, needing only the occasion afforded by sense, needing only opportunity and circumstance, to call them forth and to develop them in the consciousness. Such are the ideas of time and space, *e. g.*, as shown by Cousin. Such are also, in fact, the first principles, or necessary truths, of Reid and Stuart.

All philosophical truth, Leibnitz maintained, must be deduced by analysis from the primary truths involved in these necessary laws of the human understanding. The ideas derived from the senses cannot serve as the starting point and basis in such investigations, for the ideas thus derived are confused, indistinct, uncertain. In this he agrees with the old Grecian rationalists, the Eleatics, and also with Plato.

But how are we to distinguish the true and primitive ideas from the false and sensuous? What tests or criteria of truth? Not the Cartesian one of clearness, for that is inadequate. Instead of that, Leibnitz proposes as criteria the two great principles on which, as he says, all our conclusions rest: that of contradiction, by which, as Aristotle also held, we judge that to be false which involves contradictory statements; and that of the sufficient reason, which teaches that no assertion is true if no sufficient reason can be given why it is true. The former is a test of absolute and necessary truth, as, *e. g.*, the mathematical conceptions, which, to be true, need only come within the range of possibilities. The latter principle is the test of actual or real truths relating to contingent existence. The absolute final cause or reason of all truth is God.

In another respect, Leibnitz stands apart from the Cartesian ranks. We have seen that it was the tendency of that school, in its exaltation of the infinite, the great first cause, to lose sight of all inferior and secondary causes—of all activity in nature—in fine, as seen in Spinoza and Malebranche, to resolve all things into Deity, and lose sight of nature itself in one great object of thought, of whose grand existence all phenomena were but modes. Leibnitz perceived this tendency and set himself to counteract it, to bring back to its true place in the system the idea of activity in nature. "The capital error of the Cartesians," he says, "is that they have placed the whole essence of matter in extension and impenetrability, imagining that bodies can be in absolute repose; we shall show that one substance cannot receive from any other the power of acting, but that the whole force is preëxistent in itself." This, as Morell justly remarks, is the key to all that is peculiar in the system of Leibnitz.

In particular it explains, as it seems to me, the *monadology* of his system, so often ridiculed, so seldom understood. How shall we account for the phenomena of nature that are continually passing around us, inquires this close observer; not by the principle of extension. That would give us matter without change or alteration, no movement, no development, such as we see constantly in nature. There must be some fundamental attribute of matter, giving rise to all these changes—an inherent power in substance itself; how else can you account for the phenomena in question? unless indeed you take the ground that they are immediately and directly produced by the divine power. If there is, then, as it would seem, some inherent force, or activity, or power, in matter, where does it reside? Not in compound substances or masses, for these are infinitely divisible, and every essential attribute is independent of such combinations. Beneath these compound masses, some uncompound, simple substances must exist as the ground of the compound—exist though not recognized by sense. In the process of the infinite division of the composite mass, we reach eventually a point where every *material* property vanishes; we get down to zero, the limit of extension, and there remains only the simple idea of power or force as the basis of all existence. This substance simple and uncompound, underlying all compound masses, this simple element of *force*, the basis of existence, is what Leibnitz terms *monad*.

The monad being immaterial, unextended, indivisible, is subject of course to no external or foreign influence, and whatever changes take place in it, take place in consequence of an *inherent* energy in the monad itself, by which it has the power to modify and develop itself. The monad is indissoluble, and therefore imperishable. Each monad differs in its qualities from all others, for no two things are ever exactly alike. He specifies four distinct classes: 1, Those which compose material objects—not self-conscious, manifesting only physical qualities; 2, Those which form the souls of *beasts*, having an *indistinct* consciousness; 3, Those which compose the souls of *men*, having a *clear* and *distinct* consciousness; and finally, 4, God the original, absolute, eternal monad, the Monas Monadum, the origin of all knowledge and all being. All finite beings are aggregates of monads. Different monads have no direct influence on each other. But yet the internal changes of each monad are such as to agree with the corresponding changes in the monads with which it is immediately connected. This is effected by the Divine wisdom and power in the first constitution of the several monads, and the arrangement by which this agreement is effected he denotes by the term preëstablished harmony. He is led to this doctrine in this way. It was an old maxim of the philosophers that *like* only can act on like, *i. e.*, that things wholly unlike in their nature can exert no reciprocal influence on each other. But the monads of body and those of mind are wholly unlike. Mind and matter, then, can have no influence on each other. How then *do* they have any union or co-action? This is brought about by the divine power and skill in so *constituting* and *arranging* them that they shall correspond and work together in complete unison. This harmony is preëstablished—hence the term, all things are pre-formed, and from eternity. He who produces them perceives in them, as resulting from their *nature*, all their future movements. Hence the harmony of all things, of the past and the future, of the divine decree and human conduct.

It is evident that from this system there proceeds, as by natural and inevitable consequence, the doctrine of *philosophical necessity* in all its purity and depth. The only kind of liberty consistent with this preëstablished constitution and harmony of all things, is liberty to do that which actually is done—that, and nothing else. The only point remaining worthy of special notice, in the philosophy of Leibnitz is his celebrated doctrine of *optimism*, which is developed in his Theodicea, or treatise on theology. The object of this treatise more especially is, to defend the wisdom of the Creator against the charges brought against it on the score of the *existence of evil* in the universe. The position assumed is, that of all *possible* worlds an infinite number of which are possible, God has actually chosen the very best. Everything which is, however imperfect, in itself considered, is still, all things considered, and in its relation to all things, the very best possible. Hence the name, *optimism*, given to this doctrine and the system framed upon it. According to this system the existence of evil is no argument against the supreme wisdom and benevolence, for *metaphysical* evil—from which *natural* and *moral* evil, or *suffering* and *sin*, necessarily result—is only the *necessary limitation*, or *imperfection*, inherent in, and pertaining to the *nature of things*. *Moral* evil is based on the premise of human *freedom*, or the choice we have of one among many acts, all of which are physically possible. The future is indeed determined, and all the actions of men ; yet man is ignorant of that future and of that determination, and acts only according to reason and preference. From various causes he choses oft that which is ill—hence moral evil, or sin ; yet in the end even this shall prove for the best as regards the whole, and every being, however imperfect, and every act and event, however evil in itself, shall contribute as a necessary part to the perfection of the whole.

The close correspondence of this system with the theological tenet, that sin is the necessary means of the greatest good, and also with the theology of a more infallible standard, which asserts that all things work together for good to them that love God, is too obvious to require statement.

The system of Leibnitz as now explained, was somewhat modified subsequently by its most distinguished adherent and disciple, Christian Wolf, about the beginning of the eighteenth century. He supplied what was previously wanting, a clear, connected, methodical form, modifying somewhat the doctrine of monads, drawing a broader line of distinction between matter and mind, and limiting the preëstablished harmony to the mutual relations of soul and body, rather than to monads in general, and applying to the whole a strictly mathematical method, he first gave the whole system a complete scientific form.

The whole province of philosophy with him consists of two parts, theoretical and practical. The former comprises *logic proper*, and *metaphysics*, which latter includes *ontology, psychology, cosmology, and natural theology*. Practical philosophy comprises ethics, the law of nature, and politics. Thus improved, the system found its way into most of the universities of Europe and held sway predominant for the first half of the eighteenth century.

CHAPTER VII.

HOBBES.

THE manifest tendency of the Baconian doctrines was to give undue prominence to natural philosophy and to physical science generally, greatly at the expense of mental and moral philosophy, which, whether by design or not, yet in fact and almost inevitably, were thrown into the background. Nothing in human knowledge was held of much importance or considered as fully reliable which was not based on processes and investigations purely experimental.

The empirical element preponderated over every other, and the ultimate tendency and final result was of course decidedly in the direction of a wide-sweeping and thorough sensationalism. The practical lesson learned by the wisdom of the age from this master teacher was to fall back ultimately, and as the only safe method, upon the testimony and experience of the senses as the main if not the only sound and sure basis of knowledge. The master left the age and his disciples little more than a new and a true *method*. It was for them to apply it and discover results. Many arose to do this in the department of natural and physical research. One man alone, a warm admirer of the Baconian doctrines, appeared, to apply the empirical method to the investigation of mental and moral science. This man was Thomas Hobbes, the philosopher of Malmesbury, one of the most distinguished writers of the seventeenth century. He was born April 5, 1588, in the borough of Malmesbury. After studying at Oxford, and making the tour of France and Italy in company with the son of Lord Hardwicke, he spent several years in the family of that nobleman as secretary. Here he formed the acquaintance of Lord Bacon, Lord Herbert, and Ben Jonson, and subsequently at Paris and Pisa, during a tour to the continent, he became acquainted with Gassendi and Galileo. Returning to England he fixed his residence at Chatsworth. The prospect of political troubles soon drove him to Paris, where he resided during the wars of the revolution, and where he published most of his works. He was employed to teach Prince Charles (Charles II.) the elements of mathematical science. Returning to England he was kindly received by the Devonshire family, with whom he passed the remainder of his life, employed mostly in writing upon philosophical and political subjects. A treatise, in 1650, on Human Nature, and another, in 1658, on Man, in which he treats of the moral and intellectual faculties, are his principal philosophical writings. But the work on which his fame chiefly rests is the Leviathan, 1651, in which he treats of the matter, form, and power of a commonwealth, ecclesiastical and civil, which work greatly alarmed the ecclesiastics, and excited no little ferment in England. It was severely censured in Parliament sixteen years after its publication; so great was the disapprobation with which it was generally regarded.

His other literary labors were a translation of the Iliad and Odyssey, which passed through three editions in ten years, and a History of the Civil Wars, which did not appear till after his death. After the restoration, Hobbes was received with favor by the King, who gave him a pension of 100 pounds per annum from his privy purse. He died, December 4, 1679, at Hardwicke, a seat of the Earl of Devonshire, at the age of 91.*

* See amusing account of his personal habits, especially his smoking—Sydney Smith's Sketches of Moral Philosophy, pp. 365–366.

Perhaps no writer, unless it be Spinoza, has been more generally caluminated than the philosopher of Malmesbury. By some he is regarded as a dangerous man; by others as a shallow and superficial man. His influence has never been great, owing to the fear which has been entertained of his doctrines. Yet that very fear is a tribute to his strength, and proclaims him anything but a weak and shallow writer. "Impartial minds," says Lewes, "will always rank Hobbes among the greatest writers England has produced; and by writers we do not simply mean masters of language but masters of thought. He is profound and he is clear, weighty, and sparkling. His style, as mere style, is in its way as fine as anything in English; it has the clearness as well as the solidity and brilliancy of crystal" (Hist. Phil. ii. 495).

He is, in a word, one of those cool, collected, resolute thinkers, who in their search after truth are startled by no consequences, turned back by no results, but keep on in close pursuit of the game with all the tenacity and perseverance of the hound upon the track of the stately deer. The world at large is too lazy to keep up with such runners, too timid to follow at such a rate, a leisurely walk or jog-trot is the most it can venture, and it must be a tame and slow-footed animal that shall allow itself to be fairly overtaken in such a race.

We by no means intend by this, however, to approve the recklessness of such a writer as Hobbes, or to vindicate his conclusions.

The main features of his philosophy may be thus sketched. Bacon had relied upon *experience* as the main source of knowledge. Upon this ground Hobbes takes his stand, and so develops the principle as to make sensation the real basis of all knowledge and all thought. Hence the *material* tendency of his philosophy. By sensation we perceive only what is *material*, and as sensation is the source of all our knowledge, hence *matter is the only reality*, and what we perceive or think, we perceive as existing—what exists *to us*—is part of the material universe. Our sensation is the standard and criterion of all truth and reality. We have then to do simply with *bodies* in our search after the truth ; we can know nothing else. *This* is the substance of philosophy, its aim and province, to teach the doctrine and phenomena of *bodies*, regarded as to their existence and their changes. Under the term bodies, however, he includes mind or soul. He divides all bodies into natural and political ; including under the former the physical and mathematical sciences, psychology, logic, etc. Our ideas or thoughts, he holds to be each a "representation or appearance of some quality or other accident of a body without us, which is commonly called an object, which object worketh on the eyes, ears, and other parts of a man's body, and by diversity of working produceth diversity of appearances. The original of them all is that which we call *sense*. For there is no conception in a man's mind, which hath not at first totally or by parts been begotten upon the organs of sense. The rest are derived from that original."

According to this view of things, the mind seems to be wholly natural in its nature ; and the phenomena of consciousness are the natural and immediate result of our physical organization. "All the qualities called sensible," he says, "are in the object that causeth them but so many several motions of the matter by which it presseth on our organs diversely. Neither in us that are pressed are they any else but diverse motions. Every operation of the mind is but a transformed sensation, and sensation itself is simply the effect of material objects around us pressing on the organs of sense and on that material organization within, viz., the mind.

Hobbes divides the faculties of the mind into two classes ; cognitive, imaginative, or conceptive ; and motive. There are in our minds continually, "certain images or conceptions of the things without." We call this imagery or representation "our conception, imagination, ideas," of the external things. The faculty or power by which we can form this conception or knowledge, is what he means by the *conception or conceptive* faculty.

While *sense*, however, *furnishes our conceptions*, those *conceptions*, or sensations, do *not* correspond to any external qualities of bodies; on the contrary, the sensible qualities of bodies are but modifications of our own sentient being. This was also the doctrine of Descartes.

The imagination, according to Hobbes, is the result of the gradual ceasing of that *motion* or movement, by which sensation is produced; in consequence of which diminished movement the impression becomes fainter and fainter. "Imagination, therefore, is nothing but decaying sense." By imagination he means simply the faculty of forming *images*—the primitive sense of the term. He likens this decaying sense to the gradual going down of the waves after a storm. The cause of this decay or diminution of the sensible impression, is not the absolute decay of the motion made in sense, but the impulse of some succeeding and stronger motion, by which the former is obscured, as the *stars* go out in appearance, when the *sun* rises. Memory and imagination are the same things essentially under different names; memory denoting, not the thing itself, the decaying sense which he turns imagination, but rather the *character* of it, as something *fading* and *past*.

Hobbes gets a glimpse, though indistinct, of the great law of association of ideas: "When a man thinketh on any subject, his next thought is not altogether so casual as it seems to be. Not every thought to every thought succeeds indifferently." The reason why one follows another he says is this: All our ideas or images are *motions* in us, relics of those made in sense, and the motions that followed each other in sense follow each other in imagination or thought also, so that when the former come again to mind or occur, the latter follow them, just as water upon a plain table is drawn which way any one part of it is guided by the finger." This train or succession of thoughts he divides into two sorts: that which is spontaneous, unguided, as in men untrained to reflection; and that which is the result of, or modified by our voluntary effort.

We cannot imagine the infinite, says Hobbes, cannot conceive it; can imagine or conceive only what is within the sphere of sense. Of the infinite we can form an idea only by *faith*.

Language is, with Hobbes, a very important thing. Without it society would have been impossible, and the simplest mathematical truths indiscoverable. Our *original* knowledge is from sensation, but we use *words* to denote the things thus known, and these words we form into propositions. Understanding is the faculty that perceives the relation between words and things, and affords us thus *another* and *secondary* sort of knowledge. Truth and falsehood are only the agreement or disagreement of words among themselves.

Reasoning is merely a numerical calculation, involving and consisting in the processes of addition and subtraction, words being the *figures* used. *Error* in reasoning arises only from using the wrong words or figures, or a want of proper definition of terms.

The *ethics* of Hobbes correspond to his psychology. As thought is only transformed sensation, so *good* and *evil* are only other expressions for pleasure and pain. Nothing is in itself either good or evil simply and absolutely, but only as they affect us. Our duties practically, then, are simply to avoid the disagreeable, and seek the pleasurable, and as we cannot be otherwise affected than we are by the agreeable and the disagreeable, our volitions or desires are consequently determined by motives external, so that we are creatures of irresistible necessity. The active powers and faculties of the soul are simply our desires or wants. The will is the ultimate or final desire. The end of all our desires and wants is pleasure. This is, then, the true destiny of man, his law of action, the chief of all his rights and all his duties.

From this results his theory of civil polity. As good and evil are simply pleasure and pain, and nature teaches to desire the one and shun the other, man is by nature inclined, and instructed, to do whatever will secure and promote the greatest degree of personal enjoyment, irrespective of his fellow men. Whatever tends to this is reasonable and lawful. Right is the liberty of employing our natural powers agreeably to reason, and reason teaches to do whatever can be done to promote our own enjoyment. In other words, might makes right. But this would bring man constantly into collision with his fellows—for they are all equal; have equally the same law of self-preservation and self-enjoyment. Hence war is the natural state of man, each against his fellow. This, however, is found to be not for the highest welfare of all concerned. It is the end of repose and security and tranquil enjoyment. Self-defence is continually necessary against the encroachments of the more powerful. Hence to secure the highest attainable good, men league together for mutual defence and security—and so originates the civil compact, in which the individual merges some private rights in the public organization, and resigns part of his natural power or right into the hands of others. Thus begins society as organized—the state; the tribe; the city—in a word, *government.* It would follow from this, that if any one is powerful enough he may do *what he likes, and it is all right.*

Cousin very well objects that *all force* claims *pretence* of *justice* and *piety*. But why *so* if mere force is of itself sufficient to *justify?* He farther argues against this scheme that whatever may have been the *primitive* state of man we are not of necessity to take *that* as the *criterion* and standard of judgment in such cases. A state of barbarism may have been the primitive state of man, and out of this may have sprung the *beginning* of human government. But it is not therefore the true *foundation* and *reason* and basis on which law and society are built, nor the standard by which we are to measure them.

As the design of human government, according to Hobbes, is to keep in check the lawless and aggressive desires of the individual, otherwise destructive of the interests of his fellows, so that government is the best, answers best the end of government, which keeps man most completely in check—in other words, which is *strongest*. Such is an absolute monarchy,—the perfection of all government; and *law*, *morals*, and *religion* ought to be subject to its undisputed and irresistible sway.

We can hardly wonder that such a system met with strong opposition and awakened no inconsiderable alarm. Mr. Hallam thus sums up his estimate of the philosophy now detailed: "The political system of Hobbes, like his moral system, of which in fact it is only a portion, sears up the heart. It takes away the sense of wrong that has consoled the wise and good in their dangers, the proud appeal of innocence under oppression, like that of Prometheus to the elements, uttered to the witnessing world, to coming ages, to the just ears of heaven. It confounds the principles of moral approbation, the notions of good and ill desert, in a servile idolatry of the monstrous Leviathan it creates, and after sacrificing all *right* at the altar of *power*, denies to the Omnipotent the prerogative of dictating the laws of his own worship" (Literature of Europe, vol. iii. p. 176). Such is Hobbesism. Would Bacon have sanctioned it? By no means. Yet, as Morell justly observes, the *germ* of it is in the Baconian philosophy.

CHAPTER VIII.

LOCKE.

THE opinions of Hobbes excited no little alarm in England and awoke no little controversy. Some sought to oppose those doctrines in one way and some in another, but everywhere they were the object of attention and discussion. The most distinguished opponents of that system were Lord Herbert, Richard Cumberland, bishop of Peterborough, and Ralph Cudworth, the well known author of the "Intellectual System of the Universe," a true Platonist in philosophy. While this discussion and conflict were going on, a company of Oxford students met one day at the rooms of one John Locke, of the university. They discussed and wrangled, but to little purpose as regards the elucidation of truth, and the problems which they sought to solve. It occurred to one of them that that were pursuing a wrong method, and that, instead of analyzing things themselves, it were better to begin the search with investigating the *mind* itself, to know what it *can* and what it cannot comprehend. From that occurrence dates, the first idea and origin of a work which has awakened more thought, and received more attention probably, than any metaphysical treatise, since the days of Aristotle, viz., the "Essay on the Human Understanding." Its author was by no means, however, a mere metaphysican. He carried his philosophical genius and acumen into the science of government, political economy, and religion. His name and authority, as Cousin has well said, fill the eighteenth century.

John Locke was born at Wrington, not far from Bristol, August 29, 1632. His father took part in the political disturbances of 1640, and served as captain in the

Parliamentary army under Colonel Popham. To this officer young Locke was indebted for an introduction to the College of Westminster, at London, where he stayed till he was nineteen or twenty, and then went to Oxford. It is not improbable that these early family associations had something to do with that devotion to civil and religious liberty which breathes in all the writings and pervaded the spirit of John Locke. Oxford was then, as now, attached to the past; worshipped antiquity, gave itself to the scholastic philosophy; had little sympathy with the age and the busy world. Locke, whose cast of mind was eminently *practical,* had little sympathy with that spirit and that philosophy, and consequently paid little attention to those studies that were chiefly in vogue there, but sought a more congenial pursuit in the study of medicine and the classics. Feeble health prevented him from the practice of medicine, nor, indeed did he ever take the title, yet he seems to have attained some distinction in it as a science. The culture of this science, and of the kindred natural sciences, seems to have developed in him a habit and love of close observation, which were in truth the best foundation and training, for those still higher pursuits in which he was chiefly to distinguish himself. He continued at Oxford, it would seem, till 1664, when he accompanied William Swan, as secretary, to the court of Berlin. Returning at the end of a year to Oxford, he met for the first time with one who was to exert an important influence on his future fortunes, Anthony Ashley Cooper, first Earl of Shaftesbury. This nobleman was in ill-health, and meeting with Locke as a medical adviser, discovered in him more than ordinary abilities, and formed a strong personal attachment to him. The skill of Locke detected the true nature of his disease, and aided him to regain health. The two remained firm friends ever after. Shaftesbury was not ungrateful. The fortunes of his friend were linked thenceforth with his own.

Nor is it a little to the credit of this ambitious and brilliant man, that in his subsequent political career he remained faithful to his earlier friendship, and that he continued not only to treat Locke with due regard, but that he held so high a place in the esteem and regard of so good and truth-loving a man as John Locke. It was Shaftesbury who first discovered the ability and worth of Locke, drew him forth from his retirement in Oxford, and introduced him to the brilliant circles of literary society in London—to such men as Lord Halifax, the Duke of Buckingham, the Earl of Northumberland, the Earl of Pembroke, and others. In 1668, Locke was chosen a member of the Royal Society of Sciences. When Shaftesbury became High Chancellor in 1672, he gave Locke an honorable and important office, that of secretary of presentation to benefices. One year, however, sees them both out of office, both in again in 1679, only to see them out again shortly after. Shaftesbury is now banished from England, and dies in Holland, in 1683, whither his faithful friend had followed him. No man had done more than Shaftesbury to bring back Charles II. to the throne, yet he incurred the displeasure of that fickle and ungrateful monarch, and so fully did Locke share that displeasure, that in his retreat in Holland, Charles cuts him off from the list of members of Oxford, and even demands his person as implicated in the Monmouth conspiracy. It was only through the kindness of friends that Locke escaped being given up as a malefactor. It was in Holland that he wrote his first philosophical treatises and finished his greatest work—the Essay on the Human Understanding, although it was not published till after his return to England. The revolution of 1688, which brought in a different dynasty, enabled Locke to return to London, where he was received with every mark of favor. William gave him his confidence, and in turn Locke wrote much and did much to strengthen the hands of the governing power.

He was appointed to a responsible and lucrative office, but was obliged by failing health to resign. He retired to private life and seclusion, passed his remaining years in peaceful retirement in Oates, at the house of his friend Lady Masham, daughter of Dr. Cudworth, where he died, October 28, 1704, aged 72.

In private life and personal character Locke was justly esteemed by all as a man of accomplished manners, strict and unbending integrity, a faithful friend, an upright and amiable man. As an author his fame is coëxtensive with the English language. No writer on philosophical subjects has probably exerted so wide and lasting an influence on the thinking mind, not of England only but of all Europe. His name is justly regarded as one of the brightest ornaments of English literature and science, and of the seventeenth century. His system has been severely assailed; it has become fashionable within the present century to speak lightly and with disparagement of his philosophy; his influence is by no means what it once was; but it will be long ere those who know anything of the history of philosophy, or have any respect for the opinions and great minds of the past, will pronounce with other than profound respect the name of John Locke.

The plan of the Essay on the Human Understanding seems to have been conceived as early as 1670, but it was not until his exile in Holland that he found leisure to write out and complete the work, and it was not published until 1690, after his return. It was written consequently, not in consecutive efforts, but, as he says, "by incoherent parcels, and after long intervals of neglect resumed again as my humor or occasions permitted, and at last in retirement where an attendance on my health gave me leisure, it was brought into that order thou now seest it." He further informs us that when he first put pen to paper, he thought all he should have to say on this subject would have been contained in one sheet, but that the further he went the larger prospect he had, new discoveries still leading him on till his work "grew insensibly to the bulk it now appears in" (Epistle to the Reader. Essay, vol. i. p. 23). This fact will account, perhaps, for the somewhat disconnected character of the several parts of the work; for some inconsistencies which appear in it; for the variation in the use of terms and the different significations with which the same terms are variously employed in different parts of the treatise. He not only wrote at different times, but his views doubtless changed in many respects as he went on. He learned as he wrote. His system did not lie complete in his mind's eye when he first began. Hence he is far from precision and unvarying exactness in the use of terms or even complete consistency. Stewart conjectures with some reason that the fourth and last book was the first in order of composition, as it contains the leading thoughts of the work, as they first presented themselves probably to the author's mind when he began to reflect on the subject, while it refers but seldom to the preceding parts of the Essay. The third book, on language, its nature, use and abuse, seems to have been an afterthought. The chapter on association of ideas and that on Enthusiasm, were not added, indeed, until the fourth edition. The first and second books are of a more abstract nature, and probably, as Stewart suggests, opened gradually on the author's mind as he advanced in his work and in years. Of these books Stewart says that while they are inferior in point of general utility to the *two last*, "I do not hesitate to consider them as the *richest contribution* of *well observed* and *well-described* facts *which was ever bequeathed to this branch of science by a single individual;* and as the *indisputable* (though not always acknowleged) *source of some of the most refined conclusions* with respect to the intellectual phenomena *which have been since* brought to light by succeeding inquirers."

The same author very justly remarks with respect to

the style of the essay, "that it resembles that of a well-educated and well-informed man of the world, rather than a recluse student who had made an object of the art of composition," and he thinks this circumstance may have contributed not only to the popularity of the work, but to the design he had in view, of turning public attention to this class of subjects. Shaftesbury, who severely criticises the system, says notwithstanding, that no one has done more toward the recalling of philosophy from barbarity into use and practice of the world, and into the company of the better and politer sort, who might well be ashamed of it in its other dress. No one has opened a better and clearer way to reasoning."

It was not so much the clearness and elegance of the style, however, as it was the author's well-known character and celebrity as a firm and tried and earnest advocate of civil and religious liberty, that contributed to the general interest with which the work was received on its first publication. Four editions were printed in ten years, and in a subsequent impression the author refers to the *sixth* edition, so that the work passed through seven editions *at least* in the fourteen years preceding his death. The thirteenth edition had been issued as early as 1748. Soon after its first publication the work was translated into French, and though Descartes was preëminent in France and Holland, and Leibnitz in Germany, still Locke found not a few to appreciate and admire him, and his work gradually gained great influence on the continent. In his own country, while Oxford denied him a place on the roll of her members, and his book a place in her halls, Cambridge on the other hand bestowed on him an admiration little short of idolatry. The result of this rapid and wide circulation soon showed itself in the remarkable change which manifested itself in the philosophic writing and thinking of England, and to a great degree of the continent. It led men to make use of their own reason to a degree they had never before done. Indeed this is the characteristic feature of the essay, in the opinion of Mr. Stewart, and to this general effect of his writings in leading men to think and reason for themselves, he supposes the essay is chiefly indebted for its immense influence on the philosophy of the eighteenth century.

But it is time to inquire what was the philosophy of Locke. If we were to look for some one principle that should be regarded as the foundation of his system, doubtless it would be this, that it is useless to inquire into the great and hidden problems of philosophy, before we have first explored the human mind itself, and learned its nature, capacity, and powers ; that *psychology* must first be understood before *ontology ;* that the proper method and true instruments of investigation in this science, are *observation* and *consciousness ;* the *basis* of all our knowledge respecting it, *experience.* In this brief outline of the system, this ground-plan of it, we recognize at once the Baconian spirit and method, substituting experiment and observation in place of speculation and conjecture and theory.

Locke's great object and merit, as Tennemann remarks, was "the investigation of the origin, reality, limits and uses of knowledge." The ultimate source of all our knowledge is *experience,* which, however, is twofold in its channels—sensation and reflection. The latter term he uses to denote the perception of the operations of our minds, and speaks of it in one place as a kind of internal sense. Hence his system, built as it would seem to be, on sensation in great measure, is usually denominated—with what propriety we shall presently inquire—*sensational* or (in the philosophic sense of the term) sensual. Our ideas are of two kinds : *simple,* such as solidity, space, extension, figure, number, motion, existence, time, power, etc. ; and *compound,* deduced from the simple ones by some mental process, as comparison, abstraction, etc. Such are our ideas of accident, substance, relation, etc. (Book ii. chap. 2). The doctrine of innate ideas, as held by Descartes and others, he rejects. Of our simple ideas, some represent *primary* qualities, as extension, solidity, figure, number, etc. some *secondary*, as color, sound, scent, etc. (chap. viii. §§7, 9, 10).

The ideas of primary qualities are *resemblances* of what really exist in bodies, but the ideas we have of *secondary* qualities have no such resemblance. "There is nothing like our ideas existing in the bodies themselves," but "only a power to produce those sensations in us" (Book ii. chap. viii. §15). Our knowledge, so far as regards this part of it, is wholly *subjective*. There is no conceivable connection between these qualities of bodies, and the effects produced on us by them; they have no affinity at all with those ideas they produce in us. We know them only by experience, and can reason about them only as incomprehensible effects produced by the Creator. (As regards both primary and secondary qualities, however, and all other objects of knowledge, *all that we immediately know*, all that we *can* in fact *know* or *contemplate*, is not *things themselves*, but only *our own ideas*. *These are the real objects of our knowledge*).

There are two or three points requiring more careful investigation in connection with this system as now briefly sketched. One is the use which Locke makes of the term *reflection*, what he means by it and whether or not it really introduces an element or source of knowledge altogether distinct from sensation. Another is as to the sense in which he uses the term *idea*, whether to denote something distinct from the mind in operation, or not.

Another question of importance relates to the correctness of his views of the *origin* of our ideas, whether they are all capable of being traced to *sensation* or not, or even to sensation and reflection; more than that, whether the question of the *origin* of our ideas is a right and proper question to be entertained in psychology.

All these are disputed points, on most of them the dispute has been warm and long protracted, and according to the view taken of them is the view one takes of Locke's system as a whole. As to the first question, Locke's use of the term reflection. It is contended by many of his critics, especially Cousin, that Locke really reduces all our knowledge to sensation, that reflection, as he uses the term, introduces no new element of knowledge, that it changes not the character of the objects on which it is employed, that, after all, we have to do on this system only with *sensible* phenomena. They charge him, accordingly, with overlooking a very important class of our conceptions, those of *reason*, or rather with omitting entirely that important function, and asigning its office to reflection. This is the view generally taken of Locke by continental writers. They persist in regarding him a mere *sensationalist*, and class him in the same category with Hobbes and Gassendi, who had preceded, and with Condillac, Diderot, and Condorcet, who, professing to be his disciples and followers, carried out his principles to the extreme of materialism. The position of Locke is doubtless unfortunate in placing him thus on either side in immediate contiguity with avowed sensationalists, especially as on one side they profess to derive their views and principles from him. That he himself held these views or would allow himself to be classed with that school—notwithstanding the high authority of Leibnitz and Cousin, and the Germans, and even of those French metaphysicians who avow themselves as his disciples while they teach materialism—is, after all, very doubtful. Mr. Stewart, in his first dissertation, has been at considerable pains to show that this view is quite incorrect, that Locke is by no means a sensationalist. Lewes, himself a sensationalist but an admirer of Locke, also takes this view. But let us inquire of Locke himself. "The other fountain," he says, "from which experience furnisheth the understanding with ideas, is the *perception of the operations of our own minds within us ; as it is employed about the ideas it has got ;* which operations, when the soul comes to reflect on and consider, do furnish the understanding with another set of ideas, which could not be had from things without ; and such are perception, thinking, doubting, believing, reasoning, knowing, willing, and all the different actings of our own minds, which we, being conscious of, and observing in ourselves, do from these receive into our understandings ideas as distinct as we do from bodies affecting our senses. This *source of ideas every man has wholly in himself, and though it be not sense,* as *having nothing to do with external objects,* yet it is very like it, and might properly enough be called internal sense. But as I call the other *sensation* so I call this *reflection,* the ideas it affords being such only as the mind gets by *reflecting* on its own operations within itself" (Book ii. ch. i. §4). Plainly enough, then, Locke *does* mean to make our knowledge of *twofold* origin. He does not *intend* to trace it all to sensation. Plainly enough also, by reflection he means the attentive consideration of what passes in our own minds, of our own mental operations—in other words, consciousness. But now the question arises, whether reflection, as thus defined, does, after all, furnish us a new source of ideas, whether, as regards the *material* of thought, it really adds anything to what sensation furnishes, or simply busies itself with observing what the mind is about as it works over and makes use of these materials. This is the main question. It is very well stated and very closely pressed by Morell and Cousin. They argue with considerable clearness and force that, according to this view, the operations of the mind, which it is the province of reflection to observe, *being employed only about sensible things,* do not and cannot of themselves add anything to the materials on which they operate, so that the senses, after all, are the sole inlet of our ideas, and ultimate source of all our knowledge. Yes, Locke would say, they are so, as regards all our knowledge of the *sensible world*, but not of *all* our knowledge, for we know some things that are not *sensible*, we know *mind*. Those operations, as Locke analyzes them, about which reflection is conversant, are *perception, retention, discernment, comparison, composition, abstraction*, all of which evidently employ themselves with such ideas as are already in the mind, such *materials* of thought as they find ready at hand, which materials he is ready to admit are furnished by sensation. It does not follow, however, that by reflection, after all, we come into possession of no new material of thought other than what is furnished by the senses, for manifestly we do gain this knowledge at least, *the simple consciousness that we have such and such faculties, i. e., the knowledge of the* ME, *in distinction from the* NOT ME, and this, certainly a most important addition to our stores of knowledge, this knowledge of the mind's own faculties seems to me all that Locke intended to bring in under the term reflection. Is he then a pure *sensationalist?* Certainly not. The external world is not the only thing we know, not the only source and origin of ideas to us. What else do we know? We know our own mental faculties. How do we know these? By observation of their operations, *i. e.*, by reflection.

There is the great sensible world without, *matter*, that we know by sensation. There is the little conscious world within—*mind*—that we know by *reflection*. These *two* are the sources of our knowledge. So he says himself, "External objects furnish the mind with the ideas of sensible qualities; and the mind furnishes the understanding with ideas of *its own operations*." Nothing can be plainer. Of these two, indeed, he contends, that we know the latter much better than the former, mind better than body, more *clearly, exactly, certainly, definitely;* no *materialist*. Locke admits, however, that ideas of sensation are those first awakened in the mind;

that reflection comes in at a later period, which of course all must admit.

We pass now to the inquiry, in what sense does Locke use the term *idea*. Reid attributes to him the long-received opinion that ideas are a sort of independent and real existences, something intermediate between the mind and external objects, something distinct from the mind itself, not a modification of the mind, not the mind thus and thus affected, or thus and thus acting or thinking, but a *tertium quid*, representing to the mind whatever extrinsic to itself becomes the object of its knowledge, the doctrine, in a word, of the ancient peripatetics, and of all subsequent philosophy down to the time of Reid himself. Brown denies that Locke, or in fact any modern philosopher, held any such view, and denies to Reid the credit of overthrowing this doctrine. But Brown is unquestionably in the wrong, and entirely so, in this. Beyond all doubt Locke was a *representationist* in his theory of knowledge, a *hypothetical* realist, not a *natural* realist. Ideas with him *represent* to us the real existence without. It is only by means of them that we know anything out of ourselves. Beside the perceiving mind and the thing perceived there is the intervening idea, as the medium of communication between the two : or rather the idea is *itself* the thing really perceived, all that we *immediately* know, the real object of our knowledge. "It is evident," he says, "that the mind knows not things immediately, but by the intervention of the ideas it has of them. Our knowledge, therefore, is real only so far as there is a conformity between our ideas and the reality of things" (Book iv. chapter 4, §3). But how do we know whether there is such a conformity ? A most important question. The answer Locke gives to this question is this : Our ideas are such as *nature* and the Creator ordained ; they represent things to us just as the Creator intended they should, hence they "are not fictions of our fancies, but the natural and regular productions of things without us really operating upon us; and so carry with them all the conformity which is intended, or which our state requires, for they represent things to us under those appearances, which they are fitted to produce in us." This is a short solution of the problem. It resolves the evidence of the existence of a material world into the assumed premise that God would not constitute us with faculties fitted only to deceive, precisely the Cartesian ground. In fact in his whole philosophy, as Dugald Stewart has fully shown, Locke is much more a Cartesian than a Hobbesist; much more a Cartesian indeed, than he doubtless supposed himself to be. However that may be, in the present case, Locke's answer is no solution at all of the great problem. It simply cuts the Gordian knot, as Lewes says. It unravels no difficulty. In fact his doctrine, as now stated, contains the germ of all the idealism and scepticism of Hume and Berkeley—as we shall by and by have occasion to see. All that we *know* is our own ideas, nor have we any proof that there is anything external and real to correspond to these ideas. Thus was the text furnished by Locke from which the idealism and scepticism of the succeeding century preached *ore rotundo* its most obnoxious but inevitable conclusions.

But it is of still more moment to inquire, Was Locke *right* in ascribing the origin of all our ideas to sensation and reflection alone? Have we no ideas which cannot be thus resolved? Are our ideas of *time, space, infinity, identity, power, substance,* etc., capable of being thus disposed of? *This* is the grand question in dispute between the idealist and the sensationalist, the German and the English schools. The idea of *space,* Locke derives from sight and touch (Book ii. chap. 13, §2). It is an *inference* from the idea of body. The idea of time he derives "from reflection on the train of our own ideas," the result of our own consciousness of existence (Book ii. chap. 14, §2, §3). The idea of Infinity he derives from the continual addition of finites, "a supposed endless progression" (Book ii. chap. 17, §§3, 5, 8, 9), the negation of the finite. The idea is not positive but negative (chap. xviii. §13). Identity consists in consciousness (Book ii. chap. 27, §9). The idea of power he derives from the observation of our own motive faculty, and the effect of natural bodies on each other (Book ii. chap. 7, §8); and also from *reflection* on our own mental changes and impressions (chap. 21, §1). The idea of substance (Book ii. ch. 23, §2), is merely that of a cluster of sensations *supposed* to adhere in some imaginary *substratum.* Things are good or evil only with reference to pleasure or pain (Book ii. ch. 20, §2). Our ideas of virtue and vice are the *result,* not the basis, of ideas of reward and punishment, (Book i. ch. 3. §6). Now against all this we enter, *not* our *question,* our *doubt* merely, but, with Cousin, Morell, and others, our decided protest. Can we conceive of body without space? Of the *succession* of thought without *time*? Of our own operations *as our own* without identity? Of quality as pertaining to no substance? If *not,* then to derive the latter class of ideas from the former is absurd; we might with equal propriety derive the former from the latter—body from space, etc.

The error of Locke in this has been well pointed out by Morell and Cousin, and prior still by Kant. The origin of a thing may denote either its *occasion* or its producing cause. Locke *confounds* the two things—sensation may be the *occasion,* it may not be the *cause* of the ideas above named. A spark may be the *occasion* of the explosion of gunpowder. The chemical nature and inherent properties of the powder may be the real *cause* of the explosion, which needed but the *occasion* to develop itself in operation, which, however, *but for the* occasion would never have shown its power. So sensation may be the occasion needed and given, upon which certain faculties of the mind shall come into operation, which but for the occasion would have slumbered forever. Yet not sensation but those faculties, that inherent constitution and nature of the mind, are the true *cause* of the action. Now the *ideas* themselves may not be innate, doubtless are not, but the faculties or principles or laws of the mind which, on the given occasion, give rise to those ideas, *these* are innate, and are the true source of the ideas.

"The spirit of man," says Morell, "just like the seed, has its inherent energy within itself. The grain of wheat has in it, potentially, the ear that is to wave in the next summer's sun, and the acorn, in its little circumference, encloses the oak that is to bear the blast of ages. In the same manner does the mind at birth contain potentially all the elements of the future man, neither more nor less. But as the seed must come in contact with the soil to call its hidden powers into development, so must the mind come into contact with the world of experience, in order that its energies may unfold themselves, and produce their own proper fruits" (Hist. Phil. p. 86). This is doubtless the true doctrine. Would Locke have dissented from it? probably not. But it was a distinction which he seems to have overlooked when he undertook to derive all our ideas from experience, and made that the *source* and *origin* of all. There are certain ideas which can by no means be thus reduced within the domain of sensible experience. Our ideas of space—time, and cause, and substance; of infinity and personal identity; of right and wrong, and perhaps some thers, are of this class. They spring up in the mind by virtue of the mind's own inherent power, its native constitution, the laws of its being, so soon as the fitting occasion is furnished by experience. We may call these inherent laws of the mind *principles of common sense* with Reid, *fundamental laws* with Stewart, *principles of intuitive belief* with Brown, or with Kant the *necessary forms* of *the understanding*—whatever we call them,. they and not sensation or experience are the real cause and origin of a large *and very important* class of our ideas. There is a scientific method of stating this subject adopted by Cousin, which is clear and precise. The origin of any idea he calls the LOGICAL *condition of* its existence ; its *occasion* the CHRONOLOGICAL (Hist. de la Phil. Leçon 17). Of any two ideas, that is the *logical* condition of the other, which virtually includes or involves the other. The chronological is that we first become conscious of. Logically, e. g. the idea of space is the condition of that of body, since we cannot conceive of body but as in space ; *chronologically* it may be otherwise, the idea of body may be even the first to occur to the mind, on occasion of sensible experience. *Logically,* all our abstract ideas are primary ones and involve those of sensation and experience ; *chronologically* the ideas of sensation and experience are contemporary with the former, if not in order of time prior to them. It would be, then, scientifically more correct to say that the idea of space is the *origin* of that of body, than the reverse, since the former logically includes the latter.

It has been very generally supposed that Locke's system of philosophy was subversive of all moral distinctions. If the mind of man is a mere *tabula rasa* at birth, has no innate ideas, no innate laws of thought, then virtue and vice, good and evil, are mere arbitrary distinctions, it is said,—creations of human law. Shaftesbury accuses him of throwing all law and virtue out of the world and making the very *ideas* of these unnatural and without foundation in our minds. Dr. Beattie urges a similar complaint. Both, however, acquit him from any such *intention.* Fortunately there are passages in which Locke unequivocally avows his firm belief in the natural and immutable foundation of moral distinctions, of virtue and vice, of the idea of a God. "I would not be mistaken," he says, "as if because I deny an innate law I thought there were none but positive laws. There is a great deal of difference between an innate law and a law of nature ; between something imprinted on our minds in their original, and something that we, being ignorant of, may attain to the knowledge of by the use and due application of our natural faculties, (Book i. ch. 3. § 13). In another place, he speaks of the extreme danger of principles "taken up without due question or examination; especially if they be such as influence men's lives and give a basis to all their actions. He that, with Archelaus, shall lay it down as a principle that right and wrong, honest and dishonest, are defined only by laws and not by nature, will have other measures of moral rectitude and pravity, than those who take it for granted that we are under obligations antecedent to all human constitutions." We cannot, then, admit the justice of the charge so frequently brought against Locke, at least as regards his real opinions and his sincere intentions. Whether the *tendency*, however, of his philosophical system *on the whole* is favorable or not to sound views of truth may admit of question. It is a significant fact that the great majority of Locke's avowed disciples and followers have advocated essentially the views of Hobbes and Gassendi, as Stewart himself reluctantly admits, and that from the principles of his philosophy subsequently Hume and Berkeley derived the materials for the strongest and most impregnable system of scepticism ever constructed by man. "It must be confessed," says Morell, "that notwithstanding all the admirable lessons which his writings contain, they manifested a decided leaning towards sensationalism, and included, although unknown to himself, germs which after a time bore the fruits of utilitarianism in morals, of materialism in metaphysics, and of scepticism in religion" (Hist. Phil. p. 95). We are not surprised, on the whole, at the popularity of his writings in France—at their enthusiastic reception by Voltaire and the Encyclopedists. Yet from all this Locke would have shrunk with horror. He was a genuine lover of virtue, truth and morality. His character is of the noble, lofty sort. He was born a sage. His disinterested patriotism, his love of liberty, his personal integrity and unbending rectitude, his zeal for the advancement of true religion and manly piety, his *liberality* and tolerance, his ready forgiveness of injuries, his moderation and calmness of temper, are equalled only by the strength and acuteness of his intellect. No name is more worthy of honor, no tomb in Westminster Abbey will inspire in your bosom profounder emotion than the simple monument of John Locke in the plain country church which shelters his honored dust.

CHAPTER IX.

SUCCESSORS OF LOCKE IN ENGLAND AND FRANCE.

It has been already remarked that very many of the professed disciples of Locke were decided materialists, and while calling themselves by his name were really indebted not to him but to Hobbes and Gassendi for their principles. In order to trace the progress of philosophy from this period onward in Europe, it becomes necessary to dwell a little upon this point, and mark out more definitely the positions and doctrines of some of the more celebrated successors of Locke. Of the Deistical school of English writers which flourished at this period the main and avowed philosophy was in its essential principles a system of materialism, based upon the conclusions of Locke. Collins built on this foundation a stern and gloomy doctrine of necessity. Mandeville struck boldly at the root of all morality and virtue with the doctrine borrowed from Locke, that there are no innate principles of human action. These dangerous publications called out the strength of such controversialists as Stillingfleet, Shaftesbury, Norris and, par eminence, Clark. Into the merits of this grand controversy, wherein not so much philosophy as theology was the goddess of the strife, we cannot enter.

In the domain of speculative philosophy, Hartley stands prominent as a sensationalist, deriving his principles from the system of Locke. He was, like Locke, a physician, educated at Cambridge, and was led by the nature of his profession to give a decidedly physiological cast to his psychological investigations. He undertook to account for the phenomena of sensation, which Locke had wisely left unattempted, by the theory of vibrations. His fame rests however chiefly on his doctrine of association, a term first used by Locke, but employed in a new and much wider sense by Hartley to denote, as stated by Morell, "*any combination of thought and feeling which is capable of becoming habitual* by means of repetition." The theory is that the vibrations produced along the nerves by the action of external objects, when oft repeated, have a tendency to reproduce or repeat themselves spontaneously, even in the absence of the external object. These repetitions are *ideas,* relics of former sensations, and by mutual association they recall each other. Sensations, ideas, and muscular movements are all thus affected by the law of association. Our emotions, passions, natural and religious affections, are all traced to and included under sensation. As all our ideas and emotions are controlled according to the laws of association, man is a *passive* being, *will* is a nonentity, *necessity* rules all things. Though not himself a materialist, the system of course was decidedly of that tendency. Priestly carried out the principles of Hartley, which he adopted and maintained with enthusiasm, to their natural result—bold materialism. Thought and sensation are with him, essentially the same thing. Darwin carries out the scheme still further and banishes the idea of spirit from the universe, leaving only the powers of nature in place of God. This is the goal of sensationalism in this direction—bold atheism. In the sensational school of England there are other names of celebrity. Tooke the grammarian, Bentham the moralist and politician, Paley, the pleasing, accomplished, superficial moralist and theologian, are all of this school, building, each in his way and his department, with the essential principles of the great master of English philosophy.

More noted as metaphysicians were the *French* disciples of the school of Locke. Chief of these Condillac, next Condorcet. These writers were thorough and decided sensationalists; philosophers both of no mean reputation or merit. Losing sight of the second source of knowledge as laid down by Locke, they make all our ideas transformed sensations, and profess to follow Locke in so doing. The source of most of our mental faculties is found in *language*, the parent and origin of our distinctive intellectual powers. A statue is represented, or a perfectly organized human being enclosed in marble, which little by little comes to consciousness and sensation; first an idea is perceived, then *sensation* and *attention* are developed, next other sensations; these are remembered, compared, etc., thus step by step the whole machinery of mind comes into play, and all as the result of sensation and experience alone. Condillac is one of the chief philosophers of France of that century. Condorcet, epicurean in his philosophy, advocates strongly the perfectibility of the race by means of educational development. Diderot, D'Alembert, Voltaire, the whole school of Encyclopedists, following in the track of this system, carrying out with more or less consistency its principles, close this period of philosophy.

CHAPTER X.

BERKELEY.

THE idealism of Descartes, carried out in Spinoza, Malebranche and Leibnitz, as also the materialism of Hobbes and the sensationalism of Locke, carried out in Condillac and Condorcet in France, as well as by Hartley, Priestly, Collins and Mandeville in England, we have already traced. As the result of these opposing tendencies, but more especially of the latter, by way of natural reaction, there sprang up in England in the early part of the 18th century, a school destined to exert no slight influence on the thinking mind of Europe, and to claim a considerable notice in the history of modern philosophy. Alarmed at the materialistic and atheistic tendencies of the prevalent sensationalism, this school, by a process so natural to the human mind, revolted to the opposite extreme of absolute idealism, and carried that theory to its farthest results. The consequence was the blank denial of material existence and finally even of the mind itself.

The first distinguished advocate of the views to which we refer was George Berkeley, Bishop of Cloyne; born 12th of March 1684 in Killerin, county of Kilkenny, Ireland, educated at Trinity college, Dublin, of which he became a fellow in 1707; his first work, entitled a New Theory of Vision, appeared two years after, 1709, while the author was yet only twenty-five, and at once attracted great attention. This introduced him to the notice of distinguished and literary men. He was appointed chaplain and secretary to the earl of Peterborough, Ambassador to Sicily, and subsequently travelled over a considerable part of Europe. In 1724 he was raised to the deanery of Derry. About this time he became greatly interested in a project for the conversion of the North American Indians and the establishment of a college in the Bermuda Islands, and succeeded in interesting many others in his enterprise, among them persons of the first rank. Resigning his living of eleven hundred pounds a year, he embarks with his young wife, his library and his property, on this romantic expedition, and sets sail for Rhode Island. Parliament had promised him a stipend of one hundred pounds a year, but this promise was not fulfilled, and after seven years of fruitless endeavor, having spent the most of his personal property, he is obliged to relinquish the undertaking and return to England. He was appointed Bishop of Cloyne in 1734. In 1752 he removed to Oxford, where he died the year after, 1753, at the age of sixty-nine. His character seems to have commanded universal respect and admiration. The satirist, Pope, expressed only the common opinion of his countrymen in the line ascribing "To Berkeley every virtue under heaven." He enjoyed the regard of Swift and Addison, and the fastidious Atterbury said of him, "So much learning, so much knowledge, so much innocence and such humility, I did not think had been the portion of any but angels till I saw this gentleman."

The principal philosophical works of Berkeley, beside that already named, were the Treatise on the Principles of Human Knowledge, (London 1710,) and the Three Dialogues between Hylas and Philonous, (London 1713,) subsequently to his return from America, he also published a work entitled Alciphron, or the Minute Philosopher, (London 1732). It is in the dialogues that the peculiar philosophy of the author is most fully developed. And what was that philosophy, and how came Berkeley by those views?

As I have already intimated, the chief peculiarity of his system is its bold denial of the *reality of material existence*, and to this position he was led by observing, with regret and alarm, the dangerous extreme to which the later disciples of Locke were pushing the principles of the sensational and material school. By a natural recoil he shrank from that result, and sought a secure retreat for truth and philosophy in opinions, the farthest removed from those of the prevalent and so dangerous doctrines. In common with Descartes and all preceding philosophers, Locke had taken the ground that the mind knows and is conversant with only *its own ideas.* *These and not things external to itself are the proper and immediate, and only true objects of its knowledge,* a principle that reigned unquestioned in philosophy, from Plato down to Reid. It knows itself—its own sensations, impressions, ideas,—farther than that, as to any external *cause* of those sensations or impressions, it only infers, but not strictly *knows.* This is called by Hamilton the representative theory of perception, and those who hold it are termed representationists, in distinction from natural realism, or the doctrine of the immediate perception of external objects themselves. Here the acute eye and quick discernment of Berkeley discovered a way of escape from the all-surrounding forces of inexorable materialism. Ha, exclaims the shrewd Irishman in the close corner, we know nothing but our own ideas and sensations then! Nothing else, properly speaking, reply his antagonists. Pray how then do you *know* that there *is* anything else beside and beyond our ideas, any such thing as you call the material world, at all. Sensationalism is posed, can only answer, Why, strictly speaking, we do not know it, but only infer it.

Ha! ha! then I think I will just deny that little inference of yours, and walk out of my close corner, and now gentlemen, catch me if you can. The gentlemen aforesaid have been in hot pursuit of the Irish bishop to this day, but have not yet laid hands on him, nor ever will. The Irish bishop will be caught, if at all, only by the tactics of a very different school. Grant him his premise, his starting point, and no mortal man can ever overtake him. If your knowledge of an external world is only *representative*—only an inference,—then if any man chooses to say—I deny that inference to be either necessary or just; I demand the proof of anything really existing beyond and out of my own mental operations and impressions—you can never hinder him, he has the start of you, and though he go no faster than a tortoise, you are not the Achilles to overtake him. Only the natural realist can do that. Now this was precisely the case with the Bishop of Cloyne and the sensationalists of that age. These were representationalists, and on that account totally unable to refute the point blank scepticism of Berkeley.

Nor was Berkeley a mere metaphysical juggler and gladiator in all this, throwing up daggers and catching in his teeth just for the sport of it. He was a sincere, earnest, patient seeker after truth. In the philosophy of Locke he felt certain there was some latent error. There must be something wrong in the philosophy of sensationalism, since it led to such results. Carefully running his keen eye along the system, he discovered, as he thought, the lurking-place of that latent error—discovered the false quantity that had so deranged the whole calculation;—discovered that the passage from psychology to ontology, from the world within to the world without, from mere thought and sensation to external realities, as the cause and occasion of the same, had always been, and in all systems taken for granted, merely assumed, never demonstrated to be either necessary or possible. What if I make my attack just here, says Berkeley, what if I call in question the possibility of any such passage from the inner to the outer world; what if I deny altogether any such process and conclusion—what becomes of materialism—who can drive me from such a position? He saw his advantage, and discovered as he supposed, not merely the weak point in the opposite philosophy, but the stronghold and vantage ground of truth.

There he intrenched himself, and there his flag floated in triumph till the philosophy of common sense put to rout both him and his antagonists, by showing that both materialist and idealist were involved in one common error and mistake—that ideas were *not* in fact the sole immediate objects of knowledge.

Berkeley, in denying the reality of anything external to the mind itself, labors much to show that he is not in conflict with the common sense and commonly received opinions of mankind. An able writer in Blackwood's Magazine, (June, 1842) takes high ground in his defence upon this point, and still more recently, a writer whom we have frequently cited, Lewes, in his chapter* on Berkeley, goes fully over to this view of the case, contending that all Berkeley really denied was the existence of that unknown *substratum* termed matter, which philosophers had conceived as the *basis* underlying all sensible qualities — a mere philosophical abstraction—a metaphysical entity, and nothing more, while the qualities themselves, the things seen, felt, handled, perceived, he admits to have a real existence. To this effect he quotes Berkeley, saying: "I do not argue against the existence of any one thing that we can apprehend either by sensation or reflection. That the things I see with my eyes, and touch with my hands do exist, really exist, I make not the least question. The only thing whose existence I deny is that which philosophers call matter or corporeal substance." "That what I see, hear, and feel, *doth exist*, i. e. *is perceived by me*, (mark these last words) I no more doubt than I do of my own being." It is perfectly idle now to cite passages from Berkeley to show that he was merely at war with metaphysical abstractions and not with the common sense of mankind; that he denied not the real existence of the sensible world as it lies around and without us, but only a philosophical conception. When he says in his own behalf, and his apologists say for

* History of Philosophy. Modern Philosophy, Epoch, iv. ch. 1.

him, that he fully admits the existence of what he sees, hears, and feels, the question is *what sort* of an existence he means to allow these things—an existence *where?* as what? in the *mind* merely or out of it? as mere modes of the thinking mind or as independent existences? To this question Berkeley makes but one answer. They exist, *that is, are perceived by him,* exist as ideas exist *in the* mind, have real existence as all our thoughts and conceptions have, but only as modes of our own mental being. I fully admit the existence of what I see, hear, feel, etc., says B. But Mr. Berkeley, do you mean to say that these sensible appearances are anything more than phenomena, that they exist anywhere out of the mind that thinks and perceives them? Oh. Not at all. "It is indeed an opinion *strangely prevailing* among men that houses, mountains, rivers, in a word, all sensible objects have an existence natural and real, *distinct from their being perceived by the understanding.*" "The table I write on, I say, exists, *i. e.*, I see and feel it, and if I were out of my study I should say it existed, *meaning thereby that if I was in my study I might perceive* it, or that some other spirit actually does perceive it. As to what is said about the existence of unthinking things, without any relation to their being perceived, that is to me perfectly unintelligible. Their *esse* is *percipi, nor is it possible they should have any existence out of the minds of thinking beings which perceive them.*" Nothing can be plainer than this doctrine, unless it be the following account of precisely the same doctrine. "In a word all the choir of heaven and furniture of earth, all those bodies which compose the mighty frame of the world, have not any subsistence without a mind; their *esse* is *to be perceived or known,* and consequently so long as they are not *actually perceived by me,* or do not *exist in my mind,* or that of any other created spirit, they must either have *no existence at all* or else *subsist in the mind of some eternal spirit.*"

Berkeley, then, was, out and out, an *idealist.* He

admits the reality of things, but only as phenomena,—only as ideas in and impressions on the mind,—no other reality or existence have sensible objects. The distinction between primary and secondary qualities he breaks down and shows that both are merely sensations in us. But how are these phenomena, these sensations produced? Not by the existence of what philosophers call matter, but by the direct agency of Deity, acting upon us through *laws of nature* by Him established, thus giving permanency and constancy to our sensible impressions.

Such is the substance of Berkeley's system. On the ground of the then prevalent philosophy, we fully admit that it was unanswerable. No theory of representative knowledge can stand its onset. Realism alone can cope with it.

CHAPTER XI.

HUME.

WITH the autobiography of this celebrated man, as prefixed to the History of England, it may be presumed that every one tolerably familiar with English literature is already acquainted. No one, I am sure, has ever read that little memoir without admiring its simplicity and beauty, and without feeling an interest in the writer. There is no need, then, in this connection to do more than simply advert to the leading events of his life, before we pass to consider his philosophy.

David Hume was born at Edinburgh, April 26, 1711. His father dying while he was yet in early life, the care of his education devolved wholly on his mother, who seems to have been a woman of more than ordinary ability. He was destined for the law, but so strong was his passion for literature, that he neglected his professional studies, and finally retired to France, where he spent three years in privacy, wholly devoted to his favorite pursuits. In 1737 he went to London and published his "Treatise on Human Nature," which met with no attention or success whatever. In 1742 he published, at Edinburgh, his "Essays Moral and Political," which attracted more attention. In 1746 he offered himself as candidate for the professorship of Moral Philosophy at Edinburgh, but was defeated by the vote of the Presbytery on account of his known scepticism. That year he accompanied General Sinclair, as his secretary in his expedition against the French coast, and the year following on a military embassy to Vienna and Turin. During his absence he recast his treatise on Human Nature and published it under the title of "an Inquiry concerning the Human Understanding," but with no better success. His "Principles of Morals" shared the same fate, but his "Political Discourses" were better received. In 1752 he was appointed librarian to the Faculty of Advocates at Edinburgh. Here he conceived the idea of writing history. His first publication in this line, embracing the history of the House of Stuart, was received, he says, with one cry of reproach, disapprobation and even detestation. It was universally decried and neglected. Hume's equanimity and perseverance, however, prevailed at last. He kept on writing, and England kept on reading and abusing, until he fairly won the victory and achieved for himself a place among the standard authors of English Literature. Subsequently, he attended Lord Hertford as ambassador to Paris, where he was received with open arms as a man of letters and philosophy.

He remained there as Chargé d' Affaires for some time after Lord Hertford's departure, and on returning to England became, in 1767, under secretary of state, under Conway, which post he held till 1769. He then retired to Edinburgh on a fortune of one thousand pounds per annum, and died in 1776, August 25, in his sixty-fifth year.

It has been well said that the influence of Hume as a philosopher has been as much owing to the general alarm excited by his doctrines, as to the ingenuity with which they were maintained. It is to be remembered, however, that Hume is merely a sceptic, not a dogmatist. He takes as his premises, the current philosophy of the time, and simply shows that on the basis of that philosophy such and such things must be true. He places that philosophy thereby in a sad dilemma, it is true, lands it in inevitable scepticism. But he surely is not to blame for that. What were the premises furnished by the prevalent philosophy of the age? Locke had shown that all our knowledge was dependent on experience, and that we know nothing immediately but our own ideas. Berkeley had shown that we have no experience of an external world independent of perception, that we perceive in reality only our own ideas, and that these ideas give us no information, no experience of that world, nor can do so, in a word, that we have no experience of anything beyond certain sensible qualities, which are in fact only impressions or ideas made upon our senses, that the substratum, which we call matter and in which we suppose those qualities to inhere, is only a figment of the imagination. Hume found philosophy thus far on her way to scepticism; the path before her was a plain and obvious one; there was no mistaking it, no turning aside. She must either retrace her course, and starting anew, pursue quite another route, or keep on over the precipice. Hume thought she might as well keep on, now she had come so far, and, taking the reins where Berkeley dropped them, like a bold and reckless charioteer, dashed on and over into the bottomless abyss of utter scepticism. He did not choose the road; is not responsible for its having been chosen and so far pursued; is not responsible for the final overturn, any further than that he fearlessly and consistently forced the result which he saw to be inevitable.

Believing with Locke that our ideas are the only objects of knowledge, and with Berkeley that our ideas give us no reason to conclude the existence of anything beyond and out of ourselves, he saw that there was but one step more wanting to carry out the system and make it complete, and that step must be taken. If there is no evidence, said he, of any occult substratum called matter, as its basis of the qualities that strike our sense, what hinders me from denying also that occult substratum called mind, in which our thoughts and impressions are commonly supposed to inhere? If all that I know is simply my ideas themselves, then what becomes not only of matter as a basis of sensible qualities, but of mind as basis of mental phenomena? suppose I deny the latter altogether? Philosophy stands aghast at the dilemma, but perceives no way of escape. There is the precipice and over she must go, and over she goes, all the world of course cursing the charioteer, as being the sole author and cause of the mischief. Dr. Brown himself could have done no better, however,—admits that the reasoning by which this conclusion is reached is unanswerable. And so indeed it is for all who, with Brown and Locke and the earlier philosophers, admit that ideas are the only *immediate* objects of our knowledge. Drive in at that gate and there is no escaping the precipice. Nor does it make the least difference, as Sir W. Hamilton has well shown, whether you regard ideas, with Plato and Descartes, as something other than simple modes of the mind itself, or whether, with Brown and others, you regard them as mere modifications of mind, in either case the result is inevitable. All *evidence* is gone of anything as reality to correspond to these our ideas, and if any man, choosing to be consistent, *denies* that reality, no answer remains nor is possible. Neither Hume nor Berkeley, it is to be remembered, denied the subjective reality of sensible impressions, but only their objective reality. Their appearance as phenomena both fully admitted, but refused to admit anything more than that. Both declare that the common belief in these phenomena as real existences is not only universal but inevitable; that we are so constituted that we must proceed upon that principle. Hume expressly declares that neither he nor any other man ever rested in the positive disbelief of material and mental existence. But at the same time he can give no reason for that belief, though he finds himself compelled to act upon it,—nay perceives that it is altogether without a reason. This is the amount of his scepticism. Manifestly we have reached the end of philosophy in this direction. Nothing remains but to seek for it a new and entirely different route.

CHAPTER XII.

THE SCOTCH PHILOSOPHY. DR. THOMAS REID.

THE greatest errors are not unfrequently of the greatest use and service to poor mankind. Indeed it not unfrequently happens that next to a great truth the most useful thing in the world is a great error; since it prepares the way for and gives rise to great truths. So it has been in physical science; so in speculative philosophy. Of all the great and profoundly reflecting minds whose opinions we have hitherto sketched in the progress of these lectures, no one had with greater boldness and logical consistency followed out to extreme and dangerous conclusions, premises and principles, then almost universally received in philosophy, and thus demonstrated the inherent falsity of those principles, than David Hume. Men started as from a dream, when they perceived whither their own cherished philosophy was leading them. They looked about for some way of escape from conclusions so formidable. Everybody fell to combating Hume. Theologians, young and old, metaphysicians, men of all professions and of none, pressed into the lists to break a lance with this Goliath of scepticism ; the welkin rang with the sound of their blows, as one after another each new champion tried his weapons on the steel-plate armor of the redoubtable sceptic. Ere long it was discovered that Hume's coat of mail was perfectly proof against all such assaults, that the difficulty and error lay back of the conclusions, among the premises which he assumed and the philosophy which others had furnished to his use; that if these conclusions were to be successfully assailed they must begin by assailing the premises and principles on which the conclusions were built, must begin in fact, *not* with David Hume, *but with John Locke,* and the preceding philosophers. The only way was to retrace the steps and seek for a sure and safe path in some other direction. Such a movement, accordingly, now commenced. Simultaneously in Scotland and in Germany, commenced such a movement. Two distinguished men, patient, profound, truth-loving, earnest men, much unlike each other, quite unknown at the outset to each other, but animated by one common impulse, set about the work of constructing anew, and on an entirely different basis, the philosophy of the human mind. That German was Immanuel Kant; that Scotchman, Thomas Reid. A brief sketch of the life of the latter will form a fitting introduction to the remarks we have to offer upon his philosophy.

Thomas Reid was born on the 26th of April, 1710, at Strachan, a country parish in Scotland, about twenty miles from Aberdeen. His father was for fifty years clergyman of this parish ; a man of piety, benevolence, unostentatious learning and love of letters, purity and simplicity of manners, virtues inherited from a long line of ancestors, most of whom, like himself, had been ministers of the church of Scotland. For several generations had his ancestors distinguished themselves by a marked fondness for the cultivation of letters, and a propensity to the learned professions. One of them was surgeon to King Charles I., another, distinguished as a philosopher and a poet, after extensive travel, became secretary to King James in the Greek and Latin tongues. By the maternal side, also, the ancestry of Dr. Reid were somewhat distinguished by the same tastes and pursuits.

His mother was of the family of Gregorys, noted as mathematicians, one of them the inventor of the reflecting telescope; one of her brothers was professor of astronomy at Oxford, and an intimate friend of Sir Isaac Newton; another was professor of mathematics at St. Andrews, and another still at Edinburgh. Thus descended from families of such hereditary worth and genius, it would have been a natural and pardonable ambition that should have prompted Reid to show himself worthy of his ancestry. After two years at the parish school, he was sent to Aberdeen for classical study, and at the age of twelve or thirteen entered Marischal college, where he studied philosophy for three years under Dr. George Turnbull. The sessions of the college at that time were short, however, and the instruction superficial, says Mr. Stewart. His residence at the university was prolonged, it would seem, beyond the usual period, by his appointment as librarian, which afforded him the opportunity he desired for quiet study. While thus employed, he formed an acquaintance with Mr. John Stewart, afterward professor of mathematics. The two friends, in company, prosecuted with great ardor this their favorite study, and read together with no little delight the Principia of Newton for the first time. In 1736, Reid resigned his office, and in company with his friend visited England, forming the acquaintance of literary men in Oxford, Cambridge and London. In 1737, he was presented to the living of New Machar, in Scotland. His parishioners, prejudiced and irritated by the system of patronage, received him not very cordially, stoutly resisted his coming in fact, and even fought to drive him away. He incurred not merely violent opposition, but personal danger. This prejudice, however, was soon subdued by his winning manners, his mildness, benevolence and patient, faithful attention to his duties, so that when he was called, some years after, to another situation, the same persons who had so stoutly resisted his first ministrations followed him with their prayers and their tears and their earnest blessings. At New Machar, Reid employed his retired and leisure hours in intense and diligent study, particularly in relation to the laws of perception and the fundamental principles of human knowledge.

In 1752, he was elected professor of philosophy in Kings college, Aberdeen. Here he devoted himself with ardor to the pursuits which were to occupy the remainder of his life and energies. A literary society was soon formed where a number of kindred spirits met weekly for literary and philosophic discussions and criticisms. From this source emanated at nearly the same time the writings of Reid, Gregory, Campbell, Beattie, Gerard.

The Inquiry into the Human Mind was published in 1764, but the plan was formed and the subject had been deeply studied years before. It was the publication of Mr. Hume's treatise on Human Nature that first led him to the investigations which resulted in this work. He had in his youth admitted without examination, the established opinions on which that scepticism was built; indeed, had embraced, as he informs us, the whole Berkeleyan system, till finding other consequences to flow from it that gave him more uneasiness than the want of a material world, he began to inquire what evidence there was for the doctrine *that all the objects of our knowledge are ideas in our own minds.* That we know only our own thoughts, that all our knowledge is *subjective,* is, as we have seen, the basis of the idealism of Berkeley and the scepticism of Hume. But it was a principle that had come down unsuspected and unchallenged from a remote and venerable antiquity, and had received the imprimature of Descartes, Leibnitz

14*

and Locke. But, thanks to Mr. Hume, the time had now come when either this fundamental principle of so many different and diverse systems must be given up, or philosophy itself must be abandoned as hopeless. Patiently and with sincere love of truth, Reid set about the work of thoroughly exploring and constructing anew the foundations of science. For more than forty years, he diligently pursued his toil, and the Essays on the Intellectual Powers published in 1785, and on the Active Powers, in 1788, were the ripe and finished results of these years of thought.

Anxious not to misunderstand or misrepresent his opponent, before the publication of his first philosophical treatise, the Inquiry, he submitted portions of it, from time to time, through the medium of a mutual friend, Dr. Blair, to the inspection of Hume himself. Had all controversies been thus candidly conducted, how much bitter and bellicose writing had been spared. Mr. Hume seems not, at first, to have relished the idea of another antagonist. "I wish," says he, "that the parsons would confine themselves to their old occupation of worrying one another, and leave philosophers to argue with temper, moderation, and good manners." After the perusal of the manuscript, however, he seems to have formed quite a different opinion, as the following letter to the author indicates :

"By Dr. Blair's means, I have been favored with the perusal of your performance, which I have read with great pleasure and attention. It is certainly very rare that a piece so deeply philosophical is wrote with so much spirit, and affords so much entertainment to the reader." After adverting to some obscurities, which he attributes to the circumstance that he had seen the work only in detached parts, he continues, "for I must do you the justice to own that, when I enter into your ideas, no man appears to express himself with greater perspicuity than you do, a talent which, above all others, is requisite in that species of literature which you have cultivated." Professing to forbear criticism till the whole work is before him, he adds, "I shall only say, that if you have been able to clear up these abstruse and important subjects, instead of being mortified, I shall be so vain as to pretend to a share of the praise; and shall think that my errors by having at least some coherence, have led you to make a more strict review of my principles, which were the common ones, and to perceive their futility. As I was desirous to be of some use to you I kept a watchful eye, all along, over your style; but it is really so correct, and so good English, that I found not anything worth the remarking."

The candor and generosity of this communication are at once remarkable and rare, and go far to raise Mr. Hume in our estimation. I cannot forbear to subjoin in this connection a part at least of Reid's reply to this letter. After due and handsome acknowledgment of the courtesy and kindness of his antagonist, he says, "whether I have any success in this attempt or not, I shall always avow myself your disciple in metaphysics. I have learned more from your writings in this kind, than from all others put together. Your system appears to me not only coherent in all its parts, but likewise justly deduced from principles commonly received among philosophers—principles which I never thought of calling in question, until the conclusions you drew from them in the treatise on Human Nature made me suspect them. If these principles are solid, your system must stand; . . . I agree with you, therefore, that if this system shall ever be demolished, you have a just claim to a great share of the praise, both because you have made it a distinct and determined mark to be aimed at, and have furnished proper artillery for the purpose." In a note on this passage, Hamilton observes, "Kant makes a similar acknowledgment." "By Hume," he says, "I was first startled out of my dogmatic slumber." Thus Hume is author, in a sort, of all our subsequent philosophy.

For out of Reid and Kant, mediately or immediately, all our subsequent philosophy is evolved.

The work of Dr. Reid was well received, at first of course chiefly by the few who were prepared to appreciate it. Venerable professors, who had spent their lives in teaching views and theories which this work wholly subverts, gave it a cordial reception.

In 1763, Dr. Reid was elected to the professorship of moral philosophy in the University of Glasgow, where he found a large number of choice and congenial spirits. His course of instruction here employed five hours every week, for six months in the year. His elocution was not attractive. He read exclusively from his written manuscript, nor was his manner of reading impressive, but the clearness of his style, the importance of his themes, and the great respect which his character commanded, procured him numerous and attentive listeners. Mr. Stewart admits that his course was wanting in comprehensive and systematic order and arrangement.

Anxious to perfect his great work, he resigned his post, while yet in vigor of body and mind, withdrew from public labors, and at the age of seventy and upwards, devoted himself to the completion of his principal works, the Essays on the intellectual and moral powers of man. He died October, 1796, in his eighty-sixth year.

Doctrines of Reid.

Mr. Stewart is of opinion that the distinguishing feature of Dr. Reid's philosophy is the steady adherence with which in all his inquiries, he follows the Baconian method; that to recommend this plan to others was his constant aim and favorite topic in his conversation with his friends and pupils. Dr. Reid himself, in a letter to Dr. Gregory, says of Bacon, I am very apt to measure a man's understanding by the opinions he forms of that author.

"We are not surprised, accordingly, to find him abandoning the high *a priori* road, as it has been called, and confining himself in his philosophical writings to the *simple facts* and evident phenomena of observation and experience respecting the laws and operations of the human mind. We are not surprised to find him attaching great importance to those first principles and maxims, which lie at the foundation of belief, and which it is of the highest moment to ascertain and establish. His efforts in this direction have given a name, in fact, not to his system alone, but to the philosophy of that entire school of which he stands the undoubted head and founder, the philosophy of common sense. The *name* is perhaps not happily chosen, the *thing signified* by the name is worthy to be made the foundation of a philosophic system. If the Baconian method, so called, is of any value in the acquisition of truth, if it admits of application to the philosophy of the mind, as well as to that of the material world, then is credit due to Reid as the first distinctly to apply, and successfully and systematically to carry out, this method of investigation in the department of psychology. This is beyond question the characteristic feature of his philosophy, cool, cautious, distrustful, even to a fault perhaps, of theories and hypotheses, seeking only for facts, trusting only to careful observation of, and careful reflection on the palpable and obvious phenomena of the human mind as reported by consciousness and the experience of mankind, it seeks by a careful induction of these facts to arrive at certain general conclusions, and with these it is content and rests satisfied, not seeking to penetrate farther and conjecture the unknown and the unknowable.

It has been objected that to combat the sceptic with appeals to common sense, is to degrade philosophy by reducing the problems of speculative thought to the tribunal and judgment of the vulgar and uneducated mass, utterly incompetent to decide such questions. This is not so. The appeal is not made to the vulgar against the learned, or to the common prejudices of unthinking men, against the doubts of the speculative reasoner. The tribunal to which the appeal is made is a different and far higher one than this. There are in the constitution of human nature certain ground-principles of all belief and all action, on which we always, and all proceed in the uniform conduct of life, and without which all the intercourse of society, all the transactions of business, all reasoning, all forethought, all judgment of past or future, would be at an end,—principles which require no proof,—which *admit* of none, in fact,—universally received, universally acted on by men,—common at once to the philosopher and the illiterate. These are the fundamental maxims or principles to which, under the name, not altogether felicitous, of maxims of common sense, the appeal is made by Reid, and on which as a secure basis he erects his philosophical system. It is to be regretted, as Mr. Stewart himself seems disposed to admit, that Dr. Reid had not more fully elaborated this part of his system; and shown with more completeness and distinctness, what is this common sense of mankind, its nature, its claims to be regarded as the foundation of all philosophic investigation and speculation, the number and nature of those distinctive principles which find a legitimate place in this ground-work of all knowledge. This he should have done. And the want of this we regard, with Tissot and others, as a serious defect in his philosophy, regarded as a complete system.

It is hardly necessary to state in detail the distinctive and several parts of Reid's philosophy.

A few general observations and criticisms are all that is demanded.

Aside from the consideration of the method pursued in this science, and which he was the first to pursue, if not to point out, the chief merit claimed by Dr. Reid, and by his friends in his behalf, as a contribution to the science of the human mind, is that of having completely refuted and overthrown the old and widely-prevalent theory of *ideas*, according to which theory the mind perceives not external things themselves and immediately, but only certain ideas or images in the mind itself, more or less resembling external things. This, as we have seen, was the open door through which idealism and scepticism walked in, as exhibited by Hume and Berkeley. Yet it was a door which such men as Newton and Locke and Leibnitz and Descartes, to go no further back, had, without suspicion, passed, and left it as they found it, open for all future comers. It was no small merit to discover the entire groundlessness and fallacy of this assumption, and boldly to discard it, and completely overthrow it, and put it out of the way and path of philosophy for all future time. That which we see and know is not something in our own minds, image, idea, or whatever you may please to call it, but the very things themselves. Our knowledge of things external is not, as all the world has been told, has believed for ages, simply a *conjectural, mediate,* and *representative* knowledge, but *real, immediate* and *intuitive.* Such was the bold announcement with which Dr. Reid startled the repose of the speculative and reflecting world. The merit of this discovery and refutation has been indeed denied him, and that by one who should have known better, Dr. Thomas Brown, whose philosophy has been justly termed an open revolt against that of Dr. Reid, and who seems anxious to strip his distinguished countryman of an honor which justly belongs to him, by maintaining that no philosopher of note for many years had held any such doctrine as that which Reid assails,—that it was in fact, a mere man of straw, that the words, *idea, image,* etc., were merely figurative and metaphorical terms, which Dr. Reid mistook for literal expressions and magnified into a philosophical heresy. As this is a somewhat serious charge, and one which, if true, quite takes away the foundation not only of Reid's claim as a discoverer, but of his entire philosophy regarded as a distinctive system, it deserves serious investigation. No man in Europe was so well able to weigh or pass judgment on a question of this kind, as Sir W. Hamilton. Never was judgment in such a case more carefully, more clearly, more fully and decidedly given; never question and questioner more completely and fully put to silence. The result is thus expressed.* "With all our admiration of Brown's general talent, we do not hesitate to assert, that in the points at issue between the two philosophers, to say nothing of others, he has completely misapprehended Reid's philosophy, even in its fundamental position. . . . Dr. Brown is not only wrong in regard to Reid's own doctrine, he is wrong, even admitting his interpretation of that philosopher to be true, in charging him with a series of wonderful misconceptions in regard to the opinions universally prevalent, touching the nature of ideas. . . If Reid be not always correct, his antagonist has failed in convicting him even of a single inaccuracy." He then proceeds to consider the charge in detail. "It is always unlucky to stumble on the threshold. The paragraph in which Dr. Brown opens his attack on Reid, contains more mistakes than sentences; and the etymological discussion it involves supposes as true, what is not simply false but diametrically opposite to the truth. Among other errors, in the first place, the term *idea* was never employed in any system previous to the age of Descartes, to denote 'little images derived from objects without;' in the second, it was never used in any philosophy, prior to the same period, to signify the immediate object of perception." Hamilton proceeds to specify, in all, six errors of a similar nature in this one passage of Brown, respecting the history of the word *idea*. In a note he adds that, previous to the age of Descartes, as a philosophic term it was employed exclusively in a Platonic meaning and "this meaning was *precisely the reverse* of that attributed to the word by Dr. Brown,—the idea was not an object of per-

* See Edinburgh Review, Oct. 1830.

ception,—the idea was not derived from without," that neither in the schools, nor after the revival of letters, was the word used as a psychological term, by the Aristotelians or others, but had only a theological signification, that it came into use as a psychological term to denote the immediate objects of thought, and of consciousness in general, only when Descartes and his followers thus employed it. "Dr. Brown," he continues, "only fails in illustrating against Reid the various meanings in which the old writers employed the term *idea*, by the *little fact that the old writers never employed the term idea at all.*" Having disposed thus of Brown's statements respecting the use of the term by ancient authors, Hamilton proceeds to show that he is equally incorrect in his statements respecting its use by modern writers, especially by those whom Reid has cited and criticised. Brown denies that they do use the term idea in the sense Reid attributes to them. Hamilton takes up those authors one by one, Descartes, Arnauld, Locke, etc., and shows that they do each and all employ the word idea, either as distinct from or identical with the act of the mind itself, to denote the immediate object of thought, *representative* of external objects, and that so far from their doctrine being identical with that of Reid, as Brown has asserted, it is directly at variance with and fundamentally opposite to it.

While Hamilton, however, would concede to our author the full merit of overthrowing the theory of ideas then current, he admits, and justly as we think, the existence of certain inconsistencies and defects which mar the symmetry and completeness of his system. It was an error to make consciousness, as he does, a distinct faculty of the mind, since it is implied in every mental operation and is essential to every faculty, and cannot therefore be itself a faculty, coördinate with memory, imagination, etc. It was an error in him to restrict the sphere of consciousness, as he does, solely to the *operations* of the mind, exclusive of their *objects*—to perception, e. g. and not to the object perceived—to memory, but not to the object remembered—since, as Hamilton shows, we cannot be conscious of an act of knowledge, without being conscious of its object—cannot be conscious, e.g. of the perception of a rose—i.e. cannot *know* that we have said perception and of said object and *no other*, unless we know also the object itself, *that it is*, and *what* it is ; so that virtually our consciousness and our perception are one and not to be *psychologically* though they may be logically distinguished. He errs, also, in making memory to be an *immediate* knowledge of the fact, which is impossible, since that only is known immediately which is known in itself and as it is, but the past can be known only as it *was*, not as it *is*. Memory, therefore, like imagination, is a representative faculty.

Reid's acquaintance with the *history* of philosophy seems to have been very imperfect. This even his warmest friends and admirers cordially admit. In consequence his historical sketches are the least valuable and reliable portion of his works ; he not seldom mistakes the real opinions and doctrines of other authors, at least as regards the nicer points of distinction. This is particularly true in his historical sketch of the doctrine of perception, in which he fails to distinguish between the views of those who, with Leibnitz, Arnauld, Malebranche and the later Germans, regard ideas as mere modifications of the mind itself, and those who held the cruder doctrine of ideas as something distinct from the percipient mind. And this leads me to notice what must be regarded as the most serious defect in Reid's system. He nowhere draws with sufficient clearness, definiteness and precision the dividing line between the true and false doctrines of perception—between the high and only tenable position of natural realism, and the prior form of idealism, egoistical representationism, which, while it has nothing to do with ideas *as images*, still holds that ideas in the modern sense, as notions or conceptions, states of the mind, are the *immediate* and *sole* objects of our knowledge. This distinction did not probably occur to him. Nay, it is even a matter of some doubt whether he were not himself of the latter class—an egoistical representationist; though we think Hamilton has shown that the drift and general tenor of his system proves the contrary. Still it can be made out only by inference. He nowhere clearly and fully defines his position as to this point, and it is a fundamental one in his system. He nowhere says directly and explicitly, that we do in perception know immediately aught beyond our own mental states and operations. The passage from the subjective to the objective is not clearly pointed out anywhere in his works. This is unfortunate. In a system designed to rebut idealism it is absolutely essential that the opposite doctrine of realism should be sharply and clearly defined and freed from all confusion and ambiguity. It matters little, as Morell and Hamilton have clearly shown, whether in Reid's sense of the term, one regard the idea as an image of external things, a representation floating before the mind, but not of it, or whether we regard it as merely a modification of the mind itself; so long as this idea, in either case, is all that we perceive and know. What evidence have we of anything external to correspond to this idea in the mind? not the least; we concede to idealism all it asks. The main hold of that system, its strong and impregnable fortress, is just this position—all *our knowledge is subjective*, that the *ego* has no immediate knowledge of the *non-ego* as existing, but knows it only as represented to the *ego*—only as a modification of the self-conscious *ego*. We have no knowledge of anything out of our own consciousness, no cognizance of any really objective reality; we know, are conscious of certain modes or affections of our own minds, certain *mental* phenomena, and that is all. The supposition of a really existing external world to produce these mental phenomena in us, is purely gratuitous unless it can be shown that they can be produced in no other way—and this cannot be shown—nay, it is evident that in many cases our mental impressions *are* produced in other ways, self-produced as in dreams, delirium, etc.

The only way to meet this is to take the high ground of natural realism, that our knowledge is not wholly subjective, that in perception we are cognizant *not* merely of our own mental phenomena or the modification of our own minds, but also, and that immediately, of the *phenomena of matter in relation* to our minds as percipient—that there is a duality known and recognized in every act of perception, that every act of perception involves, as has been said, the union of the subjective and the objective. This is the only answer to the idealism of Hume, Berkeley, et id omne genus, and we are confident it is the only true statement of the facts in the case. It is certainly to be regretted that Reid, in laying the foundation of a new school of philosophy, should not have placed it fully and fairly and firmly upon this immovable rock of truth.

I cannot better close this discussion than by citing the words of Morell, who has well stated the case. "The position that we must assume, if we would complete what Reid so nobly commenced, is that the very essence of perception consists in a felt relation between mind and matter ; that, instead of being wholly the act of the mind, it is the union of the subjective and the objective necessarily arising from man's constitution as a being composed of soul and body. If you look to the acts of the will, you feel them to be purely personal or subjective ; if you look to an act of the reason, you feel that it refers simply to abstract truth, which the mind of itself could work out ; but if you analyze a perception, you at once detect in it another element, which does not depend upon the *will* or the *reason*, but upon some other existence out of and distinct from ourselves ; so that perception, instead of being an operation of the mind, as Reid regarded it, is in fact an intuitive, felt relation between self and nature, between the *me* and the *not me*. The one of these related terms is, in truth, as much given in every act of perception as the other, neither can we abstract either the subject or the object without destroying the very essence of the thing itself." (Hist. Phil. pp. 185, 186.)

CHAPTER XIII.

THE SUCCESSORS OF REID.

§ 1.—DUGALD STEWART.

MR. STEWART was the son of Dr. Mathew Stewart, professor of mathematics in the University of Edinburgh. Hence the allusion of Burns when he speaks of the "philosophic sire and son." Born 1753. He received his education at the University, to which he was admitted at the age of thirteen. There he enjoyed the tuition of Drs. Blair and Ferguson. He also heard the lectures of Dr. Reid at Glasgow. At the age of eighteen such was his progress, that he was associated with his father as assistant lecturer on mathematics, which place he filled until the death of the latter. In 1783 he visited the continent in company with the Marquis of Lothian. When Dr. Ferguson went to North America as secretary to the commissioners sent to conclude a peace with this country, Mr. Stewart during his absence occupied the chair of Moral Philosophy, and on the resignation of Dr. Ferguson he was appointed to fill the vacancy, a chair which he was destined to adorn for a quarter of a century with more than common reputation and brilliancy. His Elements of the Philosophy of the Human Mind was published in 1792, followed by Outlines of Moral Philosophy for the use of students, in 1793. He also published an account of the life and writings of Dr.

Adam Smith, of Dr. Reid, and of Dr. Robertson. In 1810, he was induced by delicate health, and a desire to devote himself entirely to study and the preparation of his works, to resign his office and retire from the labors of public instruction. He found a retreat at Kinneil house, about twenty miles from Edinburgh, where he continued till his death, June 11, 1828. The fruits of this leisure were the volume of Philosophical Essays, (1810), the Dissertation on the Progress of Metaphysical and Ethical Philosophy prefixed to the Encyclopedia Britannica, a truly elegant piece of philosophic writing, a second volume of the Philosophy of the Human Mind, 1813, with a continuation in 1827, and his work on the Philosophy of the Active and Moral Powers, 2 vols. 8vo., 1828, a work almost posthumous, and composed under circumstances which impart to it the deepest interest, as being the finale of a long and brilliant literary life. He died at the age of seventy-five.

It is hardly necessary for me to say that he adopted in the main the system of Reid, introducing such modifications as seemed needed to render the system more complete, and substituting, in some cases, a more appropriate phraseology, polishing and finishing with the skillful eye and hand of a critic, what the master had left in the rough, but neither adding to nor departing from the philosophy of that master in anything essential. In erudition and acquaintance with the history of philosophy, especially, he was far superior to Reid ; in profoundness and originality of mind, he was perhaps inferior to the latter. He is not so much the inventor as the elaborator of a system, not so much a philosopher as an ingenious, erudite and elegant critic on philosophy. Yet his improvements are by no means to be overlooked. His substitution of the terms, *fundamental laws of thought,* in place of the inadequate and unfortunate expressions of Reid—*common sense* and *instinct*—is in itself of the highest service to that system, and goes far to remove many of the objections brought against it. Nor did he perform a slight service to philosophy in elevating the power of attention to the rank of a distinct and coördinate faculty of the mind, and especially in developing, with a wise and masterly skill, the law of association in its relation to the various operations of the mind, and to the practical offices of life. The system as it came from his hand, possessed not only more symmetry and completeness, and a more scientific exactness, than Reid had given it, but withal a nice application to the manifold phases and movements of the mind as seen in action and developed in art—of man as in society; it was the philosophy not of mind in the abstract, but of the living, stirring world. A fine illustration of this occurs in the chapter on Association as applied to various *fine arts*, and especially as illustrative of the phenomena of reasoning, a peculiarly finished and nice specimen of the critical and elegant in philosophy.

No one has done better justice to Mr. Stewart's general merits as a philosopher, or formed, on the whole, a more correct estimate of his character and worth, than Mr. Mackintosh in his History of Ethical Philosophy. "Perhaps few men ever lived," says that accomplished author, "who poured into the breasts of youth a more fervid and yet reasonable love of liberty, of truth, and of virtue. How many are still alive, in different countries, and in every rank to which education reaches, who, if they accurately examined their own minds and lives, would ascribe much of whatever goodness and happiness they possess, to the early impressions of his gentle and persuasive eloquence! He lived to see his disciples distinguished among the lights and ornaments of the council and the senate. He had the consolation to be sure that no words of his promoted the growth of an impure taste, of an exclusive prejudice, of a malevolent passion. Without derogating from his writings, it may be said that his disciples were among his best works." As to the qualities of his style the same author remarks, "Probably no modern ever exceeded him in that species of eloquence which springs from sensibility to literary beauty and moral excellence; which neither obscures science by prodigal ornament, nor disturbs the serenity of patient attention; but, though it rather calms and soothes the feelings, yet exalts the genius, and insensibly inspires a reasonable enthusiasm for whatever is good and fair." "Few writers rise with more grace from a plain groundwork, to the passages which require greater animation or embellishment. . . . Among the secret arts by which he diffuses elegance over his diction, may be remarked the skill, which, by deepening or brightening a shade in a secondary term, by opening partial or preparatory glimpses of a thought to be afterwards unfolded unobservedly, heightens the import of a word, and gives it a new meaning without any offense against old use." A peculiar susceptibility and delicacy of touch produced forms of expression in themselves extremely beautiful, but of which the habitual use is not easily reconcilable with the condensation desirable in works necessarily so extensive. If, however, it must be owned that the caution incident to his temper, his feelings, his philosophy, and his station, has somewhat lengthened his composition, it is not less true, that some of the same circumstances have contributed towards those peculiar beauties which place him at the head of the most adorned writers on philosophy in our language." . . . "His writings are a proof that the mild sentiments have their eloquence as well as the vehement passions. It would be difficult to name works in which so much refined philosophy is joined with so fine a fancy, so much elegant literature with such a delicate perception of the distinguishing excellencies of great writers, and with an estimate, in general so just, of the services rendered to knowledge by a succession of philosophers. They are pervaded by a philosophic benevolence, which keeps up the ardor of his genius without disturbing the serenity of his mind,—which is felt in his reverence for knowledge, in the generosity of his praise, and in the tenderness of his censure. . . . Those readers are not to be envied, who limit their admiration to particular parts, or to excellencies merely literary, without being warmed by the glow of that honest triumph in the advancement of knowledge, and of that assured faith in the final prevalence of truth and justice, which breathe through every page of them, and give the unity and dignity of a moral purpose to the whole of those classical works."

I cannot close this brief notice of an author to whom personally I am so deeply indebted without mentioning one other trait conspicuous in his writings. I refer to the peculiar modesty and caution with which he differs at any time from writers of established authority, and especially from Dr. Reid. It has been well said that he "employed more skill in *concealing* his very important reforms of Reid's doctrines, than others exert to maintain their claims to originality." In this respect his writings form a marked contrast as it seems to me with those of his not less distinguished successor, who seems to glory in nothing more than in casting off allegiance to the authority of his predecessors.

ADDENDA.

The following is the only notice I have been able to find of the closing years of Mr. Stewart's life. It is from the same pen to which I am indebted for the preceding observations.

After remarking that the Dissertations on the Progress of Philosophy, Mr. Stewart's latest works, are the most highly ornamented of any of his productions, a fact which is to be accounted for in part from the nature of the subject, the writer proceeds to observe : "But the memorable instances of Cicero, of Milton, and still more those of Dryden and Burke, seem to show that there is some natural tendency in the fire of genius to burn more brightly, or to blaze more fiercely in the evening than in the morning of human life. Probably the materials which long experience supplies to the imagination, the boldness with which a more established reputation arms the mind, and the silence of the low but formidable rivals of the higher principles, may concur in producing this unexpected and little observed effect.

It was in the last years of his life, when suffering under the effects of a severe attack of palsy, with which he had been afflicted in 1822, that Mr. Stewart most plentifully reaped the fruits of long virtue, and a well ordered mind. Happily for him, his own cultivation and exercise of every kindly affection, had laid up for him a store of that domestic consolation, which none who deserve it ever want, and for the loss of which nothing beyond the threshold can make amends. The same philosophy which he had cultivated from his youth upward employed his dying hand. Aspirations after higher and brighter scenes of excellence, always blended with his elevated morality, became more earnest and deeper as worldly passions died away, and earthly objects vanished from his sight."

§ Dr. Thomas Brown.

The system of philosophy commonly known as the Scotch Metaphysics, as blocked out by Reid, matured and completed by Stewart, received a very serious modification, if not indeed a complete subversion, at the hands of Mr. Stewart's immediate successor, Dr. Thomas Brown. Of the personal history of this distinguished metaphysician, neither the limits of this lecture, nor the materials at my command, enable me to say much. He was born in 1728, and like Dr. Reid, was descended from one of those ministers in the Scottish church which, in the language of another, "after a generation or two of an humble life spent in piety and usefulness, with no more than needful knowledge, have more than once sent forth a man of genius from their cool and quiet shade, to make his fellows wiser or better, by tongue or pen, by head or hand." Like Mr. Stewart, he was educated first at the High School, and afterwards at the University of Edinburgh, in which he subsequently became professor of Moral Philosophy. While yet in his 19th year he distinguished himself by an acute and able review of Dr. Darwin's Zoönomia. This publication introduced him to the notice of some of the most distinguished men of the time, and at the age of 19 he was associated with a number of them in the formation of the Edinburgh Academy of Physics. Erskine, Brougham, Lord Seymour, Mackenzie, Jeffrey, and others, were of this number, and from this association originated the Edinburgh Review. Dr. Brown wrote for this Review the article on the Philosophy of Kant in the second number, but taking umbrage at some liberties which were taken with a subsequent paper, he withdrew entirely his connection with the work.

Dr. Brown figured somewhat as a poet, though not, it would seem, with any great success. His poetry is of that metaphysical sort, which comparatively few readers appreciate or enjoy, and which is by no means the highest order of poetry. He looked upon nature and upon man too much with the eye of a philosopher intent upon discovering the true relations of things and their moral bearings, just as he looked upon philosophy too much with the eye of a poet, intent upon discovering beauties where only nice discrimination of truth should be the object. It may be said of him without injustice, that his philosophy spoiled his poetry, and the latter avenged itself by spoiling, in turn, his philosophy. His principal poetical work was the Paradise of Coquettes, London, 1814. The prose of Dr. Brown is certainly as unphilosophical, as his poetry is unpoetical. In the somewhat severe but just language of one who was himself both a philosopher and a personal friend of Brown, "It is brilliant to excess. It must not be denied that its beauty is sometimes womanly, that it too often melts down precision into elegance, that it buries its main idea under a load of illustration, of which every part is expanded and adorned with such a visible labor as to withdraw the mind from attention to the thoughts which it professes to introduce more easily into the understanding. It is darkened by excessive brightness; it loses ease and liveliness by overdress,—and in the midst of its luscious sweetness we wish for the striking and homely illustrations of Tucker, and for the pithy and sinewy sense of Paley, either of whom by a single short metaphor from a familiar, perhaps a low object, could at one blow set the two worlds of reason and force in movement."

These very qualities, however, contributed not a little doubtless to the success of his lectures on their first delivery. Brilliant, adorned with every grace and ornament of style and fancy, sparkling with imagery, sufficiently original to wear the air of novelty, bold and daring even to a fault in differing from established authority, *analytic* withal in a very high degree, yet clothing the most abstract speculations in popular language and even poetical diction, the lectures of Dr. Brown drew large and admiring audiences, and attracted general attention. They were the result, however, not of careful and mature thought and long study, but of a brilliant and original genius trusting to its own powers of invention and analysis. They were generally written the night previous to their delivery, and of necessity were as hasty and superficial as they were brilliant and popular. Had he lived to prepare them for the press he would probably have divested them somewhat of the popular and declamatory style and clothed in a garb more fitting the chaste and sober genius of philosophy.

The personal character of Dr. Brown is peculiarly attractive. Mackintosh speaks of him "as an example of one in whom the utmost tenderness of affection and the indulgence of a flowery fancy were not repressed by the highest cultivation, and by a perhaps excessive refinement of intellect. His mind soared and roamed through every region of philosophy and poetry, but his untravelled heart clung to the hearth of his father, to the children who shared it with him, and after them first to other partners of his childish sports and then almost solely to those companions of his youthful studies who continued to be the friends of his life. Speculation seemed to keep his kindness at home. It is observable that, though sparkling with fancy, he does not seem to have been deeply or durably touched by those affections which are lighted at its torch, or at least tinged with its colors. His heart sought little abroad, but contently dwelt in his family and in his study. He was one of those men of genius who repaid the tender care of a mother by *rocking the cradle of her reposing age.*"

He died April 2d, 1820, at the age of 42. Of the philosophy of Dr. Brown we have already had occasion to speak in discussing that of Reid ; especially of the injustice which he does the latter in respect to the merit of overthrowing the established and long current theory of ideas ; and also of the historical inaccuracies with which he abounds. The most serious defect of his system is, perhaps, the doctrine which he saw fit to advocate in regard to perception. The very point on which he claims to be at one with Reid, is the very one in which he differs most essentially and entirely from him. So far is he from understanding either the history of the doctrine, or Reid's position with regard to it, or in fact, his own. Brown is, with regard to perception, what Hamilton would call a representationist of the egoistical order. The object immediately perceived is, with him, not any external thing, but a mode or modification of the mind itself. Reid, as we have seen, is a *natural realist,* the thing directly perceived is, with him, not the mind itself, not any idea in the mind or out of it, but the really existing external object. Brown misunderstands his entire doctrine on this subject and supposes him to be, like himself, a representationist. In taking this position, Brown throws the entire philosophy of the Scotch school a step backwards,—out of order into confusion, out of progress into retreat. The shadow moves a degree backward on the dial the moment that step is taken. The door is thrown open again to idealism and scepticism, and the philosophy of Dr. Brown is utterly powerless to meet these advancing foes. This so far as regards merely our belief in external realities, may not be of so much consequence, for that belief is too firm to be shaken by any theory or speculation. But the mischief wrought is chiefly in another quarter. The representation theory contradicts the universal *consciousness* of mankind, and if that be affirmed false in *one* instance it cannot, as Hamilton has well shown, be relied on in other cases. All certainty, all confidence in its testimony is destroyed, and what becomes of the validity of human knowledge of any kind and in any case? See Hamilton's argument against Brown.

The general system adopted by Brown may best be seen in his classification of the mental powers. He divides mental phenomena into external and internal *states;* including under the former the various sensations; under the latter, intellectual states, which are all reduced to simple and relative suggestion, and emotions, which comprise the passions and desires. The will has no place among these faculties. There are in fact no *faculties,* but merely *states* of the mind. The mind exists now in the state of memory, now in that of imagination, etc., just as moisture exists, now in the state of vapor, now of water, now of ice or snow. The laws by which it passes from one of these states to the other, are in either case fixed and positive, and may be, to some extent at least, definitely ascertained, and the mental, as truly as the physical phenomena, are the definite and certain results of those laws. *Activity, operation, power, faculty,* are terms not known to this system as designations of mental phenomena. The native spontaneity, the inherent activity of mind, its first chief distinguishing characteristic, in distinction from mere organized and animate or inanimate matter, is altogether overlooked. Psychology becomes merely the *physiology* of mind,—a system of mental mechanics. Against this cardinal feature of Brown's system we protest with all earnestness, as a cardinal error and blunder. The mind is not a series of *states,* but a living conscious *unity,* possessing an inherent activity of its own, possessing by its nature and constitution certain *powers,* putting forth those powers as it will, now this—now that—but always *acting,* operating, continually; and to speak of the mind thus constituted as existing merely in *certain states,* is not simply ridiculous, it is one of the grossest *libels* upon psychology,—it is to give the play of Hamlet with the character of Hamlet left out,—it is to stumble over the very threshold of the science and sprawl at full length on the first pavements. Mental physiology—mental mechanics. Procul! O procul!

We object still further to the peculiar phraseology of Brown. The *states* of mind are part internal, part *external.* But what are we to understand by an *external* state of mind! Was ever a greater absurdity of language perpetrated in all *Ireland?* Paul assures us that at one time he knew not whether he was in the body or out of it, but Dr. Brown seems to be in the same quandary as to the condition of the human mind generally. It is liable to exist at any time in an *external state.* But, overlooking the absurdity of the language, the principle of classification here involved is not the true one. The question of importance to be answered is not what is the *origin* of these so called mental *states,* as Morell very justly insists, but what are they in themselves. Nor is the principle self-consistent even were it admissible; for some of the internal states, so called, are really of external origin. The whole thing is, in fact, from beginning to end, a tissue and concatenation of blunders.

Not much better is the attempt to reduce all mental operations and faculties to the category of *single* and *relative suggestion.* What is to be gained by this? Are not these several operations and faculties of operation really distinct? Are they not essential to the mind? known by well defined names from time immemorial? Why disturb this accustomed nomenclature? I have now and had from birth a faculty of memory, of conception, of imagination, of judgment, of taste, etc. Why strip me of these, and send me out into the world, like the plucked chicken of the ancient philosopher, *two-legged* and *featherless*—a *man* with only *two* capacities; single and relative suggestion, and no *faculty* at all. What is the gain to philosophy or to the individual in particular, by any such process. It is not true moreover that all the mental powers may be thus comprised under the one general faculty, a law of suggestion—a law which, in Dr. Brown's view, plays the same part in the mental that gravitation does in the physical world. Matter gravitates; mind . . *receives suggestions.* We would beg leave in this connection to *suggest* that this is not altogether a satisfactory view of the human mind. It remains only to notice briefly two other points in this system of philosophy. Brown's theory of cause and effect and his theory of morals. As to the first, he virtually *denies* the *existence* of power other than that of the Deity, as an existing objective or subjective reality, manifesting itself as cause in the production of changes or effects. There are for him no efficient causes in nature, only immediate, invariable antecedence. Nor does he recognize power or cause in the mind itself as the efficient, voluntary producer of its own acts. Overlooking our own personal consciousness of voluntary power, effort, sensation,—the source of all our ideas of power or cause in nature, he fails of course to perceive in the material world anything of the sort, and so reduces all phenomena both mental and material to mere succession of events, connected indeed and uniform in their procedure, but of which no one is, or contains in itself, the cause or reason why another occurs. It is this idea of causation or rather the entire absence of causation which gives that peculiar hue and coloring which we have already noticed to Brown's whole theory of mind. He sees in the mind a mere passive receptivity of suggestions, a passive entity existing in certain ever changing *states* dependent for the quality and character of those states upon influences and impressions from without, and the established laws of consciousness within. The mind as a *power*, as possessing faculties, and exerting them at its own sweet will, he does not recognize, has never formed the idea of such a thing. Hence it is that the will has no place in his system. It is merely a modification of *desire*.

As to ethics, a word will suffice. Brown nowhere discusses the great problem of liberty and necessity. There was perhaps, with such a theory of mind as we have now described, very little occasion for him to take up those intricate and deep questions. They were in part already settled by the very basis of his theory. Everything goes according to fixed laws—no spontaneity, no activity, no will—of course no occasion for liberty. Such, as it would seem, would be the almost inevitable conclusion—certainly the only consistent one from such a psychology—or system of mental mechanics.

His theory of virtue is analogous to that of cause and effect; certain actions are followed by certain emotions in us, the one the antecedent, the other the consequent; that is all we know or can know of the matter. To inquire for the cause of the emotions which thus arise, or seek any adaptation in the action to produce the consequent emotion is idle, just as it is in nature to inquire for a cause of the observed connection of events. Gravitation is the name we give to this relation of events in the physical world. So in the moral world we call the relation of actions and emotions by a general name—virtue—a mere name for an unknown thing, an abstraction. We are not to ask, then, what is the ground of virtuous emotion, why we approve or disapprove certain actions; there is no ground, at least that can be known to us—nothing in the nature of human action in *itself* considered, why one emotion should follow rather than another. Were the emotions then to be reversed, were we to approve what now we disapprove, and vice versa, no reason could be shown why that would not be just as well as the present arrangement, nay, why virtue and vice would not just change places. To such a pass do we come when once we lose sight of the element of human freedom as the basis of human responsibility, and the foundation of human conscience.

I have spoken in somewhat severe terms of this entire system, because I regard it as on the whole most radically defective and unsound, and from the very genius of its author and the attractive dress in which it is clothed, all the more specious and dangerous. It is all the more to be condemned as being a move backward from a far better and nobler system, against which it sets itself in open revolt. I would by no means deny the originality and genius of its author's mind, nor his power of analysis, which is everywhere manifest. Of his personal character and worth, I have already spoken; so true is it, as a profound moralist has remarked, that men are always better or worse than their speculative opinions.

CHAPTER XIV.

THE GERMAN PHILOSOPHY.—IMMANUEL KANT.

WHILE Reid was laying the foundations of a true philosophy in Britain, and setting himself to stem the prevailing torrent of scepticism, a greater than Reid was devoting himself to the same work, and with the same design, in another land. They were contemporary writers, in some respects of kindred spirit, animated by a common desire, laboring for a common end. Both gave their lives to the great work of elaborating a system of philosophy that should prove an effectual barrier to the inroads of that scepticism which both saw and felt to be most formidable, not to philosophy alone, but to all truth and all sound principles of morality. Both were men of genius and power. Each knew little of the life and writings of the other. It was the writings of David Hume that first aroused both to undertake the work to which each devoted his life. But though animated by the same impulse, they moved in altogether independent courses. The manner in which Reid accomplished his design we have already noticed. It remains to inquire into the philosophy of his great contemporary, Immanuel Kant.

This distinguished man, second in fame as a philosopher to no other, certainly in modern times, was born in Konigsberg, Prussia, April 22, 1724. He was the son of poor but honest and respectable parents; his father a harness-maker; his mother a woman of marked character, strictly religious and not wanting in native strength of mind. She took her boy early into the fields and taught him the names of the flowers that grew by the wayside and along the meadows, and awakened in him the love of nature and the beautiful. The boy grew up and in course of time, having received his first education at a charity school in the suburbs, was sent in 1732, then only eight years old, by much sacrifice and exertion of the parents, to the college at Königsberg, named after Frederic, and in 1740, then sixteen, to the University. The mother and the son now walked forth as before into the fields,—she now to question and he to teach. For his mother he ever retained, as every truly great and noble man has ever done, the tenderest affection. Both his parents, however, were removed by death soon after he reached the age of manhood. His application to study at the college and university was unremitting, and his proficiency great. He devoted himself chiefly to philological studies at first, together with Physics and Mathematics, which were his favorite studies and recreation in subsequent life. At the university he studied theology as a profession, intending to devote himself to it as a means of livelihood, but seems never to have formed any special taste therefor. He was quite too fond of science and philosophy to devote himself to either of the practical professions as the business of life. Coleridge, the English disciple of Kant, had in early life a similar destination and went so far as actually to preach on a few occasions, once certainly on the *corn-laws,* not altogether a gospel sermon probably. Whether Kant did likewise we are not informed, but he somewhere speaks of having, as a candidate for theology, written a sermon on reconciliation with enemies from the words " agree with thine adversary quickly," etc., which however, he had never had occasion to deliver. Very early, however, must he have acquired a fondness for philosophical investigation, since we find him at the age of twenty-two assailing vigorously the systems of Leibnitz and Wolff and using the weapons of dialectic skill with no little effect against the most eminent authorities of the age in metaphysical science. Obliged to depend upon his own resources, he spent some years in retirement as private tutor in several families, where he devoted much time to reading, and marked out the plan of several of the philosophical treatises which he subsequently published. In 1755, after ten or twelve years thus employed, he returned to Königsberg, took the degree of A. M., and soon after published his celebrated work the Theory of the Heavens, or the constitution and mechanical structure of the Globe, according to the Newtonian system. This was a work of no little originality and merit, and in it he anticipates more than one of the subsequent discoveries of Herschel, as that astronomer afterwards admitted, particularly the existence of the planet Uranus. Kant now began to lecture as Doctor Docens on a wide range of subjects—natural law, metaphysics, mathematics, logic, natural philosophy, moral philosophy, natural theology, etc. He became popular with the students, but was not appointed a professor until after some fifteen years of patient toil and waiting. At length in 1770 the honor so long and richly merited was conferred on him. His publications did not attract much attention at first. The Critique of Pure Reason, his master work, lay six years almost unnoticed, and the publisher was on the point of destroying the unsold edition, when suddenly the demand increased, the value of the work became known, successive editions were quickly disposed of, and all Germany became animate with the discussion of the new philosophy. It was stoutly and learnedly assailed, as vigorously and ably defended by its friends and disciples; the thinking mind of Germany ranged itself on either side, for and against the new system. Gradually it prevailed over all obstacles. Almost every chair in the German universities was filled by a Kantist. The work was the study of twelve years, but was written in five months. Hence its defects of style, its carelessness, looseness, want of clearness, sometimes of consistency. It is such a work as none but a German could ever write, and no literary community but a German would ever tolerate. In spite of its defects of style, however, it has exerted a more powerful influence on the educated and thinking mind of Europe than probably any other book of the kind ever written.

The fame of Kant was now fully established. From all the countries of Europe men came to see and speak with the great German. One man, himself a professor, announced himself at the study door, as having travelled 160 miles to speak with Kant. Advantageous proposals from other universities were made to him, but Kant remained faithful to the home of his early life and labors. Indeed, with the exception of his private tutorship at Arensdorf, 32 miles distant, he never once quitted Königsberg, it is said, during his whole life. His habits were extremely simple. He had no ambition for display and the attentions of a crowd,—sought retirement,—lived alone, attended only by a faithful old soldier in the capacity of body servant,—in a retired house,—the domestic arrangements of which were all entrusted to his servant and his cook. There he passed his hours, days, years, till an advanced old age, content with his own best thoughts and best society. Reichardt describes him as a lean, small man—"leaner, nay, drier, none probably ever existed." A high, calm forehead, tranquil and lofty as the seat of high thought, a well-formed nose, and clear bright eyes of serene depth, gave his countenance a marked expression. Though loving retirement he was yet fond of society, and never dined without one or two invited guests. Dinner was a social and cheerful meal, in which he gave himself up to conversation, merriment, good cheer, good living. His habits were quite as regular and punctual as those of the town clock, which seemed rather to regulate its movement by his, than his by its. At five minutes before five, summer and winter, weather what it pleased, the old soldier walked with military precision into his master's bed-room, exclaimed with a bow, "Sir, it is time!" and immediately withdrew. Just five minutes after, the philosopher invariably sat down to a cup of tea, scarcely more, for breakfast. He now marked out with the precision of an astronomical diagram, his occupations for the day, and immediately entered upon them. At seven he sallied forth for lecture, frequently giving successive lectures at short intervals, through a considerable part of the morning. His lectures were full of illustration —given mostly without reference to his notes, from memory. After that he gave himself up to study till, at a quarter before one, the old soldier opened the door and announced that 12¾ had struck. Whatever else might be on hand at the moment, Kant was on hand also,—made his toilet with care—and appeared precisely at one, neatly dressed, and with a cordial greeting for his invited guests. At no other time did he see visitors. After dinner, which occupied some two hours or more, he always, and in all weathers, took his promenade of an hour, alone, or attended only by his servant,—spent the remaining afternoon in light reading,—which comprehended almost everything in almost every department of literature—but especially politics and books of travel. At six o'clock, without supper, he addressed himself to the studies of the evening, retiring at ten. Fifteen minutes before retiring, he broke off all thought and occupation that might disturb his repose, and immediately fell asleep on touching his pillow. Thus he lived till extreme old age gradually wore out his powers of labor and endurance, and he sank to his final sleep February 12th, 1804, eighty years of age. His faculties gradually wasted with his wasting form. His memory first,—his sight followed,—he became gradually unconscious of surrounding objects, and yet life still lingered at the citadel, as loth to deprive the world of one who had so well adorned and served it. After his decease, his remains were visited by immense multitudes, thronging the house for days, and his funeral solemnities were attended as few kings have been attended on their march to the sepulchre. All Germany conspired to do him honor. It would have been gratifying to have heard from the lips of so great a man, as he approached the grave, some avowal of a personal Christian faith. Alas! he was a philosopher, rather than a Christian. When asked in his closing life to what he looked forward in the future, he professed an *entire ignorance of what might hereafter await him.* The wasting energies of life filled him with sad regrets. Weary and sick of existence, which was to him full of pain and misery, he drew no consolation from the hopes of the future and of immortality, which revelation holds out to man. He was ready enough to die, and would gladly depart, but the ground of this readiness was the uselessness and misery of further existence, and the ground of his confidence was that he had never consciously injured any one. A sad death for a Christian philosopher of the 19th century. That of Socrates was a far more sublime and Christian death of the two.

Of the philosophy of Kant little more than a meagre outline can be given in the compass of a lecture, and no such outline, however full and faithful and correct, can convey an adequate and just idea of a great system of philosophy. And yet it may be of service to study an outline map before travelling over a country, and thus learn beforehand what are the prominent features of the region we are about to visit. I shall be satisfied if the exposition I am about to give shall serve as such an introduction and guide to any of you in your future study of the great author himself.

The philosophical systems that were chiefly in vogue, it will be remembered, at the time when Kant came upon the stage, were the sensationalism of the followers of Locke, the idealism of Leibnitz and his followers, together with the prevailing scepticism of Hume. These all, the latter chiefly, had left their impression on the thinking mind of northern Europe, and were producing their effects. Hume had shown triumphantly that certain ideas of the human mind, as e.g. ideas of cause and effect, are not derived from *experience*, and thence concluded that they were mere figments of the imagination, quite without *authority*. Kant saw the necessity of a profounder investigation of the fundamental laws of the mind itself, as the only way of settling truth and philosophy on a sure basis. He saw that Hume was right as to his premises in this case. He saw that the ideas of cause and effect were, however, not the only ideas that are not derived from experience, that the same thing is true of a large class of our ideas, and that instead of rejecting these ideas, with Hume, as of no authority on that account, it was necessary to admit and establish them as of the very *highest* authority. To these ideas or forms of thought not derived from experience, he gives the name transcendental; and seeks to determine their number and legitimate province. These are primitive intuitions; *a priori* conceptions, not *a posteriori*—not the result of experience—not, with Descartes, innate. The truths which are thus acquired are the only truths that are absolutely certain. The truths of experience are contingent, variable, uncertain, changing with circumstances. These *a priori* or transcendental conceptions, on the contrary, have the character of *necessary* and *universal* truths. Of such a nature are the ideas we have of substance, causality, infinity, space, time, etc. The faculty which furnishes the principles of this *a priori* cognition Kant denominates the pure reason.

It is the object of the work entitled Critique of Pure Reason to give a general theory of all the pure or *a priori* elements which enter into human knowledge. The work consists of two parts, the first of which enumerates and establishes the existence of those various elements, the second investigates their value, absolute and relative, and their right use.

All human knowledge, says Kant, is derived from two sources, equally important but essentially diverse. These two sources or fundamental faculties, are *first* the *sensi-*

bility; (sinnlichkeit), which is the capacity of receiving representations (vorstellungen) of objects by means of the impressions made on our senses,—a passive faculty—hence called the receptivity, but essential to the representation of objects, since objects are represented to us only as we *are affected in some way* by them; the representations thus received he calls also *intuitions;* (anschauungen), and their objects are appearances, phenomena (erscheinung); *second* the *understanding;* (verstand)—the faculty of knowing objects by means of the representations afforded by sense—the source of notions, or conceptions, (begriffe) as the sensibility is of *intuitions.* It is not, like the former, a mere *capacity* (fahigkeit), but an *active power,* a faculty (vermogen). Its developments are spontaneous. These two powers, differing thus in character and function, *concur* in all our knowledge. The study of the one differs from that of the other as Æsthetic differs from Logic. Now the question is, what are the pure *a priori* elements that are contained in each of these; for to determine this simply, not to treat at large of the two faculties, is Kant's sole object in the Critique. And first as to the *sensibility.* In every object of intuition, that is, in every phenomenon, we distinguish two things; the *matter* of the phenomenon,—that which is manifold, variable, that which corresponds to the sensation, and the *form,* that which is fixed and unchangeable. The former is given in sensation or *a posteriori;* the latter is independent of and prior to sensation *i. e., a priori.* On examination we discover two of these invariable elements or forms, of sensible intuition, viz., *time* and *space*—the *necessary conditions* of all sensible experience. You cannot conceive of body *without space.* It is in space that you locate it, determine its figure, size, relations. It is the indispensable condition then of sensation. It is not given in the *materials* of sensation;—annihilate all those materials, all sensation, all matter, you have not annihilated space—that still remains—must therefore be its form. It answers to the character of an *a priori* or pure element; since universal, invariable, necessary.

So of *time*. It too is a *form* of sensible intuition. All objects not only, but all consciousness or *internal intuition* is represented under this form, just as all objects are in space. We are sensible of things and conscious of things only as presented in *succession* to our sensibility. These then are indispensable conditions both,—pure forms of sensibility, with which *we invest* all the materials of sensation. Since these are given not in experience, since they are not contained in the material of sensation, but are forms of it only, they have no *objective* existence, are purely *subjective*, conceptions of the mind. They exist within us, not without—are necessary and pure intuitions of the internal sense.

Let us now examine the understanding to discover what pure *a priori* elements are there contained.

The function of this power, it will be observed, is to judge, to elevate into notions or conceptions, the perceptions furnished by the sensibility. It does this by linking diverse sensations together, reducing them to unity by means of memory, imagination, consciousness, thus forming conceptions. Without this faculty we should have no *knowledge*, only *sensations*. As the sensibility imposes the laws or forms of time and space on the objects presented to it, so the understanding imposes certain laws or forms of its own on the materials furnished by sensibility. What are these forms of the understanding, these laws of its operation? If we examine all the different methods of judging, we find them to be four—viz, *quantity*, *quality*, *relation*, *modality*—i. e., in every judgment we have regard to some one of these four things, predicate something either as to the quantity, or the quality, or the relation, or the mode of existence of the object considered. Each of these four embraces under it three distinct, pure, *a priori* conceptions. Thus, in judging of *quantity* we regard the object as a unity, plurality, or totality. In judging of quality we have to do with affirmation or reality, negation, limitation, *i. e.* we affirm or deny, or limit the thing proposed or considered. So in judging of the *relations* of an object, we have to do with the ideas of *substance,* causality and reciprocity ; while if we consider the modality or mode of existence of any object, we regard its possibility, actuality, and necessity.

These are all pure *a priori* conceptions, indispensable to experience—prior to it—the conditions and forms or laws of the understanding. Kant calls them categories.

Kant divides all judgments into two classes, analytic and synthetic. The former is a simple statement of our conception or notion of a thing, as that a triangle has three sides. The latter states some circumstance or quality not involved necessarily in the conception of the object itself, *adds* something to what is implied in the simple conception of the object, as when we say a straight line is the shortest distance between two points. These synthetic judgments may be either *a posteriori,* from experience, or *a priori,* independent of experience. Iron is malleable,—a synthetic judgment from experience. Not so that synthetic judgment already stated respecting a straight line as the shortest distance, etc. That experience can only confirm. It was true without experience, has *universality* which experience cannot bestow, since experience can only show what has been frequently found true, but cannot prove that the same is universally true. Experience may show that in numberless instances the sun has risen, or crows are black, etc., but cannot prove that no exceptions ever will occur. Nor is there any *a priori* synthetic judgment that affirms that. But that every effect must have a cause is a pure *a priori* conception, not given in experience merely, but independent of it, prior to it. Now these synthetic *a priori* judgments are *certain* and *universal.* They are the *ground* of *certitude*. The veracity of human reason rests and reposes on that certitude. Thus and therefore it is, that, while endless disputes prevail about metaphysics, men do not endlessly quarrel about mathematics, logic, or the higher physics, because these have to do with universal and *a priori* truths, not with the contingent and variable. The principles and properties of mathematical science are only so many conceptions; the rules and propositions of logic are only so many invariable *laws* of the human mind. Even in physics men follow reason while investigating nature. Reason furnishes the rules, methods, *problems* even, by which and on which they work. Science then reposes on the laws of the human mind.

Thus far we have investigated the *a priori* elements given in the sensibility and the judgment. The *Reason* also furnishes its quota. What are they?

Understanding is the faculty of judging;—Reason the faculty of ratiocination,—of drawing conclusions from premises. It reduces our various conceptions to unity, traces each up to some more general idea, and that onward to its ultimate principle. It also deduces the particular from the general. Now in our reasonings and generalizings we may proceed in either of three ways, as shown by the rules of formal logic, viz., categorically, hypothetically or disjunctively. The first regards the relations of substance and accident, and proceeding according to this method we reach at last, as the result, a subject universal and absolute, not itself the attribute of any other substance, viz., *the soul*. Proceeding hypothetically, we reach at last a supposition which supposes nothing further, something which is not an effect depending on some *anterior* effect, the absolute unity and totality of the series of phenomena, viz., the world or universe. Finally, by the disjunctive process we arrive at last at the absolute unity of all the objects of thought in general, viz., Deity. The soul, the world, God; these are three ideas or pure forms of the reason, the first, uniting in itself as unity all the phenomena of the *Ego;* the second, uniting in itself, as unity, all the phenomena of the *non-Ego;* the third, uniting in itself, as the absolute and final unity, both the other, the Ego and the non-Ego, as the source and basis of both.

Corresponding to these three ideas of the reason are three sciences: psychology, cosmology, theology; the science of the soul, of the world, of God.

As the results of the understanding are called *notions,* so the results of the reason are in this system termed *ideas.* These ideas, unlike our notions, have no objective reality, are the pure creations of the reason, are subjective merely; notions being derived, primarily, from experience and sensation, can be traced back to some objective reality, fall within the limits of perception. Not so ideas; they afford no basis of certain objective reality; they only *regulate* the use of the understanding, as that regulates the use of the faculty of sense. Such, however, is the constitution of the mind, that we do inevitably and universally proceed, as above shown, in accordance with these ideas of the pure reason; that we necessarily form the idea of a thinking subject, a soul, as the basis and unity of the phenomena of self; the idea of a substance, the universe, as basis of the phenomena of the non-Ego; the idea of a supreme substance and unity, Deity, as the ground of all secondary conditions of existence. Still, though all men do, and must and ever will reason in this way, these great ideas have, after all, only a subjective value. They demonstrate nothing, *can prove* nothing, objectively; for all proof, all certain science and knowledge, is grounded on experience. Hence all attempts to *prove,* by the *arguments usually drawn from reason and the pure metaphysics,* the personality of the soul, its immateriality, its immortality, the creation or non-eternity of the universe and the existence of God, are futile and worthless. The opposite can with equal facility be proved from the same source. What then? Scepticism? Have these things no reality, no existence, no certainty to us? They *have.* We are not left without any ground of certainty as to the reality and objective existence of these things. We have that ground, not in the pure and theoretical reason, indeed, which is merely formal, merely negative, but we have it in our practical reason, in our *moral nature.* The knowledge of the external universe, and of the soul, and of God, rests ultimately on the same firm and sure basis as the knowledge of our own present existence and thought and sensation, viz., on the basis of *consciousness.* For consciousness attests the reality and existence of our moral nature, reveals to us the supremacy within us of an absolute moral law, imperative, commanding,—the authority of the conscience, that grand practical movement of the reason, by which it sways the sceptre of lofty dominion over the soul, and regulates the conduct. This is a reality as sure and positive as any other part of consciousness. And it implies, what? Mark the answer. It implies *freedom,* without which all moral action were impossible; a future state, as the goal of human action and completion of the present; a God, as the lawgiver and judge, whence emanates this regulative and legislative principle in man. These grand truths are realities, then, founded not in theoretical reason, but in practical reason, in the *moral nature* of man, and attested by consciousness, whose testimony is never to be called in question.

Between the theoretical and the practical reason there comes in as an intermediate and connecting link the faculty of judgment, which unites the two in a common result. This faculty gives us the feeling of the sublime, the beautiful, and the reverse, also the notion of a final end,—teleology—arising from the perception of the design everywhere manifest in nature. These noble æsthetic sentiments confirm the belief of the practical reason in immorality and in God. The certainty and immutability of moral distinctions and the evidence of natural religion are thus placed on a basis as sure and valid as anything short of absolute demonstration can possibly make them.

Such are the grand outlines of the philosophy of Kant. To sum up its leading points:—He acknowledges the reality of our sense-knowledge, makes it the basis in fact of all positive science, but not the source of all our knowledge. We have beyond and above this *a priori* conceptions, not derived from experience. These are the forms of our intellections, as furnished by reason while experience or sense furnishes only the matter. But these pure *a priori* forms and conceptions are subjective only, can never lead to objective reality. The certainty of those truths which lie above and beyond the sphere of sense, and which the theoretical reason affirms but can never prove, is to be found in our moral nature.

The grand merits of this system are its clear and complete analysis of the mental processes, especially of the *a priori* elements of our knowledge; its distinction between sense and understanding; its discovery in the soul of a higher faculty than either, viz., the pure reason; its establishing morality and religion on a firm basis, the constitution of man's moral nature as attested by consciousness.

Its grand defects are, that it makes the *a priori* elements of time and space purely *subjective*, mere phenomena of ego, and assigns them to the sensibility in distinction from the understanding, as if the latter had no concern with them; and also it makes the reason and its ideas, in like manner, purely subjective and personal, thus banishing from pure philosophy the certain knowledge of the soul as immortal and immaterial, of the universe as an objective reality, and of God, making all these all-important truths rest entirely on altogether another basis, viz., that of belief in and consciousness of our moral nature. The system of Kant puts no faith in reason as a revealer of these grand truths.

With all the merits then of this system, its *tendency* to pure idealism is obvious and apparently inevitable. We shall not be surprised then to find the successors of Kant going beyond him in this direction, and with less perspicacity and less caution, boldly adventuring where his clear and gigantic intellect could find no sure resting place.

Addenda on Kant.—A Biography.

It was at the age of twenty-two that he published his first work. His teaching was in families in the environs of Königsberg. He never went out of the province of Königsberg in his life. That was to him a theatre of action, a mart and centre of commerce, a political centre and literary also, affording abundant advantages for the study of men and manners. While specially devoted to mathematics, and physical science, he was a stranger to no branch of knowledge. He was gifted with a vast memory and a great power of conception and combination. He despised *rhetoricians*, and with Montaigne regarded rhetoric as the art of *deceiving* men, yet he by no means undervalued the talent of speaking well. It was in his lectures on anthropology and physical geography, that his abundant knowledge of men and things, his accurate observation, his profound and original and just views, more conspicuously appeared, and these lectures following his other course, were attended by auditors of all ages and all ranks.

As a writer he is often embarrassed and obscure, needlessly so, but is always equal to, and often rises above his *cotemporaries* in the qualities of good writing. His distinguishing characteristic was *love of truth*; nothing stood second to *that* in his estimation, and he demanded *liberty* to think and to speak accordingly, could brook no hindrance to the free utterance of truth, demanded the strictest veracity also on the part of his friends.

He was a patriot; "Liberty, law, and the public power are elements of all social life," he says, "law and liberty without power, is anarchy. Law and power without liberty, is despotism; power alone is barbarism; liberty and law united with power is republicanism, the only good civil constitution, but which is not necessarily democracy."

In religion he seems to have been a sort of Deist. He rejected all supernatural revelation as useless and impossible, and for a long time took no part in public worship of any kind, which he regarded as needful only for the feeble-minded; yet so far from discarding the doctrines of the Bible, he bent all his energies, says Willm, to reconcile them with reason and thus established a *rational theology.* He inculcates in his writings rather a *natural* than a supernatural religion.

His personal appearance was not unprepossessing. His physical constitution was feeble, his frame not robust but small and delicate, his eye blue, at once lively and mild, indicating spirit and kindness, his forehead elevated, indicating the profound thinker.

Never was a man more systematic and exact in all his habits; and to this regularity is owing his advanced age and his vigor of mind and body until almost the last.

It is impossible, says Willm, when one has read all that his biographers relate of Kant, not to love and respect the man as much as we admire the philosopher. It is related by his biographers that his habit was to sit at evening twilight by his window and meditate on his next day's lecture, his eyes fixed abstractedly meanwhile on a neighboring tower. The gradual growth of a row of poplars, at last hid the tower from view, and occasioned so much embarrassment to the course of thought in the philosopher that he was under the necessity of prevailing with the owner to cut down the pretensions of the too aspiring poplars. It is also related of him that he was accustomed in lecturing to fix his eyes on a particular coat button of one of his auditors. One day the lecture was unaccountably confused and heavy, a perfect failure in fact. Thinking of the circumstance afterward, Kant remembered that the *button* was that day unfortunately *missing*, and coat being minus the button, the philosopher was minus his lecture.

CHAPTER XV.

SUCCESSORS OF KANT.

KANT had nicely distinguished the various faculties of the mind, but had not attempted to derive them from a common source, to trace them back to a single and primitive origin. The life of the soul, however, is a unique and single principle. It is one in its origin, and one in its end. The development of this principle is progressive, and is to be viewed in diverse aspects and results as understanding, judgment, reason, etc. What is this unity, this single fundamental principle of all psychological development, and all human knowledge ? Let us search it out, and so place the philosophy of Kant on a better foundation and give it the completeness it needs. Thus reasoned the first successors of Kant, of whom *Reinhold* and *Fichte* are more especially worthy of notice.

§ 1. REINHOLD.

Born at Vienna, 1758 ; at first a Jesuit ; after the dissolution of that order, a Barnabite monk and professor of philosophy in his convent ; in 1783 embraces protestantism ; 1787 professor at Jena. 1794 at Kiel, where he dies in 1823. He was a man of the world, a journalist, a man of brilliant and vivacious mind, but not the calm, patient, profound thinker,—not the *correct* philosopher. His thoughts were often very just and weighty, but he was content to herald and announce them merely, leaving it to others to give them the correct expression. His *influence* on the public mind, however, was very great. He adopts the philosophy of Kant at its first appearance with enthusiasm, and writes a series of letters on it which were widely read, and with which Kant himself expressed great satisfaction. Seeking to place this philosophy, however, on a firmer basis, as already explained, he discovers, as he thinks, the fundamental principle of which he is in search, in the fact of *consciousness* or of perception, and bases human knowledge on the *representative faculty.* In the representative process, there is the subject which represents, the object represented, and also the act of representation itself, which unites the two,—their synthesis in the consciousness. Representation supposes in man, or the subject, a *representative faculty,* which precedes, of course, the *exercise* or act, and which comprises under it, sensible intuition, concept, idea, sensibility, understanding even, and reason. The principle of consciousness, then, which determines the representative faculty, is the elementary principle of knowledge, and of all philosophy.

§ 2. Fichte.

That foundation which Reinhold sought thus to establish in the consciousness, Fichte, going back of that, going further than that, places in an act primitive and spontaneous, the source of consciousness itself, viz., the act by which the soul, the subject, the ego, concludes its own existence as such. This modification of the system deserves a more particular mention; but first the personal history of the man himself demands our attention.

Johann Gottlieb (or Theophilus) Fichte was born at Rammenan, May 19, 1762, of poor but respectable parents; his father a ribbon-maker, descended from a Swedish sergeant of the army of Gustavus Adolphus, a man of strict integrity, of firm, unbending will, virtues which passed over in striking degree to the inheritance of the son. Many anecdotes are related of the childhood and youth of Gottlieb, which show that he possessed a very marked character. He was little like other children, little with them, took no pleasure in the sports of his brothers and sisters. There seems to have been in him, in very childhood, a love of solitude, a power of creative imagination, vague longings for something superior to what was about him or what was in him. By himself he wanders into the fields and among the forests, pleased with the luxury of silence and his own thoughts and the deep solitude of nature, gazes into the deep sky till the sun goes down, and late in the twilight returns sadly, thoughtfully, to his home. An anecdote which is related of him shows the *self-command* of the boy. A work of fiction which fell into his hands seized so strongly on his imagination that he forgot all things else, and was punished for his negligence. Deeply stung with the consciousness of his fault and his degradation, he resolved to sacrifice forever the object which had betrayed him to this offence, and taking the book, walked deliberately to a stream that ran past the house, and lingering awhile to gather strength for the sacrifice, summoning all his resolution, threw the idol at last into the stream and as he saw it floating away forever from him, burst into tears. The act had been observed, and as the boy did not explain his conduct, his motive was misunderstood, and he was again severely punished—a prelude of what oft happened to him in after life, to be *misunderstood* and suffer in consequence. The precocity of the child attracted the attention of the Lord of Rammenan, and of his friend the Baron von Miltitz, of Saxony on the Elbe, who took charge of his education, placing him under the care of a country pastor, where he passed some of the pleasantest years of his life. Here he remained till his thirteenth year, receïving his first instruction in the ancient languages, and what was worth more to him than all languages, ancient or modern, kind and affectionate treatment. His patron now placed him at the seminary of Schulpforte. There he was harshly treated and much abused. Tyranny and force on the part of the teachers led to duplicity and cunning on the part of the pupils. The generous and virtuous elements of character were little cultivated or esteemed. The integrity and honesty and self-reliance of Gottlieb were put to a severe test. His sympathies were repressed. His tears were taught to flow in secret. He resolved to fly from the gloomy monastic walls, where life was so wretched. He was already well on his way, on foot and without resources, to Hamburg, when he remembered a saying of his old pastor, that one ought never to begin an important undertaking in life without asking Divine assistance. Kneeling by the road-side, he implores the blessing of heaven on a friendless wandering boy. The thought of his mother now occurred to him; his eyes filled with tears; wandering from his school, he was in fact wandering from his friends and home, and might perhaps return no more. This thought brought back his courage and his better principle. He resolved to return and bravely meet the punishment that might await him at Schulpforte, "that he might look once more on the face of his mother." The honesty with which he confessed his fault procured his pardon, and he was thenceforth more kindly treated. How much to the future man was that one instance of self-conquest worth in after years.

At eighteen Fichte enters the university of Jena as student of theology; and here his philosophic genius seems to have been more decidedly awakened by the grand problems of liberty, necessity and Providence, which now came before him for solution. His patron's death, which occurred soon after, threw him again on his own resources, and he became private tutor in Zurich. Here he became acquainted with Mlle. Rahn, a niece of Klopstock, his future bride. His tutorship was not altogether to his mind, nor altogether successful, and 1790 he quits Zurich to seek his fortunes in Germany. Vainly seeking employment at Stuttgart and Weimar, he comes at last to Leipsig and begins giving lessons in Greek and philosophy, and here forms his first acquaintance with the writings of Kant. It was an era in his life. "I have been living for the last four or five months," he says, "in Leipsig the happiest life I can remember. I came here with my head full of grand projects, which all burst one after another, like so many soap-bubbles without leaving me so much as the froth. At first this troubled me a little, and half in despair, I took a step which I ought to have taken long before. Since I could not alter what was without me, I resolved to try to alter what was within. I threw myself into philosophy, the Kantian, and here I found the true antidote for all my evils, and joy enough into the bargain. The influence which this philosophy, the ethical part of it particularly, has had upon my whole system of thought is not to be described." He proceeds to express his firm belief in the doctrine of free will as the only foundation for virtue and duty, and then proceeds: "I am furthermore well convinced, that this life is not the land of enjoyment, but of labor and toil—that every joy is granted to us but to strengthen us for further exertion; that the management of our own fate is by no means required of us, but only self-culture. I trouble myself, therefore, not at all concerning the things that are without; I endeavor not to *appear*, but to *be*. And to this perhaps I owe the deep tranquillity I enjoy." After various reverses and removals, Fichte visits Königsberg, attracted by his admiration for Kant. He places in the hands of that philosopher, to whom he had no introduction, a work written in eight days entitled, A Critique on all Revelation. Kant saw in the stranger his own peer, and received him cordially.

But the resources of the adventurer were nearly exhausted. His journal bears the most touching witness to many a mental conflict on this score. "I have reckoned my finances," he says under date of August 28th, "and find that I have just enough to subsist on for a fortnight.' First September, "A situation as tutor, however reluctantly I might accept it, does not even offer itself, while the uncertainty of my position does not allow me to work. I must return home. I can perhaps borrow from Kant the small sum needful for my journey." 12th September, "I wanted to work to-day but could do nothing. How will this end? What will become of me a week hence? Then all my money will be gone." But a brighter day was at hand for the poor struggling scholar, conscious of his strength and firm in his purpose. By the advice of Kant he puts his manuscript into the hands of a bookseller, who consents to publish it anonymously. So well was it written, and so fully did it fall in with the known sentiments of the great philosopher that it was very generally attributed to Kant himself. The mistake at once made the reputation and the fortune of Fichte. He marries and returns to Zurich in 1793. The applause now acquired procured him the chair of philosophy at Jena, the leading university of Germany, whither he repairs in 1794; not however to end his troubles or escape opposition, which seems to have been his fortune in life. After some years of arduous toil and brilliant success, his enemies charge him with inculcating atheistic sentiments. The government takes up the matter. Fichte in disgust throws up his appointment and retires to Berlin in 1799. There he pursued his studies with renewed energy, and published several works.

In 1805 he is appointed professor at Erlangen. The troubles with France now occurred, and Prussia lost her independence. Fichte shares the lot of the vanquished and escapes to Copenhagen. After the peace of Tilsit he returns to Berlin and accepts the rectorship of the University then just organized there. His rule was one of firmness and vigor. His labors were for the *country* quite as much as for philosophy. He lectures with all the fire and fervor of a patriot, and pronounces his celebrated discourse to the German people, while the French drums were sounding in the street beneath the windows of his lecture-room. At the commencement of the campaign of 1813, Fichte terminates one of his most eloquent lectures with these words: "This course will be suspended till the end of the campaign. We will resume them in a free country or die in the attempt." Loud shouts responded to his appeal. Fichte descends and places himself in the ranks of a corps of volunteers just departing for the field of strife. His noble wife devotes herself wholly to the care of the sick and wounded in the hospitals, and the contagion seizes her—her husband devotes himself day and night to her care, contracts the same disease and expires the 28th January, 1814, at 52. A truly heroic life is here, a truly great and noble character rises before us, like a granite obelisk piercing the clouds, defying the winds and storms.

We have lingered so long in sketching the man that we must pass rapidly over the philosophy. And as we wish merely to indicate its general outlines, and show wherein it differs from that of Kant, it will not be necessary to go into detail. Kant had admitted the objective reality of things about us in the material world, but had contented himself with saying that we cannot know them as they are in themselves, but only as they *appear* to us, only as *phenomena*. These appearances, even, are determined by our intellectual organization. The laws of nature are in fact, only the laws of our own mind, the phenomenal world is, as to its *forms* at least, only a production of our own intellect. Still it has a real and material existence independent of us. Fichte carries idealism much further than this. The *Me* only exists, and the *things* of which Kant speaks are only just so many and such as the *intelligent Me postulates* and *determines.*

The "things in themselves," so called, of Kant, are thus reduced to a simple *not-me,*—are imagination, not a reality, —devised merely to give the me the knowledge of itself. And why assume the objective existence of these so called things? Science must proceed from one self-evident position as starting-point or basis, and go on step by step, assuming nothing. Now the starting-point in philosophy, says Fichte, is not even *consciousness,* but something back of that—an act of the mind, whence our very consciousness, our knowledge of self proceeds—an act by which the ego comes to know itself. But to go no further back even than consciousness and to make that the starting-point; now are we *conscious* of external things? no;—only of our own impressions, sensations, judgments, ideas, or whatever we choose to call them,—only of these are we conscious. Whatever I *experience,* that and that only is with certainty known to me. If there be an external reality, then how can I ever *know* it? *believe* it, I may: that is another thing; but how *know* it? It must first pass through my mental experience, before I can be conscious of it, and in so doing becomes *subjective;* no longer *objective.* Is a *representation* given us by the constitution and operation of our minds? How can we verify the so called representation and know its correctness, but by comparing the said representation with the thing represented, that is, by comparing it with what is out of our consciousness and cannot therefore be known or perceived by us? But we are so formed, it will be replied, that we must accept our consciousness as a true representation of what lies beyond and without. And what is this, Fichte replies, but a purely subjective process; a law of our own minds; we do not get out of the charmed circle of self, of the ego, in this way; nor is it possible to do so, try what method we will. The very necessity of supposing, even, an external world is a necessity resulting from the very constitution of the mind, a purely *subjective* necessity.

Did Fichte, then, mean to *deny* all objective existence? Not at all. He denies merely that in *strict philosophy*, which allows us to *assume* nothing which requires certainty, and confines us to the facts of consciousness, we can ever attain a positive knowledge of such external reality. We can never *know* it. *If* it exist, it lies by the very supposition beyond our consciousness, and can only be *believed*, not known.

"He imagined the mind," says Morell, "to be as it were an intelligent eye placed in the central point of our inward consciousness, surveying all that takes place there, and it was from that point of view, (the only absolute and scientific one,) that he wished to give an account of our moral and intellectual history, detailing the rise, the progress, and all the events of our real inward life from its commencement to its maturity. Whether the scenes which take place within this subjective circle betoken any objective existence or not, that was to him a matter of no consequence, and he knew that if this were the case, it was only just in proportion as the objects could lay aside as it were, their objectivity, and transport within the subjective sphere of the mind's vision, that they could be observed and known; or, what is the same thing, that *to us* they could *exist*. The real history of every man, urged Fichte, is the history of his mind, the flow of his conscious existence; for what are to us woods, mountains, trees, or stars, but names we attach to certain parts of our consciousness? What are all forms of the material world but certain visions which have passed through our own minds—sensations which we have inwardly experienced?"

Which now is the primitive, which the cause of the other, the subjective or the objective? Have we subjective phenomena because there is an objective world to produce them, or do we suppose such a world because we have the former? Manifestly the *subjective* comes first. I am conscious of sensations; to explain these I infer the objective reality. The mind then is *the sphere of its own operations.* It is at once subject and object. Such is, in popular language, a general outline of his system.

The technical method in which he established logically and scientifically the foundation principles of this system is sufficiently curious and sufficiently unintelligible to all but the initiated. Science, being one, must repose on some one absolute, unique, sovereign principle, the source of all knowledge and all reality, and that must be discovered by reflection. Now on looking carefully we can find nothing more incontestible and certain than this proposition, A=A; in saying which I affirm nothing as to the existence of A, but only that *if* it is, it is *what* it is. Yet in even this I pass a *judgment,* and thereby propose or affirm *myself,* for all judgment implies the existence of him who judges. This is, in fact, the "*cogito ergo sum*" of Descartes, scientifically stated. But further, in thus affirming itself, the *me* first becomes *conscious* of itself, nay, produces itself, for there is no Me without and prior to consciousness, and no consciousness prior to this proposition or affirmation of itself.

It is because it affirms itself, and it affirms itself because it is. The Me affirms primitively its own being. This is the first act of the Me, and the absolute principle of all science. By a second act, the Me affirms, or opposes to itself a not Me, both absolute; or—A is not=A. In the first case it viewed itself as absolute subject. In the second it become absolute object. The one proposition is absolute affirmation, the other absolute negation. The last proposition however is as truly primitive as the first; to say Me is to distinguish that which is so called from something which is not itself. But this last proposition is contradictory of itself and of the first, for the Me and the not-Me are both affirmed as *absolute,* which is impossible. To reconcile the two a third is necessary, as the union of the positive and the negative, viz., the principle of limitation, thus: the Me and the not-Me are both affirmed by the Me as *reciprocally limiting each other*. The subject limits the object and the object the subject. So, then, we have here three elementary principles, affirmation, negation and limitation ; or thesis, antithesis, and synthesis, the primitive processes of the mind, the absolute principles of all science. "In thus hovering between subject and object, all our knowledge lies cradled."

The idea of the not-me is then only a modification of the me—a creation of it, arising from the fact that the me perceives itself limited, and supposes, out of itself, a cause of that limitation, yet in turn does itself define and limit that cause. All the sensations, ideas, etc., of the Me proceed from its own activity, and the not-Me itself is produced by the Me, proceeds from it and has no existence in fact but in it.

This is pure absolute idealism. Beyond this can no mortal go, one is ready to exclaim ; but of this we can never be sure till we know what the next German that comes after is to teach. What becomes of creation and the Creator on this system ? one asks. Simply this becomes of it. The mind is the true creator of all things out of itself, since all things out of itself are only its reflected existence, itself *objectified*. Of God, as an essential and personal existence, this philosophy knows nothing. Nay, to have an idea of God, says Fichte, is to limit him, and thus destroy the notion of him as an *infinite* being. How then, is Fichte an atheist ? Not at all. As a man he believes in God, but as a philosopher, does not know him. The region of philosophy,—he would say,—is pure *science ;* the region of faith is quite another realm and domain from that. We cannot *know* God, cannot demonstrate him, cannot philosophize him, but practically we believe in him, just as practically we believe in an external world, so soon as we step out of the realm of science into that of faith. It is a sad mistake, however, to construct a philosophy which does not admit a God; nor can we be surprised at the charge of atheism which occasioned him so much trouble and led to his retirement from Jena.

The great error of this system is obvious. It makes self the centre and circumference of all being and all knowledge. The sphere of thought, and the sphere of being are synonymous. The difference between those ideas and operations which depend solely on the mind's own activity, as memory, judgment, etc., and those which depend on something without the mind, and which we call perceptions, is altogether ignored. That which SEEMS to be an objective element, a not-me, is admitted in what we call perception, but the fact is explained by the supposition of certain laws or limits in the very constitution of our minds, which make it necessary for us to create for ourselves such an objectivity as a limit of our own free activity.

This point was never cleared up, and never could be. Nor was it ever shown why we should admit the reality of the *me,* rather than of the *not-me;* why we should admit the one and deny the other. Nor was it ever shown what could be the ground and basis of all the phenomena of sense; what the ground of the limitations and laws and activities of the mind itself; what the foundation of all these subjective phenomena. This was ever asked, never answered. We are not surprised to learn, accordingly, that Fichte, on further reflection, essentially modified his whole system, and instead of making conscious self the sole existence, the sole reality, a mere activity perceiving and thinking while there is nothing to be perceived or thought, he so far changed his stand-point as to admit, not indeed a *duality* of existence, subject and object both real, independent existences, but on the contrary one sole and absolute existence, which is the same in both subject and object, and of which both are but forms. This one absolute existence is the divine mind or reason,—Deity himself, of which existence both what we experience within, and what we see without are equally and only manifestations. Still, however, mind is the only reality. The only objectivity is mind in some or other of its forms and manifestations. Such, first and last, is the system of Fichte. We agree on the whole with Morell, that notwithstanding the results to which his philosophy led, it is still impossible to withhold our "admiration at the powerful eloquence, the unwearied energy of thought, the close and almost pitiless logic, with which he compels you on from one conclusion to another. So far from answering to the idea of a mystic recluse, dreaming away life in the midst of the ethereal and shadowy creations of his own fancy, we venture to affirm that never was there a man more intensely practical; never one more formed to struggle with the stern and bitter sufferings of life; never one who was more able to dispel the shadows and phantoms that deluded the world, and to gaze upon everything in its naked reality; never a mind more clear, more deep, more sternly logical, more solemnly earnest, than was that of Fichte."

ADDENDA.

The following passage from his works will convey an idea at once of his eloquent and earnest thought, and of the depth and sincerity of his religious sentiments.

"I am free; and it is not merely my action but the free determination of my will to obey the voice of conscience, that decides all my worth. More brightly does the everlasting world now rise before me, and the fundamental laws of its order are more clearly revealed to my mental sight. My will alone lying hid in the obscure depths of my soul, is the first link in a chain of consequences stretching through the invisible realms of spirit. . . . The will is the efficient cause, the living principle of the world of spirit, as motion is of the world of sense. I stand between two worlds, the one visible, in which the act alone avails, and the intention matters not at all; the other invisible and incomprehensible, acted on only by the will. In both these worlds I am an effective force. The divine life as alone the finite mind can conceive it, is self-forming, self-representing will, clothed to the mortal eye with multitudinous sensuous forms, flowing through me, and through the whole immeasurable universe, here streaming through my veins and muscles, there pouring its abundance into the tree, the flower, the grass. The dead heavy mass of inert matter, which did but fill up nature, has disappeared, and in its stead, *there rushes by the bright, everlasting flood of life and power from its infinite source.*

The eternal Will is the creator of the world, as he is the creator of the finite reason. . . . The infinite reason alone exists in himself, the finite in him; in our minds alone, has he created a world, or at least that by and through which it becomes unfolded to us. In his light, we behold the light and all that it reveals. *Great living Will! whom no words can name,* and *no conception embrace!* Well may I lift my thoughts to thee, for I can think only in thee. In thee, the Incomprehensible, does my own existence and that of the world become comprehensible to me; all the problems of being are solved, and the most perfect harmony reigns. *I veil my face before thee,* and *lay my finger on my lips.*"

CHAPTER XVI.

SUCCESSORS OF KANT.

WE have extended the course already so far beyond the limits originally intended, that what remains to be said of German philosophy must be compressed within the smallest reasonable limits, although the complete works of Hegel alone occupy 20 vols. 8vo., and the analysis of his system is itself a full-sized octavo volume.

§ 3. SCHELLING.

Frederic William Joseph Schelling was born Jan. 27, 1775, at Leonberg in Würtemberg, educated at the university of Tübingen, where he became acquainted with Hegel; studied medicine and philosophy at Leipsig, and afterward at Jena, where he was the pupil of Fichte; in 1798 was chosen to fill the chair vacated by Fichte at Jena, and lectured with great success; in 1807 removed to Munich, and the same year was made member of the Munich Academy of Sciences; there he remained with honor till 1841 or 2, when he was invited by the King of Prussia to Berlin, and went thither; where as late as 1845 he still continued to lecture, at that time seventy years of age and upwards, but still hale and vigorous and full of enthusiasm. At Berlin, however, he met with much opposition from the disciples of Hegel, and subsequently resigned his post, in order to end his days in peace. He died at the Baths of Ragaz, in Switzerland, Aug. 20, 1854.

The philosophy of Schelling may be briefly designated as the philosophy of the *absolute*. Fichte, as we have seen, had carried the subjective view to its furthest extreme, had merged all reality in the Ego,—had made the object dependent entirely on the subject and *created* by it,—had found it necessary, in a measure, to retrace subsequently, his own steps, and admit the existence of an essential reality as the foundation of the Me and the not-Me, of which reality with subject and object are but forms, themselves in part identical. The principle now named, that of identity of object and subject in one absolute essence or existence, while it certainly constitutes the essential feature and peculiar modification of the later philosophy of Fichte, was fully adopted and made the basis of a complete system by Schelling. The merit of the discovery of this principle is warmly contested between the two, by their respective friends and disciples.

We may proceed, says Schelling, in either of two ways in philosophizing ; with Fichte we may construct the objective out of the subjective ; or we may with equal propriety and equal success reverse the process, and construct the subjective from the objective, deduce the Me from the universe. Now both the ego and the material world or nature are realities, the one as much as the other. They have each a common basis. There is one essential absolute existence that underlies them both. They are in truth both but forms and aspects of the *absolute,* in which both exist, indivisible and *identical.*

Before either nature or the ego existed, this one great, absolute thought or being—viz. Deity—existed and filled all space. This self-existent one is the only absolute reality—not substance, as Spinoza held, but *mind.* To know him is to know all real existence and without knowing him we take not the first step in philosophy. The faculty by which we may know him and that immediately is the faculty of *intellectual intuition.* All forms of being, all reality, are but the several forms of self-development of this absolute reality. The knowledge of the absolute is the highest knowledge, and alone deserves the name of philosophy. In distinction from this knowledge of the absolute by means of intellectual intuition, or ideas, there is the knowledge of the *conditional,* the *divisible,* the *individual,* by means of our ordinary conception; this Schelling terms inferior or secondary knowledge.

All things are but the development of this absolute principle of being, every mind an image of the eternal mind, man a microcosm, and by gazing steadfastly into our own consciousness, and observing how our own minds develop, we may learn the universal process. Now in our consciousness we find subject and object combined and these are not in fact distinct, but rather, when properly viewed, the *two-fold* law of our mind's operation; the one movement, that in which thought predominates, we call subject, the other, in which existence is the principal notion, we call object; but this mode of thinking is both unphilosophical and untrue, and creates a distinction between the soul and the world without, which does not really exist. From whichever of these opposite poles we set out we must arrive at the other. From the objective we may deduce the subjective, and vice versa. There are in fact too philosophies, then, two fundamental sciences, the philosophy of nature and the philosophy of spirit, from each of which we may construct the other.

Now what is the law of self-development, according to which the absolute and all things else unfold themselves?

This law comprises three movements or, as he terms them, *potencies.* The first is the Reflective Movement, the attempt of Infinite to embody itself in the Finite. The second is that of *Subsumption,* the attempt of the Absolute thus embodied, to return to the Infinite. The third movement, that of *Reason,* is the union of the two former, in which the subjective and the objective movements are blended.

By the first of these movements, the Infinite Being, containing in itself potentially all that it ever becomes actually, striving after self-development, embodies its own attributes in the finite, produces finite objects, reflections of itself, nature, which is thus the Infinite objectified.

By the second movement the finite returns to the infinite, nature becomes absolute again, and reassumes the nature of the eternal, becomes *conscious,* becomes *mind* as we see it in *man,* which is only nature striving to find its way back to the Infinite and eternal.

These two movements have given us object and subject. The third movement unites the two in the divine reason, and gives us God, not in his *original potential* state but in his self-developed existence, as comprising the universe of *mind* and *being.* Thus out of the absolute we construct nature or object, mind or subject, and their reunion or God in his *realized* existence.

In like manner, we may proceed to unfold both *nature* and *mind* according to the same law of development, and in so doing we find again three movements or potencies in each, giving use to *three spheres of being,* each exhibiting the same general law, viz. two opposite potencies and a point of indifference or reunion of both. The movements by which nature (i. e. the absolute essence viewed objectively,) unfolds itself, Schelling calls real, and those of mind ideal. Looking at the real, or the philosophy of nature, the first movement gives us the sphere of *matter,* the union of the infinite with the finite. Matter is the emanation of the eternal mind ; it is that mind in its reflective movement, making itself finite in order to become the object of its own contemplations and privity. This is the first movement, and its potencies are : 1. *repulsion,* or the expansive power, 2. *attraction* or the returning toward the centre and source, and 3. *gravity,* or the indifference of the two.

The second grand movement of nature, the *subsumptive,* by which it returns from the finite toward the Infinite again, gives us the second sphere, that of *light,* which is to matter what soul or mind is to body. This has its three potencies also: 1. *magnetism*, the going forth in opposite poles, 2. *electricity*, the return, the unity of the positive and negative poles, 3. *galvanism*, the combination of the two.

The third grand movement of nature, the reunion or combination of the two first, gives us the third sphere, that of *organization* or life, in which *matter* and *light* are combined. Its three potencies are: 1. reproduction, 2. irritability or self-movement, 3. sensibility, which combines the two previous principles. This brings us to the point where matter or nature ends, and spirit begins.

It will be observed, that all these movements and potencies follow the same regular law, and correspond perfectly to each other; first, the going forth, second, the regress, third the combination of the other two.

Turning now from the real to the ideal, from nature to mind, we find the same grand law of development.

The first grand movement is the going forth of mind, enbodying itself in the finite—making itself objective—giving rise thus to the sphere of *knowledge*. In *knowing* anything, the mind finds itself a *limit*, becomes *finite*. This sphere corresponds to that of *matter* on the *objective* or *real* side. The three potencies in this sphere are: 1. *sensation*, the mind going forth and embodying itself in an object or image, 2. *reflection*, the mind returning to self-consciousness of its own operation in the process, 3. *freedom*, the union of the two other.

The second grand movement, the regress from the finite toward the infinite, gives us the second sphere of mind, viz., that of practice. As in knowledge essence expresses itself in a *form*, so in action the *form* returns to the essence. The three potencies here are: 1. Individuality, or the single individual mind, which is merely one moment of the infinite intelligence, just as a single thought is one moment of the whole mind. 2. The State. 3. History, which combines the freedom of the one, with the necessary development of the other.

The third movement blends together the two preceding, combines knowledge and practice, gives us the sphere of *art*, which *is* the combination of theory and practice. This, moreover, being the highest point of self-development of the absolute, the *ultima Thule* of the process combines the two departments, the subjective and objective, the real and ideal, unites the two, brings matter and mind into combination, gives unity to the two. The finite and the infinite here unite, and this is what we see, the infinite, the beau-ideal, shadowed forth by the artist in the finite production. Here, then, we reach the end of the grand process.

Such is a very brief outline of the system of Schelling. You perceive at once the perfect symmetry and completeness of the theory. A more perfect and comprehensive webwork of theory was probably never spun out of the human brain. You perceive the perfect *pantheism* of the system. This was its great defect and crime. Schelling subsequently modified the theory in several respects to meet this difficulty, giving a *positive* in distinction from *previous* or negative philosophy. We have neither time nor inclination to follow him in these successive modifications. Suffice it to say, he carries the threefold potency already explained into the field of revelation, and explains by the same general law the doctrines of Trinity, fall of man, redemption, and the entire religious history of the world.

§ 4. Hegel.

We have seen in Fichte and Schelling the two opposite phases of idealism, the subjective and objective; the one making self the starting point and origin of all things; the other resolving self and all things into the one existence, the absolute. It remains to notice a movement in philosophy still beyond these, more radically and thoroughly ideal than either, which, denying alike the subjective and the objective as realities, resolves both and all things into a mere logical process, mere thought. I mean the absolute idealism of Hegel.

George William Frederic Hegel was born in Stuttgard, in 1770, went to the university of Tübingen at the age of seventeen, where he studied theology and philosophy, and formed the acquaintance of Schelling, with whom he remained ever after on terms of intimacy; spent some time as private tutor in Switzerland and Frankfort; went to Jena in 1801, where he enjoyed the friendship and society of Goethe and Schiller, published a *dissertation,* and began lecturing with a regular audience of four persons, fit audience they were, however, though few. On Schelling's quitting Jena, Hegel filled the vacant chair for one year. His first important philosophical work was finished on the night of the memorable battle of Jena, while the artillery was roaring under the walls, the rapt philosopher unconscious of any special disturbance. On his way to the publishers, next morning, he encounters the French soldiery in the streets, who without further ceremony proceed to lay his ideality under arrest. Subsequently we find him editing a paper at Bamberg; then rector of a college at Nuremberg; in 1816, called to the chair of philosophy at Heidelberg, and finally, in 1818, to that at Berlin, the most important in Germany, where he lectured with great favor for thirteen years till his death by cholera, November 24, 1831, in his sixty-first year.

Hegel began as a firm advocate of the philosophy of Schelling, and sought only to give system and unity to his views. But he soon diverged, or rather passed on beyond him and out of sight. Schelling had not denied the primary existence of the absolute, previous to all development, lying beyond the region of thought, the basis of all existence, apprehended by means of intellectual intuition. Hegel allows no such existence whatever. He *begins with pure nothing.* Schelling had admitted experience as the means by which we come to know the law of the universe and of all being,—experience as regards self, nature and history. Hegel discards all this and makes thought itself, *pure logic*, the revelation of the absolute,—nay, itself the sole *existence*, itself *the very process in which the Absolute, or God, consists.* Subject and object, thought and existence are absolutely identical, and in the mutual relation of the two consists the only reality. For example, I see an object, viz. a tree ; that tree, says Fichte, is merely a creation of your mind, your subjective activity *objectifies* itself thus. That tree, so called, is not a real only an ideal thing. No, says Schelling, the object and the subject are both real, both forms of the one infinite and absolute essence. No, says Hegel, neither the tree nor the perception, neither the object nor the subject, has any real existence, in and by itself, or can have ; the only reality is the *idea,* the *relation of the two.* Ideas are the only concrete realities. This is the substance and essential character of his philosophy. The absolute is with him, as Morell has well stated, not the infinite substance of Spinoza, nor the infinite subject or Ego of Fichte, nor the infinite mind of Schelling, but infinite and eternal thought, a *perpetual Pono,* without beginning or end.

In order to philosophy, then, we must gain a clear conception of the laws of thought, the process of knowledge. The process by which we arrive at the knowledge of anything, we find on close examination to involve a threefold movement : first, the mind is in the state of mere consciousness or *sensation,* in which condition it is *one with the object,* it merely *feels,* but does not distinguish between itself as subject and the thing or object felt ; secondly, the mind objectifies the sensation and refers it to some external existence or cause ; thirdly, the mind perceives, on reflection, that this object is, after all, a product or process of its own activity, and so returns again to complete union and identity with it. The first of these movements is produced by sense, the second by understanding, the third by reason. This general threefold movement or law pervades the *universe of thought.* We have first the infinite idea *in itself, bare thought;* next the idea in its objective form, thought making itself external and objective, as in *nature;* lastly, the idea in regress, thought returning to itself, mind. Hence philosophy has three grand divisions; 1. logic, or the philosophy of pure thought; 2. the philosophy of nature; 3. the philosophy of mind.

1. Logic, the province of abstract thought, of the *idea in itself* (Idee an sich).

Here again we find the *same threefold law at work.* All knowledge consists in separating one thing from another, setting it off by itself, distinguishing it from some other thing, e. g. finite stands opposed to infinite, *subjective* is known only as distinguished from *objective,* so north implies south, etc., etc. No one thing can be known in itself alone, no notion as mere *unity* can be conceived, but must consist of two opposite sides, *positive* and *negative,* and these must be combined in order to form a *complete* idea. This is what Hegel calls the doctrine or law of *contradiction,* which lies at the basis of his system, and which is the key to the whole. It corresponds to and carries out in the logical domain, that threefold movement which takes place, as already stated, in the *mind,* in the process of its attaining to the knowledge of anything, the two opposites answering to the first and second movements of mind, the union of these opposites in one answering to the third and highest movement.

Logic, then, divides into three parts. I. Doctrine of Being, thought in its *immediacy;* II. Doctrine of Essence, thought in communication; III. Doctrine of Notion, thought in regress; or the subjective, the objective, and the union of the two. In each of these divisions, again, we find the operation of this same threefold law or rhythm.

I. Doctrine of Being comprises *three categories,* Quality, Quantity, Measure.

(A) Quality. Nothing is the opposite of Being, and without the idea of nothing you could not have that of *Being,* and vice versa: they are the two *opposite poles* of thought. The two opposites combined form the idea of *Becoming* or of Existence, the production of something out of nothing. Hence the proposition so paradoxical, that Being=Nothing, (i.e. in their *unlimited* state, as opposites) and that Being and Nothing constitute existence; or Becoming is the identity of Being and non-Being. But this process now goes over again. Existence, in order to become a distinct reality must be still further subject to negation. Mere existence by itself is vague, undetermined; negative it, say it is not so, or not so, and you make it definite, it becomes this or that, becomes some *distinct* existence. A rose is a rose, only by virtue of this negation, i. e. because it is *not* a lily or some or *any other* flower than just this particular one.

We have, then, these three steps: 1. Being, which combined with Nothing gives, 2. Becoming or Existence, which, still farther negatived, gives 3. definite or independent existence. (Seyn, Deaseyn, Für-sich-seyn.)

These make the category of *Quality.* Then comes (B) the category of quantity, which consists of 1. pure quantity, 2. particular quantity, 3. the union of the two forming degree. The combination of the categories of quality and quantity gives us (C) Measure.

II. Doctrine of Essence. Thought no longer abstract; being as *concrete* and *real* existence—(corresponding to the second movement of mind by which the understanding separates the object from its consciousness). Here again a threefold division—1. Essence, as ground or substratum, 2. as phenomenon or attribute; 3. as reality, or the union of substratum and attribute.

III. Doctrine of Notion; threefold again; 1. *subjec-*

tive, the operating of the mind in (a) simple *apprehension* (b) *judging*, (c) *reasoning*; 2. *objective*, our conceptions of (a) *mechanical* powers of nature; (b) *chemical* powers; (c) *organization* or *design:* 3. the union of the subjective and the objective in the *Idea*, (a) of *life*, (b) *intelligence;* (c) the *absolute*. Thus we reach by a logical and perfectly symmetrical process the highest step of pure thought, viz., the *absolute idea*—Deity,—and to do this we start, it will be remembered, from *nothing*.

Thus far we have considered only the first grand division of philosophy, *i. e.*, Logic. We now approach the second, and find the same grand law applying also here. Our progress will now be easier, since we know the path.

II. *Philosophy of Nature*. Nature is thought—but only not *subjective*—thought externalizing itself.

1. Nature in its undetermined forms—corresponding to what in logic was termed doctrine of Being—gives us what we call *mechanics*, comprising, (a) *mathematical* properties of matter as existing in time and space, (b) *mechanical* properties, as *gravitation*, etc., *absolute* or *actual* properties which regulate the motion of the various bodies in space.

2. *Physics*, comprising, (a) the general forms of matter, as air, water, light, etc., (b) the relative forms, as cohesion, elasticity, etc., (c) specific forms, as acids, alkalies, etc.

3. *Organism*, combining the other two, viz., matter and form, comprising, (a) the geological, (b) the vegetable, (c) the animal structure.

III. This brings us to the third grand division—to *Philosophy of the mind*. Here we find the two former, the *subjective* and the *objective* processes, combined. The steps are similar to those in the preceding divisions.

1. Mind viewed *subjectively*—comprising (a) anthropology; (b) psychology; (c) will—three separate branches of *mental* science.

2. Viewed *objectively*, mind in its relations to what is without, or the range of *Moral Philosophy*; comprising, (a)

the rights of person and property, or what is termed *jurisprudence,* (b) rectitude of actions, or what is termed *morals,* (c) politics, or duties domestic and public.

3. Mind in its *absolute* form, as belonging not to the individual but the race, comprising in its several stages of development, (a) *art* or æsthetics, (b) religion, (c) philosophy.

Such is the single brief outline of the complete system of philosophy as marked out by Hegel.

With regard to revealed religion, Hegel carries his system fully out in the explanation of the leading doctrines of revelation, making a complete rational theology. The personality of God in our sense of the word, is not admitted, however; for God is the absolute, and to make the absolute a person would be a contradiction in terms. He is not a person, but rather the absolute, total personality, as realized in every individual mind and consciousness of man. The Trinity finds its rational explanation by his threefold law. The Father is pure thought and self-existence. The Son is this pure thought, or existence, objectified, manifest in the flesh. The *Spirit* is the *reunion* of the *two.* Redemption is the reunion of man's spirit, as individualized, with the Spirit of eternal truth. By faith we become mystically one with God, members of his spiritual body.

The great contest of Hegelianism has been a theological contest, questions of this nature absorbing every other in the system. The followers of Hegel are themselves divided in opinion on these questions.

The right, the centre, and the left, as these divisions are termed, hold views widely divergent from each other. The right is the least rationalistic—regards our religious consciousness, our intuitive perceptions of religious truth, as of equal validity and authority with the deductions of reason. Of this class are Gabler, Erdmann and others. The centre makes these religious feelings and intuitions of *secondary* importance, uses them to *illustrate* the logical conclusions of reason—no more. Rosenkrans and Marheineke are of this class. The left discards these entirely, is purely pantheistic and rational. Of this class are Strauss, Bauer, Feuerbach. The results of this rationalism have been disastrous in the extreme. It were unfair, however, to charge these results upon Hegel himself, or even upon his philosophy as a system, for many most excellent and evangelical men have been firm adherents of that philosophy. Its tendencies, however, and its final *results* have been most pernicious in Germany and on the continent.

The lectures of Hegel were published after his death—according to his desire—by some of his most distinguished pupils, and they have also done much to defend and illustrate the system, but it is now on the wane, and what will be the next type of German philosophy is known only to him who knows the future.

CHAPTER XVII.

THE RECENT PHILOSOPHY OF GREAT BRITAIN.

Two opposing schools may just now be said to be disputing the empire of British thought; that of the *Scotch* philosophy, as represented by *Sir William Hamilton,* and that of the *positive,* or as it is often termed the *material* philosophy, as represented by *John Stuart Mill* and *Herbert Spencer,* as also by Bain, Maudsley, Huxley and others of that class, men of great learning and industry, devoted chiefly to scientific pursuits.

§ 1. Sir William Hamilton and the Scotch Philosophy.

This most distinguished of modern metaphysicians was born in Glasgow in 1788. He was educated at Baliol College, Oxford; in 1821 appointed Professor of History in the University of Edinburgh, and in 1836 called to the chair of Logic and Metaphysics in the same institution, which position he held till his death in 1856. He first attracted the attention of the philosophic world by a brilliant and searching review of the philosophy of Cousin, which appeared in the Edinburgh Review in October, 1829, and which drew from Cousin himself the highest encomium. This was followed in the succeeding year by an article in the same magazine on the philosophy of perception; and three years after by the famous review of Whateley and the English logicians. His fame as a critic and philosophical writer were now fully established. No one can peruse either of these articles and not be struck with these two things,—the distinguishing peculiarities of Sir William Hamilton, as shown in all his writings,—his immense erudition, which seems to have laid the whole world of learning under contribution, and his remarkable power of analysis. The most subtle and perplexed problems of thought seem to resolve themselves at once into their simple elements before his clear and searching glance. With these qualities he combines a precision and elegance of style, that command the admiration of the reader. *Cousin* pronounces him "the greatest critic of our age;" (Fragmens Philosophiques); and *M. Persse,* the French translator of his principal essays, says of him "there is not perhaps in Europe a man who possesses a knowledge so complete and so minute, so profound an understanding of the books, the systems, the philosophers of Germany." (Fragmens de Philosophie par Sir W. Hamilton.)

In personal appearance, Hamilton was dignified and commanding—I speak from recollection of him as seen at his house in High-King street, Edinburgh, in 1854, two years before his death—in stature somewhat above ordinary, and with a countenance at once prepossessing and impressive. That lofty brow and that repose of manner seemed to indicate a kingly soul conscious of its power; while yet a genuine modesty and Christian humility marked all his deportment.

A glance at the prevalent philosophy of Europe at the time when Hamilton came upon the stage may enable us the better to estimate his position and his influence. At the close of the last and the beginning of the present century, as we have seen, the philosophy of Locke, as carried out by Condillac in France, and, as to its general principles, by Hume in England, had led in its prevalence to results which at once awakened and alarmed the public mind, both in Great Britain and on the Continent. As the result there came naturally, almost necessarily, a reaction. Kant in Germany, and Reid in Scotland, working quite independently of each other, but with the same spirit and to the same end, had laid the foundations of a different philosophy. The fame of the former already, at his death, in 1804, filled all Europe; while the works of the latter, though less famous, philosopher, as edited by Jouffroy and advocated by Royer Collard, in France, were exerting no inconsiderable influence on the Continent, as well as in England. Such were the influences prevalent in the philosophic world at the time when Hamilton was first turning his attention to the great problems which in all ages have profoundly exercised the human mind. Fichte had followed Kant; Schelling and Hegel were just coming into notice; Cousin in France was attracting the gay and pleasure-loving Parisians by thousands to his eloquent expositions. At this juncture appeared the articles in the Edinburgh Review, of which I have already spoken, and which indicated the rising of a new star of the first magnitude on the philosophic horizon.

In the main Sir William Hamilton may be said to be a disciple of Reid and the Scotch school; yet not more a disciple of Reid in reality than of Kant; and not more of either than of Aristotle. These three were his chief masters, while he sat also at the feet of all antiquity. It is to be regretted that he left no work in which his own system is fully and methodically developed. His lectures on metaphysics, designed for the class room, and written, *currente calamo,* often on the night preceding their delivery, never subsequently rewritten, nor even revised for publication by the author, but given to the public since his death, cannot, valuable as they are, be regarded as the results of his mature and later thought, but rather of his earlier and cruder speculations. His dissertations appended to his edition of the works of Reid, contain his more elaborate statements ; yet even in these most admirable essays his doctrines are rather indicated than fully and systematically developed.

In common with the great body of modern philosophers Hamilton adopts the threefold division of the powers of the mind into intellect, sensibility, and will ; classing, however, the desires with the will under the head of *conative* powers. Consciousness he regards, not as a distinct faculty of the mind, but as involved in all intelligence, and the basis of all. We are conscious, he holds, not of self alone, but of the external world as well, of the non-ego just as really as of the ego. Attention, he regards as a mere modification of consciousness ; the voluntary direction of consciousness to a particular object. He does not, however, make consciousness co-extensive with knowledge, or with all our mental states and operations, but holds that there are modifications of mind which do not come within the sphere of consciousness, latent states and operations of which we are not cognizant except in their effects. This unconscious mental activity, he maintains, shows itself in our acquired habits, as the knowledge of a language or a science which we are not at the moment making use of ; in acquisitions of former years, which though long since passed out of the recollection come back to consciousness in certain abnormal states, as in delirium, somnambulism, and the like ; and also in the operations of the senses which construct that of which we are conscious out of a multitude of impressions of which we are unconscious (Lectures pp. 241, 2).

The doctrine of unconscious perception, or unconscious mental modification, first announced by Leibnitz in Germany and advocated by Wolff, as also by some recent French philosophers, has not received the attention it deserves at the hands of English psychologists. Hamilton is also the first distinctly to announce the grand law of the relation of knowledge to sensation in the act of sense-perception, a law indicated, but not definitely determined, by Kant—that is, that in any act of the senses the element of knowledge is in the inverse ratio to the degree of feeling or sensation, and vice versa; that as the one increases the other diminishes (Lectures, p. 335). In Logic, Hamilton maintains with great earnestness and ability the doctrine,—not indeed original with him, but first by him fully set forth and defended,—of the *quantification of the predicate* in syllogistic reasoning, a most important modification of the Aristotelian syllogism, but one not as yet generally accepted by logicians.

But the great merit of Hamilton, that on which his fame as a philosopher must chiefly rest, is his clear and complete analysis and full elaboration of the doctrine of *perception*. It had been, as we have seen in the previous lectures, the widely received doctrine of the various schools of philosophy, however divergent in other respects, that in the act of perception the mind is directly cognizant only of its own ideas.

This doctrine of representative perception, as we have seen, was boldly assailed by Reid, who ably maintained the opposite doctrine, that of the immediate cognizance of external objects by the mind in the act of perception. But the true philosophy of perception, though clearly indicated, was not fully elaborated by Reid, who failed to discriminate between different forms of the doctrine of representative perception. It remained for Hamilton thoroughly to analyze this doctrine and to reduce to a system its various modifications. This work he has most thoroughly and completely done. The true doctrine of perception, according to Hamilton, is that which fully admits the veracity of consciousness, and the reality of the antithesis of mind and matter as the two factors always and necessarily given in every act of perception. This doctrine he calls *natural realism.* If we deny the reality of this antithesis, we have the theory of *absolute identity* of the subject and object in perception. If we admit reality of the subject, and derive the object from it, we have *idealism.* If we make the object the real and original factor, and derive the subject from it, we have *materialism.* If we deny the reality of both, we have *nihilism.* If with the great majority of philosophers from the earliest to the latest times we *admit the reality* of the external or objective world, while at the same time we *deny its immediate cognizance in the act of perception,* we have the scheme of *cosmothetic* or *hypothetic realism.* This is only one form of the theory of representative perception, as Hamilton very clearly shows, a theory unnecessary, not in accordance with the facts, and in reality destructive of all evidence of the existence of an external world; since the only evidence we have of such existence is the testimony of consciousness, in the act of perception, which evidence the theory in question sets aside as unreliable. The doctrine of natural realism he shows to be the true and only tenable ground, recognizing in every act of perception the direct and immediate cognizance of self as percipient, and the external reality as object perceived; while the rejection of this doctrine in any form, consistently carried out, leads to idealism, materialism, or nihilism, according to the shape which the denial assumes.

There is yet another feature of the Hamiltonian philosophy which should not be entirely passed over in this brief outline of his system. I refer to his philosophy of the *conditioned.* All our knowledge is relative, says Hamilton. We know and can know anything, only as it stands in some way related to our faculties. If these were different our knowledge would be different. We know and can know only the limited, the definite. *To know* IS *to limit, to define.* Hence the wholly unlimited, the infinite and absolute, we cannot know nor even conceive. So Hamilton; and his friend and disciple Mansel (Bampton lectures—Limits of Religious Thought). True, says Kant; we cannot know the infinite, and absolute, but we can conceive them. We may *both know* and *conceive* them, says Cousin, as within the sphere of consciousness. No, not as coming within the sphere of ordinary consciousness, says Schelling; and yet we may know them by that faculty of the higher reason, or intuition, which transcends the understanding and consciousness. The infinite and absolute can neither be known nor conceived, replies Hamilton, by the finite human mind; for this is to limit the wholly unlimited; it is to make the less contain the greater.

The application of this philosophy of the conditioned to theology, is obvious and important. It presents to the mind the God whom we adore as infinite and absolute, as a being in reality incomprehensible by the mind that adores Him. A God that can be comprehended, says Hamilton, is no God; "a Deity understood would be no Deity at all" (Lectures, p. 531). "Canst thou by searching find out God? Canst thou find out the Almighty to perfection?"

This philosophy of the conditioned is applied by Hamilton to the *law of causality,* and also to the *idea of freedom,* as accounting for both. We cannot conceive the *absolute commencement* of anything that exists in time; hence we are compelled to the belief that every event *has* and *must have a cause.* It is the result of our inability to think the unconditioned. For the same reason we cannot conceive a volition wholly undetermined, or a cause not itself caused. Freedom is therefore inconceivable. But so likewise is its opposite, necessity. We *know* that we are free; consciousness assures us that we are so; but *how* such a thing as moral liberty is possible to man or God, we are utterly unable to understand. (Wight's Philosophy of Sir W. Ham., pp. 508–512.)*

§ 2. The Positive or Material Philosophy, as represented by J. Stuart Mill, Spencer and Bain.

This phase or tendency of modern speculative thought, empirical in psychology, and utilitarian in ethics, numbers among its followers not a few of the ablest and most eminent British thinkers; among whom we may rank first and foremost, John Stuart Mill, son of James Mill, a philosophical writer of some repute of the utilitarian school. J. S. Mill is well and widely known as a writer on logic and political economy, in which departments of science his works have won just renown. In metaphysics he is best known by his "Examination of Sir William Hamilton's Philosophy," a very able and searching critique of the system of that philosopher. The advocates of the empirical philosophy, whether of the positive type of Comte and Spencer, or the materialists of the school of Hobbes, Hume, Priestley, found themselves, as a matter of self-defence, under the necessity of attacking the authority and destroying the prestige of Sir William Hamilton as an acknowledged leader of British thought. He was too formidable and too earnest an opponent to be let alone. Resolutely and earnestly the foremost champion of the opposing system, J. S. Mill, girded himself for the

* For a fuller discussion of Hamilton's philosophy than could be given in these pages, and especially for a consideration of his theory of causality and of freedom, I must refer the reader to my "Studies in Philosophy and Theology," article, Philosophy of Sir W. Hamilton.

attack. That he has succeeded in demolishing the system of his great antagonist can hardly be claimed, even by his ardent admirers; while on the other hand even his opponents must concede the fairness and candor, as well as the ability, of his attack.

In common with all the philosophers of the empirical or sensational school, as Hobbes, Locke, Hume, Priestley, Bentham, Hartley, Paley, and others of more recent fame, Mill derives all our ideas from experience, denying all innate or connate ideas, and *a priori* truth. All our knowledge comes primarily from the senses and is the result of experience. Our ideas of right and wrong, of truth, beauty, duty, honor and the like, are of empirical origin. Nothing is true necessarily and *a priori*. In this he stands opposed not only to such thinkers as Descartes, Leibnitz, Kant, Cousin, Coleridge, and others of the so called transcendental school, but to the Cambridge Platonists as well, and to the sturdy common sense of the Scotch philosophers, Reid, Stewart, Mackintosh, and others of that type. But to no one of all these does the empirical or sensational philosophy stand more directly and squarely opposed than to Sir William Hamilton. No one has more distinctly and earnestly contended for the supreme importance in philosophy of *a priori* ideas and convictions. It is one of the distinguishing features of his system, as the denial of it is of that of his opponent. This denial is complete and thorough-going. It is only by experience that we know that two straight lines cannot enclose a space, or that the whole is greater than a part, or that one action is right and another wrong. And as experience is the source of our ideas of this sort, so expediency or utility is the *ground* of morals, the reason why we come to pronounce one action right and another the reverse.

With respect to the *reality* of our knowledge, the doctrines of Mill are essentially opposed to those of the Hamiltonian or Scotch philosophy. All our knowledge, says Hamilton, is relative, in the sense that it stands related to our faculties of knowing; but it is none the less real and true knowledge. All our knowledge is relative, says Mill, in this higher and further sense, that it is merely the report of our faculties as to what seems to be so and so; whether the thing is what it seems to be, whether our knowledge is real or only apparent and illusive, we are not and cannot be certain. The only thing certain is that we have such and such impressions; things seem to us so and so. To us, constituted as we are, two and two are four, and a straight line is the shortest distance between two points. But because it is so in our experience, it does not follow that it is so in the nature of things; because it is so to us, it does not follow that it is so everywhere and always. In other parts of the universe, and to beings otherwise constituted, all this may be changed; two and two may be five, or a part may be equal to the whole; and their knowledge may be as correct and as real as ours. All certitude and reality of truth seems to be by this doctrine utterly destroyed. We are out on a wide sea of conjecture, and can know nothing positively.

As regards the perception of external things by the senses, Mr. Mill of course rejects the doctrine of *natural realism*, or the immediate cognizance of the external world in the act of perception, which is the distinguishing feature of the Hamiltonian system. We have impressions and sensations—that is all. From these we *infer* the existence of an external something capable of producing these impressions. It is an inference, a connection forced upon us by our sensations, not a direct and positive knowledge. Matter is "a permanent possibility of sensation," as he expresses it. In this, he is even more an idealist than Berkeley, for not even *mind* is here given as a real entity.

As to the idea of, and belief in, a personal God as first cause of all things, Mr. Mill says nothing definitely, but leaves it an open question, on which the positive philosophy may take one side or the other without detriment to its principles. He thinks, however, that there may be a religion without a belief in the existence of God (Critique on Comte, p. 133).

As to the freedom of the will, Mill assails Hamilton's theory. Moral responsibility does not, he thinks, involve freedom of the will, as Hamilton maintains. The feeling of accountability is to be traced not to the possession of freedom, but to the fact that the evil-doer is liable to be called to account, and that he knows the punishment which awaits him is just and well deserved. Volition follows its moral causes just as physical events follow their physical causes. He does not affirm that they *must* do so; only that they always do. He disapproves the use of the word necessity to express this relation, and understands by that term, when he employs it, as do Edwards and most necessitarians, the simple *certainty* of events. (Examination of Hamilton, vol. II. pp. 281, 300.) Necessity is to be carefully distinguished from fatalism, which teaches that a superior power overrules our destiny, and that our characters are formed *for* us, not *by* us.

In ethics Mr. Mill is of the utilitarian school. Virtue is an enlightened and refined expediency. The principle of greatest happiness is the ruling motive of human conduct.

It need hardly be remarked, that the system now sketched,—as in fact any scheme that derives all our ideas from sensation, and makes our knowledge relative in the sense above explained, must inevitably do,—fails to solve the great problems of human thought, or even to account for some of the most important mental phenomena. If, as Mr. Mill holds, the mind is a mere series of feelings tending to associate according to certain laws, how is it that this series of feelings recognizes itself as a series, and as having an existence in the past? In other words, how is the fact of memory to be explained? And whence these laws of association which govern the series? And whence the whole class of our *moral* feelings and judgments, the sense of duty or obligation? Whence this MUST, that plays so important à rôle in the mental phenomena? Here the philosophy in question wholly fails. It cannot explain by any laws or principles of association, this grand characteristic feature of our moral nature, "the conversion," to use the language of Masson, "of the *prodest* into the *oportet*; the evolution of the participle in *dus* out of never so much of the past participle passive."*

If we regard Mr. Mill as, in some sense, the leading representative of the positive and material school of thought in Great Britain, at the present day, it must be conceded that *Herbert Spencer* ranks hardly second to him as an advocate of the same essential principle. Mr. Spencer's writings cover a wider range of topics, and are perhaps, even more widely read, in this country at least, than are those of Mr. Mill. With various modifications, the philosophy of Mr. Spencer is, in its essential features, substantially the same as that already sketched. In common with Mill, he denies all primitive, universal and *a priori* truth, making all such or so called truths, as for example the axioms of geometry, to be only the inductions of our experience. He differs from Mill as to the ultimate test of belief, which he makes to be the inconceivableness of the opposite, or the inability to think the alleged truth to be false. With him, as with Mr. Mill, what we call knowledge or cognition, is simply the relation subsisting among our feelings. We know and can know only phenomena; of the hidden causes of phenomena we know and can know nothing. He divides our cognitions, or intellectual powers, into *Presentative*—as localizing sensations—*Presentative-Representa-*

* For a more complete statement and criticism of this system the reader is referred to the Author's "Studies in Philosophy and Theology," article "Mill versus Hamilton."

tive, as when the sight of an object calls to mind its various qualities;—*Representative,* as memory; and *Re-Representative*—as the higher abstractions of mathematics, designated by symbols. His classification of the emotions runs parallel to that of the intellectual powers.

With the same school essentially, may be classed *Alexander Bain,* professor of Logic and Philosophy in the University of Aberdeen, though in some respects he seems to approach more nearly the idealism of Berkeley, than the materialism of the positive philosophy. He treats the mind from a physiological stand-point throughout. His division of the faculties is into I. Antecedents of Intellect, 1. muscularity, 2. the senses; II. The Intellect, with its three functions, 1. discrimination or difference, 2. agreement or similarity, 3. retentiveness. The physical sensations of pleasure and pain are classed with the mental emotions of fear, love, etc., under the general designation of the feelings, every feeling having its physical as well as its mental side. No distinctive place is assigned among the feelings or emotions to the moral faculty. In common with Mill and Herbert Spencer, Bain argues at length against the existence of innate or intuitive ideas. *Matter,* and *mind,* are distinguished as the two great departments of our knowledge, Object and Subject, the former distinguished by the quality of *extension,* the latter by the absence of that quality. As regards the perception of an external object, Professor Bain is not far removed from the position of Berkeley when he affirms that in ascribing separate and independent existence to the object, "we not only forget that the object qualities are still modes of conscious experience, but are guilty besides of converting an abstraction into a reality" (Mental Science, p. 202). "The prevailing doctrine is that a tree is something in itself, apart from all perception; that by its luminous emanations it impresses our minds and is then perceived; the perception being an effect, and the unperceived tree the cause.

But the tree is known only through perception. What it may be anterior to, or independent of, perception we cannot tell" (Mental Science, p. 198).

As to the will, the law of causality reigns there no less than in the realm of physical events; freedom is an illusion and a myth.

§ 3.—Certain Later Forms of Materialism.

Of late, Materialism has assumed a more direct and distinctly avowed form in the writings of modern scientists of note. The doctrines announced by *Cabanis,* and endorsed by *Vogt,* that "the brain secretes thought as the liver secretes bile," or, as expressed by *Moleschott,* that thought is a motion of matter, and by *Büchner,* that "mental activity is a function of the cerebral substance," "emitted by the brain as sounds are by the mouth, as music is by the organ," has not been without its adherents in England. Spencer says: "That no idea or feeling arises, save as a result of some physical force expended in producing it, is fast becoming a common-place of science" (First Principles, 217). The tendency to resolve the phenomena of thought into material agency, and to identify matter and mind as essentially one and the same thing under different phases, is quite marked among English scientists. Professor *Tyndall* disclaims materialism, and believes in the existence of mind as associated with the phenomena of matter; but affirms that "thought, as exercised by us, has its correlative in the physics of the brain," and considers it probable "that for every fact of consciousness, whether in the domain of sense, of thought, or of emotion, a certain definite molecular condition, is set up in the brain; that this relation of physics to consciousness is invariable, so that, given the state of the brain, the corresponding thought or feeling might be inferred" (Address before the British Association). *Huxley* in like manner declares himself no materialist; but it is on the ground that neither matter nor mind are to be regarded as substances, apart from our own sensations and impressions. "What after all do we know of this terrible 'matter,' except as a name for the unknown and hypothetical cause of states of our own consciousness? And what do we know of this 'spirit, over whose threatened extinction by matter a great lamentation is arising, like that which was heard at the death of Pan, except that it is also a name for an unknown and hypothetical cause or condition of the states of consciousness?" (Physical Basis of Life.)

All that we know, in other words, is simply our own mental states and impressions; matter and mind, self and not-self are mere hypotheses devised to explain those states and impressions. "Nor is our knowledge of anything we know or feel more or less than a knowledge of states of consciousness.", "Strictly speaking, the existence of a self and a not-self are hypotheses by which we account for the facts of consciousness." It is evident that if all real knowledge of an external world vanishes on these principles, so also does all real knowledge of the internal or spiritual world, as well. We stand, not with Berkeley merely, but with Hume. Yet in this sense, at least, must Huxley be content to take his place with the materialists; he makes use of a terminology entirely materialistic, and he establishes a purely physical basis for the phenomena of mind. "All vital action," he declares, "is the result of the molecular forces of the protoplasm which displays it." "Even those manifestations of intellect, of feeling and of will, which we rightly name the higher faculties," are not exceptions to the rule, but are known, to every one but the subject of them, only as "transitory changes in the relative positions of the parts of the body." (Physical Basis of Life.)

Perhaps no modern English writer, however, has more distinctly advocated the doctrines of materialism as regards the philosophy of the mind, than Dr. Maudsley, an English physician of reading and culture, who, as superintendent of the Manchester Royal Lunatic Asylum, has had special opportunities for the study of abnormal conditions of the mind, and has devoted particular attention to psychology in connection with these conditions. In a work of much ability, entitled *Physiology and Pathology of Mind,* he traces the various forms of mental derangement to pathological causes, and shows the influence of a disordered brain upon the operations of the mind. From this he is naturally, though incorrectly, led to the conclusion—a conclusion not warranted by the facts adduced—that as disordered and abnormal states of mind may be traced to physical causes, so all psychological states and processes may be accounted for in like manner. Thought, feeling, volition, are certain modifications of the brain, certain processes "which take place in the minute cells of the cortical layers." So delicate, however, are these processes as to be quite beyond our power of investigation in the present resources of science. The system thus developed is wholly and avowedly material. The doctrine is not that the brain cells are the organ of thought, as all admit, but that they manufacture thought, emotion, and the various operations of what we call the mind. This is their function as really as it is that of the certain other organs to secrete bile, or gastric juice. To think and to feel is as truly the function and province of the brain cells, as it is that of the stomach to digest food.

These various mental operations we are to study not by the old method of consciousness, but by observation, not subjectively, but objectively, by careful investigation of the states of the brain and nervous system as affected by these processes. Self-consciousness he regards as a method wholly unreliable. If the mind is for any reason disordered, the consciousness partakes of the disorder, and reports accordingly, that is *falsely*. The man is conscious that he is a king; or that he is made of glass; and the like. It cannot therefore be trusted. (Physiology, etc., p. 25.)

This however is wholly a mistake. Consciousness never testifies falsely. Its office is simply to report our own present sensations and impressions, not to vouch for the correctness of those impressions. And this it does, and does correctly. It affirms that we *feel* warm or cold, not that we *are* so ; it says that we think and believe ourselves to be such and such personages, not that we are so. Even the most decided sceptics have admitted the testimony of consciousness as valid and trustworthy ; nor is it possible on any other principle to lay the foundation of any system whatever, not even of materialism, or nihilism, since whatever we affirm or deny, the truth of our affirmation or denial must rest ultimately on the veracity of consciousness.

Dr. Maudsley denies the unity of the soul. It is one only in the sense in which a tree or a house is one, by the combination and co-operation of the several parts of which it is composed. It is one, only as the brain cells co-operate to produce a given effect, and the ceasing thus to act, the disorder or dissolution of the cells which constitute mental activity, would be the dissolution of that unity, and in fact of the soul itself. This is materialism in its most direct and decided form.

THE END.

INDEX OF PRINCIPAL TOPICS.

SHAW'S NEW SERIES

ON

ENGLISH AND AMERICAN LITERATURE.

I.

Shaw's New History of English and American Literature. Price $1.50. This book has been prepared with the greatest care by Prof. TRUMAN J. BACKUS, of Vassar College, using *as a basis Shaw's Manual*, edited by Dr. WILLIAM SMITH. The following are the leading features of the book:

1. It has been put into the ***modern text-book form.***
2. It is printed in ***large, clear type.***
3. Many parts of the book, which were not very clear, have been ***entirely rewritten.***
4. The history of ***great Authors*** is marked by the use of larger-sized type, which indicates to the scholar at once the important names in English and American literature.
5. It also contains diagrams, showing the easiest way to ***classify and remember the eras*** in English literature. We believe that this is the ***best text-book on this important subject*** ever offered to the American public.

II.

Shaw's Specimens of American Literature, and Literary Reader. GREATLY ENLARGED. By Prof. BENJ. N. MARTIN, D.D., L.H.D., Professor in the University of the City of New York. 1 vol. 12mo. Price $1.50.

This book contains specimens from all the chief American writers. Especially those authors who have given ***tone and character to American literature*** are so represented that scholars may obtain a just idea of their style.

As a ***LITERARY READER*** for use in our Higher Seminaries, it is believed that ***no superior book can be found.***

III.

Shaw's Choice Specimens of English Literature. *A Companion Volume to the New History of Literature.* Selected from the chief English writers, and arranged chronologically by THOS. B. SHAW and WM. SMITH, LL.D. Arranged and enlarged for American students by BENJ. N. MARTIN, D.D., L.H.D., Prof. of Philosophy and Logic in the University of the City of New York. 1 vol. large 12mo. Price $2.00.

We shall still continue to publish

Shaw's Complete Manual of English and American Literature. By THOS. B. SHAW, M.A., WM. SMITH, LL.D., author of Smith's Bible and Classical Dictionaries, and Prof. HENRY T. TUCKERMAN. With copious notes and illustrations. 1 vol. large 12mo, 540 pp. Price $2.00.

FRENCH AND GERMAN.

PROF. KEETELS' NEW FRENCH SERIES.

The Oral Method with the French. By Prof. JEAN GUSTAVE KEETELS, Author of "Keetels' New Method with the French." In three parts, 12mo, cloth, each 75 cents.

[*The student is saved the expense of a large book in commencing the study.*]

The Oral Method of Teaching living languages is superior to all others in many respects.

It teaches the pupil to speak the language he is learning, and he begins to do so from the first lesson.

He never becomes tired of the book, because he feels that, with moderate efforts, he is making constant and rapid progress.

The lessons are arranged so as to bring in one difficulty at a time. They are adapted to class purposes, and suitable for large or small classes, and for scholars of all ages.

The teacher, with this book in his hand, is never at a loss to profitably entertain his pupils, without rendering their task irksome.

In fine, the Oral Method works charmingly in a class. Teachers and pupils are equally pleased with it; the latter all learn—the quick and the dull—each in proportion to his ability and application. It is our opinion that before long the Oral Method will find its way into every school where French is taught.

"I find that pupils understand and improve more rapidly under the Oral Method of Keetels' instruction than any other heretofore used."—A. TAYLOR, *Elmwood Seminary, Glenn's Falls, N. Y.*

A New Method of Learning the French Language. BY JEAN GUSTAVE KEETELS, Professor of French and German in the Brooklyn Polytechnic Institute. 12mo. Price $1.75.

A Key to the above. By J. G. KEETELS. Price 60 cents.

This work contains a clear and methodical *exposé* of the principles of the language, on a plan entirely new. The arrangement is admirable. The lessons are of a suitable length, and within the comprehension of all classes of students. The exercises are various, and well adapted to the purpose for which they are intended, of reading, writing, and speaking the language. The Grammar part is complete, and accompanied by questions and exercises on every subject. The book possesses many attractions for the teacher and student, and is destined to become a popular school-book. It has already been introduced into many of the principal schools and colleges in the country.

PEISSNER'S GERMAN GRAMMAR.

A Comparative English-German Grammar, based on the affinity of the two languages. By Prof. ELIAS PEISSNER, late of the University of Munich, and of Union College, Schenectady. New edition, revised. 316 pages. Price $1.75.

BULLIONS'S

NEW SERIES OF GRAMMARS,

ENGLISH, LATIN, AND GREEK,

ON THE SAME PLAN.

CAREFULLY REVISED AND RE-STEREOTYPED.

BULLIONS'S SCHOOL GRAMMAR............................ $0 50

This is a full book for general use, also introductory to

BULLIONS'S NEW PRACTICAL GRAMMAR............ 1 00

EXERCISES IN ANALYSIS, COMPOSITION AND PARSING. By Prof. JAMES CRUIKSHANK, LL.D., Ass't Sup't of Schools, Brooklyn... 0 50

This book is supplementary to both Grammars.

BULLIONS & MORRIS'S LATIN LESSONS............... 1 00

BULLIONS & MORRIS'S LATIN GRAMMAR............ 1 50

BULLIONS'S LATIN READER. New edition................ 1 50

BULLIONS'S CÆSAR; with Notes and Lexicon............ 1 50

BULLIONS'S CICERO; with Notes......................... 1 50

These books contain direct references to both Bullions's and Bullions & Morris's Latin Grammars.

BULLIONS & KENDRICK'S GREEK GRAMMAR..... 2 00

KENDRICK'S GREEK EXERCISES, containing easy Reading Lessons, with references to B. & K.'s Greek Grammar, and a Vocabulary.. 1 00

☞ Editions of Latin and Greek authors with direct references to these Grammars and Notes are in preparation.

BULLIONS'S LATIN-ENGLISH & ENGLISH-LATIN DICTIONARY, the most thorough and complete Latin Lexicon of its size and price ever published in this country.................. 5 00

"Dr. Bullions's system is at once scientific and practical. No other writer on Grammar has done more to simplify the science, and render it attractive." —*National Quarterly Review.*

"Dr. Bullions's series of Grammars are deservedly popular. They have received the highest commendations from eminent teachers throughout the country, and are extensively used in good schools. A prominent idea of this series is to save time by having as much as possible of the Grammars of the English, Latin, and Greek on the same plan, and in the same words. We have taught from these Grammars successfully, and we like their plan. The rules and definitions are characterized by accuracy, brevity, and adaptation to the practical operations of the school-room. Analysis follows etymology and precedes syntax, thus enabling the teacher to carry analysis and syntax along together. The exercises are unusually full and complete, while the parsing-book furnishes, in a convenient form, at slight expense, a great variety of extra drill. The books deserve the success they have achieved."—*Illinois Teacher.*

www.ingramcontent.com/pod-product-compliance
Lightning Source LLC
LaVergne TN
LVHW021150110826
845150LV00005B/1179

* 9 7 8 1 4 2 5 5 4 7 3 7 0 *